Intellectual Property Rights and Competition in Standard Setting

Competition and intellectual property rights (IPRs) are both necessary for a market to work efficiently and to promote consumer welfare. Properly applied, intellectual property rules define a legal framework which allows undertakings to profit from their inventions. This in turn encourages competition among firms and enhances dynamic efficiency, to the benefit of consumer welfare. Standard setting represents one of the fields where the interaction between competition law and IPRs clearly comes to light. The collaborative goal of standard setting organizations (SSOs) is to adopt and promote standards that either do not conflict with anyone's right or, if they do, are developed under condition that patents are licensed under defined terms.

This book examines the tension between IPRs and competition in the standard-setting field which can arise when innovators over-exploit the rights they have been granted. The book compares EU and US jurisdictions with a particular focus on the IT and telecommunication industries. It scrutinizes those practices which could harm standard setting and its goals, looking at misleading conducts by SSO members which may breach the EU and US antitrust provisions on abuse of market power. Recent developments in EU and US standard setting are analyzed, highlighting the differences in enforcement approaches. The book considers how the optimal balance between IPR and industry standards can be struck, suggesting a policy model which takes into account both innovators' interests and SSO goals.

Valerio Torti is a Post-Doctoral Research Fellow at the Centre for Law and Business of the National University of Singapore.

Routledge Research in Intellectual Property

Available:

Intellectual Property Policy, Law and Administration in Africa
Exploring continental and sub-regional co-operation
Caroline Bongiwe Ncube

Intellectual Property Rights and Competition in Standard Setting
Objectives and Tensions
Valerio Torti

Re-thinking Intellectual Property
The Political Economy of Copyright Protection in the Digital Era
YiJun Tian

The Development of Intellectual Property Regimes in the Middle East
David Price

Intellectual Property, Community Rights and Human Rights
The biological and genetic resources of developing countries
Marcelin Tonye Mahop

Intellectual Property in Global Governance
The Crisis of Equity in the Knowledge Economy
Chidi Oguamanam

Intellectual Property Overlaps
Theory, Strategies, and Solutions
Robert Tomkowicz

Private Copying
Stavroula Karapapa

The Law and Economics of Intellectual Property in the Digital Age
The Limits of Analysis
Niva Elkin-Koren & Eli Salzberger

The Politics of Patent Law
Crafting the Participatory Patent Bargain
Kali Murray

Copyright Industries and the Impact of Creative Destruction
Copyright Expansion and the Publishing Industry
Jiabo Liu

Health Technologies and International Intellectual Property
A Precautionary Principle
Phoebe Li

Intellectual Property, Traditional Knowledge and Cultural Property Protection
Cultural Signifiers in the Caribbean and the Americas
Sharon Le Gall

Intellectual Property and Traditional Knowledge in the Global Economy
Translating Geographical Indications for Development
Teshager W. Dagne

The Object of Copyright
A Conceptual History of Originals and Copies in Literature, Art and Design
Stina Teilmann-Lock

Well-Known Trade Marks
A Comparative Study of Japan and the EU
Hiroko Onishi

Forthcoming:

Intellectual Property and Conflict of Laws
Moral Rights and Alternatives to the Copyright Qualifications
Hanan Almawla

Intellectual Property Rights and Competition in Standard Setting

Objectives and Tensions

Valerio Torti

Routledge
Taylor & Francis Group
LONDON AND NEW YORK

First published 2016
by Routledge

2 Park Square, Milton Park, Abingdon, Oxfordshire OX14 4RN
711 Third Avenue, New York, NY 10017

Routledge is an imprint of the Taylor & Francis Group, an informa business

First issued in paperback 2018

British Library Cataloguing in Publication Data
A catalogue record for this book is available from the British Library

Library of Congress Cataloging-in-Publication Data
A catalog record has been requested for this book

ISBN: 978-1-138-94157-1 (hbk)
ISBN: 978-1-138-61448-2 (pbk)

Typeset in Baskerville MT Pro by
Servis Filmsetting Ltd, Stockport, Cheshire

Contents

Acknowledgements

One of the joys of having completed this project is to look over the journey past, the many places and academic institutes that I have visited (from London, to Singapore, Hamburg, and New York), and remember all the colleagues and friends who have helped and supported me along this long but fulfilling road. My gratitude goes especially to my parents and my sister, for all their support and encouragement during my life and academic path.

I would like to express my sincere gratitude to the academic and administrative staff of the National University of Singapore and, in particular, to Professor Tan Cheng Han (Chairman of the Centre for Law and Business) and Professor Stephen Girvin (Vice Dean of the Faculty of Law), who made the realisation of this ambitious research project possible. The opportunity to contribute to the NUS academic environment and interact with scholars of exceptionally high calibre was an incredibly priceless experience. My gratefulness equally goes to my supervisor, Professor Renato Nazzini (King's College London), for all his contributions of time and ideas that made my PhD experience productive and stimulating, and for giving me the possibility to explore and further develop my academic interests. His high standards have been a constant source of motivation to complete the task.

Finally, I owe particular gratitude to Associate Professor Andrea Lista (University of Exeter) and Associate Professor Johanna Hjalmarsson (University of Southampton), both inspirational and supportive guides; to Associate Professor Burton Ong, my mentor at NUS; to the staff of the University of Wisconsin Law School and, in particular, Professor Peter Carstensen, for the many intellectually challenging debates we had during a summer spent in Wisconsin; to the staff of Fordham New York Law School, where part of the research was conducted; to all my friends and PhD colleagues at the University of Southampton Law School, who have been invaluable in creating a very intellectually stimulating environment; and to the entire editorial and production team at Routledge, who made this book possible. I gratefully acknowledge the funding support of the Centre for Law and Business – National University of Singapore (NUS).

Forewords

It is with great pleasure that I write a foreword for *IPRs and Competition in Standard Setting: Objectives and Tensions* by Valerio Torti.

The book is published at a time when the perceived tension between the protection of intellectual property rights and competition law could not be more problematic, especially in the area of standard setting. On the other hand, there is now a reasonable amount of case law and enforcement practice in this area and a vast literature on the subject. Thus, this book can draw on experience and existing scholarship and gives a comprehensive and rigorous account of the problems. By way of example, the reader will find valuable accounts of the *Samsung* and *Motorola* cases in the EU and of the *Qualcomm* and *Rambus* litigation in the US. The different approaches to FRAND that have been adopted in practice or proposed by scholars are also thoroughly discussed.

The value of this book is that it goes much further than providing a thoughtful review of the existing knowledge. It does so, I think, in two ways. Firstly, the author understands the importance that the objectives of competition law and intellectual property law play in shaping rules and practical solutions. But the author also demonstrates, convincingly in my view, that the objectives of competition law and intellectual property protection are by no means necessarily in conflict. It is indeed not only desirable, but quite possible, to design rules that promote competition while remaining faithful to the need to protect investments that is the foundation of the recognition of intellectual property rights. Secondly, on the strength of this analysis, the author puts forward his own solution to the problem: *ex ante* disclosure of maximum royalties and other key licensing terms to be incorporated in the policy of standard setting organisations. As any solution that purports to be of general application, it is bound to be controversial. But the author is right that it does solve, if not all, many of the problems associated with *ex post* enforcement models such as an imaginative use of competition law that may have the undesirable effect of discouraging participation in standard setting organisations. In the author's model, competition law still has a role to play. But it is a role that is much better defined by the yardstick of compliance with the policy of the standard setting organisation rather than by vague and controversial concepts such as the EU law catch-all doctrine of "competition on the merits".

Dr Torti's book is a contribution to the scholarly debate on standard setting and competition law, but also, more generally, to the role of competition law in the globalised economy. From a somewhat specialist perspective, the book goes deep and wide in understanding law and policy in complex, ever-evolving areas. Because of this, it is to be commended to scholars and practitioners alike.

Professor Renato Nazzini
King's College London
London, 25 May 2015

Competition law is an extremely complex area of law in constant evolution, and whose underpinning principles cross paths with economics and market theories. Its pervasive effects embrace every aspect of the market economy including the intellectual property sector, where the impact of competition law is particularly controversial. Indeed, much debate traditionally surrounds the interaction between competition law and intellectual property law, as the impelling and atavistic desire for ownership protection of intellectual property rights inevitably must do battle with the need for competition and enhancement of technological process.

Within the area of intellectual property rights, standard setting has now assumed a preponderant role. The aim of standard setting organisations is to develop, coordinate and promulgate technical standards intended to address the needs of a wide base of affected adopters. Standards can cover various issues, such as standardisation of different grades or sizes of a particular product, standardisation of production processes or methods, or technical specifications in markets where compatibility and interoperability with other products or systems is essential. In a globalised economy, standards are more important than ever, as they often facilitate economies of scale, and secure multiple supply sources. Standards have their biggest impact on technology markets by providing the very foundation of interoperability. The development of electronic communications networks has seen a rise in the importance of interoperability between equipment used, between services provided, and between data exchanged. Most standards are voluntary in the sense that they are offered for adoption by people or by an industry without being mandated in law. Some standards become mandatory when they are adopted by regulators as legal requirements in designated domains. Within the European internal market, standards provide the additional benefits of contributing to the achievement of market integration within the EU. Common standards, be they of a governmental or private nature, help eliminate restrictions to trade among Member States.

Despite the existence of extensive literature unfolding the issues revolving around the tension between competition law and intellectual property rights, not enough attention has been paid until now to the issue of standard settings. This is surprising, as in this area the conflict between competition law and intellectual property rights becomes particularly exacerbated and interesting. Standard setting agreements may be ultimately beneficial for consumers, as they may lead to the creation of new or better products. In the presence of competing technological solutions, it may well be more efficient for society to rely on one agreed technological standard instead of having to choose between the competing alternatives. Nevertheless, the setting of standards also gives rise to serious competition concerns. In order to introduce a new standard, standard setting organisations rely on standard setting agreements, which may represent an ideal opportunity to reduce or eliminate competition, by excluding competing technological solutions. This scenario may also ignite an opportunity for patent holders relevant to the standard to achieve excessive market power, enabling them to overexploit the rights they have been granted.

This book explores in detail the complexities arising from the application of competition law to standard setting, analysing the interplay between competition law and intellectual property rights, the tension between the application of competition law to standard setting organisations arising from the EU and US scenarios, and finally theorising a paradigm attempting to reconcile competition law and standard setting. The book is of an unwavering high standard. It is the most comprehensive, and perhaps also the most important work on the subject to appear in print in England. All who wish to understand more about the application of competition law to standard setting, from practitioners to academics and students alike will find this book invaluable. I am pleased to be able to welcome its appearance, and to warmly commend its contents.

Dr Andrea Lista
Associate Professor in Commercial Law
University of Exeter, UK

Table of cases

China

European Union

United States

Table of legislation

European Union

United States

Others

Introduction

1 The problem

This book seeks to resolve the tension that may potentially arise in the field of standard setting between intellectual property rights (IPRs) and competition law. On the one hand, IPRs are exclusive rights which confer on innovators the power to exclude other firms from the protected business or invention. IPRs represent the incentives undertakings need in order to invest in costly and time-consuming innovation. On the other hand, competition rules aim to ensure a level playing field in the marketplace, prohibiting conduct that may lead to any abuse of market power. Their ultimate goal is to enhance consumer welfare and societal growth.

The products developed by innovators may be eventually included in standards, which are documents "established by consensus that provide, for common and repeated use, rules, guidelines or characteristics for activities or their results, aimed at the achievement of the optimum degree of order in a given context." Standards, it is well known, facilitate the dissemination of knowledge and allow interoperability between different products. However, tension between IPRs and competition in the standard-setting field may arise when innovators over-exploit the rights they have been granted, to achieve unfair economic advantage. Such tension highlights the clash between the private character of IPRs and the public nature of standards. As innovators continue to contribute to standard-setting development, concerns may arise as to the exact boundaries between appropriate and illegitimate conduct. It is clear that any misleading or deceptive behavior by IPR owners may seriously harm standardization. In this regard, a typical example of harmful conduct is patent hold-up, an anticompetitive practice which leads to manipulation of the whole process.

2 Research questions

Given this premise, one question may legitimately be posed: how to strike the optimal balance between innovators' interests and standard-setting objectives and between IPRs and industry standards? This seems to be the core problem behind hold-up, which affects the effectiveness of standardization activities. In order to answer this question, however, it is essential to address further related issues. First, the intersection between competition and IP laws must be scrutinized, both in terms of objectives and of principles emerging from the case law. Several disputes addressing the interaction between these two fields of law have established principles that may potentially find application in standard setting. Second, the concept of standards needs to be examined; standards have been classified in various ways, so those at issue must be distinguished. Along the same lines, it seems essential to analyze the policies developed by standard-setting organizations (SSOs). Indeed, the effectiveness of standardization activities is closely related to the implementation of robust regulations. In particular, criteria are needed to define an ideal IPR policy framework for SSOs. Moreover, how the current judicial systems in the US and the EU have addressed the anticompetitive risks affecting standards is also an aspect that must be investigated. To sum up, the main research questions are as follows:

- What are the ultimate goals of competition and IP laws? How can they be reconciled?
- How can standards be defined and classified? What are their anticompetitive risks?
- How did the judicial systems in the US and EU tackle abusive conduct in standard setting?
- What is the optimal policy model which may ensure effective standardization?
- How could this optimal model be eventually enforced?

3 The structure of the inquiry

This book is structured in three Parts. In Part One, Chapter 1 will consider the objectives of competition law. The literature and the jurisprudence have identified several potential goals. However, it is not always possible to reconcile all of them at once. Therefore, it seems crucial to choose one optimal objective, which may theoretically differ from the enforcement test adopted. The selected goal will be justified also in light of the need to ensure the proper functioning of standard setting. Chapter 2 will look at the goals of IP law, trying to understand how these aims may be reconciled with those pursued by competition rules. By examining the interaction between these two fields of law, the chapter will delve into the meaning and scope of those legal principles that may apply also to standard setting conduct. Finally, Chapter 3 will explore the concept of standard and the possible classifications. The chapter will also study the main rules implemented so far by standard-setting organizations. Successful standardization, indeed, requires the adoption of robust regulations that clearly identify the participants' duties.

In Part Two, Chapter 4 will scrutinize those practices that may harm standard setting and its goals. The chapter will examine misleading conduct by SSO members that may breach the EU and US antitrust provisions on the abuse of market power. It will explain that the very existence of unclear policies may ultimately encourage the participants to implement deceptive behaviors. The solutions proposed by the literature have not proved to be effective in limiting the risks existing in SSOs. Chapter 5 and Chapter 6 will consider how the judicial systems of the EU and the US have addressed deceptive practices by SSO members. The detailed analysis developed therein represents the empirical evidence of the failure of the current policy system. These chapters will thoroughly investigate the recent history and developments of standard setting in the EU and the US, comparing the laws of these jurisdictions and highlighting the differences in the enforcement approaches. Collectively, the recent disputes on the scope of injunctions and the landmark cases of *Dell, Unocal, Rambus* and *Qualcomm* raise important questions that are relevant in the comparison of the two approaches to hold up. Differences exist as to the role of exclusionary and exploitative conduct, the role of deception by non-dominant firms, and the role of intent in assessing the conduct.

Finally, in Part Three, Chapter 7 will suggest a policy model which may strike *ex ante* the optimal balance between innovators' interests and SSO goals. The right balance needs to be shaped with respect to search, disclosure and licensing duties. From an *ex post* perspective, the chapter will explain how this optimal model may be enforced. In this respect, the role of competition and of private law remedies will be examined.

4 Limitations

The analysis of these issues will be mainly led by comparing the EU and US jurisdictions, as these legal systems have developed considerable experience in the field of standard setting. The first examples of SSOs have been found in the United States. Further limitations regard the concepts of standard and of IPR. As to the former, the research will mostly concern standards in high technology industries, characterized by network effects, due to their key role to innovation and societal growth. They have been the subject of most of the cases examined. High technology standards usually read on patents; the latter will be generally referred to also as "IPRs". When a different right is discussed, as in the case of copyright, this will be clarified in the text. On a final note, the book is up to date as of March 2015, and includes some sections whose earlier versions appeared in articles published – in the author's name – by *European Competition Law Review* and *European Intellectual Property Review*.

Part One

IPRs, competition and the standards

1 The objectives of competition law

1 Interpreting the goals of competition

Competition, in a commercial context, can be regarded as a process encompassing firms that strive to win the customers' business in the market place.[1] This process may lead to a firm succeeding in seeing off its competitors, by being the most efficient and innovative towards its customers' needs. An undistorted competitive system should bring better outcomes than those achieved in a monopolistic market: lower prices and better products, wider choice for consumers and greater efficiency.[2]

As pointed out by the UK Government, "competition helps consumers get a good deal. It encourages firms to innovate by reducing slack, putting downward pressure on costs and providing incentives for the efficient organization of production."[3] Thus, vigorous competition between firms may be considered as a fundamental tool in order to develop strong and efficient markets.

1.1 Different policies and different objectives

Enhancing efficiency,[4] however, is not the only objective of competition law, but other goals may be identified. These include the promotion of consumer welfare[5]

1 See UK Competition Commission, "Merger References: Competition Commission Guidelines" (June 2003, CC 2), §1.20; and UK Competition Commission, "Market Investigation References: Competition Commission Guidelines" (June 2003, CC 3), § 1.16.

2 R. Whish and D. Bailey, *Competition Law* (7th edn, Oxford University Press, Oxford 2012) Ch. 1.

3 UK Department of Trade and Industry, "Productivity and Enterprise: a World Class Competition Regime" (Cm 5233, 2002), §1.1.

4 C. Bellamy and G. Child, *European Union Law of Competition* (7th edn, Oxford University Press, Oxford 2013) Ch. 3; J. Faull and A. Nikpay, *The EU Law of Competition* (3rd edn, Oxford University Press, Oxford 2014) Ch. 1; V. Korah, *An Introductory Guide to EC Competition Law and Practice* (9th edn, Hart Publishing, London 2007) 11; R. Posner, *Antitrust Law* (2nd edn, University of Chicago Press, Chicago 2001); R. Whish and D. Bailey (n 2) Ch. 1; K. Heyer, "Welfare Standards and Merger Analysis: Why not the Best?" (2006) 2 *Competition Policy International* 29; H.B. Wellford, "Antitrust Issues in Standard Setting" (Speech at *2nd Annual Seminar on IT Standardization and Intellectual Property*, China Electronics Standardization Institute, Beijing – 29 March 2007).

5 See P.E. Areeda, "Introduction to Antitrust Economics" (1983) 52 *Antitrust Law Journal* 536; R.H.

and consumer choice,[6] the achievement of market integration[7] and the encouragement of economic freedom, fairness and equality in the market.[8] Uncertainty, then, has recently arisen as to the opportunity to consider the promotion of an effective competitive process as a means to achieve these goals or as an objective of competition *per se*.[9]

More generally, there is vigorous debate among competition authorities and governmental bodies as to the objectives of competition law.[10] It is difficult to find a common view also in the literature and in the jurisprudence on what the aims of competition policy have been until now. Although it seems clear that greater weight is now given to economic rather than political objectives, there is no definitive answer or consensus on the issue.[11]

For instance, while in the United States relevant authorities have more than once identified the maximization of consumer welfare as the proper legitimate aim of competition policy,[12] in other jurisdictions the emphasis on such a goal is less obvious. In this sense, the European Commission, while recognizing the protection of consumer welfare as one of the predominant objectives of modern competition law, has nevertheless referred also to other goals to be achieved through the enforcement of competition policy.[13] This can be easily explained by considering that EU competition policy has so far been highly influenced by the legislative framework of the EC Treaty of Rome,[14] which set out a number of additional goals.[15]

Lande, "Wealth Transfers as the Original and Primary Concern of Antitrust: the Efficiency Interpretation Challenged" (1982) 34 *Hastings Law Journal* 65; S.C. Salop, "Question: What is the Real and Proper Antitrust Welfare Standard? Answer: The True Consumer Welfare Standard" (Paper presented to the Antitrust Modernization Commission – 4 November 2005).

6 Consumer choice is usually included in the concept of consumer welfare. However, an alternative would be to consider it as an autonomous competition goal, on the ground that maximizing consumer welfare does not always lead to maximization of consumer choice.

7 D.J. Gerber, *Law and Competition in Twentieth Century Europe – Protecting Prometheus* (Clarendon Press, Oxford 1998) 334; R. Whish and D. Bailey (n 2) Ch. 1; V. Korah, "EEC Competition Policy – Legal Form or Economic Efficiency" (1986) 39 *Current Legal Problems* 85.

8 M. Furse, "The Role of Competition Policy: a Survey" (1996) 17(4) *European Competition Law Review* 250; V. Korah (n 4) 14.

9 On this topic, see below section 2.1.

10 Unilateral Conduct Working Group, "Report on the Objectives of Unilateral Conduct Laws, Assessment of Dominance/Substantial Market Power, and State-Created Monopolies" (6th Annual Conference of the International Competition Network (ICN) – Moscow, May 2007).

11 J.B. Kirkwood and R.H. Lande, "The Fundamental Goal of Antitrust: Protecting Consumers, Not Increasing Efficiency" (2008) 84 *Notre Dame Law Review* 191.

12 US Department of Justice and Federal Trade Commission, "Horizontal Merger Guidelines" [Revised 1997], reprinted in 4 Trade Reg Rep (CCH) §§13, 104 (April 1997). See also *Reiter v Sonotone*, 442 US 330 (1979), at 343; *Business Electronics v Sharp Electronics*, 485 US 717 (1988), at 723; *Leegin Creative Leather Products v PSKS*, 551 US 877 (2007); *Brooke Group v Brown and Williamson Tobacco*, 509 US 209 (1993), at 224.

13 V. Korah (n 7) 85. Here, the author focuses on one of these other goals (i.e. market integration).

14 Treaty of Rome establishing the European Economic Community (1957), as amended in accordance with the consolidated version of the Treaty of Nice, [2002] OJ C 325/1.

15 J. Galloway, "The Pursuit of National Champions: The Intersection of Competition Law and

Contrasts have also arisen in the literature, where several authors have mentioned different and potentially conflicting goals for EU competition policy. Bishop and Walker, for instance, identify two main objectives: market integration and the economic goal.[16] Motta, then, considers efficiency and European market integration as the main aims of competition, although he recognizes the role of social and political reasons.[17] Ahlborn and Padilla instead identify three groups of objectives: fairness, welfare and efficiency, and market integration.[18] Along the same lines, Monti indicates three core aims of EU competition law: efficiency, market integration and the protection of economic freedom.[19]

All these views seem to confirm that "EU competition law is a bit like a multiple personality, fascinating but complicated."[20] A debate may arise, *inter alia*, on whether market integration is an intermediate goal, which in turn should achieve the ultimate welfare objective, or whether it is itself an ultimate goal. A second question, what is more, could also be posed in relation to the optimal standard that should be adopted in the enforcement of competition rules: should the legal test directly reflect the need for market integration or should it be better based on a *welfarist* approach? In this second case, should the enforcement test pursue consumer or total surplus? It is undoubted that it would be difficult to reconcile, in the legal enforcement standard, all the various objectives that may potentially be assigned to competition policy.

The discussion on the objectives of competition policy, further developed in the next sections, is thus relevant as far as it helps to understand which test should be applied in the enforcement of the competition rules. The enforcement test, indeed, may diverge from the ultimate competition policy aim.

The optimal solution finally suggested reveals its clear effectiveness also when applied in the context of standard setting. In particular, the importance of the test selected will be further explained in light of the aim to guarantee the optimal functioning of standardization processes, although a more effective policy framework seems also to be necessary to this purpose. In that particular environment, the interests of IPRs owners, consumers and licensee-manufacturers could be often at odds. The adoption of one legal test over another, when enforcing competition law against anticompetitive practices, may lead to very different outcomes, which may eventually boost or compromise the whole standardization process.

Industrial Policy" (2007) 28(3) *European Competition Law Review* 173; G. Monti, "Article 81 EC and Public Policy" (2002) 39(5) *Common Market Law Review* 1057; C. Townley, *Article 81 EC and Public Policy* (Hart Publishing, London 2009) Ch. 5.

16 S. Bishop and M. Walker, *The Economics of EC Competition Law* (3rd edn, Sweet & Maxwell, London 2010) Part I.

17 M. Motta, *Competition Policy, Theory and Practice* (Cambridge University Press, Cambridge 2004) 15.

18 C. Ahlborn and A.J. Padilla, "From Fairness to Welfare: Implications for the Assessment of Unilateral Conduct under EU Competition Law" in C.D. Ehlermann and M. Marquis, *European Competition Law Annual 2007: a Reformed Approach to Article 82 EC* (Hart Publishing, Oxford 2008) 55.

19 G. Monti (n 15) 1057.

20 L. Parret, "Shouldn't We Know What We Are Protecting? Yes We Should! A Plea for a Solid and Comprehensive Debate about the Objectives of EU Competition Law and Policy" (2010) 6(2) *European Competition Journal* 376.

Hence, it is clear the need to identify *a priori* the ultimate objective of competition law and the optimal test in the enforcement of the rules. The next sections are therefore devoted to define the scope of the debate and to identify possible answers to the mentioned questions.

2 Competition law as a means to achieving different aims

A report of the International Competition Network (ICN) Unilateral Conduct Working Group has taken into consideration some interesting issues concerning competition.[21] The document, based on the responses of different ICN members and non-governmental advisors to a questionnaire developed by the group, has analysed the objectives of unilateral conduct rules as described by the respondents. This report may be used as a starting point for a catalogue of the possible goals of competition law more generally.[22]

Among these goals, it usually appears more reasonable to identify a primary objective.[23] The better view, indeed, seems to be that the pursuit of different goals as primary objectives may not always be achieved and reconciled at the same time. Other socially desirable objectives may thus be achieved through competition law, but only in so far as they are consistent with the primary aim. These considerations hold true even when applied in the analysis of conduct in standardization processes.

The most part of respondents identified several goals of unilateral conduct laws, regulations and policies, namely: ensure an effective competitive process; promote consumer welfare; enhance efficiency; ensure economic freedom; ensure a level playing field for small and medium-sized enterprises; promote fairness and equality; promote consumer choice; achieve market integration; promote competitiveness in international markets.[24] To the list, a further objective not mentioned by the respondents should be added: promoting total welfare.

As a premise, the goals of Articles 101 and 102 TFEU (former Articles 81 and 82 of the EC Treaty) should be read in a harmonious way, being the origin of these rules identical. The same concept holds for the antitrust provisions of the US Sherman Act, Section 1 and Section 2. Differences, however, may arise between the various systems of competition policy, such as the US, the EU and the UK.[25] This means that competition is the expression of the values and concerns of a particular society. Therefore, its objectives may vary with the change of political

21 Unilateral Conduct Working Group (n 10).

22 See also OECD Secretariat, "The Objectives of Competition Law and Policy and the Optimal Design of a Competition Agency" (2003) 5 *OECD Journal of Competition Law and Policy* 7.

23 R. Nazzini, "Welfare Objective and Enforcement Standard in Competition Law" in A. Ezrachi and U. Bernitz, *Private Labels Brands and Competition Policy* (Oxford University Press, Oxford 2009) 387, 390–391.

24 Unilateral Conduct Working Group (n 10) 2.

25 On this point, see P. Jebsen and R. Stevens, "Assumptions, Goals and Dominant Undertakings; the Regulation of Competition under Article 86 of the European Union" (1996) 64 *Antitrust Law Journal* 443.

thinking and societal needs.[26] The latter, it must be remembered, also form the basis of standard setting developments.

2.1 Ensuring an effective competitive process

First, a critical question needs to be addressed: what is an effective competitive process? Concerns, indeed, may arise about its exact meaning. While the legislator of some countries concluded that the meaning of "free competition" should be left to the judiciary interpretation, others suggested that effective competition can be deemed to exist where all firms have an opportunity to succeed or fail, according to their potentiality to compete.[27] It could be further defined as a process of rivalry among firms on a given market (a definition, however, that according to some authors, would not provide a proper standard for distinguishing between anticompetitive and non-anticompetitive conduct).[28] Such a process, then, seems to be a dynamic and (potentially) self-initiating market phenomenon, where products are supplied by firms able to produce them in the most efficient way.[29] Accordingly, antitrust enforcement agencies should intervene only in those cases where the "spontaneously-occurring competitive process falters as result of anti-competitive conduct."[30]

Competition law, in other words, should ensure that a free undistorted competitive process be maintained in the marketplace, while it should not be enforced in case an undertaking legitimately strengthens its economic position. In this sense, for instance, the Protocol introduced by the Lisbon Conference refers to the need to maintain a system ensuring that competition is not distorted.[31] This requirement, as confirmed in *Metro*, implies, *inter alia*, the existence of workable competition, which is the degree of competition needed in order to ensure the achievement of the objectives of the European Union.[32]

2.1.1 Effective competition: a means or an aim?

Whether ensuring an effective competitive process should be recognised as a means to achieve other goals (e.g. the protection of consumers' interests) or as a primary objective of competition law *per se* has been a controversial issue. As stated by Advocate General Kokott in *British Airways*:

26 See also E.M. Fox, "The Kaleidoscope of Antitrust and its Significance in the World Economy: Respecting Differences" in B. Hawk (ed.), *International Antitrust Law & Policy: Fordham Corporate Law Institute* (Juris Publishing, New York 2001) 597.

27 See Unilateral Conduct Working Group (n 10) 30.

28 R. Nazzini (n 23) 387.

29 However, certain sectors which are in origin state monopolies would need a government's intervention, in terms of privatization and liberalization, to be subject to competitive forces.

30 See Unilateral Conduct Working Group (n 10) 30.

31 Protocol on Internal Market and Competition, Annexed to the Treaty on the European Union (TEU) and the Treaty on the Functioning of the European Union (TFEU), [2007] OJ C 306/156.

32 Case 26/76 *Metro v European Commission* [1977] ECR 1875.

> Article 82 EC, like the other competition rules of the Treaty, is not designed only or primarily to protect the immediate interests of individual competitors or consumers, but to protect the structure of the market and thus competition as such (as an institution), which has already been weakened by the presence of the dominant undertaking on the market. In this way, consumers are also indirectly protected. Because where competition as such is damaged, disadvantages for consumers are also to be feared.[33]

This position has been confirmed by the Court of Justice in *GlaxoSmithKline*, where it was held that "competition law aims to protect not only the interests of competitors or of consumers, but also the structure of the market and, in doing so, competition as such."[34] This notwithstanding, the cited view must be compared with the position of the EU Commission, which has often observed that the protection of competition cannot be considered as a goal *per se*.[35]

More generally, some antitrust agencies believe that the protection of competition may play an important role as a crucial antitrust objective, while others affirm that it may be only considered as a means to achieve other goals.[36] According to certain authorities, furthermore, the protection of a competitive process could be interpreted both as an objective and as a vehicle, mainly for protecting consumers and maximizing efficiency.[37]

Apart from the considerations expressed by both the competition agencies and the courts in the case law, it is necessary to recall the concept that competition should be developed in order to achieve a primary goal. The latter, of course, may vary in accordance to the policy objectives of a system. However, it seems reasonable to support the view that any public policy should be addressed and implemented so as to maximize the well-being of the society as a whole.[38]

That is why competition systems and their enforcement processes should not aim at the protection of rivalry *per se*. The protection of the competitive process as

33 Opinion of Advocate General Kokott of 23 February 2006, in Case C-95/04 P *British Airways v European Commission* [2007] ECR I-2331, at 44, citing Case 85/76 *Hoffmann-La Roche v European Commission* [1979] ECR 461, at 91; Case 322/81 *Michelin v European Commission* [1983] ECR 3461, at 70; Case 31/80 *L'Oréal v De Nieuwe AMCK* [1980] ECR 3775, at 27; Case C-62/86 *AKZO v European Commission* [1991] ECR I-3359, at 69. In the *British Airways* judgment, however, the ECJ did not explicitly support Kokott's arguments on this point.

34 Case C-501/06 P *GlaxoSmithKline v European Commission* [2010] ECR I-9291.

35 See for instance N. Kroes, "European Competition Policy: Delivering Better Markets and Better Choices" (Speech at *European Consumer and Competition Day*, London – 5 September 2005); M. Monti, "European Competition for the 21st Century" in B. Hawk (ed.), *International Antitrust Law & Policy: Fordham Corporate Law Institute* (Juris Publishing, New York 2001) 257; and P. Lowe, "The Design of Competition Policy Institutions for the 21st Century – The Experience of the European Commission and DG Competition" (2008) 3 *Competition Policy Newsletter* 1.

36 Unilateral Conduct Working Group (n 10) 7–8.

37 In this sense, see the Netherlands Competition Authority's position.

38 See C. Ahlborn, "Competition Policy in the New Economy: Is European Competition Law Up to the Challenge?" (2001) 22(5) *European Competition Law Review* 156; and C. Ahlborn and A.J. Padilla (n 18).

an institution may result under certain circumstances in the protection of competitors, leading then to a loss of welfare.[39] Rather, the protection of the competitive process or free competition should be strictly interpreted in the light of a further primary goal.[40]

In the context of standard setting, the enforcement of a legal test merely focused on the protection of rivalry may have undesirable effects for certain categories of consumers. Once the standard-setting body has selected a specific technology, indeed, the patent owner may try to license its rights under supra-competitive royalties and breach any terms previously subscribed. In case there is no evidence of harm to the competitive process (e.g. if the standard-setting organization (SSO) could not select an alternative technology), the IP owner may escape antitrust liability.

This means that the application of a test mainly based on harm to the competitive process would probably lead to exclude pure exploitative abuses from the range of prohibited conduct. Therefore, a IPRs owner could finally charge exorbitant fees without incurring the risk of being fined by the competition enforcers. The ultimate effect could be detrimental to the welfare of consumers.

2.2 *Promoting consumer welfare and consumer choice*

Rivalry, that is the process of competing between firms seeking to win consumers and drive competitors out of the business, should be protected in so far as it brings an improvement in the well-being of society. A long-standing debate has developed around the concept of the welfare standard to apply. What is the proper standard? Should competition maximize consumer welfare or total welfare? On the one hand, some authors refer to the aggregate economic welfare standard (also called total surplus or efficiency standard).[41] On the other, a different doctrine usually favors the consumer welfare standard (or consumer surplus standard).[42] The following sections will summarize the objections arisen against both standards. The most relevant issue is to understand whether a consumer surplus test, as enforcement standard, could be more desirable for maximizing societal welfare as a competition policy objective.

39 R. Nazzini (n 23) 388. Consider, for instance, the case where the protection of the competitive process would mainly lead to preserve the activities of highly inefficient firms.

40 On the issue, see H. Vedder, "Competition Law and Consumer Protection: How Competition Law can be Used to Protect Consumers Even Better – or Not?" (2006) 17 *European Business Law Review* 83. See also J. Stuyck, "EC Competition Policy after Modernization: More than Ever in the Interest of Consumers" (2005) 28 *Journal of Consumer Policy* 1.

41 See D.W. Carlton, "Does Antitrust Need to Be Modernised?" (2007) 21 *The Journal of Economic Perspectives* 155; and K. Heyer (n 4) 29.

42 See S.C. Salop (n 5); R.H. Lande (n 5) 65; R.H. Lande, "Proving the Obvious: The Antitrust Laws Were Passed to Protect Consumers (not Just to Increase Efficiency)" (1999) 50 *Hastings Law Review* 959; and R. Pittman, "Consumer Surplus as the Appropriate Standard for Antitrust Enforcement" (2007) 3(2) *Competition Policy International* 205.

2.2.1 *Consumer welfare v total welfare*

The total welfare standard takes into consideration the aggregate welfare of both consumers and producers. In contrast, consumer welfare only focuses on consumers and does not consider conduct harming rival undertakings. Consumer welfare, in particular, is the difference between what consumers are willing to pay for certain goods and what it is finally paid. Total welfare, instead, considers also producer surplus, the economic profit a company may realise in selling goods and services.

Regardless of which should be the optimal test, a welfare standard should be usually appraised on a long-term basis, rather than on a short-term framework. As evidenced by Porter, by referring to a long-term basis it is possible to take into account any potential benefit deriving from dynamic efficiencies, which may finally lead to productivity growth.[43]

2.2.2 *Welfare standards in the EU and the US*

A consumer welfare standard seems to be supported by many national antitrust authorities, among which the European Commission.[44] Former commissioners and officials of the institution defined consumer welfare as the standard the Commission applies when appraising infringements of the Treaty rules on cartels and monopolies, and recognised the important role of the market and of competition in guaranteeing consumer surplus and enhancing efficiency.[45] Consumer welfare, it has been held, could be interpreted as strictly related to the general economic welfare purpose that was at the basis of articles 2 and 3 of the EC Treaty, and that is now reflected in the new Treaty on the European Union.[46] What is more, other provisions of the Treaty on the Functioning of the European Union (formerly the EC Treaty) directly refer to consumer welfare by requiring EU institutions to take into consideration the protection of consumers when developing their policies.[47]

43 M.E. Porter, "Competition and Antitrust: Toward a Productivity-based Approach to Evaluating Mergers and Joint Ventures" (2001) 46 *Antitrust Bulletin* 934–935.

44 See the European Commission's "Guidelines on the application of Article 81(3) of the EC Treaty" [2004] OJ C101/97, at 13; "DG Competition Discussion Paper on the Application of Article 82 of the Treaty to Exclusionary Abuses" (Public Consultation, December 2005), at 4; "Guidelines on the Assessment of Horizontal Mergers Under the Council Regulation on the Control of Concentrations Between Undertakings" [2004] OJ C31/5, at 8 and 12; "Guidelines on the Assessment of Non-horizontal Mergers Under the Council Regulation on the Control of Concentrations Between Undertakings" [2008] OJ C 265, at 10 and 21. See also B. Allan, "Article 82: A Commentary on DG Competition's Discussion Paper" (2006) *Competition Policy International* 49.

45 See N. Kroes (n 35); M. Monti (n 35) 257; and P. Lowe (n 35) 1.

46 R. Nazzini, "Article 81 between Time Present and Time Past: a Normative Critique of 'Restriction of Competition' in EU Law" (2006) 43 *Common Market Law Review* 497.

47 See for instance Article 12 (former 153(2) EC Treaty), Treaty on the Functioning of the European Union, O.J. 2010 C 83/47.

The jurisprudence of the EU, however, is undoubtedly less clear in defining the welfare standard and, more in general, the main objective of competition policy. In *GlaxoSmithKline*, the Court of First Instance (after Lisbon, "General Court") clearly opted for consumer welfare as the main driver of EU competition policy.[48] This case represented one of the few examples of a court expressly mentioning consumer welfare as the optimal standard to be applied. However, in the appeal of that case, the Court of Justice raised some doubts about this supremacy. The court observed that:

> there is nothing in Article 81(1) to indicate that only those agreements which deprive consumers of certain advantages may have an anticompetitive object ... Article 81 EC aims to protect not only the interests of competitors or of consumers, but also the structure of the market and ... competition as such.[49]

Hence, the Court of Justice made an important, albeit disputable, point where it clarified that competition as an institution is not simply a means and cannot be excluded from the goals of antitrust. This recalls what had been previously held by Advocate General Kokott in *British Airways*, where it was stated that competition law is not designed to protect only or primarily individual competitors or consumers, but also the structure of the market.[50]

In the United States, instead, there is strong consensus for a consumer welfare standard as the optimal goal of antitrust policy.[51] The Department of Justice, the Federal Trade Commission and the US Supreme Court have clearly held that competition should be for the protection of consumers, not competitors.[52] Nevertheless, some authors support the view that antitrust laws should prohibit conduct reducing total welfare.[53] Which test should be applied has been at the heart of an intense debate, and objections could be raised for both of them.

2.2.3 Consumer surplus as enforcement standard

Different arguments have been proposed both in favor of consumer and of total welfare standards. These, however, are not completely convincing for justifying one or the other as the only legitimate test. Redistribution of wealth has been cited by those supporting a consumer welfare standard, on the basis that the latter would achieve a more equal distribution of wealth in the society, in comparison

48 Case T-168/01 *GlaxoSmithKline Services Unlimited v European Commission* [2006] ECR II-2969. In *GlaxoSmithKline*, in particular, the CFI observed that "the objective assigned to Article 81(1) EC.... is to prevent undertakings....from reducing the welfare of the final consumer of the product in question".

49 *GlaxoSmithKline* (n 34).

50 *British Airways* (n 33), at 68.

51 S.C. Salop (n 5); R.H. Lande (n 5) 65; R.H. Lande (n 42) 959; R. Pittman (n 42) 205.

52 *Reiter* (n 12), at 343; *Business Electronics* (n 12), at 723; *Leegin Creative* (n 12); *Brooke Group* (n 12), at 224; *Brown Shoe v US* 370 US 294 (1962), at 320.

53 D.W. Carlton (n 41) 155; K. Heyer (n 4) 29.

to a total welfare standard.[54] However, this cannot be a concern of competition policy; rather it should be addressed by other tools of public policy, such as tax and subsidy schemes.[55] On a further different ground, supporters of a consumer welfare standard also argue that a total surplus test may be perceived as politically unpopular, since it does not focus entirely on consumers.[56] In addition, as they hold, the monitoring of competition policy would be easier under a consumer welfare standard than under a total surplus test, as in the latter case it could be difficult to calculate the offset between consumer harms and claimed producer efficiencies.[57] However, the fact that a consumer surplus test is more observable, administrable and politically favored does not seem a relevant benchmark in the assessment of the optimal standard for competition policy.[58]

The justifications developed by the literature in support of a total welfare standard mainly concern the alleged positive effects of such a test on gross domestic products. Carlton argues that it is not reasonable to ignore producer surplus, as efficient economic activities that raise gross domestic product usually can make everyone better off.[59] However, this conclusion seems no more than an assumption which lacks robust evidence. It is difficult to understand why an increase in the welfare of producers should be automatically passed to consumers, for instance in the form of reinvestments enhancing dynamic efficiency and consumer choice, rather than being dissipated and used (at least partially) for producers' self-interests.[60] Rather, it seems more reasonable to sustain that increased consumer welfare may subsequently benefit producers, than to assert that increased producer welfare may then make everyone better off. Keynes's economic theories, indeed, lead to the conclusion that consumers benefiting from an increased welfare (comparable to a higher income) may then be encouraged in purchasing further goods and services, to the benefit also of productivity and producer surplus.[61] These observations, of course, cannot necessarily lead to sustain that consumer

54 R. Ahdar, "Consumers Redistribution of Income and the Purpose of Competition Law" (2002) 23(7) *European Competition Law Review* 341; R. Pittman (n 42) 205; S.C. Salop (n 5); R.H. Lande (n 5) 65.

55 J. Farrell and M.L. Katz, "The Economics of Welfare Standards in Antitrust" (2006) 2 *Competition Policy International* 3. See also F.M. Scherer, "Antitrust, Efficiency and Progress" (1987) 62 *New York University Law Review* 998.

56 S.C. Salop (n 5) 23.

57 Ibid., 22–23. See also C.F. Rule and D.L. Meyer, "An Antitrust Enforcement Policy to Maximize the Economic Wealth of All Consumers" (1988) 33 *Antitrust Bulletin* 677.

58 On the relationship between politics and antitrust, see G. Amato, *Antitrust and the Bounds of Power: The Dilemma of Liberal Democracy in the History Market* (Hart Publishing, Oxford 1997).

59 D.W. Carlton (n 41) 158.

60 J. Farrell and M.L. Katz (n 55) 12.

61 J.M. Keynes, *The General Theory of Employment, Interest and Money* (Macmillan, London 1936). The author elaborated the function of consumption in the following terms: $C = C^{\circ} + cY$, where C° is the basic level of consumption, c is the marginal tendency to consumption and Y is the level of income. Keynes noted that an increase in the level of income leads to a raised consumption. However, such raise in consumption proportionally diminishes as the income continues growing.

surplus should be valued more than producer welfare.[62] However, the question still stands. What is the optimal standard? Is there a test under which both producers and consumers, i.e. the society as a whole, may benefit from antitrust policy?

What has been noted in the previous sections, on consumers' and producers' behaviors, may suggest recalling the view of those authors that distinguish between the enforcement test and the ultimate policy aim of antitrust, on the ground that the latter could not necessarily coincide with the enforcement standard to be applied by competition authorities and courts.[63]

The policy objective, as the ultimate goal pursued by competition law, could be distinguished from the enforcement standard as the analytical framework or criteria applied to determine which behavior is prohibited. By supporting this position, the appropriate goal of competition law should be identified in the maximization of long-term societal welfare, which must be distinguished from the concept of total surplus. According to Carlton, total welfare is enhanced as long as the aggregate between consumer and producer surplus is positive. Increased societal welfare instead means that both producer and consumer welfare have been raised. In order to reach the goal, courts and competition authorities could adopt long-term consumer surplus as the enforcement standard, as this may provide a workable test that guarantees a maximized long-term societal welfare. The main argument for supporting consumer surplus as enforcement standard lies on Keynes' model on the theory of consumption: the promotion of consumer welfare is likely to determine an increase in consumers' consumption, and hence lead to maximize the societal well-being.

The relevance of societal welfare, as ultimate objective of competition, seems to have been recognised (perhaps indirectly) by the recent judgment of the Court of Justice in *TeliaSonera*.[64]

2.2.4 Societal welfare as ultimate aim

In brief, maximization of societal welfare should be the ultimate objective of competition policy, as there appears to be no strong reason to value consumer surplus more than producer welfare, and vice versa. In order to achieve the objective, a total welfare enforcement test does not seem the optimal standard, in light of the considerations made in the previous sections. Directly enforcing a societal surplus test may then be complex, as a conduct for instance may apparently harm producers in the short term but may have unpredictable benefits in the long-term. Competition policy should aim to maximize societal welfare by enforcing

62 See R. Bork, *The Antitrust Paradox* (Basic Books, New York 1978) 110. Bork is among those authors believing that no distinction should be made as "producers are consumers too."

63 R. Nazzini (n 23) 405. See also J. Farrell and M.L. Katz (n 55) 32–33.

64 Case C-52/09 *Konkurrensverket v TeliaSonera AB* [2011] ECR I-527, at 22. The court, in particular, held that the function of competition rules "is precisely to prevent competition from being distorted to the detriment of the public interest, individual undertakings and consumers, thereby ensuring the well-being of the European Union."

a consumer surplus test, which bans conduct harming consumers and reduces competitive pressure on firms.

Competitive pressure, it is well known, functions as an incentive for firms to reduce prices, increase output and invest in new innovative products. To appraise whether effective competitive pressure has been eliminated, it is appropriate to pay attention to the effects of the conduct under investigation on price, output and innovation. In case these elements are unaffected, then it can be presumed that firms are still subject to a healthy competitive pressure that forces them to pass to their customers any benefits resulting from harm to rivals. In case such factors are negatively affected (i.e. increase of price, reduction of output) as a result of the diminished competitive pressure, consumer surplus is harmed. This, in turn, may discourage consumers' consumption of goods and services, and consequently industrial productivity, to the detriment of the welfare of the society as a whole.[65]

The context of standard setting, as it will be later seen in the next chapters, represents a good example to explain the importance of a *welfarist* approach in competition policy. The enforcement of a test focused on consumer surplus ensures that also standards institutes may perform optimally their functions and achieve their ultimate objectives: the enhancement of consumer welfare and societal productivity. Under a consumer welfare enforcement test, indeed, undertakings which agree to be involved in standardization processes and subscribe the organizations' policies rules may well be prevented from behaving in a misleading way and undermining the scope of the selection procedure.

Instead, the enforcement of a test merely focused on total welfare may lead to non-optimal outcomes. By applying such a test, patentees who manipulate the standard-setting process in order to charge supra-competitive fees for their licenses may escape antitrust liability. Indeed, as long as patentees' gains equal or exceed consumers' losses, total welfare would not be lowered. Thus, the misleading conduct would finally pass antitrust scrutiny, to the detriment of the standardization aims in terms of enhanced societal growth and productivity.

2.3 Enhancing efficiency

Enhancing efficiency can be considered as another desirable goal of competition law. Many antitrust agencies in the world have recognized that, in order to promote competition for the long-term welfare of consumers, it is important that resources are best allocated in a competitive market. The process of rivalry between undertakings must ensure that efficiency in the use of resources (e.g., capital, investment, labor, raw materials) be maximized.[66]

Efficiency, therefore, seems to be closely related to the concept of welfare. As Heyer says, "an economy is operating at maximum efficiency when society is squeezing the greatest value – the highest level of welfare – out of its scarce

65 J.M. Keynes (n 61).

66 See Unilateral Conduct Working Group (n 10) 13.

resources."[67] In that situation, usually typical of a perfectly competitive market, undertakings strive to win new customers by producing those products that consumers value most. They try to do so by putting down costs at the lowest possible level and by reducing prices towards the marginal cost of production. In the famous words of Adam Smith, such a competitive process could be interpreted as driven by an "invisible hand," without the need for any governmental intervention in the marketplace.[68] In a perfectly competitive market, where neither producers nor consumers may substantially influence its structure, three types of efficiency are deemed to be maximized: allocative efficiency, productive efficiency, and dynamic efficiency.

2.3.1 Allocative, productive and dynamic efficiency

First, allocative efficiency refers to the model in which resources are allocated between different products in a way that it is not possible to make anyone better off without harming someone else.[69] Second, economists then believe that, in a perfectly competitive structure, productive efficiency is at its largest. Productive efficiency, in particular, refers to the model in which goods and services are produced in the least costly way.[70] Third, with reference to the last concept of efficiency, perfect competition is also deemed to maximize dynamic efficiency.[71] The latter refers to the model in which producers constantly innovate and develop new products. They are stimulated in doing so by the vigorous struggle for winning new customers.[72] The famous economist Schumpeter described it as "competition from the new commodity, the new technology, the new source of supply, the new organization."[73]

In this context, it can be argued that there is little dynamic efficiency in a perfectly competitive market since economic profits will never be so large as to incentivize production of new technologies. Rather, only an undertaking with some market power would be stimulated in investing in expensive research and development.[74] In particular, the pursuit of market power – and in the ultimate analysis monopoly – is what attracts firms and influences their business strategy

67 See K. Heyer (n 4).

68 A. Smith, *The Wealth of Nations* (Strahan and Cadell, London 1776). The metaphor of the "invisible hand" was used by Adam Smith in order to demonstrate that an individual maximizing his own self-interest, thus driven by greed, also maximizes the total revenue and good of the society as a whole. This observation may be reconciled with the view that promoting consumer welfare as enforcement standard can lead to maximize the societal welfare as a whole.

69 See F.M. Scherer and D. Ross, *Industrial Market Structure and Economic Performance* (Houghton Mifflin, Boston 1990).

70 R. Whish and D. Bailey (n 2) Ch. 1.

71 S. Bishop and M. Walker (n 16).

72 On the concept of dynamic efficiency, see in particular M.E. Porter, *Competitive Strategy: Techniques for Analyzing Industries and Competitors* (The Free Press, New York 1980).

73 See J. Schumpeter, *Capitalism, Socialism and Democracy* (Allan & Unwin, London 1943).

74 See J. Galbraith, *American Capitalism: The Concept of Countervailing Power* (Houghton Mifflin, Boston 1952).

in terms of investment in research and development.[75] In brief, the higher the market power (and thus the profits) of a company, the higher the incentive to enhance innovation and dynamic efficiency as a whole.[76] These considerations will be recalled in the analysis of standard-setting bodies. In that context, it will be explained that, in order to encourage IPRs owners' participation, it is crucial to preserve their interests in being rewarded for investments in innovation.

2.3.2 Monopoly and the pursuit of efficiencies

The position of a firm enjoying some market power, but still subject to competitive pressure, must be distinguished from the case of a monopolist. An undertaking already enjoying monopolistic revenues, it has been held, could simply sit on monopoly profits due to the lack of rivalry and of incentives to change the *status quo*. According to Leibenstein, as the monopolist is usually immune from the forces of competition, this would finally lead to inefficiency.[77] In particular, a monopolist would be able to raise prices and reduce the production, increasing in the end the profits. The result would be allocative inefficiency as the output would be lower than it would have been in a perfectly competitive market. The company, moreover, would become "x-inefficient," since also productive efficiency will generally be reduced, as it is unlikely that costs would be held to the lowest possible level.[78] The outcome would finally lead to the use of resources for the right product, but in a less productive way. These considerations explain why monopoly has for long been considered harmful for consumers, while a perfectly competitive system has been deemed to maximize the societal welfare.[79]

It is noteworthy, however, that nowadays the US and (to a minor extent) the EU jurisprudence have developed a more nuanced approach towards monopoly, recognizing that monopolies may present dynamic advantages to the benefit of the society. The *Verizon* case clearly explains why monopoly may be desirable.[80] As Schumpeter realised, "within big units (conscious) policy towards demand and taking a long-term view towards investment becomes possible."[81] One may argue that the *raison d'être* of competition is the struggle for market leadership, and thus a (super) dominant position that may lead to potential benefits should be carefully appraised rather than automatically prohibited. Such intervention could be better

75 On the relationship between market power and dynamic efficiency, see the *Microsoft* saga (Case T-201/04 *Microsoft v European Commission* [2007] ECR II-03601). Here, however, the CFI (after Lisbon, "General Court") finally established that the alleged efficiencies achieved by Microsoft's business strategy did not outweigh the negative effects on consumer welfare.

76 S.M. Willimsky, "The Concept(s) of Competition" (1997) 1 *European Competition Law Review* 54–57.

77 H. Leibenstein, "Allocative Efficiency vs. 'X-Efficiency'" (1966) 56 *American Economic Review* 392.

78 R. Frantz, "X-Efficiency: Past, Present and Future" in K. Weiermair and M. Perlman, *Studies in Economic Rationality* (University of Michigan, Ann Arbor 1990). See also G. Stigler, "The Existence of X-Efficiency" (1976) 66 *American Economic Review* 213–216.

79 On the negative effects of monopoly, see also R. Lande (n 5) 65.

80 *Verizon Communications v Trinko*, 540 US 398 (2004).

81 J. Schumpeter (n 73).

justified, for instance, by the presence in the market of high entry barriers that would facilitate anticompetitive conduct.

For the sake of clarity, no one contests that monopoly *per se* is not unlawful and that competition law should rather sanction abuses of monopolistic power. However, it appears more complex to support the view that monopoly may substantially increase efficiency, to the final benefit of the societal well being.

Rather, it seems more reasonable to state that monopoly, due to the total absence of competitive pressure, would seldom enhance efficiency. At the same time, it seems equally legitimate to doubt that such an aim could be achieved in a perfectly competitive market. In the situation of perfect competition, it is well known, no firms enjoy considerable market shares. More importantly, as Porter observes, perfectly competitive markets can be regarded as utopian, due to the many distortions that generally characterize all markets in the current economy and that prevent high levels of efficiency being reached.[82] Investments require profits. Hence, some market power is needed in order to incentivize a company (still subject to competitive pressure) in investing in research and development to the benefit of efficiencies.[83]

2.3.3 Efficiency and the objective of competition law

Apart from discussing the effects of monopoly on efficiency, the main question to be addressed concerns the role of efficiency as a goal or as a means.[84] The analysis developed in the previous sections has evidenced the need to identify a primary objective of competition policy, as the goals of welfare, efficiency or competitive process may not always be pursued or reconciled at the same time. The arguments presented above have already shown that the optimal primary aim of competition should be societal welfare, best achieved by authorities and courts through the enforcement of a consumer surplus test. An efficiency primary objective, instead, would lead competition enforcers to focus their analysis only on whether firms are producing goods that are most valued by consumers, whether they are doing this at the lowest possible cost of production, and whether firms are reinvesting their profits in innovation.[85] This complex analysis would consequently focus less on the impact of firms' conduct in the marketplace. In particular, such an approach, exclusively focused on allocative productive and dynamic efficiency, would pay insufficient attention to the level of price finally charged to the final consumer. For this reason, it is preferable to enforce a test that would pay more attention to the effects of conduct on consumer surplus, focused on potential increases and

82 M.E. Porter (n 72). See also H.B. Wellford (n 4). As Wellford argues, "perfect competition is impossible to determine, much less regulate, and heavier government intervention in search of perfection is self-defeating."

83 S.M. Willimsky (n 76) 54–57; J. Galbraith (n 74).

84 O. Odudu, *The Boundaries of EU Competition Law: the Scope of Article 81* (Oxford University Press, Oxford 2006) Ch. 6.

85 See for instance O. Williamson, "Economies as an Antitrust Defence: the Welfare Trade-Offs" (1968) 58 *American Economic Review* 18.

reductions of price and output. By enforcing a consumer surplus test aiming at the maximization of societal welfare, also efficiency could be achieved as an indirect objective.[86] Increased consumer welfare, indeed, may have a positive effect on the demand and consumption of goods and services, increasing productivity and enhancing also efficient mechanisms of production.

Such a virtuous mechanism may also be reflected in the functioning of standards institutes. For instance, a standard setting process which ultimately leads to the adoption of an innovative technology licensed at competitive levels will probably lead to final products purchased at not excessive prices, to the benefit of consumers. The latter may then be more motivated in reinvesting their savings in the purchase of further goods and services, determining an increase of productivity and encouraging the enhancement of efficient production methods.

In conclusion, efficiency, rather than being reflected in the immediate legal test adopted by competition enforcers, should be interpreted as an indirect, despite socially desirable, goal to be better achieved through the pursuit of the distinct objective of societal welfare.

2.4 *Pursuing market integration*

The promotion of market integration is what makes the European competition law system unique.[87] Its role is particularly important as the effects of the abolition of trade barriers in the EU can be compromised by firms implementing anticompetitive conduct.[88] Ehlermann rightly noted that the EC Treaty was designed to eliminate all national barriers and to create a Community market characterized by conditions similar to those present at national level.[89]

In order to achieve such a goal, the EC Treaty included provisions on the free movement of goods and services, ensuring the latter could freely flow from one Member State to another, from a low-price area to a high-price area, thus making it impossible for higher prices to be maintained. However, this effect might be limited, for instance, by undertakings entering into agreements that forbid retailers to sell outside a defined territory. Therefore, the competition provisions – in particular Article 101 TFEU – may be considered as supporting those rules in preventing barriers being re-erected by private agreements.[90] The recently amended Article 3(1)(b) TFEU confirmed that competition rules are paramount in the achievement of the Treaty's market integration goal. This objective has for long been viewed as the most relevant goal of EU competition policy.[91]

86 R. Nazzini (n 23) 391–392.

87 L. Parret (n 20) 346.

88 V. Korah (n 7) 85.

89 C.D. Ehlermann, "The Contribution of EC Competition Policy to the Single Market" (1992) 29 *Common Market Law Review* 257.

90 See C. Bellamy and G. Child (n 4) Ch. 2.

91 See S. Wilks and L. McGowan, "Competition Policy in the European Union: Creating a Federal Agency?" in B. Doern and S. Wilks, *Comparative Competition Policy: National Institutions in a Global Market* (Clarendon Press, Oxford 1996).

2.4.1 *The positions of the EU Commission and the courts*

In the debate on the role of market integration, it is worth mentioning the position expressed by the European Commission. In the early days of competition policy, the authority used to pay relevant attention to integration issues. In the last decade, however, the Commission has emphasized the need to give more importance to consumer welfare, and to consider at the same time the protection of competition and market integration as means to enhance consumer surplus and allocative efficiency.[92] However, the jurisprudence of the EU courts still demonstrates that market integration is not simply a means, as it has not lost its crucial value in the scale of the objectives of the EU. The importance of protecting the market has been highlighted by the Court of Justice in the recent judgments *Syfait II* and *GlaxoSmithKline*.[93]

2.4.2 *The relation between welfare and market integration*

It cannot be denied that a close connection exists between integration and the welfare objective, since the protection of the market – by condemning for instance international cartels aimed at territorial allocations – usually has relevant beneficial effects on consumer surplus.[94] A debate could arise as to whether market integration should be interpreted as an intermediary goal, necessary to achieve the *welfarist* aim, or as an ultimate objective itself. The recently ratified Treaty on the European Union reaffirmed the importance of sustainable development of the internal market among the aims of the EU, but has not specified the nature of the connection between welfare and integration.[95]

A different question is whether these two objectives may always be reconciled and whether they may both be reflected in the enforcement legal test. The need to reconcile market integration with the currently more prominent aim of protecting consumers is indeed one of the challenges of EU competition law.[96] First, as already noted, the prohibition of international cartels is undoubtedly beneficial from a *welfarist* perspective. Consumers are indeed penalized by those agreements between suppliers aimed at restricting or eliminating competition. Similarly, beneficial effects for consumers may also derive from the prohibition of vertical restraints, especially those restricting parallel trade across the EU.[97] As

92 European Commission, "Guidelines on the Application of Article 81(3) of the EC Treaty" [2004] OJ C101/97, at 13; European Commission, "DG Competition Discussion Paper on the Application of Article 82 of the Treaty to Exclusionary Abuses" (December 2005), at 4.

93 *GlaxoSmithKline* (n 34); Cases C-468/06 to C-478/06 *Sot. Lelos Kai Sia EE and Others v GlaxoSmithKline AEUE Farmakeftikon Proionton* (*Syfait* II) [2008] ECR I-07139, at 4 and 6. See also Case C-295/04 *Manfredi v Lloyd Adriatico Assicurazioni SpA* [2006] ECR I-6619, at 41.

94 Case T-202/98 *Tate & Lyle v European Commission* [2001] ECR II-2035; Case T-213/00 *CMA CGM v European Commission* [2003] ECR II–913.

95 Article 3(3), Treaty on the European Union (TEU), OJ 2010 C 83/13.

96 See, for instance, *GlaxoSmithKline* (n 34).

97 See Joined Cases 56/64 and 58/64 *Consten & Grundig v European Commission* [1966] ECR 299.

Motta argues, however, concerns may arise in the context of other practices, as in the case of *ad hoc* price discrimination across national borders.[98] The author refers to this practice to evidence the potential tension between the political objective of integration and the economic goal of welfare. Prohibiting price discrimination, as the argument goes, would not be rational under a *welfarist* perspective. Along the same lines, Bishop and Walker seem to confirm the existence of a possible conflict between integration and economic welfare.[99] These views suggest that it may be difficult to reconcile these goals under all circumstances, and that the evaluation of trade-offs may sometimes be necessary.

On the same grounds, it is reasonable to believe that an enforcement legal standard focused on both welfare and market integration may be difficult to apply. Even enforcing a test exclusively focused on market integration does not seem desirable. On the one hand, this test may successfully lead to challenge anti-competitive practices in EU-wide standard setting contexts, which usually play an important role in market integration dynamics. On the other, however, the application of such a test would make competition policy a useless tool in several other circumstances which negatively affect only consumer welfare. This may happen, for instance, in case of national standard-setting institutes developing technical specifications only valid and applicable in local contexts. The choice of a test exclusively based on market integration may leave certain practices (harmful for consumers) out of the scope of competition enforcement.

2.4.3 Market integration and the role of competition

Finally, it is worth remembering that the various amendments of the treaties have also opened a debate on the exact role of competition policy, which seems to have been reconsidered after the Lisbon conference. The function of competition has been subjected to the achievement of the market integration goal.[100] The question, thus, relates to how the EU courts will consider such a policy change (supposing that it should be appraised as a policy change) and whether they will continue referring to competition as a fundamental tool of the Union.[101]

Despite the new language of the Treaty, it seems that these amendments do not justify a substantial shift in the role of competition policy and in the hierarchy of the objectives. Competition policy, as already held, was and still is a means to achieve the aims of the European Union: i.e. societal welfare and market integration.

With reference to the former, the amended Treaty on the EU has confirmed the importance of pursuing balanced economic growth, scientific and technological

98 M. Motta (n 17) 23.

99 S. Bishop and M. Walker (n 16).

100 See Article 3(1)(b) of the Treaty on the Functioning of the European Union (TFEU), OJ 2010 C 83/47. This article now refers to "establishing competition rules necessary for the functioning of the internal market."

101 See *TeliaSonera* (n 64), at 21. Here, the court clearly highlighted the role that competition rules play for the functioning of the internal market.

developments, and a highly competitive social market economy. This suggests that societal welfare continues to be highly considered as a priority of the Union.[102] At the same time, however, reference to a sustainable development of the internal market, price stability and balanced economic growth also suggests that these elements cannot be appraised as unrelated to the market integration issue.

The debate is open, of course, as to the exact nature of the relationship between market integration and welfare objectives. In any case, enforcing a consumer surplus test, aimed at enhancing societal welfare, may have substantial beneficial effects for trade development and market stabilization.

3 Conclusion

EU competition and US antitrust laws have always, and still have, various goals. A compromise approach may mean that all the different cited objectives should be reconciled as much as possible. However, this may prove to be a very difficult task for competition authorities. In enforcing the law, it is often necessary to trade off between different conflicting objectives; and this could require complex and time-consuming analysis. In the United States, there is strong consensus for a consumer welfare standard as the optimal test in antitrust policy. In the EU, also the Commission has referred – especially in the last decade – to consumer welfare as the primary objective of competition law. However, recent judgments of the Court of Justice (e.g. *TeliaSonera*)[103] and the new amendments of the Treaty of Lisbon have not confirmed this view.[104] Which goals should competition policy pursue? The considerations made in the previous sections lead to conclude that the main driver of competition and antitrust policies should be the maximization of societal welfare, through the enforcement of a consumer surplus test; a standard focused on price, output and innovation. By applying such a test, the welfare of the whole society could be maximized. Societal welfare should hence be distinguished from the concept of total welfare adopted by the literature. The achievement of societal surplus indeed implies that both consumers and producers may benefit in the long run.

As it will be explained in the next chapters, the pursuit of consumer and societal welfare is central in the functioning of standards institutes, whose main aim is to develop standards by means of a collaborative process often involving IPRs owners. Standardization can be defined as "the reaching of an agreement on technical or quality requirements, with which current or future products, production processes or methods may or must comply."[105] Standards are crucial in today's knowledge-based economy, as they facilitate the dissemination of knowledge,

102 Article 3(3) of the Treaty on the European Union (TEU), OJ 2010 C 83/13.

103 *TeliaSonera* (n 64), at 22.

104 Treaty of Lisbon, amending the Treaty on European Union and the Treaty establishing the European Community (2007), [2007] OJ C 306/01.

105 C. Koenig and K. Spiekermann, "EC competition law issues of standard setting by officially-entrusted versus private organizations" (2010) 31(11) *European Competition Law Review* 449.

ensure the interoperability of products, and hence make consumers' lives easier.[106] Antitrust policies enforcing a consumer welfare test may work as effective *ex post* remedies to abusive behaviors in SSOs, and may guarantee the optimal functioning of standard setting and the achievement of societal surplus.

The enforcement of a consumer welfare standard may further lead to achieve efficiency, which should be better considered as an indirect, despite desirable, objective of competition rules. Antitrust laws, on a further ground, should not pursue the protection of the competitive process *per se*, as an institution, despite the content of some recent judgments. The protection of competition as a goal may lead in some circumstances to the protection of competitors, and finally to a loss of welfare. Rather, the protection of competition should be better considered as a means to achieve the primary objective.

Other goals of competition have then been cited. Among these, market integration has been recognized as a crucial objective by the amended Lisbon Treaty, in the "multi-valued tradition of European competition law."[107] In this context, competition policy has been clearly subjected to the achievement of the integration goal. However, the new provisions cannot justify the enforcement of a legal test focused on both consumers and market integration. By enforcing such a standard, conflicts could arise and trade-offs would often be necessary, as it is not always possible to reconcile both objectives. Despite the emphasis on integration as one of the Union core aims, therefore, a legal test solely focused on consumer welfare seems preferable. The application of this standard would not necessarily lead to disregard the integration issue. The test, indeed, could also be effective in contrasting those practices that hinder market integration and harm consumers at the same time (e.g. international cartels between producers or vertical restraints between suppliers and distributors).

Finally, among the aims of competition, the literature has also mentioned the concepts of competitiveness, the need to ensure a level playing field for small and medium-sized enterprises, and the promotion of freedom fairness and equality in the marketplace. Again, these goals should be better considered as indirect desirable effects of a *welfarist* competition policy, rather than aims to be directly encompassed in the enforcement legal test.

106 J.L. Contreras and D.L. Newman, "Developing a framework for arbitrating standards-essential patent (SEP) disputes" (2014) American University WCL Research Paper n. 2014–20.

107 R. Van den Berghe and P.D. Camesasca, *European Competition Law and Economics: a Comparative Perspective* (2nd edn, Sweet & Maxwell, London 2006) 39.

2 Goals of IP law and interplay with competition

1 Introduction

It has often been held that competition and intellectual property rights (IPRs) are tools in conflict with themselves. From an *ex ante* point of view, before an investment is made, IPRs promote competition and rivalry as firms strive to receive the benefits of IP protection. From an *ex post* perspective, instead, intellectual property laws are deemed to limit competition, as firms owning IPRs may legitimately exclude rivals from the marketplace. The overlap between these branches of law, therefore, is not completely unexpected. A balance between property rights and competition has been partially achieved by granting an IPR only for a limited amount of time.

However, although a superficial tension exists between the exclusivity awarded by intellectual property and the price-reducing competition pursued by antitrust rules, competition and IPR policies are harmonious in purpose. This means that they promote consistent goals and are complementary rather than discordant. Both bodies of law, indeed, strive to promote consumer welfare and efficiencies, and work together to bring innovation in the marketplace.

The interaction between IP and competition rules has been at the core of several investigations led by the European Commission and the EU courts. The latter have explored the dynamics of such relationships in various disputes, which have highlighted that the mere existence of an exclusive right cannot constitute an abuse, but the way in which such right is exercised may lead to liability. Also in the United States, courts and authorities have dealt with the issue, and have similarly contributed in several circumstances to the heated debate. On a parallel ground, in the last few decades, there has been a substantial amount of EU and international initiatives to promote harmonization of IP law systems. This notwithstanding, it is difficult to find in the law or in the jurisprudence of the EU and, similarly, of the US specific and generally accepted principles that clarify the nature of such interaction.

The main aim of the chapter is twofold: on the one hand, to identify the objectives of IPRs and compare them to the ones pursued by antitrust; on the other, to explore the grounds on which the complementary nature of competition and IP laws may be justified. The discussion on the legal principles emerging from case law will be used as a platform to achieve both goals.

The conclusions of the chapter are particularly relevant, as they will inspire research on standard setting functioning in the core part of the book. Here, the intersection between IPR (in particular, patents) and competition will be scrutinized with a focus on the EU and US standardization contexts.

2 Intellectual property rights (IPRs)

An intellectual property right (IPR) is a negative right granted for the protection of intangible things, such as ideas, signs and information.[1] It can be interpreted as a right to stop others doing certain things (e.g. to stop counterfeiters, imitators and even in some cases third parties who have independently reached the same ideas) from exploiting them without a license from the right owner.[2] The shift from an industrial to a knowledge-based society, increasingly based on the exchange of information, has strengthened the relevance of IPRs due to their key role in promoting innovation and creativity.

Three main categories of IPRs may be identified, each with different rules and different aims: patents, copyrights and trademarks. Patents are usually granted up to 20 years for inventions and technological improvements which satisfy certain criteria, based on novelty, inventive step and industrial applicability.[3] Copyright covers original literary and artistic works, for the author's life plus (depending on the jurisdiction) a period of time between 50 and 70 years.[4] Trademarks protect symbols or signs as long as these are used by businesses, in order to allow consumers to distinguish different brands from each other.[5]

It is beyond the scope of this study to explore thoroughly the doctrinal and normative issues related to each of these three categories of IPRs. Rather, it seems more pertinent to discuss their scope and justification, and understand whether their objectives may be reconciled with the goals of antitrust. In the following chapters, a more prominent role will be given to patents and the dynamics relating to their exploitation; this is due to the key function patents play in influencing and directing standardization activities.

1 H.K.S. Schmidt, "Article 82's 'exceptional circumstances' that restrict intellectual property rights" (2002) 23(5) *European Competition Law Review* 210.

2 See W.R. Cornish, D. Llewelyn and T. Aplin, *Intellectual Property: Patents, Copyrights, Trademarks and Allied Rights* (8th edn, Sweet & Maxwell, London 2013) Part I.

3 See L. Bently and B. Sherman, *Intellectual Property Law* (4th edn, Oxford University Press, Oxford 2014); D. Bainbridge, *Intellectual Property* (8th edn, Longman, Harlow 2010); A.L. Durham, *Patent Law Essentials – A Concise Guide* (4th edn, Praeger Publishers, Westport 2013); and J.H. Park, *Patents and Industry Standards* (Edward Elgar, Cheltenham 2010).

4 See W.R. Cornish, D. Llewelyn and T. Aplin (n 2) Part IV; and H. Laddie, P. Prescott, M. Vitoria, *The Modern Law of Copyright and Designs* (4th edn, Butterworths, London 2011).

5 See P. Torremans, *Holyoak and Torremans Intellectual Property Law* (7th edn, Oxford University Press, Oxford 2013); and J. Phillips, *Trademark Law – A Practical Anatomy* (Oxford University Press, Oxford 2003).

2.1 Justification and scope of IPRs

One of the central questions relates to the underlying *raison d'être* and purpose of IP rights. Two main justification theories deserve careful attention. The first highlights the role of IPRs in encouraging firms to invest in innovation. It is based on the fact that, without a reasonable protection of the inventor against the possible exploitation of rivals, there will accordingly be little incentive to invest in the ideas or information and the consumer may be correspondingly the poorer.[6] This would explain the IPRs' monopolistic nature. The second is based on the need to reward innovators for the efforts they have put into their invention. From an historical perspective, this view emanates from the philosopher John Locke's famous arguments about the origins of property and how "intellectual property is seen as a suitable reward for intellectual labour."[7] It should not be necessary for a deeper examination of these concepts to understand that these theories are inextricably intertwined, and ultimately identify the desirable function of IPRs for the society.

On the other side of the spectrum, various objections have been raised against IPRs. Firstly, it has been questioned whether other non-exclusionary systems, with fewer social and economic costs, exist as incentives to innovate.[8] From this perspective, the monopolistic character of IPRs has been seen as a serious threat for societal welfare. Secondly, it has been said that several works of art may still be created even in the absence of IPRs, as these are not always necessary for some products to appear in the marketplace.[9] The criticisms, however, do not seem persuasive. It is true that some works may still be produced in the absence of IPRs, and that other means to encourage innovation may exist (e.g. tax incentives). However, these views cannot be generalized. Legal protection has a strong impact on the willingness to engage in time-consuming and costly research activities, which would not otherwise be undertaken.[10]

The debate on the justification for IPRs inevitably recalls the discussion on the scope of intellectual property and on the need to set its boundaries. In this context, there is a very fragile relationship between the interests of the creator and those of society.[11] On the one hand, the innovator must be incentivized to invest in the production of IP works by providing effective legal protection. On the other hand, these products must find their way into the public domain. Put differently, it is essential to guarantee that the public is ultimately able to access the fruit of

6 See W.R. Cornish, D. Llewellyn and T. Aplin (n 2) Part I.

7 C. May, *A Global Political Economy of Intellectual Property Rights: The New Enclosures?* (Routledge, New York 2000) 7.

8 On the argument, see B. Gurel, "An External Method for Establishing the Balance in Intellectual Property Rights' Scope: Article 102 of the TFEU" (2010) 3 *Global Antitrust Review* 53.

9 L. Bently and B. Sherman (n 3).

10 A. Brown, J. Cornwell, S. Kheria, C. Waelde and G. Laurie, *Contemporary Intellectual Property: Law and Policy* (3rd edn, Oxford University Press, Oxford 2013); D.G. Swanson and W.J. Baumol, "Reasonable and Non-discriminatory (RAND) Royalties, Standards Selection, and Control of Market Power" (2005–2006) 73 *Antitrust Law Journal* 2.

11 B. Gurel (n 8) 54.

human creativity.[12] Without this, society will not benefit from the innovative nature of works of art. In order to reach a reasonable balance between public and private interests, restrictions on the duration of IPRs have been set. This internal mechanism has contributed to define the boundaries of their scope. However, other factors may also have an influence.[13]

2.2 Objectives of IPRs

Having discussed the scope and justification of IPRs, it is crucial to take a step further and explore their aims from a broader standpoint. From this perspective, it is legitimate to question how IPRs may affect consumer and societal welfare, as well as dynamic efficiency and the competitive processes. Further questions may also arise with respect to the relationship between property rights and market integration goals. All these objectives have been ascribed by the literature to competition policy, albeit to different extents.[14]

2.2.1 Promotion of competition

First, an initial assessment of the goals of IPRs leads to evaluate the effects they have on the promotion of competition. In this regard, the literature has developed a traditional approach, interpreted as something more than a mere philosophical exercise.[15] From an *ex ante* perspective (before an investment is made), IPRs encourage competition as firms are incentivized to strive in the market and get the benefits of IP legal protection. From an *ex post* standpoint (after the grant of the right), IPRs reveal their exclusionary nature as they allow holders to legitimately exclude competitors from certain business. This kind of influence on competition dynamics is ambiguous; it cannot be generalized under just one perspective. However, the promotion of competition *per se* should not be considered as a desirable goal. Rather, rivalry should be interpreted as a means to achieve more relevant social aims.[16] The *ex ante–ex post* perspectives do not seem to shed substantial light on the true objectives of IP rights.

12 On the objectives of IP protection and enforcement, see also Article 7 of the Agreement on Trade Related Aspects of Intellectual Property Rights (TRIPs), Annex 1C to the Marrakesh Agreement establishing the World Trade Organization (WTO), 33 ILM 1197 (1994).

13 See C. May (n 7) 7–8; V. Korah, "The Interface between Intellectual Property and Antitrust: the European Experience" (2002) 69 *Antitrust Law Journal* 801; and D.A. Balto and A.M. Wolman, "Intellectual Property and Antitrust: General Principles" (2003) 43 *IDEA: The Journal of Law and Technology* 395.

14 See above, Chapter I sections 2.1, 2.2, 2.3, 2.4.

15 On the issue, see for instance M.A. Lemley, "Ex Ante versus Ex Post Justifications for Intellectual Property" (2004) UC Berkeley Public Law Research Paper n. 144.

16 See Chapter I, section 2.1.

2.2.2 *Dynamic efficiency*

Among the goals which may be potentially ascribed to IPRs, dynamic efficiency certainly plays a more significant role. IP law systems indeed may be interpreted as the strongest "tools available to stimulate and channel innovation."[17] Driven by the aim of getting the benefits of IP protection, undertakings give rise to the innovation cycle, characterized by three steps: the creation of the innovative work; the subsequent adoption and diffusion of the invention in the society; and the ultimate phase in which the work becomes part of the public domain, after the expiry of legal protection.[18] This dynamic cycle, which flows from exclusivity to accessibility, finally brings a "great ocean of knowledge in the accessible domain."[19] The aforementioned balance between private and public interests is thus reflected in these three steps.[20]

These considerations seem to suggest that the pursuit of dynamic efficiency (i.e. the development of new innovative products) through the grant of IPRs should not be appraised as an objective in itself. Rather, it should be interpreted as being closely related to a more relevant goal, centered on the concept of welfare.

2.2.3 *Consumer and societal welfare*

As concepts, consumer and societal welfare are intrinsically intertwined. The enhancement of the former inevitably has a positive impact on the latter. This conclusion has been thoroughly justified in Chapter 1, in the examination of the goals of competition.[21] Keynes's economic model has been used as a platform to validate this assertion.[22] In brief, the bedrock of the theory lies on the likely reaction consumers would have in case of increases of their welfare. It has been explained that consumers would be incentivized to spend more money in the purchase of further products. This mechanism would benefit also producers, finally leading to the enhancement of the societal welfare.

Given this premise, the key question is whether and to what extent these goals may be ascribed to IPRs. The relationship between competition and IP laws, indeed, ultimately depends on their core objectives and on the possibility of reconciling them. One traditional opinion has been that this creates an irreversible conflict due to the opposite approaches competition and IP laws have towards exclusivity. This position, however, cannot be endorsed. It should not be forgotten that "all the systems of intellectual property rights are based on the premise that a restraint of competition is necessary to increase ultimately competition in the

17 M.A. Gollin, *Driving Innovation: Intellectual Property Strategies for a Dynamic World* (Cambridge University Press, Cambridge 2008) 12.

18 B. Gurel (n 8) 55.

19 M.A. Gollin (n 17) 19.

20 See also J.H. Barton, "The Balance between Intellectual Property Rights and Competition: Paradigms in the Information Sector" (1997) 18 *European Competition Law Review* 443.

21 See Chapter I, section 2.2.1.

22 J.M. Keynes, *The General Theory of Employment, Interest and Money* (Macmillan, London 1936).

public interest."[23] The public interest must be identified in the welfare of consumers. In other words, the exclusivity initially granted by IPRs must be interpreted as a tool to encourage further competition, to the benefit of successful innovation and consumer surplus. Therefore, even if there appears to be a *prima facie* tension, no irremediable conflict exists.[24] Rather, these two legal systems are harmonious in purpose, and should be "reconciled by emphasising their common goal of promoting overall consumer welfare."[25] As will be seen below, Microsoft clearly highlighted the apparent tension between competition and IPRs; at the same time, it also emphasized their common ultimate aim.

The fact that the achievement of this aim has a likely positive impact on the well-being of the whole of society leads to the conclusion that both consumer and societal welfare should be taken as the true objectives of IPRs. Among these, instead, there should be little room for market integration because the exclusionary nature of IPRs may facilitate (as in the case of patents) dynamics of territorial protection, ultimately running counter to any integration purpose.

3 IPRs and Article 102 TFEU

Albeit harmonious in purpose, competition and IP laws tend to pursue their objectives using different means. This may give rise to the well-known tension examined above. It has been explained that IP law systems usually have their inner balancing mechanisms, which regulate what can be protected and for how long. However, in order to reach a proper balance between private and public interests, other external "forces" must also be taken into account. One of these "forces" is represented by competition law.

Article 102 of the Treaty on the Functioning of the European Union (TFEU) may indeed be determinative and limit attempts to over-exploit IPRs.[26] This provision, in particular, prohibits any abuse[27] by one or more undertakings of a dominant position[28] within the internal market or a substantial part of it, in so far

23 I. Govaere, *The Use and Abuse of Intellectual Property Rights in EC Law* (Sweet & Maxwell, London 1996) 29.

24 B. Gurel (n 8) 57.

25 A.S. Gutterman, *Innovation and Competition Policy* (Kluwer Law International, London 1997) 11. *Cf.* E. Ramirez and L. Kimmel, "A Competition Policy Perspective on Patent Law: the Federal Trade Commission's Report on the Evolving IP Marketplace" (2011) *The Antitrust Source* 1.

26 Article 102, Treaty on the Functioning of the European Union (TFEU), OJ [2010] C 83/89.

27 On the concept of abuse, see Case 85/76 *Hoffmann-La Roche v European Commission* [1979] ECR 461, at 91; Case 322/81 *Michelin v European Commission* [1983] ECR 3461, at 70; Case C-62/86 *AKZO v European Commission* [1991] ECR I-3359, at 69; Case 31/80 *L'Oréal v De Nieuwe AMCK* [1980] ECR 3775, at 27; Case T-30/89 *Hilti v European Commission* [1992] ECR II-1439, at 8; and Case C-333/94P *Tetra Pak v European Commission* [1996] ECR I-5951, at 37.

28 On the concept of dominant position, see Case 27/76 *United Brands v European Commission* [1978] ECR 207, at 65; *Hoffmann-La Roche* (n 27), at 38; *Michelin* (n 27), at 29; Case 30/87 *Bodson v Pompes Funebres* [1988] ECR 2479, at 26; Joined Cases C 395/96 P & 396/96 P, *Compagnie Maritime Belge Transports v European Commission* [2000] ECR I-1365, at 34; Case T-282/02 *Cementbouw Handel v European Commission* [2006] ECR II-319, at 195; Case C-280/08 *Deutsche Telekom AG v European Commission* [2010] OJ C 346, at 170; Case T-321/05 *AstraZeneca AB v European Commission*

as it may affect trade between Member States. It is beyond the the scope of this book to examine exhaustively the doctrinal and normative issues related to dominance and abuse.[29] Rather, the analysis of these concepts and of the jurisprudence on Article 102 TFEU is relevant to the research project as long as it concerns the interaction between IP and competition laws.

Getting back to the core problem of this chapter, not everyone agrees that competition is a proper remedy to constrain innovators' IP strategy. For instance, it has been suggested that IPRs should be immunized against competition law enforcement, since exclusivity derives from the very nature of these rights.[30] On a further note, it has been added, limitations on the exercise of IPRs by competition would be questionable from a policy perspective, as there might be a lower interest in investing in innovation.[31] Finally, it has been questioned whether competition authorities may be well suited to oversee the objectives of IP laws.[32]

Although these criticisms may have an element of truth, it seems more reasonable to argue that IP rules should be subject to competition intervention in the same way as they must comply with other fields of law; examples come from "environmental laws, health and safety laws and drug safety laws, that restrict the free exercise of these rights in the public interest."[33] In particular, the risks of IPRs misuse by innovators do justify the enforcement of competition in the interest of consumer and societal welfare. Such enforcement, however, should be triggered only in those exceptional circumstances in which IP law's own mechanisms do not resolve the tension.[34]

The next sections will be devoted to examine the legal principles emerging from case law. The Commission and the EU courts have extensively contributed to the debate on the intersection between IP and competition laws. It must be seen, however, how they have interpreted the delicate relationship between these two fields of law, above all the conduct of refusal to license or deal by dominant innovators. The conclusions will be further recalled in Chapter 7, on standard setting

[2010] OJ C 221, at 239; and Case C-52/09 *Konkurrensverket v TeliaSonera AB* [2011] ECR I-527, at 23.

29 On these concepts see, *inter alia*, R. Nazzini, *The Foundations of European Union Competition Law – The Objective and Principles of Article 102* (Oxford University Press, New York 2011) 107; M.M. Dabbah, "Conduct, Dominance and Abuse in 'Market Relationship': Analysis of Some Conceptual Issues under Article 82 EC" (2000) 21(1) *European Competition Law Review* 47; and D. Sinclair, "Abuse of Dominance at a Crossroads – Potential Effect, Object and Appreciability under Article 82 EC" (2004) 25(8) *European Competition Law Review* 492.

30 See C. Ritter, "Refusal to Deal and Essential Facilities: Does Intellectual Property Require Special Deference Compared to Tangible Property?" (2005) 28(3) *World Competition* 291.

31 V. Korah, *Intellectual Property Rights and the EC Competition Rules* (Hart Publishing, London 2006).

32 See B. Gurel (n 8) 58.

33 S. Anderman, "Does the Microsoft Case Offer a New Paradigm for the Exceptional Circumstances Test and Compulsory Copyright Licenses Under EC Competition Law?" (2004) 1(2) *Competition Law Review* 22. See also R. Hewitt Pate, "Competition and Intellectual Property in the US: Licensing Freedom and the Limits of Antitrust" (Speech at *EU Competition Workshop*, Florence – 3 June 2005).

34 See R. Dreyfuss, D.L. Zimmerman and H. First, *Expanding the Boundaries of Intellectual Property: Innovation Policy for the Knowledge Society* (Oxford University Press, New York 2001) 312.

enforcement. Below, a synthetic overview of the main disputes on this practice will try to shed light on the EU approach. As to the second relevant conduct, the charging of excessive fees for licensing IPRs, the EU approach will be thoroughly examined in the chapters on standardization.[35]

3.1 Volvo

Volvo[36] is known as the first case in which a refusal to license IPRs was scrutinized under EU competition law. The question was whether a refusal to license by the proprietor of a protected design could amount to an abuse of dominance, contrary to Article 102 TFEU. The court first said that the use in a normal manner of an IPR does not usually lead to abusive practice. It explained that the proprietor of a protected design was not obliged to license to third parties, even in return for a reasonable royalty. It then concluded that, as the conduct constituted the "very subject matter of the exclusive right," it could never be, in itself, an abuse of dominance.[37] The finding of an infringement should require further elements in the conduct under investigation. Among these, the Court of Justice mentioned the charging of unfair prices, or the arbitrary decision to stop supplies or production of certain demanded products.[38] This meant, in the Court's view, that refusal to supply or license IPRs could be unlawful only under specific circumstances, to be assessed on a case-by-case basis.[39] However, as part of the literature observed, the decision seemed to be generally unclear as to when the exercise of IPRs may be deemed abusive.[40]

3.2 Magill

The dispute in *Magill*, when compared to *Volvo*, certainly reveals a more restrictive approach on the part of the Commission and the EU courts in defining the scope of IPRs protection.[41] The decision, upheld by the Court of First Instance and Court of Justice, required the broadcasters for television programme listings to grant a license to third parties willing to publish a comprehensive weekly guide. First, the firms under investigation were found to enjoy a *de facto* monopoly over the information used to compile listings. Second, their refusal to license was interpreted as an abuse of their dominant position, preventing the appearance of

35 See Chapter 4, section 4.3, and Chapter 6, section 4. Among the most relevant cases on excessive pricing in general, see for instance *United Brands* (n 28) and *Bodson* (n 28).

36 Case C-238/87 *AB Volvo v Erik Veng* (UK) [1989] 4 CMLR 122.

37 Ibid., at 8.

38 Ibid., at 9. See also J.H. Park (n 3) 62.

39 On the concept of abuse in relation to IPRs, see also Case 24/67 *Parke, Davis & Company v Probel and Others* [1968] CMLR 47, at 4.

40 See A. Jones and B. Sufrin, *EU Competition Law: Text, Cases & Materials* (5th edn, Oxford University Press, New York 2014) Ch 7.

41 Joined Cases C 241-242/91 P, *Radio Telefis Eireann & Independent Television Publications v European Commission* [1995] 4 CMLR 718.

a new product for which there was potential consumer demand. This approach was also supported by the fact that there was no actual or potential substitute to the product and that there was no justification for a refusal. Rather, the IPRs owners were reserving for themselves the secondary market of weekly TV guides, by excluding all competition through denial of access to basic information – the raw material indispensable for the compilation of such a guide.[42] All these factors represented "exceptional circumstances," which ultimately led the Commission to apply Article 102 TFEU and impose on the broadcasters a compulsory license.[43]

However, the case also raised several doubts and criticisms. First, at least at the time of the judgment, it was not clear whether these conditions had to be interpreted as cumulative or whether each of them could separately constitute an abuse.[44] Second, it was observed that the final decision had given no guidance on the defences IPRs holders may oppose (e.g. in terms of objective justifications).[45] Finally, from a more general perspective, doubts arose as to the likely negative effects that the case would have had on the innovators' incentives to invest in costly and time-consuming research.[46]

Despite the criticisms, *Magill* also clarified a few crucial concepts. On the one hand, it acknowledged that the mere ownership of an IPR cannot automatically confer a dominant position. When dominance is found, instead, only the exercise of an IPR may lead to an infringement of competition law.[47] On the other hand, the case deserves consideration for having taken a step further in exploring those "exceptional circumstances" which may justify competition enforcement. The test developed therein strongly influenced further judgments of the EU courts, which in turn contributed to expand the scope of *Magill*.

3.3 Tierce Ladbroke

The relevance of *Tierce Ladbroke* lies in the attempt to solve one of the issues that *Magill* had left open.[48] In the dispute, concerning a refusal to license copyright for televised pictures and sound commentaries on horse races, the Court of First Instance interpreted the "exceptional circumstances" identified in *Magill* as

42 M. Angelov, "The Exceptional Circumstances Test: Implications for FRAND Commitments from the Essential Facilities Doctrine under Art. 102 TFEU" (2014) 10(1) *European Competition Journal* 45.

43 On compulsory licences and exceptional circumstances, see G. Julian Arnold, "International Compulsory Licensing: the Rationales and the Reality" (1993) 33 *IDEA: The Journal of Law and Technology* 349; and L. Zhang, "Refusal to License Intellectual Property Rights under Article 82 EC in Light of Standardisation Context" (2010) 32(8) *European Intellectual Property Review* 404.

44 See A. Jones and B. Sufrin (n 40); T.C. Vinje, "The Final Word on *Magill*" (1995) 6 *European Intellectual Property Review* 297; and J.H. Park (n 3) 64.

45 S. Anderman, "EC Competition Law and Intellectual Property Rights in the New Economy" (2002) *Antitrust Bulletin* 293–294.

46 D. Aitman and A. Jones, "Competition Law and Copyright: Has the Copyright Owner Lost the Ability to Control His Copyright?" (2004) 26(3) *European Intellectual Property Review* 137.

47 *Radio Telefis Eireann* (n 41), at 46–50.

48 Case T-504/93 *Tierce Ladbroke SA v European Commission* [1997] ECR II-923.

alternative, rather than cumulative. In particular, it ruled that an abuse of dominance by an IPR owner may occur either when the refusal to license impedes the appearance of a new demanded product, or where the refusal concerns a product which is essential for activities in a related market.[49] As none of these conditions were deemed to exist, the court did not enforce Article 102. The interpretation articulated in *Tierce Ludbroke*, however, was not upheld by other rulings also focused on the intersection between IPRs and competition.

3.4 Oscar Bronner

One of these cases was *Oscar Bronner,* which did not directly concern IPRs but a refusal to supply a tangible good, considered by the claimant as an essential facility.[50] Contrary to the ruling in *Tierce Ladbroke*, *Oscar Bronner* interpreted *Magill* as requiring that all the exceptional circumstances should be present before Article 102 could be applied to confine the ambit of IPRs. By interpreting the conditions as cumulative rather than alternative, it would be more difficult to find liability on the part of IPRs owners. On a further ground, the ruling is relevant as it held that *Magill* was applicable not only to IPRs but also to other types of property rights, thereby expanding its scope. Thus, it is clear why *Oscar Bronner* with its strict test has been considered as a step towards "legal predictability and concern for the stronger firm's incentives to invest."[51]

Even more interesting was the reasonable analysis made in the case by the Advocate General Jacobs, which concerned the rationales of IPRs. In addressing the issue, he highlighted the importance of developing a proper balance between IP and competition laws; a balance reflecting the need to protect the efforts made by firms in investing in innovative research. On the basis of this premise, the Advocate General confirmed that refusal to license IPRs or supply an essential facility (e.g. an infrastructure) should be treated as an abuse only when exceptional conditions justify limitations to the right "to choose one's trading partners and freely dispose of one's property."[52]

49 Ibid., at 131. See also J.H. Park (n 3) 64–65.

50 Case C-7/97 *Oscar Bronner GmbH and Co KG v Mediaprint Zeitungs* [1998] ECR I-7791. On the concept of essential facility, see C. Stothers, "Refusal to Supply as Abuse of a Dominant Position: Essential Facilities in the European Union" (2001) 22(7) *European Competition Law Review* 256; I. Nagy, "Refusal to Deal and the Doctrine of Essential Facilities in US and EC Competition Law: a Comparative Perspective and a Proposal for a Workable Analytical Framework" (2007) 32(5) *European Law Review* 664; M. Furse, "The Essential Facilities Doctrine in Community Law" (1995) 16(8) *European Competition Law Review* 469; and J. Turney, "Defining the Limits of the EU Essential Facilities Doctrine on Intellectual Property Rights: the Primacy of Securing Optimal Innovation" (2005) 3 *Northwestern Journal of Technology and Intellectual Property* 179.

51 M.A. Bergman, "The Bronner Case – A Turning Point for the Essential Facilities Doctrine?" (2000) 21(2) *European Competition Law Review* 63.

52 Opinion of Advocate General Jacobs delivered on 28 May 1998, in *Oscar Bronner* (n 50), at 56.

3.5 IMS Health

The arguments of the Advocate General in *Oscar Bronner* were further explored in *IMS Health*.[53] The case concerned a "1860 brick structure" developed by IMS and aimed at providing data on regional sales of pharmaceutical products in Germany. The intervention of the Court of Justice was triggered by a preliminary reference of a national court about the interpretation of Article 102 TFEU in refusal to license IPRs disputes. In this case, indeed, IMS had refused to license copyright covering its invention, widely adopted by the market.[54]

Leaving aside the complex procedural background, the relevance of the case lies in the fact that the Court of Justice substantially followed *Magill*. In particular, it explained that the factors mentioned in *Magill* are cumulative and that all of them must be satisfied to find a competition violation. The element of the emergence of a new product, for instance, was discussed in-depth by the Court, which rejected the choice of a compulsory license in case competitors only propose to "clone" the main item. Only the advancement of innovative processes, through the development of new products, may justify a limitation of IPRs through the grant of a license.[55] In the Court's words, a refusal:

> may be abusive only where the undertaking which requested the license does not intend to limit itself essentially to duplicating the goods or services already offered on the secondary market by the owner of the copyright, but intends to produce new goods or services.[56]

In this sense, the Court seems to have struck properly the balance between IPRs holders' interests and competition objectives. Indeed, preventing the appearance of a new demanded product would run counter to the aim of promoting innovation, yet encouraged by both IP and competition laws.[57] Ultimately, this would have a negative impact on both consumer and societal welfare. At the same time, the imposition of a compulsory license in case of "clones" may considerably undermine the innovators' incentives to invest, and may consequently limit competition among them.

53 Case C-418/01 *IMS Health GmbH v NDC Health GmbH* [2004] 4 CMLR 28.

54 J.H. Park (n 3) 67. See also C. Ahlborn, D.S. Evans and A.J. Padilla, "The Logic and Limits of the 'Exceptional Circumstances Test' in *Magill* and *IMS Health*" (2005) 28 *Fordham International Law Journal* 1109; and B. Ong, "Anticompetitive Refusal to Grant Copyright Licenses: Reflections on the IMS Saga" (2004) 26(11) *European Intellectual Property Review* 505.

55 See S. Anderman (n 33) 13; and M. Angelov (n 42) 47.

56 *IMS Health* (n 53), at 49.

57 E. Derclaye, "The IMS Health Decision and the Reconciliation of Copyright and Competition Law" (2004) 29(5) *European Law Review* 687.

3.6 Microsoft

Among the cases on refusal to license IPRs, *Microsoft* is certainly the most interesting and, perhaps, the most controversial.[58] The scope of the legal matters addressed, the amount of the sanction ultimately imposed, and the criticism it attracted are all elements which contribute to explain the strong impact it had on the legal environment. Besides the refusal to license issue, the dispute also concerned a further abuse, which was the tying of two different products. However, due to the objective this book aims to achieve, this subsection will focus only on the first issue (i.e. Microsoft's refusal to license interoperability information to its competitors). This type of conduct, indeed, will be further examined in the core part of the book, dealing with standard setting and anticompetitive practices. Microsoft, in particular, had a dominant position in the markets of PC operating systems and work group server operating systems. These markets typically emerge as a result of time-consuming and costly investments, and are characterized by the necessity of interoperability information between hardware and software components of computer systems. Microsoft's unique position was interpreted as super-dominant or quasi-monopolistic, and could be explained in light of the network effects usually arising in these high technology markets.[59] Its products were seen as standards *de facto*, which means widely adopted goods emerging through the mediation of the market.[60] Thus, as a firm "more dominant" than the others,[61] Microsoft was expected to bear an even higher level of responsibility towards its rivals for not abusing this position.

The first relevant issue on Microsoft's refusal to license concerned the "new product" requirement, which had been set in *Magill* and restated in *IMS*. These cases, however, had not given a precise definition of the concept of "new product."[62] The decisions of the Commission and Court of First Instance in *Microsoft* gave an interpretation which increased uncertainty and attracted criticism. Indeed, there was no thorough explanation of such a concept. Rather, as Geradin noted, Microsoft's behavior was considered as preventing the emergence of "unspecified future new products."[63] It seems that the Court of First Instance had simply broadened that requirement by interpreting it as a "limitation to technical development to the prejudice of consumers under Article 102(b)."[64] Accordingly, as long as those rivals developing some new technical features on

58 Case C-3/37.792 *Microsoft* [2007] OJ L32; and Case T-201/04 *Microsoft v European Commission* [2007] ECR II-03601.

59 J.H. Park (n 3) 70. Network effects increase the value of a product with each additional user.

60 On the concept of *de facto* standard, see Chapter 3, section 2.1.

61 J. Appeldoorn, "He Who Spareth His Rod, Hateth His Son? Microsoft, Super-dominance and Article 82 EC" (2005) 26(12) *European Competition Law Review* 653.

62 E. Derclaye (n 57) 687.

63 D. Geradin, "Limiting the Scope of Article 82 of the EC Treaty: What can the EU Learn from the US Supreme Court's Judgment in *Trinko* in the wake of *Microsoft*, *IMS*, and *Deutsche Telekom*" (2004) 41 *Common Market Law Review* 1538.

64 Case T-201/04 *Microsoft v European Commission* [2007] ECR II-03601, at 647.

the same product were able to show potential consumer harm in case of limited access, their requests of IPRs licenses should have been accepted.[65] As the working group servers of Microsoft's competitors were considered to have better technical features, the Court – following the Commission's approach – had found it reasonable to impose a compulsory license on Microsoft.[66] As mentioned above, however, this approach has been seen as one which may easily weaken the balance between IP and competition.[67] Indeed, under these criteria, rivals will have a substantially higher possibility of getting access to the dominant firm's IP portfolio. This is because, in high technology industries driven by fast innovation and short lifetime products, they would almost always be in the position to claim that better technical features can be developed.

Besides the "new product" requirement, a further subject in *Microsoft* drew the attention of the critics. This concerned the objective justification which may be opposed by a defendant to reject a competition law infringement. During the investigations, Microsoft had simply stated that the very existence of IPRs should be interpreted as an objective justification to refusal to license.[68] As the outcome of substantial investments, it was contended, IPRs constitute the very incentive that leads firms to develop innovative goods and services. However, these arguments were rejected by both the Commission and the Court of First Instance. The former applied an "effect-based" approach in an attempt to understand whether "possible negative impact of an order to supply on Microsoft's incentives to innovate is outweighed by its positive impact on the level of innovation of the whole industry."[69] The Court of First Instance, then, approved the Commission's analysis and confirmed that Microsoft had developed "vague, general and theoretical arguments."[70] Such an effect-based approach appeared to be in line with the modernization process of EU competition law, which seemed to promote an appraisal of conduct not merely based on the form but more focused on the ultimate effects.[71] Of course, an effect-based analysis may, in theory, provide for less legal certainty for the dominant firms, as these would have weak guidance to know whether they are abusing their position or not.[72] However, this approach seemed to respond better to the need to ensure that only conduct harming consumer (and consequently societal) welfare may be captured by Article 102 TFEU. From this perspective, the merit of the Commission's line of reasoning could not be denied.

65 S. Anderman, "Microsoft v Commission and the Interoperability Issue" (2008) 30(10) *European Intellectual Property Review* 399; M. Angelov (n 42) 49.

66 *Microsoft* (n 64), at 650.

67 See B. Gurel (n 8) 66; and J.H. Park (n 3) 75.

68 In the US case, the DC Circuit had ironically held that the notion that copyright is a complete defense to an antitrust offense is "no more correct than the proposition that use of one's personal property, such as a baseball bat, cannot give rise to tort liability" (*US v Microsoft*, 253 F3d 34).

69 Case C-3/37.792 *Microsoft* [2007] OJ L32, at 783.

70 *Microsoft* (n 64), at 698.

71 A. Jones and B. Sufrin (n 40).

72 D. Geradin (n 63) 1553. See also D. Geradin, "Pricing Abuses by Essential Patent Holders in a Standard-Setting Context: a View from Europe" (2009–2010) 76 *Antitrust Law Journal* 329.

In conclusion, despite the reasonableness of the effect-based test, the *Microsoft* judgment was criticized: (a) for having failed to make clear once and for all what constitutes a "new product"; and (b) for having developed an approach too biased towards follow-on inventors. Nevertheless, the importance of the case for the analysis developed on the interaction between competition and IPRs cannot be forgotten. In this context, it is made clear that, despite the superficial tension which may arise together with the need to set a balance, the ultimate goal (consumer surplus) of competition and IPRs is concordant.[73]

4 IPRs and Section 2 of the US Sherman Act

On the other side of the Atlantic, US courts have frequently been involved in the assessment of potentially abusive practices by IPRs owners. Section 2 of the Sherman Act is the relevant provision addressing conduct of monopolization and attempted monopolization.[74] Monopoly power has been defined as "the power to control prices or exclude competition."[75]

The concept of monopolization, however, differs from the attempt to monopolize. The former is based on the possession of monopoly power and on the wilful acquisition or maintenance of it through improper means.[76] The attempt to monopolize, instead, is based on the anticompetitive conduct, a specific intent to monopolize, and the dangerous probability of achieving monopoly power.[77] Therefore, unlike monopolization, it is not necessary to succeed and gain monopoly.[78] Although it seems to have a more limited scope, Section 2 can be considered as the corresponding provision to Article 102 TFEU.

US courts have often applied Section 2 to cases involving the tension between IPRs and antitrust. *Kodak*[79] and *Xerox*[80] are among the most interesting disputes on the intersection between these two fields of law.[81] In comparison with EU case

73 For further analysis of Microsoft's conduct, see M. Muller, "The European Commission's Decision against Microsoft: A Violation of the Antitrust Agreements between the United States and the European Union?" (2005) 26(6) *European Competition Law Review* 309; W.H. Page, "Mandatory Contracting Remedies in the American and European *Microsoft* Cases" (2009) 75(3) *Antitrust Law Journal* 787; and S. Vezzoso, "The Incentives Balance Test in the EU *Microsoft* case: A Pro-innovation Economics-based Approach?" (2006) 27(7) *European Competition Law Review* 382.

74 15 USC § 2. Section 2 condemns "[e]very person who shall monopolize, or attempt to monopolize, or combine or conspire with any other person or persons, to monopolize any part of the trade or commerce among the several States, or with foreign nations."

75 *Aspen Skiing v Aspen Highlands Skiing*, 472 US 585 (1985).

76 S.W. O'Donnell, "Unified Theory of Antitrust Counterclaims in Patent Litigation" (2004) 9 *Virginia Journal of Law and Technology* 22.

77 See J.H. Park (n 3) 25; and M.A. Lemley, "Antitrust and the Internet Standardization Problem" (1996) 28 *Connecticut Law Review* 1066–1067.

78 On the analysis of Section 2 requirements, see also Chapter 5, section 2.

79 *Eastman Kodak v Image Technical Services*, 504 US 451 (1992); and *Image Technical Services v Eastman Kodak*, 125 F3d 1195 (C App 9th Circuit, 1997).

80 *Independent Service Organizations v Xerox Corp.*, 203 F3d 1322 (C App Federal Circuit, 2000); and *SCM v Xerox Corp.*, 645 F2d 1195 (C App 2nd Circuit, 1981).

81 See also *United States v Microsoft*, 97 F Supp 2d 59 (D. District of Columbia, 2000); and *United States v*

law, both similarities and divergences can be found. On the one hand, differences arise when interpreting the mere charging of excessive fees for licensing IPRs. As it will be explained, such exploitative conduct would seldom fall under US antitrust scrutiny, as the Sherman Act only contemplates exclusionary practices.[82] On the other hand, further elements highlight parallel approaches between the two legal systems. In particular, a few basic principles have been accepted in both jurisdictions. For instance, similarly to what had been held in *Volvo*,[83] in *Westinghouse Electric* the US Court of Appeals had clarified that the exercise of IPRs (including a refusal to license) does not lead to an abuse *per se*.[84] This notwithstanding, also in the US, uncertainties exist on the boundaries between antitrust and IPRs. The next sections will delve into the courts' approach, with a specific focus on refusal to deal and license IPRs.

4.1 Xerox

The *Xerox* litigation concerned issues of both refusals to deal and to license IPRs. In the first dispute, the US Court of Appeals for the Second Circuit had to decide whether Xerox's refusal to license IPRs covering its plain paper copying technology had infringed Section 2.[85] In this context, the Court said that:

> [i]f the threat of treble damage liability for refusing to license were imbedded in the minds of potential patent holders as a likely prospect incident to every successful commercial exploitation of a patented invention, the efficacy of the economic incentives afforded by our patent system might be severely diminished … [W]here a patent has been lawfully acquired, subsequent conduct permissible under the patent laws cannot trigger any liability under the antitrust laws.[86]

In brief, the Court of Appeals held that, when IPRs are lawfully obtained (e.g. without fraud on the patent office), innovators are entitled to refuse to license them unilaterally. This line of reasoning influenced further judgments, which confirmed that "the holder of a patent retains the power to exclude others from manufacturing, using, and selling his inventions without running afoul of antitrust laws."[87]

The second relevant case, instead, concerned Xerox's refusal to sell.[88] Xerox had refused to sell the equipment parts for its patented products to independent

Microsoft, 253 F3d 34 (C App DC Circuit, 2001). In the *Microsoft* litigation, US courts had concerns mainly around bundling/tying practices. In the final settlement (2006), Microsoft also agreed to disclose to rivals interoperability information on its operating systems.

82 See Chapter 4, section 4.3, and Chapter 5, section 3.2. On the issue, see R. Hewitt Pate (n 33).

83 *Volvo* (n 36), at 8.

84 *United States v Westinghouse Electric*, 648 F2d 642 (C App 9th Circuit, 1981).

85 *SCM v Xerox* (n 80).

86 Ibid., at 1206. See also *Automatic Radio Mfg v Hazeltine Research*, 339 US 827 (1950), where the Supreme Court held that even "the mere accumulation of patents … is not in and of itself illegal."

87 See *Miller Insituform v Insituform of North America*, 830 F2d 606 (C App 6th Circuit, 1987).

88 *Independent Service Organizations v Xerox* (n 80).

service organizations (ISOs). The latter were consequently impeded in competing in the related market for repairing and servicing. The Court first argued that "the patent holder may enforce the statutory right to exclude others from making, using or selling the claimed invention free from liability under the antitrust laws."[89] From this point of view, it opted for an approach in favor of innovators.[90]

As the Court added, it was not necessary to inquire into Xerox's subjective motivation for exerting the IPRs, "even though his refusal to sell or license his patented invention may have an anticompetitive effect, so long as that anticompetitive effect is not illegally extended beyond the statutory patent granted."[91] Hence, the Court first rejected the need of a justification requirement. Then, however, it remarked the importance of not using (lawfully obtained) IPRs to extend power in other markets. From this perspective, therefore, it seems that *Xerox* followed the EU practice in limiting IPRs over-exploitation in secondary markets. At the same time, it departed from the EU approach by denying the need of objective justifications as a defense against liability.

4.2 Kodak

Similarly to *Xerox*, also *Kodak* concerned a refusal to sell products to ISOs, limiting their ability to compete in the market for repair and servicing of Kodak's products.[92] Unlike *Xerox*, however, the company was ultimately found guilty under Section 2 of the Sherman Act, and was condemned to sell to ISOs. Kodak's argument that its IPRs had not been properly considered was rejected.[93] The Supreme Court observed that "power gained through some natural advantages such as a patent, copyright or business acumen can give rise to liability if a seller exploits this dominant position in one market to expand his empire into the next."[94] The Supreme Court, therefore, identified a serious threat for competition in Kodak's expansion into the secondary market.

In a following case concerning the same parties (*Kodak II*),[95] the Court of Appeals for the Ninth Circuit importantly noted that two principles on the intersection between antitrust and IPRs should be taken into account. On the one hand, IPRs owners are not immune from antitrust liability. On the other, IPRs holders can refuse to sell or license protected works.[96] In appraising Kodak's refusal to deal, the Court of Appeals further held that:

> while exclusionary conduct can include a monopolist's unilateral refusal to license a [patent or] copyright, or to sell its patented or copyrighted work, a

89 Ibid., at 1327–1328.
90 H.K.S. Schmidt (n 1) 216.
91 *Independent Service Organizations v Xerox* (n 80), at 1327–1328.
92 *Eastman Kodak v Image Technical Services* (n 79).
93 See H.K.S. Schmidt (n 1) 215.
94 *Eastman Kodak v Image Technical Services* (n 79), at 29.
95 *Image Technical Services v Eastman Kodak* (n 79).
96 Ibid., at 1215.

> monopolist's desire to exclude others from its [protected] work is a presumptively valid business justification for any immediate harm to consumers.[97]

In the Court of Appeals' view, however, this presumption could be rebutted in three specific circumstances: (i) where a monopolist changed its practice after freely licensing its IPRs in a competitive market; (ii) where a monopolist obtained its IPRs unlawfully; or (iii) where protection of IPRs was merely a pretext, and the real reason for the refusal to license or deal was anticompetitive. As Kodak's justifications based on the legitimacy of the refusal were considered pretextual, the Court of Appeals finally found the company liable. It is worth noting that the first of those conditions had been established in *Aspen Skiing*, a landmark case concerning a refusal to deal by a monopolist.[98] There, the Supreme Court had first held that, where there is no purpose to create or maintain a monopoly, Section 2 does not "restrict the long recognised right of a trader or manufacturer engaged in an entirely private business freely to exercise his own independent discretion as to parties with whom he will deal."[99] However, it was observed, a refusal to deal by a monopolist could lead to breach Section 2 when such refusal gave rise to an important change not justified by normal business reasons. Among the factors to examine, the Supreme Court included the impact of the conduct on both consumers and competitors.[100]

In conclusion, albeit not directly focused on IPRs, the *Kodak* litigation confirmed that a refusal to deal or license does not necessarily lead to a breach of Section 2. It is the right of the IPRs holder, indeed, to choose the business parties. This presumption, however, can be rebutted under the circumstances cited above. The relevance of the rebuttable presumption theory was also confirmed in other judgments.[101] Despite the merits for having further explored on the intersection between IPRs and antitrust, *Kodak II* was also criticized by part of the literature. It was argued, in particular, that the Ninth Circuit's ruling was incompatible with the US Patent Act.[102] The latter provides that no patent owner should be denied relief for the infringement of a patent or be deemed guilty of misuse or illegal extension of the patent right by reason of a refusal to license or use the IPR.[103] This notwithstanding, it seems that this criticism failed to acknowledge the normative role of the judiciary in limiting the tension which sometimes inevitably arises between different fields of law.

97 Ibid., at 1218.

98 *Aspen Skiing* (n 75).

99 Ibid., at 601–602. See also *United States v Colgate*, 250 US 300 (1919), at 307.

100 J.H. Park (n 3) 29; J.E. Lopatka and W.H. Page, "Bargaining and Monopolization: In Search of the Boundary of Section 2 Liability between *Aspen* and *Trinko*" (2005) 73 *Antitrust Law Journal* 115.

101 See *Data General v Grumman Systems Support*, 761 F Supp 185 (D. Massachusetts, 1991).

102 See S. Baches Opi, "The Application of the Essential Facilities Doctrine to Intellectual Property Licensing in the European Union and the United States: Are Intellectual Property Rights Still Sacrosanct?" (2001) 11 *Fordham Intellectual Property, Media and Entertainment Law Journal* 485.

103 35 USC § 271(d). On effective actions against IPR infringements, see also Article 41 of the Agreement on Trade Related Aspects of Intellectual Property Rights (TRIPs), Annex 1C to the Marrakesh Agreement establishing the World Trade Organization (WTO), 33 ILM 1197 (1994).

4.3 Other relevant cases and principles

The cases discussed above concerned the refusal to license IPRs or sell products covered by them. These disputes have heavily contributed, albeit sometimes controversially, to setting the boundaries between IP and antitrust laws in the United States. In this context, however, attention should also be paid to further cases, where two relevant doctrines were developed: (a) the essential facility doctrine; and (b) the monopoly leveraging doctrine. Although these legal principles did not concern the enforcement of patents or copyright, they could be interpreted as theoretically applicable also in IPRs-related cases.[104]

4.3.1 *Essential facility doctrine*

First, the essential facility doctrine imposes on the monopolist a general obligation to deal. It applies to those circumstances where a company which has control over a facility essential to its competitors denies the latter access to that facility.[105] This doctrine has its origin in *Terminal Railroad,* a case concerning a Section 1 violation;[106] it was applied to a Section 2 infringement only in *Otter Tail Power*, a dispute on a refusal to deal by a monopolist.[107] The specific elements of the essential facility doctrine were established even later. In *MCI*, the Court of Appeals identified four conditions: (i) the control of the essential facility by a monopolist; (ii) a competitor's inability practically or reasonably to duplicate the essential facility; (iii) the denial of the use of the facility to a competitor; and (iv) the feasibility of providing the facility.[108]

It is true, however, that this doctrine has been rejected in many other cases, where US courts had underlined, *inter alia*, the risks of reduced incentives to invest on the part of innovators.[109] More interestingly, the Supreme Court has never endorsed the essential facility doctrine in relation to IPRs and refusal to license cases.[110] Perhaps this could be explained in light of the difficulties which may arise in interpreting IPRs as essential facilities which cannot be duplicated.

104 On the issue, J.H. Park (n 3) 33–34; and P.E. Areeda, "Essential Facilities: an Epithet in Need of Limiting Principles" (1989) 58 *Antitrust Law Journal* 841.

105 H.J. Hovenkamp, M.A. Lemley and M.D. Janis, *IP and Antitrust: an Analysis of Antitrust Principles Applied to Intellectual Property* (Aspen Law & Business, New York 2008) Ch. 13.

106 *United States v Terminal Railroad Association,* 224 US 383 (1912).

107 *Otter Tail Power Co v United States,* 410 US 366 (1973).

108 *MCI Communications Corp v AT&T Corp,* 708 F2d 1081 (C App 7th Circuit, 1983). See also *Alaska Airlines v United Airlines*, 948 F2d 536 (C App 9th Circuit, 1991).

109 *Data General* (n 101); *Intergraph Corp v Intel Corp,* 195 F3d 1346 (C App Federal Circuit, 1999).

110 J.H. Park (n 3) 34. See also R. Pitofsky, D. Patterson and J. Hooks, "The Essential Facilities Doctrine under U.S. Antitrust Law" (2002) 70 *Antitrust Law Journal* 443.

4.3.2 Monopoly leveraging doctrine

The monopoly leveraging doctrine, instead, applies to those situations "where a company uses or leverages its monopoly power in one market to obtain a competitive advantage in a second market, or to monopolise or attempt to monopolise the leveraged market."[111] It was established in *Berkey Photo*, where the Second Circuit had identified the core elements of the doctrine in: (i) the existence of monopoly power in one market; and (ii) the exercise of such power to the detriment of competition in a second market.[112] Therefore, according to the Second Circuit, there might be a violation of Section 2 of the Sherman Act even in the absence of an attempt to monopolize the second market.[113] This doctrine, however, was rejected in other judgments. In *Alaska Airlines*, for instance, the Ninth Circuit held that merely obtaining a competitive advantage in the second market was not enough. Rather, as it was argued, the plaintiff had to show evidence of all the elements required for a claim of monopolization or attempted monopolization.[114] The Supreme Court in *Trinko* overruled the monopoly leveraging doctrine, by holding that "to the extent the Court of Appeals dispensed with a requirement that there be a 'dangerous probability of success' in monopolising a second market, it erred."[115] This means that the monopoly leveraging doctrine could only play a role in the context of monopolization or attempted monopolization claims already proving the factors set in Section 2.[116] This holds true even when considering the doctrine in the context of IPRs (i.e. where the IPRs holder uses his monopoly power in a primary market to leverage such power in a secondary related market). Therefore, similarly to what has been held in relation to the essential facility doctrine, this theory seems to have limited application in constraining innovators' behaviors.

5 Conclusion

It has been said that competition and IP laws tend to pursue concordant aims: the enhancement of consumer and (consequently) societal welfare. In terms of objectives, the tension between these two fields of law is apparent. Nevertheless, conflict may arise as competition and IP laws work through different means. On the one hand, indeed, IPRs confer on the holders a position of exclusivity, as a reward for firms' investment in innovation. On the other hand, competition is aimed at constraining exclusionary mechanisms and limiting the harmful effects of monopolies. It may happen, then, that IPRs owners try to over-exploit the rights they have been granted, to the detriment of market competition. Under these circumstances, the internal balancing system (as the limited duration) of IPRs may not be sufficient to

111 J.H. Park (n 3) 39.
112 *Berkey Photo v Eastman Kodak*, 603 F2d 263 (C App 2nd Circuit, 1979).
113 Ibid., at 276.
114 *Alaska Airlines* (n 108).
115 *Verizon Communications v Trinko*, 540 US 398 (2004), at 415.
116 J.H. Park (n 3) 40.

solve the tension. Should a solution be left to IP-reforming mechanisms, or should it be given by competition rules? When IP law's own mechanisms no longer fulfill their function, intervention by competition enforcers seems to be justified. This is necessary to balance between competition goals and innovation incentives, and ultimately achieve a better outcome for the whole society. Such interference, however, should be allowed only under exceptional conditions.

A typical situation in which a tension between IP and competition laws may arise is when IPRs holders refuse to license relevant rights to competitors. From the EU case law examined above, it emerged that refusal to license or deal cannot, in itself, constitute an abusive conduct. Rather, the disputes attested to the need for exceptional circumstances to impose a compulsory license. In *Oscar Bronner*, *IMS Health* and *Microsoft,* the EU courts confirmed that all the identified exceptional conditions must be present for Article 102 TFEU to apply. For instance, in order to trigger the competition enforcers' intervention, both the risk of expanding a dominant position in a secondary market and the prevention of the appearance of a new product must be found. In addition, no objective justification must exist for the refusal. It has been contended that this strict application of the exceptional circumstances is necessary to strike the optimal balance between IPRs and competition. Nonetheless, there are still uncertainties on the meaning of these concepts. On the one hand, the case law has not made definitively clear the meaning of the "new product" requirement, but seems to have interpreted the test in a broadened way. *Microsoft*, in this sense, has probably done little to clarify the scope of the concept. On the other, it is still unclear what can be accepted as a reasonable justification for refusing to license IPRs. As this test has also been mentioned by the Court of Justice, it could be, in theory, invoked by innovators to escape liability. However, the case law has not yet shed light on the conditions which may make a justification acceptable. Furthermore, it could be questioned how EU courts may appraise an objective justification in case all the other exceptional circumstances are fulfilled. Access to the market, it must be remembered, may be equally important as granting IP protection, due to the benefits which may derive from follow-on innovation. A case-by-case approach could be, perhaps, a reasonable way to handle this delicate relationship between innovators' incentives and competition objectives.

With respect to the US jurisprudence, then, it seems that *Xerox* made it difficult for a defendant in a patent infringement suit to argue that the refusal to deal or license IPRs was an antitrust violation.[117] The *Xerox* litigation, indeed, suggested that IPRs owners have broad rights to refuse to license lawfully obtained IPRs or sell patented products, even when the refusal has an anticompetitive effect. An abuse, instead, may be found where the effect consists in the expansion of market power in a secondary market. This condition was endorsed in the *Kodak* litigation, which also identified other circumstances leading to a Section 2 infringement. Nevertheless, it is clear that, in the United States too, the cases justifying an order

117 On this point, see N. Oettinger, "In re Independent Service Organizations Antitrust Litigation" (2001) 16 *Berkeley Technology Law Journal* 332–333.

to license or deal are limited and difficult to prove. Similarly, the essential facility and monopoly leveraging theories do not seem solid tools for those rivals requiring these remedies.

The exceptional circumstances and the other legal principles emerging from the case law may theoretically find application also in the context of standardization processes. Here, the selected innovator may refuse to grant a license after having subscribed to the policy of the standard-setting organization. How should this conduct be assessed? Should it be seen as the legitimate refusal of the IPRs owner, or as an abuse not justifiable under any legal principles?[118] Before delving into the problem, it is first necessary to define the concept of a "standard" and understand how the standardization processes work.

118 See Chapter 7, section 6.2.

3 IPRs and standard setting: functions and rules

1 Introduction

The advent of today's knowledge-based economy has increased the importance of intellectual property rights and made greater the prominence in the players' business strategy of the role of standards. Several firms have started to consider their patent portfolios as valuable profit centers and have begun to market the latter, exclusively focusing on innovation and technology licensing as their core business.[1] IPRs holders are more and more interested in generating profits from licensing their rights than from selling products.[2] In a context of increasing attention towards IPRs licensing, standardization processes are of strategic importance.[3] Standard-setting organizations (SSOs) represent the most common vehicle to develop industry standards. They have been considered in the United States as key instruments which wield "great power in the Nation's economy."[4] The crucial function of standard setting has also been recognized in Europe, where the Commission has clarified that "a stronger role for standardization in support of innovation is important for the European effort to address economic, environmental and social challenges."[5] As held by a former EU Commissioner for competition policy, in addition, "standards are clearly more important than ever," as "they often facilitate economies of scale."[6] Indeed, everyone nowadays seems to be familiar with standards, from the most basic to the most sophisticated. Consider

1 G. Ohana, M. Hansen and O. Shah, "Disclosure and Negotiation of Licensing Terms Prior to Adoption of Industry Standards: Preventing Another Patent Ambush?" (2003) 24(12) *European Competition Law Review* 644.

2 S. Sattler, "Standardization under EU Competition Rules – the Commission's New Horizontal Guidelines" (2011) 32(7) *European Competition Law Review* 344.

3 M.C. Naughton and R. Wolfram, "The Antitrust Risks of Unilateral Conduct in Standard Setting, in the Light of the FTC's case against Rambus Inc." (2004) 49 *Antitrust Bulletin* 699.

4 *American Society of Mechanical Engineers v Hydrolevel*, 456 US 556 (1982), at 570.

5 European Commission, "Towards an Increased Contribution from Standardization to Innovation in Europe", (Communication) COM 133 final, 11 March 2008.

6 N. Kroes, "Being Open about Standards" (Speech at *OpenForum Europe*, Bruxelles – 10 June 2008). On the role of standards, see also D.G. Swanson and W.J. Baumol, "Reasonable and Non-discriminatory (RAND) Royalties, Standards Selection, and Control of Market Power" (2005–2006) 73 *Antitrust Law Journal* 3.

those developed in the fields of electrical equipment (e.g. the three-prong plug), video communication and recording (e.g. the DVD standard) and information and communication technology (e.g. the GSM and the LTE standards). How can we define a standard? What are the rules characterizing their adoption? Should innovators be rewarded for their standardized technologies?

The chapter aims to answer these important questions, which are the cause of heated debates among several authors. There is still uncertainty about both definitions and the optimal legal framework to be implemented in standard-setting environments. What is more, not everyone agrees on the effects of rewarding IPRs owners' efforts in innovative products.

2 Standards

Standards play a central role in our global and knowledge-based economy. They facilitate trade, allow cost savings for firms, increase economic efficiency and contribute significantly to economic growth.[7] Further effects on the market concern the creation of network externalities,[8] and the reduction of what economists term informational transaction costs.[9] Especially in high-tech markets, they can help achieve interoperability between different products and allow firms to concentrate on producing innovative goods.[10] Hence, by coordinating technology development and by structuring the way markets develop, standards provide a powerful engine for change and progress.[11]

More in general, their importance comes to light in several daily events (e.g. standards regulating traffic light signals). Standards allow us to deal with the environment in an almost unconscious way.[12] When successful, they usually go unnoticed. They are like "keys always hung at the same nail – they free up our mind for more useful thoughts."[13] We notice them only when they do not perform as expected and are not complied with (e.g. in the case of driving on the wrong side of the road), as well as when they change (e.g. standardized time and geographic zones). To be of value, standards need to be stable at least for a certain period

7 T.M. Egyedi and K. Blind, *The Dynamics of Standards* (Edward Elgar, Cheltenham 2008) 4.

8 J. Farrell and G. Saloner, "Standardization, Compatibility, and Innovation" (1985) 16 *Rand Journal of Economics* 70; D.G. Swanson and W.J. Baumol (n 6) 8.

9 C.P. Kindleberger, "Standards as Public, Collective and Private Goods" (1983) 36(3) *Kyklos* 377.

10 P. Hellstrom, T. Kramler and F.W. Bulst, "Holding Standardization to Competition Law Standards" (2010) 1 *Concurrences* 24. Mobile phones, computers and network devices depend on standards to interoperate with other complex products (e.g. the Small Computer Systems Interface (SCSI) specifies how computer processors communicate with external devices).

11 S.K. Schmidt and R. Werle, *Co-ordinating Technology: Studies in the International Standardization of Telecommunication* (MIT Press, Cambridge, MA 1998) Ch. 4.

12 M.S. Royall, "Standard Setting and Exclusionary Conduct: The Role of Antitrust in Policing Unilateral Abuses of Standard-Setting Processes" (2003–2004) 18 *Antitrust* 44.

13 J. Hurd and J. Isaak, "IT Standardization: the Billion Dollar Strategy" (2005) 3 *International Journal of IT Standards & Standardization* 68.

of time. However, standards are not static but dynamic, as they can be revised, extended, withdrawn, reinstated and replaced.[14]

Several areas and specifications are affected by standard setting, from health and environment to safety and ICT (information and communication technology) sectors. Possible criteria of classification take into account the subject matter standards address, the way standard-setting processes are developed (e.g. open or restricted participation), and how standards are used.[15] With reference to the definition of standard, different authors have dealt with the issue and various opinions have been expressed, all of which with their values and constraints.[16] Grindley, for instance, has defined three different types of standards:[17] (1) minimum attributes that cover basic product requirements and minimum quality;[18] (2) interface requirements that enable interoperability when products are connected;[19] and (3) standards in the sense of standard product characteristics, which are features defining a group of similar products.[20] For the purposes of this book, I will mainly refer to those technological standards that enable interoperability between technological products in ICT industries.

Besides the abovementioned classifications and definitions it is possible to distinguish in the literature between more general categories of standards. As a premise, it is worth noting that the various theories and interpretations developed are evidence of a lack of uniform terminology. The following sections are hence devoted to the analysis of these main classifications, in an attempt to shed some light on the issue and avoid possible misconstructions.

2.1 De facto v de jure *standards*

First, standards can fall into two categories: *de jure* and *de facto*. *De jure* standards are based on cooperation between interested parties, thus they have been defined in the literature as cooperative or committee standards.[21] A cooperative standard is a very specific type of agreement; it can be interpreted as a specification developed by committees for repeated use.[22] The GSM (Global System for Mobile Communication) protocol in telecommunications is an example of cooperative

14 T.M. Egyedi and K. Blind (n 7) 1. See also T.M. Egyedi, "On the Implications of Competing Standards" in *The Pro & Cons of Standard Setting* (Swedish Competition Authority, 2010) 12.

15 H. de Vries, "IT Standards Typology" in K. Jacobs (ed.), *Advanced Topics in Information Technology Standards and Standardization Research* (IDEA Group Publishing, Hershey 2006) 1–26.

16 H. de Vries, *Standardization: a Business Approach to the Role of National Standardization Organizations* (Kluwer Academic Publisher, Dordrecht 1999) 159.

17 P. Grindley, *Standards, Strategy and Policy: Cases and Stories* (Oxford University Press, Oxford 1995).

18 Safety standards are a well-known example.

19 For instance, consider the HTTP standard, which enables web browsers to communicate with web servers. Interoperability standards, in particular, have paved the way for introducing many important innovations into the market, including mobile computing devices and networks.

20 E.g., the WinTel PC.

21 T.M. Egyedi and K. Blind (n 7) 2–3.

22 In the United States, for instance, it is estimated that there are about 50,000 standards developed by over 600 private sector industry groups.

standard, as it "was drawn up as a result of collective activity within the framework of a standards institute, in which the leading actors in the telecommunications sector took part."[23] One commentator has defined a cooperative standard as "a written document establishing technical specifications for good, services, or processes, resulting from a consensus, and whose application is voluntary."[24] From this definition, the author infers the four main characteristics of a cooperative standard: (a) they are the result of cooperation among interested parties; (b) they are based on scientific and technical data; (c) they are driven by consensus; and (d) their application is usually voluntary.[25] A further definition is given by the International Standardization Organization (ISO), according to which a legal standard is a:

> document established by consensus and approved by a recognised body that provides, for common and repeated use, rules, guidelines or characteristics for activities or their results, aimed at the achievement of the optimum degree of order in a given context.[26]

However, the element of "approval by a recognised body" in this definition only covers standards adopted by formal standardization bodies, such as the ISO. Standards, instead, may be developed also by *consortia* (e.g. the World Wide Web Consortium [W3C]) and by professional organizations (such as the Institute of Electrical and Electronics Engineers [IEEE]). Therefore, the definition given by ISO seems to be reductive.[27]

The importance of cooperative standards lies in the fact that, where a good, service or procedure is concerned, a written document is usually needed to define the form it should take.[28] In this context, cooperative standards play a crucial role, as they enable products to circulate and be compatible with other goods, services or procedures. Thus, they are also beneficial to the enhancement of free trade. The importance of their role is even clearer if we consider that standards nowadays affect and influence several economic activities, and that their extension is closely related to economic globalization and transformation of regulatory processes at the international, regional and national levels.[29]

23 B. Lelong and A. Mallard, *Reseaux: Dossier sur la Fabbrication des Normes* (Hermes Science Publications, Paris 2000) 21. According to ETSI IPRs database, around 4,700 patents have been declared essential to the GSM standard. These are owned by several different companies.

24 O. Borraz, "Governing Standards: the Rise of Standardization Processes in France and in the EU" (2007) 20(1) *Governance: an International Journal of Policy, Administration and Institutions* 57. The author interprets standards as supplements to legislation and models of co-regulation.

25 Ibid., 60. On the attributes of effective standards, see also the *Standards Development Organization Advancement Act of 2004*, 15 USC § 4301 (2004). The Act, in particular, recalls the principles of openness, transparency, consensus and balance of interests.

26 International Standardization Organization (ISO)/International Electro-technical Commission (IEC), "Standardization and Related Activities – General Vocabulary" (2004) 8.

27 T.M. Egyedi and K. Blind (n 7) 3.

28 O. Borraz (n 24) 57.

29 T.M. Egyedi (n 14) 12. Egyedi also examines the risks deriving from lack of coordinated standard

From cooperative or *de jure* standards it is possible to distinguish *de facto* standards. The latter have been defined as "widely adopted (specifications or company standards that underlie) products, services or practices."[30] From a further point of view, *de facto* standards have been interpreted as standards resulting from a unilateral act and emerging through the mediation of the marketplace.[31] In brief, as clearly explained by Lelong and Mallard, "the dynamic in which purchasers on a market take up particular products finally leads to one or more lasting standards being selected from among diverse possible alternative technologies."[32] Examples of *de facto* standards are represented by the software and hardware architecture of personal computers. *De facto* standards usually have a significant market share, albeit they are often subject to changes (e.g. software updates). Of course, they may be processed by standards bodies and become cooperative standards.[33]

The distinction between cooperative and *de facto* standards does not exhaust the possible classifications based on the way standardization can be achieved. Several authors, indeed, have opted for a more specific subdivision. Within *de jure* or cooperative standards, for instance, some commentators have identified and distinguished those standards adopted by formal bodies (recognized standard-setting institutes) from those developed by industrial *fora* and *consortia*.[34] The importance of the latter, which generally lack formal approval from recognized bodies, has led the EU Commission to adopt a white paper in which it proposes to enable "the referencing of specific *fora* and *consortia* standards in relevant EU legislation and policies."[35] Farrell and Saloner also propose a further classification, and distinguish between (*de facto*) standards adopted by the market, (cooperative) standards developed by standardization bodies, and standards achieved by a combination of the two, in which unilateral actions and negotiations are allowed.[36] Regardless of these differences, standards developed by both formal bodies and private networks have led to investigations by EU and US antitrust enforcers.

setting, which may happen in the absence of standardization (i.e. no standard at all) or when two or more standards overlap (e.g. see the case of Betamax vs VHS video tape formats).

30 T.M. Egyedi and K. Blind (n 7) 3.

31 O. Borraz (n 24) 58.

32 B. Lelong and A. Mallard (n 23) 20.

33 This happened to the portable document format (PDF) specification of Adobe and to the Office Open XML file formats of Microsoft. These standards were formalized in 2008 by the International Standardization Organization (see, respectively, ISO 32000 and ISO/IEC 29500).

34 J. Gstalter, "Open Standards and Competition Law: an Overview" (2010) 1 *Concurrences* 1–4; J.Y. Art and U. Decker, "Openness and Standards – How do (Open) Standards Affect Competition?" (2010) 1 *Concurrences* 18–20.

35 European Commission, "Modernising ICT Standardization in the EU – The Way Forward", (Communication) COM 324 final, 3 July 2009, § 2.5.

36 J. Farrell and G. Saloner, "Coordination through Committees and Markets" (1988) 19(2) *Rand Journal of Economics* 235.

2.2 Proprietary and open standards

Further relevant classifications cited by the literature distinguish between proprietary and non-proprietary standards, and between closed and open standards. These classifications have caused heated debates, which have concerned, in particular, the meaning of an "open" standard. Defining the openness of a standard, indeed, often raises more questions than it gives answers.[37] It is the most difficult and controversial step, and different interpretations showing similarities as well as opposing approaches have been adopted by *consortia*, formal standard-setting bodies and commentators.[38] Some authors interpret the concepts of proprietary and openness as being not necessarily mutually exclusive. Hence, there might be both open and closed proprietary standards, depending also on the definitions adopted.[39] At the same time, alternative theories hold that proprietary standards are typically closed, as they require access to firms' IPRs, and link the concept of openness only to non-proprietary standards, which do not read on any rights.[40] The next sections are devoted to better understanding the meaning of these terms, and to shed light on a debate which has so far created some confusion.

2.2.1 Proprietary v non-proprietary standards

The notion of "proprietary" does not refer to the context in which the standard has been developed. It refers, instead, to its content. A standard may be defined as proprietary when its implementation requires access to and the right to use intellectual property rights.[41] According to Grant, then, a standard is proprietary when a firm owns patents or other proprietary technology that give it ownership and control of the standard.[42] De Vries, furthermore, defines proprietary standards as those often protected by intellectual property rights (e.g. patents or copyright).[43] On the other hand, when a standard is non-proprietary, there is no need to negotiate licensing agreements or ask for permission to use or develop the technology. Consequently, no payment of licensing fees is required. As clarified by Kroes, former EU competition policy Commissioner, non-proprietary standards "avoid subjecting the future development of the standard and the technology

37 M. Valimaki, "Two Types of Openness in Information Technology Standards and Competition Policy" (2010) 1 *Concurrences* 5–6.

38 See, for instance, M. Bolhuis, "Open Standards and the Internet – The Way Forward" (2010) 1 *Concurrences* 21–23; K.J. Koelman, "An Exceptio Standardis: Do We Need an IP Exemption for Standards?" (2006) 37(7) *International Review of Intellectual Property and Competition Law* 840–841; M. Dolmans, "A Tale of Two Tragedies – A Plea for Open Standards, and Some Comments on the RAND Report" (2010) 1 *Concurrences* 7; J. Gstalter (n 34) 1–4; J.Y. Art and U. Decker (n 34) 18.

39 P. Hellstrom, T. Kramler and F.W. Bulst (n 10) 24–26.

40 On the argument, see N. Kroes (n 6) 2.

41 P. Hellstrom, T. Kramler and F.W. Bulst (n 10) 24–26.

42 R.M. Grant, *Contemporary Strategy Analysis* (8th edn, Wiley, New Jersey 2013).

43 H. de Vries and I. Oshri, *Standards Battles in Open Source Software* (Palgrave Macmillan, London 2008) 26.

to the commercial interests of the technology's originator."[44] This would also explain why they are usually preferred by many *consortia* and formal SSOs. It should not be forgotten that non-proprietary standards have driven excellent technical development, as in the case of the internet (e.g. the HTTP and HTML standards).[45] However, a legitimate question arises: would the adoption of non-proprietary standards lead to fewer firms investing in innovation? IPRs owners, it is noteworthy, usually aim to be rewarded for their investments in research and development.

2.2.2 *Open v closed standards*

As mentioned above, the most difficult step in the analysis of standards concerns the definition of openness. Indeed, there is no general consensus about what constitutes an open standard. It seems clear, however, that this concept should be appraised at two different levels: access to the standardization process and access to the standard once adopted.[46]

First, the process of standard setting refers to the development and approval of the standard by the firms involved.[47] Access to a standardization process can be interpreted as being open when: (a) interested firms are not excluded from the process, and are admitted on the basis of objective criteria; (b) the process is based on consensus and collaboration; and (c) procedures are transparent.[48] The importance of these elements has also been confirmed by resolutions of different international SSOs, such as the Global Standards Collaboration (GSC)[49] and the International Telecommunication Union (ITU).[50] The transparency of procedures and the implementation of consensus-driven activities should usually be granted by the SSOs' policy rules. However, as argued in the next chapters, misleading and unfair conduct by the participants may undermine these objectives and, more generally, the scope of the standard-setting process. The effect would be detrimental to the enhancement of innovation, and may harm consumer and societal welfare. In view of these considerations, it seems crucial to ensure that access to standardization should be open for all interested firms.

Second, the concept of openness should be appraised with respect to the access to the standard. In this context, it is possible to distinguish between access to the documentation of a standard and access to the implementation of a standard.

44 N. Kroes (n 6) 2.

45 Ibid.

46 J. Gstalter (n 34) 1–4.

47 Ibid.

48 See European Commission, "Modernising ICT Standardization in the EU – The Way Forward", (Communication) COM 324 final, 3 July 2009, § 2.1; EU Parliament and Council Regulation n 1025/2012, [2012] O.J. L 316/12, Annex II. See also M. Dolmans, "Standards for Standards" (2002) 26(1) *Fordham International Law Journal* 163; M. Dolmans (n 38) 7–17; P. Hellstrom, T. Kramler and F.W. Bulst (n 10) 24–26; and J.Y. Art and U. Decker (n 34) 18–20.

49 Available at: www.itu.int/ITU-T/gsc/gsc14/documents.html.

50 Available at: www.itu.int/ITU-T/othergroups/ipr-adhoc/openstandards.html.

The former can be limited by the existence of trade secrets or copyright (e.g. in relation to software components),[51] while the latter is usually influenced by the role of patents.[52] Access to the documentation of a standard may sometimes be limited by trade secrets, which are usually used as effective tools to keep the documentation closed and confidential. Another way to keep a standard confidential has sometimes been represented by copyright, although several authors and institutions nowadays bring into question the "copyright-ability" of standards.[53] If documentation is covered by trade secrets or copyright, the standard cannot be called open. A similar conclusion should also be reached when there is no documentation available.[54]

The most controversial aspect in defining the concept of openness regards the open implementation of the standard. The latter is nowadays often compromised by firms requiring high fees for licensing their patents.[55] This situation is typical, for instance, in the telecommunications and IT sectors, where several patent disputes in standard setting have arisen over the last decade. There are two different interpretations on the concept of open implementation. On the one hand, some authors argue that a standard is openly implemented only when it is non-proprietary or when the firm owning IPRs authorizes the use of the standard through free or open source license.[56] This theory interprets open access as an access which is not associated with licensing restrictions. The user of the standard, therefore, has no duty to pay royalties.[57] This interpretation has been supported by the free and open source community, which advocates a definition of open standard as non-proprietary or, at least, royalty free.[58] On the other hand, other authors and institutions consider the implementation of a standard open both when there are no licensing restrictions (as in the case of non-proprietary standards or proprietary standards licensed for free) and when the access to intellectual property rights essential to the implementation of the standard is subject to fair reasonable and non-discriminatory terms (FRAND).[59] FRAND (or, alternatively, RAND)

51 Many SSOs (ITU, ANSI) set policies covering the inclusion of copyrighted software in standards. The role of copyright, however, has not been very significant in standard-setting litigation.

52 J. Gstalter (n 34) 1–4; M. Valimaki (n 37) 5–6. On the role of IPRs and their effect on business models, see A. Layne Farrar, "Business Models and the Standard Setting Process" in *The Pro & Cons of Standard Setting* (Swedish Competition Authority, 2010) 39.

53 On the scope of copyright protection, see the Directive of the European Parliament and of the Council 2009/24/EC, [2009] OJ L111/16.

54 M. Valimaki (n 37) 5–6. The author mentions, by way of example, the DVD playback algorithm (protected documents) and some of Microsoft's *de facto* standards (complete lack of documentation).

55 Ibid., 18.

56 J. Gstalter (n 34) 1–4; M. Valimaki (n 37) 5–6; M. Bolhuis (n 38) 21. Bolhuis, *inter alia*, remarks the key role of open standards for the internet (i.e. cloud computing and data portability).

57 In the IT sector, a well-known example of technology not restricted by patent royalties is represented by *Linux*, which is licensed under GNU General Public License.

58 See for instance the Ministerial Declaration on eGovernment, 18 November 2009. Available at: https://ec.europa.eu/digital-agenda.

59 See J.Y. Art and U. Decker (n 34) 18–20; P. Hellstrom, T. Kramler and F.W. Bulst (n 10) 24–26.

licensing terms represent material restrictions to the access of the standard, and are usually set by SSOs' IPRs policies.[60]

In brief, there is no straightforward answer in defining an open standard. On the one hand, the concept of open access to standardization processes does not seem to raise many questions. On the other, the issue concerning open access to the standard and its open implementation has been at the core of an intense debate. While some standard-setting bodies provide open access to the process and allow patent licensing under FRAND or RAND conditions, other institutes and *consortia* exclude IPRs exploitation from standard development. The main doubt, therefore, is whether standards can be interpreted as open even when they read on patents which are not licensed for free but under established (FRAND or RAND) licensing terms. The answer may be relevant for those formal standards institutes and *fora* which have a policy interest to keep a standard proprietary (hence, covered by exploitable IPRs) while maintaining the positive image of openness. However, the importance of the debate is not merely linked to the meaning of openness *per se*. Rather, the different arguments made by the literature focus on a much more relevant issue, which calls into question the very essence of the relationship between competition and IP laws: the need to align the economic contribution of a standard to innovation with the effective reward for the innovator.

2.2.3 *Benefits of rewarding standards*

The key policy question, in particular, is whether allowing patent licensing in standard setting may benefit the industry and its final consumers. As some authors have rightly noted, "a truly patent-free standard is not always as open to competition as a standard with reasonable licensed patents."[61] If SSOs were to exclude patent licensing from standard setting, there would be fewer firms entering the market. It should not be forgotten that IPRs owners are incentivized to invest resources in innovation as long as they are rewarded for their economic efforts. Rewards may consist in running royalties (based on sold units or total revenues), upfront lump sum fees, or cross-licenses in case of vertically integrated firms (firms holding IPRs and manufacturing downstream).

Exclusion of IPRs licensing from standardization may hence lead to less innovation and less competition within the standards.[62] In other words, the immediate consequence could be a reduced number of standards and of a lower quality.[63] The ultimate effect could be detrimental to the welfare of consumers, and may impact negatively on their consumption levels. Decreased consumer demand

60 On the general scope and meaning of (F)RAND licensing rules, see below section 3.3.3.

61 M. Valimaki (n 37) 5–6.

62 *Cf* J. Bessen, "Open Source Software: Free Provision of Complex Public Goods" in J. Bitzer and P. Schroder, *The Economics of Open Source Software Development* (Elsevier, Amsterdam 2006) 57–81.

63 J.C. De Vellis, "Patenting Industry Standards: Balancing the Rights of Patent Holders with the Need for Industry-Wide Standards" (2003) 31 *AIPLA Quarterly Journal* 301; and D. Lim, "Misconduct in Standard Setting: the Case for Patent Misuse" (2011) 51(4) *IDEA* 562–563.

may then lower production levels, thus harming societal welfare as a whole. A slightly different position has been adopted by Kroes, which has argued that IPRs should not be included in a standard when there are no demonstrable benefits over free non-proprietary alternatives. Nevertheless, the former EU competition policy Commissioner at the same time recognized that the "patent system is a tremendously effective mechanism to create incentives to innovate, and reward successful innovation."[64]

3 Standardization processes

As seen in the previous section, standards can be developed by interested parties on a cooperative basis or can derive from dominant firms emerging in the market. Reference to the dynamics that lead to establish *de facto* standards has been made in Chapter 2 of the book, during the analysis of the *Microsoft* case, which represents a well-known example of specifications chosen by the market.[65] Cooperative or *de jure* standards are either adopted in formal standard bodies or in private *fora* and *consortia*. Unlike the latter, which usually gather firms from the private sector and lack governmental approval, formal standard organizations may either be public or private bodies accredited or appointed by governments or other governmental institutes. On a similar ground, Krechmer defines a formal standard-setting body as one that is recognized directly or indirectly by a government entity.[66] Depending on the legal system considered, these two models of standardization have expanded in very different ways. While the US has usually favored competing solutions within private industry-created networks,[67] the European Union has instead adopted a more uniform and formalized standard-setting approach.[68]

3.1 Fora *and* consortia

Industry-created *fora* and *consortia* can be defined as communities or networks devoted to the development of standards on a cooperative basis. As mentioned above, they usually lack official approval by governments or other recognized organizations. This notwithstanding, several standards have been adopted in this context. Important standard-setting developments, for instance, have been

64 N. Kroes (n 6) 2–4.

65 See Case C-3/37.792 *Microsoft* [2007] OJ L32; Case T-201/04 *Microsoft v EU Commission* [2007] ECR II-03601. In the US, *United States v Microsoft*, 253 F3d 34 (C App DC Circuit, 2001), at 59.

66 K. Krechmer, "The Meaning of Open Standards" (2006) 4(1) *The International Journal of IT Standards and Standardization Research* 43. On the difference between formal and informal SSOs, see also S. Sattler (n 2) 345.

67 M. Maher, "An Analysis of Internet Standardization" (1998) 3 *Virginia Journal of Law and Technology* 5. For an overview of US standardization principles and definitions, see also the *Standards Development Organization Advancement Act of 2004*, 15 USC § 4301 (2004).

68 A. Neumann, "The European Regulatory Framework for Standardisation in the Telecommunications Sector" in C. Koenig, A. Bartosch and J.D. Braun, *EC Competition and Telecommunications Law* (Kluwer Law International, London 2002) 624.

achieved in different sectors by IETF,[69] DVB,[70] IEEE,[71] OASIS[72] and W3C.[73] In the US, standardization processes are typically conducted by *fora* and *consortia* instead of governmental institutes.[74] Of course, official standards institutes do exist in the United States (e.g. the American National Standards Institute). However, industry-created private networks are growing rapidly and consistently, especially in those industries characterized by a rapid technological development. These private networks usually gather together competing firms with different degrees of influence in the marketplace, and promote the development of standards.[75] In the context of *fora* and *consortia*, standardization is faster, more effective and less formal than the processes of officially entrusted SSOs. This is because private industry-created bodies usually have fewer procedural safeguards, and fewer members which often have a relevant influence in the market concerned and may even control the improvements of the standard-setting process.[76] This may often happen when dominant firms try to exclude from standardization those rivals that would probably make the whole process slower and difficult.

These characteristics of private competing networks, at the same time, may determine risks under competition and antitrust laws. Concerns for competition enforcement agencies may arise if a few firms with high market power or joint dominance control and direct standardization activities, from the procedure to

69 The Internet Engineering Task Force (IETF) is a large open international community of network designers, operators, vendors, and researchers concerned with the evolution and operation of the Internet (www.ietf.org).

70 The Digital Video Broadcasting (DVB) is a European consortium designing open technical standards for the global delivery of digital television and data service (www.dvb.org).

71 The Institute of Electrical and Electronics Engineers (IEEE) is an international professional organization for the advancement of technology related to electricity (www.ieee.org).

72 The Organization for the Advancement of Structured Information Standards (OASIS) is a *consortium* that drives the development, convergence and adoption of open standards for the global information society (www.oasis-open.org).

73 The World Wide Web Consortium (W3C) is an international community which develops standards to ensure the long-term growth of the web (www.w3.org).

74 P. Staniszewski, "The interplay between IP rights and competition law in the context of standardization" (2007) 2(10) *Journal of Intellectual Property Law and Practice* 668.

75 C. Shapiro, "Setting Compatibility Standards, Co-operation or Collusion?" in R. Dreyfuss, D.L. Zimmerman and H. First, *Expanding the Boundaries of Intellectual Property: Innovation Policy for the Knowledge Society* (Oxford University Press, New York 2001) 81. On the role played by private *fora* and *consortia*, see also the EU Parliament and Council Regulation n 1025/2012, [2012] OJ L 316/12 (the "European Standardization Regulation"). The regulation sets out a new regime for the use in public procurement of certain standards in the ICT sector, and specifically recognizes the possibility for *fora* and *consortia* standards to be included in ICT public procurement tenders.

76 See R. Werle, "Institutional Aspects of Standardisation: Jurisdictional Conflicts and the Choice of Standardisation Organisations" (2001) 8(3) *Journal of European Public Policy* 392; C. Koenig and A. Trias, "Some Standards for Standardization: A Basis for Harmonization and Efficiency Maximization of EU and US Antitrust Control of the Standard Setting Process" (2010) 32(7) *European Intellectual Property Review* 322; and J. Baron and T. Pohlmann, "Who Cooperates in Standards Consortia – Rivals or Complementors?" (2013) 9(4) *Journal of Competition Law and Economics* 905.

the structure and composition of the SSOs.[77] These risks, as explained below, seem of more limited scope in the context of formal SSOs. This does not mean that no potential risk of subversion of the process exists in formal bodies.

3.2 Formal standard-setting organizations

Formal standard-setting bodies represent the most common vehicle for standard-setting processes; they can be found at national (e.g. ANSI,[78] DIN,[79] AFNOR[80] or BSI[81]), European (e.g. CEN,[82] CENELEC,[83] ETSI[84]) or international level (e.g. ISO,[85] IEC,[86] ITU[87]). Especially in Europe, officially entrusted organizations develop the main part of standards in different industries. Like *fora* and *consortia*, these formal bodies provide incentives for firms, which may otherwise compete among themselves, to collaborate in the selection of the standards. The collaborative goal of SSOs, in particular, is to adopt and promote standards that either do not read on anyone's right (non-proprietary) or, if they do, are developed under the condition that IPRs are licensed under defined terms, usually fair reasonable and non-discriminatory terms (FRAND, or alternatively RAND).[88] In the latter

77 C. Koenig and K. Spiekermann, "EC Competition Law Issues of Standard Setting by Officially-entrusted Versus Private Organizations" (2010) 31(11) *European Competition Law Review* 451.

78 The American National Standards Institute (ANSI) is a US private body promoting the development of voluntary consensus standards for products, services, processes and systems (www.ansi.org).

79 The "*Deutsches Institut fur Normung*" (DIN) is the German organization for standardization, and represents Germany before the International Standardization Organization (www.din.de).

80 The "*Association Francaise de Normalisation*" (AFNOR) is the French national organization for standard setting. It is a member of the ISO (www.afnor.org).

81 The British Standards Institution (BSI) is a business services provider focused on the production of standards and the supply of standard-related services (www.bsigroup.com).

82 The European Committee for Standardization or "*Comité Européen de Normalisation*" (CEN) is a non-profit organization aimed at fostering the European economy in global trading and the welfare of European consumers by promoting the development, maintenance and distribution of coherent sets of standards and specifications (www.cen.eu).

83 CENELEC ("*Comité Européen de Normalisation Électrotechnique*") is the European Committee for Electrotechnical Standardization, and is responsible for European Standardization in the area of electrical engineering. Together with ETSI (telecommunication) and CEN (other technical areas), it forms the European system for technical standardization (www.cenelec.eu).

84 The European Telecommunications Standards Institute (ETSI) is an independent, non-profit, standardization organization in the telecommunications industry (equipment makers and network operators) in Europe, with worldwide projection (www.etsi.org).

85 The International Organization for Standardization (ISO) is an international standard-setting body composed of representatives from various national standards organizations. It promulgates worldwide proprietary industrial and commercial standards (www.iso.org).

86 The International Electro-technical Commission (IEC) prepares and publishes international standards for all electrical, electronic and related technologies (www.iec.ch).

87 The International Telecommunication Union (ITU) is a UN agency responsible for information and communication technology issues. ITU works to improve telecommunication infrastructure in the developing world and establishes worldwide standards (www.itu.int).

88 A. Layne Farrar, A.J. Padilla and R. Schmalensee, "Pricing Patents for Licensing in Standard-Setting Organizations: Making Sense of Frand Commitments" (2007) 74 *Antitrust Law Journal*

case, owners and users of patents are incentivized to cooperate and establish standards which should facilitate the production of interoperable end products reading on patented technologies.[89]

From a procedural perspective, formal standard-setting processes usually involve close cooperation between different working groups and standards committees. Standardization activities may begin with discussions among participants on a particular subject worthy to be considered for a standard. Different proposals may then be elaborated by members and submitted for a ballot vote. Once the parties identify a potential project, a working group, comprised of technical experts and supervised by a committee, evaluates the possible approaches to the new standard and reaches an initial agreement. This is then published as a draft standard and made available for public comments. The results may be examined by the standards committee, before the final adoption and publication of the standard.[90] Of course, to successfully complete the selection process, the interested parties must comply with specific rules, which work as safeguards for all members of a standard institute.

4 Policy rules

Both private *fora* and officially entrusted SSOs have developed – sometimes to a different extent – policy rules regulating the various procedures which follow in the adoption of a standard. These provisions should also function as an incentive to participate in the standard setting process, as the participants need to be able to rely on the declarations of their fellow SSOs members that they are fully disclosing the existence of any rights related to the chosen standard and are respecting any established licensing terms. Without this assurance, firms would seldom be part of standardization; this outcome would consequently lead to an inefficient result in the development of standardized technologies.[91]

The abovementioned rules are of three different types: search, disclosure, and licensing rules.[92] The specific content of these typical provisions may vary from one standard-setting body to the next, making it difficult to generalize about the precise extent of their meaning. SSOs' participants, what is more, may sometimes find it difficult to identify clearly the policy provisions with which they are required

671–672; P. Chappatte, "FRAND commitments – the case for antitrust intervention" (2009) 5(2) *European Competition Journal* 336.

89 J.G. Sidak, "Patent Hold-up and Oligopsonistic Collusion in Standard-Setting Organizations" (2009) 5(1) *Journal of Competition Law and Economics* 124.

90 See C. Koenig and K. Spiekermann (n 77) 450 (citing the procedure before DIN, "Deutsches Institut fur Normung", the German Institute for Standardization); and K. Hussinger and F. Schwiebacher, "The value of disclosing IPR to open standard setting organizations" (2013) ZEW Discussion Paper n. 13-060.

91 M.C. Naughton and R. Wolfram (n 3) 702.

92 Ibid., 759. See also J. Farrell, J. Hayes, C. Shapiro and T. Sullivan, "Standard Setting, Patents, and Hold-Up" (2007) 74 *Antitrust Law Journal* 624.

to comply. As held by Lemley, "most technology companies face a hodgepodge of rules and obligations of which they are only dimly aware."[93]

This notwithstanding, these rules are particularly important as they aim to neutralize any potential risk of misleading and unfair conduct, consisting for instance in patent ambush (also known as patent troll) or in the mere application of supra-competitive licensing fees by the IPRs owners. These behaviors may both be referred to as "patent hold-up." Whether or not hold-ups are frequent is a controversial issue due to the lack of detailed empirical studies; however, there is growing consensus that there is a problem that needs to be addressed. As will be better explained in Part II, patent ambush occurs when a member of a standard-setting body withholds information about the existence of IPRs it owns (or intends to file) related to the standard, and subsequently asserts that those rights have been infringed by use of the adopted standard.[94] As a consequence, the IPRs owner may finally obtain exorbitant fees from the firms using the standard to license its IPRs.[95]

Of course, stronger policy rules may mitigate the patent ambush problem, but may also discourage some IPRs owners from participating in standardization processes. Lerner and Tirole have considered and analyzed the existing connection between SSOs' membership and policies.[96] The importance of striking an optimal balance in SSOs policy rules, so as to preserve the interests of all the parties (innovators, users and implementers) involved in the process, is clear. In general, search, disclosure and licensing rules play a crucial role as they function as constraints on SSOs' members. From a policy perspective, they are important as the choice of the relevant rules and the response given to those by the members directly reflect the tension between the risks of anticompetitive conduct and the incentive to protect IPRs.[97]

4.1 Search rules

Search rules require the SSO members to search within their IPRs portfolio for any rights (usually patents) that may potentially cover the standard under exami-

93 M.A. Lemley, "Intellectual Property Rights and Standard-Setting Organizations" (2002) 90 *California Law Review* 1943.

94 D. Geradin and M. Rato, "Can Standard Setting Lead to Exploitative Abuse? A Dissonant View on Patent Hold-Up, Royalty Stacking and the Meaning of FRAND" (2007) 3 *European Competition Journal* 159; M.S. Royall, A. Tessar and A.J. Di Vincenzo, "Deterring 'Patent Ambush' in Standard Setting: Lessons from *Rambus* and *Qualcomm*" (2009) 23(3) *Antitrust* 34; C.B. Hockett and R.G. Lipscomb, "Best FRANDs Forever? Standard-setting Antitrust Enforcement in the United States and the European Union" (2009) 23(3) *Antitrust* 19.

95 G. Ohana, M. Hansen, O. Shah (n 1) 645; J.G. Sidak (n 89) 123; J. Gstalter (n 34) 1–4.

96 J. Lerner and J. Tirole, "A Model of Forum Shopping" (2006) 96 *American Economic Review* 1107; B. Chiao, J. Lerner and J. Tirole, "The Rules of Standard Setting Organizations: an Empirical Analysis" (2007) 38(4) *Rand Journal of Economics* 905.

97 M.C. Naughton and R. Wolfram (n 3) 703. See also R. Bekkers and A. Updegrove, "IPR Policies and Practices of a Representative Group of Standard Setting Organizations Worldwide" (2012) Social Science Research Network 1.

nation.[98] However, only a few organizations have included search or inquiry rules.[99] The vast majority indeed explicitly disavow any search requirement.[100] The main reason lies in the fact that firms, in particular in high-technology sectors, usually send engineers, not patent lawyers to represent them before SSOs. Engineers have a deeper understanding of the subject matter that will be at the core of the discussion. At the same time, however, engineers seldom have extensive knowledge about their firms' patent portfolios. The actual knowledge of the firms' IPRs is usually limited, especially when a firm has hundreds of patents which may potentially cover a proposed standard.[101] Thus, a SSO establishing a clear duty to search would impose on members a high burden that could deter them from participating in the standard-setting process.[102]

A second reason that may dissuade standard-setting bodies from including search rules in their policy is related to the difficulty of determining when a company is required to search for potentially conflicting IPRs.[103] Standard setting, indeed, is a process *in itinere*, where the standard evolves from the status of proposal to the final form adopted by the organization. Therefore, standard-setting bodies may rather opt to include in their policy only a duty to disclose those potentially conflicting IPRs within the actual knowledge of the members' representatives. Under such a limited duty, a member failing to disclose relevant IPRs to the standard-setting body, which are not within the actual knowledge of its representative, would not breach the policy rules of the SSO.

It is true, however, that the undefined notion of "actual knowledge" may raise several interpretative doubts. For instance, it could be questioned whether SSO members should be immunized from liability even when they "wilfully blind" their representatives from knowledge about their relevant IPRs. Should the "actual knowledge" protection stop if innovators willfully fail to inform their representatives about the firms' interests in the standard?[104] A plausible answer to the issue seems perhaps to depend on the effectiveness in SSO contexts of a good faith duty, although its scope and boundaries are still uncertain. More reasonably, and as attested also by the arguments developed in the next chapters, a solution may derive from the implementation of robust policy regulations encouraging full disclosure of relevant IPRs in the first place.

98 M.C. Naughton and R. Wolfram (n 3) 759.

99 The VMEbus International Trade Association (VITA) requires a member to make "a good faith and reasonable inquiry into his or her company's patent holdings." However, this does not mean that members have to search their entire patent portfolio (see VITA, "Standards Organization – Policies and Procedures" (2011)).

100 E.g. the American National Standards Institute (ANSI) and the European Telecommunications Standards Institute (ETSI) do not include in their policies any duty of search conflicting IPRs.

101 M.A. Lemley (n 93) 1907; D.J. Teece and E.F. Sherry, "Standard Setting and Antitrust" (2003) 84 *Minnesota Law Review* 1945–1946; H.J. Hovenkamp, "Competition in information technologies: standards-essential patents, non-practicing entities and FRAND bidding" (2012) University of Iowa Legal Studies Research Paper nn 12–32.

102 M.C. Naughton and R. Wolfram (n 3) 761.

103 D.J. Teece and E.F. Sherry (n 101) 1947.

104 M.C. Naughton and R. Wolfram (n 3) 771–772.

Turning back to the risks related to search provisions, Teece and Sherry have also identified a further practical reason which may lead standard-setting bodies to omit a duty to search in their policy rules. "[I]mposing a duty to disclose known patents," the authors argue, "is relatively costless, while imposing a duty to search for potentially relevant patents can be quite costly to firms with significant patent portfolios."[105] Perhaps, as Teece and Sherry observe, "imposing disclosure rules without requiring a patent search may do little or nothing to protect other SSO participants, or users of the standard, from future patent infringement claims."[106] However, as Naughton and Wolfram observe, this is the degree of protection that firms usually seek and that may incentivize their participation in standard-setting activities.[107]

In brief, the imposition of extensive search rules could certainly help standardization environments to achieve a more transparent and competitive process. On the other hand, as Teece and Sherry rightly asserted, search requirements may drastically reduce the number of innovators participating to SSOs processes. Which meaning, then, would standardization have in the absence of those very firms investing in new innovative products? Reduced participation from IPRs owners would probably lead to the development of lower quality standards or to a higher risk of patent litigation. Indeed, the higher the number of innovators not involved in SSOs processes, the higher the risk that adopted standards may conflict with those firms' rights.

In light of these observations, the effectiveness of search rules seems more than doubtful. It is not surprising, therefore, that different SSOs have been so far reluctant to impose on members a duty to search. This has been confirmed by a survey led in the field of network industries by Lemley, which has scrutinized several SSOs dealing with interface standards in the IT (information technology), TMT (telecommunication) and semiconductors sectors. Of these SSOs, only a very small percentage required members to search for relevant IPRs.[108]

4.2 Disclosure rules

Disclosure rules impose on the participants of standard-setting bodies to reveal the existence of any rights related to the standard. These provisions are established by SSOs with the intent to limit patent ambush and, more in general, misleading and unfair conduct of the participants.[109] Typically, the disclosure duty concerns only essential IPRs: those rights that would be infringed in case of implementation of the standard. IEEE (Institute of Electrical and Electronics Engineers) defines essential rights as those that are necessarily infringed by either mandatory or

105 D.J. Teece and E.F. Sherry (n 101) 1951.
106 Ibid.
107 M.C. Naughton and R. Wolfram (n 3) 761.
108 M.A. Lemley (n 93) 1904. Only four of 43 SSOs surveyed included search duties in their policies.
109 J. Farrell, J. Hayes, C. Shapiro and T. Sullivan (n 92) 624.

optional portions of the standard.[110] This definition has been recently endorsed and shared by the US jurisprudence.[111]

4.2.1 Timing of disclosure

SSOs policies usually promote early disclosure, although they seldom clarify the optimal timing to reveal the existence of essential IPRs. One institute, for instance, simply advises IPRs holders to act "as soon as reasonably feasible," but prior to the approval of the standard.[112] However, disclosure only when a standard is close to being approved may be too late as, in the meantime, costs may have become sunk and partial commitments may have been made. At the same time, disclosure when a process has just begun may also be problematic for IPRs owners, as in the early stages the SSO may consider too many alternatives.[113] It is clear, then, why the EU Commission has urged SSOs to shed light on the problem and clearly define the meaning of "timely" disclosure in their policies.[114] It seems crucial to set a disclosure timing which takes into account both the need to preserve the optimal functioning of SSOs processes and the need to enable innovators to know exactly what type of IPRs might conflict with the proposed standard. Striking the right test implies, once more, the well-known need to balance between IPRs owners' interests and SSOs' objectives.

4.2.2 Subject of disclosure

A further relevant issue, then, concerns the distinction between disclosure of pending and of issued IPRs. Lemley noted that, in case of patents, most SSOs usually require disclosure of issued patents only. Members, instead, are seldom required to disclose pending patent applications.[115] The author, in particular,

110 See IEEE-SA, "Standards Board Bylaws" (2015) § 6.1.

111 *In Re Innovatio IP Ventures*, Case n. 11-9308, 2013 WL 3874042 (ND Illinois, 2013), at 8. As the court held, the definition of essentiality requires that: "(1) at the time of standard's adoption, the only commercially and technically feasible way to implement a particular mandatory or optional portion of … the standard was to infringe the patent claim; and (2) the patent claim includes, at least in part, technology that is explicitly required by or expressly set forth in the standard."

112 IEEE-SA, "Standards Board Bylaws" (2015) § 6.2.

113 J. Farrell, J. Hayes, C. Shapiro and T. Sullivan (n 92) 628. On patent disclosure strategies in SSOs, see also B. Ganglmair and E. Tarantino, "Patent disclosure in standard setting" (2011) NET Institute Working Paper n. 11-15; and A. Layne Farrar, "Is the patent ambush prerequisite met? Assessing the extent of ex ante IPRs disclosure within standard setting" (2011) Social Science Research Network 1. Farrar's analysis for instance reveals that, in relation to ETSI projects, *ex post* disclosure of essential IPRs is usually the norm. According to the author, while many of the average delays are small, late declarations are an industry-wide practice in ETSI.

114 European Commission, "Commission Welcomes Changes in ETSI IPR Rules to Prevent 'Patent Ambush' " (12 December 2005) Press Release IP/05/1565.

115 M.A. Lemley (n 93) 1904–1905.

found that only a few of the SSOs surveyed required disclosure of both issued and pending IPRs (among these, JEDEC,[116] ETSI,[117] W3C[118] and ITU[119]).

As Naughton and Wolfram observed, there are both practical and policy reasons why SSOs do not establish a duty to disclose pending patent applications.[120] First, it is difficult enough for firms' representatives to determine whether an issued patent may potentially be related to a proposed standard. It would be all the more difficult in pending patent applications which may often undergo revision. In consideration of the fact that a proposed standard may also change before a final version is approved, firms' representatives would find themselves in the position of having "to hit not one but two moving targets."[121] Second, it has been contended that requiring firms to disclose pending patent applications in standard-setting contexts would unjustifiably compromise firms' trade secret rights.[122] Disclosure of pending patent applications would indeed sacrifice the protection the applicant enjoys as long as it keeps the information confidential. A rival informed of the applicant's invention, for instance, may try to obtain patents to improve that invention. In other words, disclosure of an application would make competitors aware of the applicant's competitive strategy; this could jeopardize the applicant's ability to obtain coverage from the patent office in a timely manner.[123]

In light of these arguments, the vast majority of standard-setting bodies do not usually require their members to disclose pending patent applications potentially

116 The Joint Electron Devices Engineering Council (JEDEC) requires disclosure of any patents, granted or pending (see JEDEC, "Manual of Organization and Procedure, JM21-R" (2015) § 8).

117 The European Telecommunications Standards Institute (ETSI) explicitly refers, in its IPRs policy, to issued patents and patent applications (ETSI, "Guide on IPRs" (2013) § 1.3). On ETSI policy, see D. Geradin and R.G. Brooks, "Interpreting and enforcing the voluntary FRAND commitment" (2011) 9(1) *International Journal of IT Standards and Standardization Research* 1; and I. Liotard and R. Bekkers, "European Standards for Mobile Communications: The Tense Relationship between Standards and Intellectual Property Rights" (1999) 21(3) *European Intellectual Property Review* 110.

118 The World Wide Web Consortium (W3C) requires disclosure of published patent applications. It also requires disclosure of unpublished patent applications in case the application's claims refer to information gathered from a W3C working group or document (see W3C, "Patent Policy" (2004) § 6).

119 The International Telecommunication Union (ITU) requires disclosure of known essential patent and patent applications (see the "Guidelines for Implementation of the Common Patent Policy for ITU-T/ITU-R/ISO/IEC" (2015) § 3).

120 M.C. Naughton and R. Wolfram (n 3) 763.

121 Ibid., 764. See also R.A. Skitol, "Concerted Buying Power: Its Potential for Addressing the Patent Hold-up Problem in Standard Setting" (2004–2005) 72 *Antitrust Law Journal* 731; and J. Hurwitz, "The Value of Patents in Industry Standards: Avoiding License Arbitrage with Voluntary Rules" (2008) 36(1) *AIPLA Quarterly Journal* 37.

122 R.J. Taffet, "Patented Technology and Standard Setting: a Standard Development Organization View" in American Bar Association, *A Year in the Life of a High Tech Standard Setting Organization* (ABA Section of Antitrust Law, Chicago 2002) 5; D.G. Swanson and W.J. Baumol (n 6) 51–52. As the latter argue, "requiring innovators to accept disclosure obligations [...] that are inimical to trade secret protection is costly [...] also through its chilling effect of diminishing future incentives to invest in innovation."

123 M.C. Naughton and R. Wolfram (n 3) 764–765.

related to a proposed standard. Despite the logic of the reasoning, however, Lemley takes a slightly different view. He argues that a duty to disclose pending patent applications would seldom be a concern for the applicant's trade secret rights. As the argument goes:

> [o]nly the existence and scope of the patent or patent application and not the technical know-how of the invention itself normally must be disclosed to an SSO. While the very existence of a patent application may sometimes be a valuable secret, in the context of a publicly adopted standard the legitimate value of this particular secret does not seem very high.[124]

It is indisputable that disclosure of sensitive information may make rivals aware of the fields into which the applicant is pouring its resources and those in which it is not.[125] However, it cannot be taken for granted that experts (e.g. engineers) in a given field could infer the substance of an invention without access to the related technical know-how. Therefore, the mere disclosure of the existence and scope of a pending claim may still preserve the applicant's business while granting the SSO sufficient information to adopt the optimal decision. In this sense, Lemley's arguments do seem persuasive. These observations lead to the conclusion that disclosure requirements should include, beyond issued IPRs, also a partial description of pending rights. Such description, as further explained in Chapter 7, may enable a standards institute to preserve the fairness and transparency of the whole process, and reduce the risk of misleading behavior. Indeed, innovators may potentially use to their advantage the undisclosed pending status of their claims, and try to charge (once the right is granted and the standard selected) excessive fees. That is why any policy proposed in this context should include rules which may effectively tackle also the risks deriving from originally pending rights. Such a policy, in addition, should incentivize members to disclose other participants' and third parties' IPRs of which they are aware. However, it could be argued, obstacles may still arise in case of disclosure of invalid or non-essential IPRs (so-called "over-disclosure").[126] In this regard, as SSOs are usually ill-suited to thoroughly examine the validity of IPRs, only a judicial intervention may effectively shed light on the matter.

4.3 Licensing rules

Search and disclosure rules are not the only tools that standard-setting bodies may adopt. SSOs policies, indeed, usually include also licensing rules. The latter require that participants license, under specific terms, any IPRs they own which is essential to the proposed standard.

Licensing provisions usually try to solve the alleged tension between IPRs and antitrust by requiring SSO members either to license their patents for free or,

124 M.A. Lemley (n 93) 1943.

125 M.C. Naughton and R. Wolfram (n 3) 767.

126 See *Nokia v InterDigital Technology*, [2007] EWHC 3077; *Nokia v IPCom*, [2009] EWHC 3482.

alternatively, to charge licensees under fair reasonable and non-discriminatory terms (FRAND) or reasonable and non-discriminatory conditions (RAND).[127] Lemley's survey seems to confirm the relevance given to these licensing terms by SSOs policies.[128]

If IPRs owners do not agree to comply with these rules, it has been held, "the SSO will often refuse to adopt the proposed standard or will withdraw the standard if it has already been promulgated."[129] Besides, in case the SSO decides to maintain the standard reading on patents of firms committed to (F)RAND terms, a court would not necessarily grant these firms an injunction, which is an order compelling a party (e.g. implementers) to do or refrain from specific acts.[130]

For the sake of clarity, some standard-setting organizations refer to FRAND terms while others mention RAND in their licensing policies.[131] However, there is apparently no difference between the terms.[132] The real problem concerns the exact meaning of (F)RAND, which still remains vague despite scholars and practitioners having been struggling with it for quite some time. As held by Lemley, it is all well and good "to propose that SSOs require licensing on reasonable and non-discriminatory terms. But without some idea of what those terms are, reasonable and non-discriminatory licensing loses much of its meaning."[133]

What appears to be a fair and reasonable royalty in the eyes of IPRs owners, indeed, may appear entirely unreasonable and unfair to other members.[134] Similar concerns have been expressed by the US Department of Justice, which emphasized the high risk that SSOs members may disagree on the meaning of reasonable royalty once the standard has been set.[135] Standard-setting bodies

127 M. Valimaki, "A Flexible Approach to RAND Licensing" (2008) 29(12) *European Competition Law Review* 690. FRAND terms are also cited in the Commission's "Guidelines on the Application of Article 81 of the EC Treaty to Technology Transfer Agreement" [2004] OJ C101/2, at 167.

128 M.A. Lemley (n 93) 1906. The author, for instance, noted that more than half (32) of the SSOs considered (43) required or simply requested their members to license IPRs on RAND terms.

129 D.J. Teece and E.F. Sherry (n 101) 1953.

130 M.A. Lemley (n 93) 1932–1933; J.S. Miller, "Standard Setting, Patents and Access Lock-In: RAND Licensing and the Theory of the Firm" (2007) 40 *Indiana Law Review* 358; C. Shapiro, "Injunctions, Hold-Up and Patent Royalties" (2010) 12(2) *American Law and Economics Review* 280; S. Gallasch, "The Referral of Huawei v ZTE to the CJEU: Determining the Future of Remedies in the Context of Standard-essential Patents" (2013) 34(8) *European Competition Law Review* 443; D.H. Ginsburg, T.M. Owings and J.D. Wright, "Enjoining Injunctions: The Case against Antitrust Liability for Standard Essential Patent Holders who Seek Injunctions" (2014) *The Antitrust Source* 1. On the grant of injunctive relief in standard setting litigation, see also Chapter 4 section 5.

131 On the one hand, for instance, ETSI, IEEE and OASIS usually refer to FRAND. On the other hand, IETF, IEC, ITU and ISO consider RAND licensing terms.

132 M. Valimaki (n 127) 691. As held by the author, the term "fair" does not change the meaning of RAND. A similar interpretation has been given by the US Judge Posner, in the case *Apple Inc v Motorola Inc*, 869 F Supp 2d 901 (ND Illinois, 2012).

133 M.A. Lemley (n 93) 1964.

134 P. Treacy and S. Lawrence, "FRANDly Fire: Are Industry Standards Doing More Harm than Good?" (2008) 3(1) *Journal of Intellectual Property Law & Practice* 22.

135 R. Hewitt Pate, "Competition and Intellectual Property in the U.S.: Licensing Freedom and the Limits of Antitrust" (Speech at *EU Competition Workshop*, Florence – 3 June 2005).

do not usually specify when licensing terms are (F)RAND. One exception is represented by the Internet Engineering Task Force (IETF), which states that when "significant implementation and successful operational experience" of the standard in question has been achieved, IETF considers the licensing terms of intellectual property in the standard to be RAND.[136] However, this seems to be a rather abstract definition, which does not strike the quantitative evaluation. The reluctance of SSOs to define (F)RAND lies on the fact that any proposal may lead to an unfruitful policy battle which may eventually discourage participation in SSOs processes.[137] Thus, SSO policies tend to leave the definition of (F)RAND terms to the private bilateral discussions between implementers and IPRs owners, which usually take place not *ex ante*, but after the standard is selected. In case of disagreement, as Lemley noted, "an unspecified reasonable royalty term does not leave unbridled discretion with the IP owner to set the terms. Rather, courts will determine what royalty is reasonable based on industry custom."[138]

4.3.1 FRAND – meaning of fair and reasonable terms

Different options emerge from both the judicial environment and the economic literature. For instance, the US case *Georgia Pacific* is well-known for having proposed 15 factors which may potentially contribute to define the fair and reasonable prong of FRAND.[139] At the same time, some interesting considerations emerged from the proposal of the complainants in *Qualcomm*, before the EU Commission, introducing the "numeric proportionality rule."[140] On the other hand, several economists have tried to develop models in an attempt to identify the meaning of FRAND, implementing different criteria. Finally, a further possible method may also involve the use of arbitration.

4.3.1.1 THE *GEORGIA PACIFIC* TEST

In *Georgia Pacific*, the New York District Court enumerated several elements which could play a role when calculating a reasonable royalty rate for the purposes of determining damages. First, the court referred to the royalties received by the innovator from other firms, for the licensing of the patent in suit.[141] Such a price, in the court's view, could represent a reasonable benchmark. However, this factor

136 Internet Engineering Task Force (IETF), "Intellectual Property Rights in IETF Technology" (2005) § 4.1. A more specific definition was recently given in IEEE-SA, "Standards Board Bylaws" (2015) § 6.1; in defining reasonable rates, IEEE refers, *inter alia*, to the value that an essential patent claim contributes to the "smallest saleable compliant implementation" that practices that claim.

137 Policy battles on licensing rules affected the works of W3C (2002), IETF (2003), OASIS (2005).

138 M.A. Lemley (n 93) 1914. On the judicial interpretation of FRAND, see L. Zhang, "How IPR policies of telecommunication standard-setting organizations can effectively address the patent ambush problem" (2010) 41(4) *International Review of Intellectual Property and Competition Law* 397.

139 *Georgia-Pacific v United States Plywood*, 318 F Supp 1116 (SDNY, 1970).

140 Case 39247 *Texas Instruments v Qualcomm* [2009].

141 *Georgia-Pacific* (n 139). See also *Monsanto v McFarling*, 488 F3d 973 (C App Federal Circuit, 2007).

may not always seem appropriate, as licensees may have accepted to pay supra-competitive fees in order to avoid lengthy litigation.

A second factor considers the treatment of patents of similar scope in related industries.[142] Also this method does not seem faultless. A patent of similar scope, provided that it exists, may have been undervalued or overpriced in the course of negotiations or previous judicial assessments, and may not always represent an optimal benchmark for determining the price of another IPR in a related industry.

A third criterion, then, may take into consideration the price that would have been hypothetically negotiated by the SSOs' participants before the formal adoption of the standardized technology.[143] This price would differ from the level of royalties that could be negotiated *ex post*, once the members commit themselves to using the patented technology.[144] As authors argue, a court's decision on the matter would seldom reflect all the different interests of the players involved as a negotiated solution could instead do.[145] This aspect may be taken into account by SSO members to avoid litigation on the meaning of (F)RAND.[146] Nevertheless, this criterion seems to raise serious doubts, mainly due to the difficulties that may arise in interpreting what price level would have been set by the members before the adoption of the standard.

A fourth method for defining (F)RAND, what is more, could also lead a court to establish an independent expert assessment of the relevant IPRs portfolio's objective quality and centrality to the standard at issue. However, experience in patent litigation attests that two independent experts may have conflicting views on the value of a specific patent portfolio.[147]

The *Georgia Pacific* judgment, then, identified other potentially relevant factors, among which:

(a) the nature and scope of the license (e.g. exclusive or non-exclusive, restricted or non-restricted);
(b) the licensor's policy to maintain its patent monopoly by not licensing others to use the invention or by granting licenses under special conditions established to preserve the monopoly;
(c) the commercial relationship between the licensor and licensee (e.g. whether they are competitors or not);
(d) the effect of selling the patented product in promoting sales of other products

142 M.A. Lemley (n 93) 1914.
143 See *Rambus Inc*, FTC Docket n. 9302, Opinion of the Commission on Remedy (5 February 2007).
144 J. Farrell, J. Hayes, C. Shapiro and T. Sullivan (n 92) 637; P. Chappatte (n 88) 388.
145 On the argument, see D.G. Swanson and W.J. Baumol (n 6) 10; and A. Layne Farrar, A.J. Padilla and R. Schmalensee (n 88) 671.
146 J. Farrell, J. Hayes, C. Shapiro and T. Sullivan (n 92) 637.
147 ECLF Working Group on Horizontal Agreements, "Comments on the Draft Guidelines on the Applicability of Article 101 of the Treaty on the Functioning of the European Union to Horizontal Cooperation Agreements" (2010) 6(2) *European Competition Law Journal* 518.

of the licensee, and the existing value of the invention to the licensor as a generator of sales of his non-patented items;
(e) the duration of the patent and the term of the license;
(f) the commercial success, popularity and profitability of the product made under the patent;
(g) the utility and advantages of the patent property over any old devices used for working out similar results;
(h) the nature of the patented invention, and the character of the commercial embodiment of it as owned and produced by the licensor;
(i) the extent to which the infringer has made use of the invention, and any evidence probative of the value of that use;
(j) the portion of the realizable profit that should be credited to the invention, as distinguished from non-patented elements, the manufacturing process or business risks;
(k) and the portion of the profit or selling price that may be customary in the particular business to allow for the use of the invention.[148]

Also these further factors and their complex interaction may potentially raise doubts as to the way they should be interpreted to set a fair and reasonable price.

More recently, in *Microsoft v Motorola*, a US court adopted a modified version of the *Georgia Pacific* test to recreate a hypothetical negotiation between the parties.[149] In order to determine the level of RAND fees, the court evaluated (1) the importance of the patents to the standard at issue and (2) the importance of the standard and the patents to the product at issue. As Judge Robart held, a RAND royalty rate should reflect "the contribution of the patented technology to the capabilities of the standard, and in turn, the contribution of those capabilities of the standard to the implementer and the implementer's product."[150] In the court's view, moreover, the proper method for determining a RAND royalty rate should minimize the risk of hold up, and should consider the value the patent had before the adoption of the standard when alternatives presumably existed.[151]

148 *Georgia-Pacific* (n 139).
149 *Microsoft v Motorola Inc.*, Case n. 10-1823, 2013 WL 2111217 (WD Washington, 2013). Motorola owned essential patents in relation to two different standards, adopted by ITU (standard H.264 for video coding) and IEEE (standard 802.11 for wireless local area networking). In the dispute, Motorola argued that several of Microsoft's products employed both standards. Motorola's licensing terms were refused by Microsoft, which sued Motorola for breach of contract. Microsoft claimed that Motorola breached its RAND promise by making unreasonable licensing offers. Judge Robart eventually found that Motorola breached its RAND commitments and determined RAND royalty ranges for the standards as between 0.55 and 19.5 cents $ per unit.
150 Ibid., at 20.
151 Ibid., at 12–19. See also *Hynix v Rambus Inc*, Case n. 00-20905, 2013 WL 1915865 (ND California, 2013), at 19; *In Re Innovatio* (n 111); *Realtek Semiconductor Corp v LSI Corp*, Case n. 12-3451, 2013 WL 2181717 (ND California, 2013); *CSIRO v Cisco System*, Case n. 6:11-CV-343, 2014 WL 3805817 (ED Texas, 2014); and *Apple* (n 132), at 913, where Judge Posner held that "the patentee's bargaining power surges because a prospective licensee has no alternative to licensing the patent."

Further relevant judgments that followed *Georgia Pacific* and contributed to the debate on the meaning of fair and reasonable terms include *Laser Dynamics* and *Lucent*.[152] Here, the Federal Circuit considered the scope of the "entire market value rule" ("EMVR"), a principle historically developed by courts as a guide for awarding lost profits in cases where the patent covered only some portion or component of an end product. To recover all lost profits from foregone sales, the patentee had to prove that the entire market value of the end product was attributable to the patented component. The Federal Circuit eventually held that, absent this proof, reasonable rates should not be based on the entire product under the "EMVR", but on the "smallest saleable patent-practicing unit."[153]

However, the test set in *Georgia Pacific,* as further revised by the recent US jurisprudence, seems to give broad guidelines without prescribing an absolute and unquestionable method for setting reasonable fees. In a dispute on licensing terms, it is likely that each party will propose its own assessment of these criteria, which may be finally accepted or disregarded by the judge. This happened, for instance, in *Apple v Motorola,* where Apple stated that it would not necessarily accept a license on court-determined RAND terms. Apple rather sought a cap on the potential license rate that it could use in negotiations with Motorola.[154]

4.3.1.2 THE NUMERIC PROPORTIONALITY RULE

Besides *Georgia Pacific* and the other recent US disputes, the EU case *Qualcomm* deserves attention for a proposal given on the assessment of FRAND licensing terms.[155] In *Qualcomm,* in particular, the complainants had argued that all patents essential to a standard should be considered as equally valuable and treated symmetrically as they all give IPRs owners the same degree of market power *ex post.* Following this line of reasoning, they argued that licensing terms are FRAND when royalties are proportional to the number of essential patents included in the standard. In a standard-setting environment, numeric proportionality rules may be beneficial as long as they reduce transaction costs, due to an easier way to calculate royalties.

However, there might be disadvantages related to the implementation of such a mechanism. For instance, disputes may arise when members owning IPRs start discussing which patents are essential. It follows that a numeric proportionality

152 *Laser Dynamics Inc v Quanta Computer Inc,* 694 F3d 51 (C App Federal Circuit, 2012); and *Lucent Technologies Inc v Gateway Inc.*, 580 F3d 1301 (C App Federal Circuit, 2009).

153 Ibid. On the scope of the rule, see T.F. Cotter, "Four principles for calculating reasonable royalties in patent infringement litigation" (2011) 27 *Santa Clara Computer & High Technology Law Journal* 725; and D. Geradin and A. Layne Farrar, "Patent value apportionment rules for complex, multi-patent products" (2011) 27 *Santa Clara Computer & High Technology Law Journal* 763. On a further ground, this principle seems to have inspired the new version of IEEE-SA bylaws, which try to define reasonable rates (IEEE-SA, "Standards Board Bylaws" (2015) § 6.1).

154 *Apple Inc v Motorola Inc.*, Case n. 11-178, 2012 WL 7989412 (WD Wisconsin, 2012), at 2–3. On the determination of RAND royalties, see also *Ericsson Inc v D-Link System,* Case n. 6:10-CV-473, 2013 WL 949378 (ED Texas, 2013); and *Uniloc USA Inc v Microsoft Corp.*, 632 F3d 1292 (C App Federal Circuit, 2011).

155 *Texas Instruments v Qualcomm* (n 140). See also Chapter 6 section 4.

system may not work well in those contexts where the patents ultimately disclosed are not all truly essential or valid. Under those circumstances, the calculated rates would seldom reflect a fair and reasonable price. Moreover, this mechanism may encourage members to file and disclose as many (relevant or not) IPRs as possible, in an attempt to gain a larger share of the royalties paid by the licensees. As some authors pointed out, this rule may "encourage a proliferation of patenting of minor innovations."[156] Also further considerations seem to confirm that a numeric proportionality rule would seldom be a sound solution to the FRAND problem. Indeed, this system fails to consider the different technical contribution that each patent may bring to the standard. In other words, this means that a merely numerical assessment of the patents, disregarding their scope and relevance, may likely lead to disproportionate payments.[157]

4.3.1.3 ECONOMIC MODELS

As to the economic literature, several mechanisms have been developed in the attempt to define FRAND licensing terms. Some of these have taken into consideration transaction costs, incremental values[158] and patent validity.[159]

Carlton and Shampine, for instance, argue that a reasonable licensing royalty is the price that would have been negotiated *ex ante*, before the patented technology at issue had been standardized and prior to the licensees incurring sunk costs.[160] According to them, such *ex ante* price should be based on the incremental value that the technology brings to the licensee compared to the next best alternative available.[161] However, it is not always possible to elaborate an accurate estimation

156 A. Layne Farrar, A.J. Padilla and R. Schmalensee (n 88) 683–685.

157 See P. Chappatte (n 88) 340; D. Geradin and A. Layne Farrar (n 153) 779; and H.J. Hovenkamp (n 101). In estimating FRAND royalty rates, Hovenkamp argues that the "identification of a reasonable royalty in infringement cases has become an extremely costly and often indeterminate process." As the author further holds, "in general, the royalty must reflect a base that identifies the functionality to which that particular patent is tied. Second, it must include a realistic apportionment of the overall number of patents included in a device."

158 See F. Leveeque and Y. Meniere, "Technology Standards, Patents and Antitrust" (2008) 9(1) *Competition and Regulation in Network Industries* 29. Their theory is reflected in the equation: R = c + (V1-V2)p, where "c" is the incremental cost of licensing, (V1-V2) is the gain for selecting the best technology over the second one, and "p" is the probability that the patent is valid.

159 On the problem of patent validity and "over-disclosure," see the cases *Nokia v InterDigital* (n 126); and *Eon-Net LP v Flagstar Bancorp.*, 653 F3d 1314 (C App Federal Circuit, 2011), where the court found litigation misconduct by a patent owner based on the filing of baseless patent claims.

160 D.W. Carlton and A.L. Shampine, "An economic interpretation of FRAND" (2013) 9 *Journal of Competition Law and Economics* 531. See also C. Shapiro (n 130) 280.

161 On the concept of "next best alternative," see also T.F. Cotter (n 153) 743. Under Cotter's example, "suppose that use of the patented technology is expected to reduce costs by $10,000, whereas a license to use the next-best alternative is expected to cost $4,000 and to reduce costs by $6,000. The value of the patent to the user is not $4,000 ($10,000 minus $6,000), but rather $10,000 minus the *net* value of the next-best alternative ($6,000 minus $4,000 = $2,000); in other words, the value to the user is $10,000 minus $2,000 = $8,000. $8,000 is the maximum that a rational user would be willing to pay for the use of the patented invention … If the patented invention is no better than the next-best alternative – in the preceding example, if it reduces expected costs by

of these variables. The licensing of intellectual property rights may involve costs of negotiation, contracting, accounting, monitoring and auditing; it may also frequently involve the costs of instruction and training. In this regard, it seems that these economic models are abstract and theoretic solutions which cannot always find application easily.[162]

Another author proposes a screening test to assess whether a breach of FRAND has occurred. Under this model, four conditions must be satisfied: (i) *ex ante*, an alternative to the selected standard exists; (ii) *ex ante*, prospective licensees cannot anticipate the licensor's *ex post* requests; (iii) *ex post*, the licensor requests worse licensing terms than *ex ante*; and (iv) *ex post*, the licensee is locked into the technology.[163] If, on the basis of the preliminary evidence provided, a competition authority finds that all the conditions are met, then it is plausible to conclude that the IPRs owner may have breached the FRAND commitment. As a consequence, the matter should be further investigated in order to establish an infringement and potential remedies. However, this model eventually suggests the application of the cited *Georgia Pacific* factors. Even more problematic is the conclusion of the author, where he argues that "the definition of the new terms and conditions could be left to the parties, who would restart their negotiation process and … use private litigation as a tool to solve any upcoming issue."[164]

A more interesting and plausible option, perhaps, has been given by Swanson and Baumol, who developed a market-efficiency-based framework for the evaluation of (F)RAND licensing royalties.[165] According to their system, standard-setting organizations should involve innovators in an auction mechanism, where the price of the technology ultimately chosen would reflect the competition existing *ex ante* between the different alternatives. It follows, in the authors' view, that the level of royalties finally asked by the selected IPRs owner would likely reflect a fair and reasonable licensing rate. These arguments certainly deserve some merit, as long as they recognize the importance of a unilateral *ex ante* determination of the price of patents. However, this model has been criticized as it only considers standards based on one single patent, while most standards are typically based on several complementary IPRs. This means that the question of how to allocate fees between different selected innovators in the SSO context has not been addressed by the authors.[166]

only $6,000 – the user should be willing to pay no more than $4,000 (that is, the cost of a license to use the next-best alternative). Note, however, that according to this logic, if the next-best alternative is no worse than the patented invention and is in the public domain (meaning here that the cost to use it equals 0) the value to the user of a license to use the patented invention is 0."

162 M. Valimaki (n 127) 689.

163 M. Mariniello, "Fair, reasonable and non-discriminatory (FRAND) terms: a challenge for competition authorities" (2011) 7(3) *Journal of Competition Law and Economics* 523.

164 Ibid., 540. See also G. Langus, V. Lipatov and D. Neven, "Standard essential patents: who is really holding up (and when)?" (2013) 9(2) *Journal of Competition Law and Economics* 253. These authors examine the parties' incentive to litigate and argue that this is usually influenced by the patent validity, the litigation costs and length.

165 D.G. Swanson and W.J. Baumol (n 6) 1.

166 A. Layne Farrar, A.J. Padilla and R. Schmalensee (n 88) 688. On the analysis of economic

4.3.1.4 ARBITRATION

Finally, commentators have also invoked the use of arbitration mechanisms in order to unveil the mystery surrounding the meaning of fair and reasonable licensing terms.[167] According to some authors, arbitration could be used to resolve other disputes arising in SSOs contexts, concerning for instance the validity or essentiality of patents.[168] Among the benefits, they mention the potential savings of cost and time that arbitration could achieve over litigation.[169] Arbitration, together with mediation and negotiation processes, is an example of alternative dispute resolution ("ADR"). It usually occurs when parties mutually agree to forgo judicial resolution of a dispute in favor of private resolution.[170] Different institutions around the world have developed arbitration rules in order to adjudicate patent disputes.[171] However, it seems that the number of patent cases submitted to arbitration is relatively small.[172] This is even more so in the context of standard-setting bodies, where arbitral mechanisms may be possibly implemented in order to address disagreements on the validity, infringement and value of essential patents.

models appraising methods to distribute royalties between several innovators, see L.S. Shapley, "A Value for N-Person Games" in H.W. Kuhn and A.W. Tucker (eds.), *Contributions to the Theory of Games* (Princeton University Press, Princeton 1953); R. Gilbert, "Competition Policy for Industry Standards" in R.D. Blair and D.D. Sokol (eds.), *The Oxford Handbook of International Antitrust Economics* (Oxford University Press, New York 2015) 554; and P. Dehez and S. Poukens, "The Shapley value as a guide to FRAND licensing agreements" (2013) CORE Discussion Paper n. 2013/12. Under the "Shapley Value," a fair and reasonable method of allocating fees in a cooperative game considers the *ex ante* incremental contribution of each member, regardless of any efficiency considerations. Cooperative games cover situations in which a group of individuals cooperate on a common project with the aim of maximizing collective welfare and allocating it between the members.

167 M.A. Lemley and C. Shapiro, "A simple approach to setting reasonable royalties for standard-essential patents" (2013) 28 *Berkeley Technology Law Journal* 1135; M.A. Lemley, "Ten things to do about patent hold-up of standards (and one not to)" (2007) 48 *Boston College Law Review* 149; K. Kuhn, F. Scott Morton, H. Shelanski, "Standard setting organizations can help solve the standard essential patents licensing problem" (2013) *CPI Antitrust Chronicle* 1.

168 On the general use of arbitration in patent disputes, see also K. Petrakis, "The role of arbitration in the field of patent law" (1997) 52 *Dispute Resolution Journal* 24.

169 See, *inter alia*, J.L. Contreras and D.L. Newman, "Developing a Framework for Arbitrating Standards-essential Patent (SEP) Disputes" (2014) American University WCL Research Paper n. 2014-20.

170 Ibid. See also G.B. Born, *International Commercial Arbitration* (2nd edn, Kluwer Law International, London 2014). According to Born, "the foundation for almost every international arbitration is an international arbitration agreement. Absent a valid agreement to arbitrate, there is generally no basis for requiring arbitration or for enforcing an arbitral award against a party."

171 Consider for instance the American Arbitration Association (AAA), or the World Intellectual Property Organization (WIPO). WIPO, in particular, is an agency of the United Nations that promotes protection of intellectual property throughout the world. In 1995, WIPO established an Arbitration and Mediation Center, and has implemented arbitral norms designed for IP disputes.

172 M.M. Lim, "ADR of Patent Disputes: A Customized Prescription, Not an Over-The-Counter Remedy" (2004) 6 *Cardozo Journal of Conflict Resolution* 155.

Indeed, only few organizations have incorporated alternative dispute resolution rules in their policies.[173]

There are different theories explaining why arbitration is used infrequently in patent cases, despite the high cost and lengthy duration of patent litigation. Some factors concern the limited rights of appeal against an arbitration award, a lack of authority to compel discovery or the perceived tendency for arbitrators to find solutions which leave no clear winner in a dispute.[174] In the context of standard setting, moreover, there is little guidance as to the optimal means to implement and enforce arbitration mechanisms.[175] Several questions indeed may be raised.

For instance, it may be legitimate to inquire whether: (a) arbitration in SSOs should be mandatory or on a voluntary basis; (b) SSOs members should be required to arbitrate all standard disputes that arise with other members, or with all potential licensees (whether or not they are SSO members); (c) arbitration should concern only the calculation of (F)RAND royalties, or also patent infringements and patent validity or essentiality; (d) arbitrators may decide also on ancillary claims, concerning for instance antitrust, breach of contract or fraud; (e) the results of (F)RAND arbitration should be kept confidential or be subject to public disclosure; (f) the arbitral award should bind also other SSO members; (g) the parties concerned would be barred from seeking injunctions during the pendency of arbitration.[176]

Some of these questions have been addressed by Lemley and Shapiro, who proposed best practices for standard-setting bodies based on "baseball-style" or "final offer" arbitration.[177] Under their model, IPRs owners agree to license their entire portfolios of pending and issued standard essential patents on FRAND terms. Notably, any FRAND promise should follow the patent, which means that any future purchaser of the patent at issue should be bound by the FRAND commitment.

The model may require a reciprocity clause, under which the implementer makes a reciprocal FRAND commitment for any essential patents it owns that read on the same standard. In order to facilitate negotiations, the patent holder

173 Among these, the DVB Project Association (active in the field of digital television broadcasting), VITA (the VMEbus International Trade Association), the Blu-Ray Disk Association (responsible for the Blu-Ray optical audiovisual disk format), and ETSI (the European Telecommunications Standards Institute). These organizations encourage, albeit to different extents, the use of arbitration and mediation as a means to resolve patent licensing disputes. On the issue, see J.L. Contreras, "Technical Standards and ex ante Disclosure: Results and Analysis of an Empirical Study" (2013) 53 *Jurimetrics* 163.

174 See B.A. Tulis, "Final Offer Baseball Arbitration: Contexts, Mechanics & Application" (2010) 20 *Seton Hall Journal of Sports and Entertainment Law* 85; E.M. Meth, "Final Offer Arbitration: A Model for Dispute Resolution in Domestic and International Disputes" (1999) 10 *American Review of International Arbitration* 383.

175 J.L. Contreras and D.L. Newman (n 169).

176 Ibid. As the authors remark, besides these crucial issues, a standard-setting organization would still need to select a reputable arbitration association with unbiased arbitral rules, the location where the arbitration would be conducted, and the number of arbitrators forming the panel.

177 M.A. Lemley and C. Shapiro (n 167) 1135.

should first make an initial offer to any willing licensee and disclose the terms under which it has already licensed other parties. If a patent holder and an implementer do not agree on FRAND terms, the patent owner is obligated to enter into binding arbitration with any willing licensee to determine the royalty rate. At this stage, no litigation is allowed, as the IPRs owner has promised to forgo court enforcement in favor of arbitration. Each party then submits its final offer to the arbitrator, who must choose one of the two proposed prices.[178] The arbitration decision, which can be appealed in only limited circumstances (i.e. legal error or any procedural deficiency), is eventually disclosed to any willing licensees. According to Lemley and Shapiro if an (unwilling) implementer refuses to accept a reciprocal commitment or to submit to and accept the result of binding arbitration, then the IPRs holder may lawfully enforce its patents before a court and ask for damages or injunctive relief.[179]

The path proposed by these authors is certainly noteworthy. However, it should not be forgotten that it may be particularly difficult for a standard-setting body to implement an arbitration policy which could be easily accepted by all the SSO members, patent owners and implementers. The thorny issues concerning the confidentiality, the content, the scope or the preclusive effect of an arbitral award may well be an obstacle to the participants' will to resort to arbitration.

4.3.2 FRAND – meaning of non-discriminatory royalties

Further questions have been posed by the literature on the interpretation of the non-discrimination requirement of (F)RAND licensing policies.[180] Standard-setting organizations, indeed, do not usually explain when the royalties charged by IPRs owners can be considered non-discriminatory. Price discrimination occurs when a firm charges, to different clients for the same goods or services, dissimilar rates which are not cost-reflective.[181] Several cases have been decided in this context by the EU Commission and courts under Article 102(c) TFEU.[182] However, understanding when licensing fees are discriminatory may be much more complex. The Court of Justice of the EU has recently confirmed that the charging of

178 Ibid., 1145. As the authors argue, when examining which of the offers is more reasonable, the arbitrator should consider the likelihood of validity, essentiality and infringement of the patent.

179 On the use of injunctions in standard setting disputes, see Chapter 4 section 5.

180 A. Layne Farrar, A.J. Padilla and R. Schmalensee (n 88) 671; M. Valimaki (n 127) 686; D.G. Swanson and W.J. Baumol (n 6) 25; L. Zhang (n 138) 401.

181 V. Korah, *An Introductory Guide to EC Competition Law and Practice* (9th edn, Hart Publishing, London 2007) Ch. 5; R. Whish and D. Bailey, *Competition Law* (7th edn, Oxford University Press, Oxford 2012) Ch. 18; S. Bishop and M. Walker, *The Economics of EC Competition Law* (3rd edn, Sweet & Maxwell, London 2010) 224; R.J. Van den Bergh and P.D. Camesasca, *European Competition Law and Economics: a Comparative Perspective* (2nd edn, Sweet & Maxwell, London 2006) Ch. 7.

182 See Case 40/73 *Suiker Unie v European Commission* [1975] ECR 1663; Case 85/76 *Hoffmann-La Roche v European Commission* [1979] ECR 461; Case 27/76 *United Brands v European Commission* [1978] ECR 207; Case 322/81 *Michelin v European Commission* [1983] ECR 3461; Case C-95/04 P *British Airways v European Commission* [2007] ECR I-2331; Case T-228/97 *Irish Sugar v European Commission* [1999] ECR II-2969.

different royalties, calculated as a percentage of revenues, can lead to a discriminatory practice.[183] Nevertheless, it could be difficult to establish whether "two-part tariffs discriminate against smaller licensees or whether royalties assessed as a percentage of the licensee's revenues discriminate against licensees who sell more expensive products."[184] A further obstacle may arise when the parties involved agree to cross-license their IPRs, as in this case it could be difficult to appraise the value of each license.

This notwithstanding, some authors argue that limiting discriminatory licensing by imposing (F)RAND terms may finally help with the patent hold-up problem.[185] A non-discrimination requirement could dissuade SSO members from engaging in complex individual negotiations of the *ex ante* fee level, and could make them complacent about uniform marginal rates which could be passed to the ultimate consumers.[186] This could potentially eliminate the risk of lengthy multiple negotiations between licensees and IPRs owners.

A non-discrimination requirement may also be interpreted as forbidding free cross-licensing between IPRs owners, as firms owning several patents could benefit from the practice much more than those undertakings with a limited patent portfolio.[187] Discrimination in cross-licensing, of course, may be deemed to exist only after a careful assessment of the values of licenses has been made. However, it is not certain that royalty-free cross-licensing could be harmful in light of the aims of standard-setting processes.

Finally, a non-discrimination requirement could be read as prohibiting vertically integrated patent owners from favoring their own downstream firms over downstream competitors.[188] This effect, as Swanson and Baumol have asserted, may be seen as the main justification for the non-discrimination requirement.[189]

In order to ensure that IPRs owners charge downstream rivals what they charge themselves for use of the patented technology, the authors elaborated the "efficient component pricing rule" (ECPR). Under this rule, the royalty charged would be discriminatory if it exceeds the difference between the IPRs owner's price of the downstream good and its incremental cost of inputs other than the patent.[190] In other words, discrimination would occur in case the patent holder,

183 Case C-52/07 *Kanal 5, TV 4 AB v STIM* [2009] OJ C 32. On fair or excessive royalty levels, see also Case 395/87 *Ministère Public v Jean-Louis Tournier* [1989] ECR 2521.

184 J. Farrell, J. Hayes, C. Shapiro and T. Sullivan (n 92) 638.

185 Ibid., 639. See also D.W. Carlton and A.L. Shampine (n 160). In their analysis of discriminatory licensing conduct, Carlton and Shampine refer to the position of "similarly situated firms."

186 D.J. Teece and E.F. Sherry (n 101) 1956–1957; J. Farrell and R.P. Merges, "Incentives to Challenge and Defend Patents: Why Litigation Won't Reliably Fix Patent Office Errors and Why Administrative Patent Review Might Help" (2004) 19 *Berkeley Technology Law Journal* 954; J. Farrell and C. Shapiro, "How Strong Are Weak Patents?" (2008) 98(4) *American Economic Review* 1347.

187 J. Farrell, J. Hayes, C. Shapiro and T. Sullivan (n 92) 640.

188 However, it is worth noting, the existence of non-disclosure licensing clauses between IPRs holders and licensees may sometimes make it difficult to discover discrimination.

189 D.G. Swanson and W.J. Baumol (n 6) 25.

190 Under the Swanson and Baumol formula: $Pi = Pfi - ICri$ (reasonable license price = the IP owner's final product price – the IP owner's incremental cost of remaining inputs).

by charging itself what it charges downstream rivals, would lose profit on its downstream production.[191] The effectiveness of this model, however, has been criticized by different authors, who argued that a vertically integrated firm under certain circumstances may still pass the "ECPR" test by charging discriminatory royalties.[192] Doubts, in particular, exist on the application of this mechanism to those contexts where complementary rights are included in the standard and cross-licensing may be necessary.[193] In addition, as Geradin noted, identifying the incremental cost of a product might be a very difficult task.[194]

In conclusion, it is evident that the meaning of (F)RAND is all but obvious and clear.[195] These terms have been scrutinized by several commentators, which have tried more than once to define what fair, reasonable and non-discriminatory mean. The debate is directly linked to the arguments made by the literature on excessive rates, which may lead to an infringement under EU competition law. The issue posed several questions which the literature has tried to address.[196]

This notwithstanding, confusion still reigns. The *Georgia Pacific* test and its later developments, the numeric proportionality rule, and the cited economic models were not able to identify a precise roadmap which may work under all circumstances. A change in the SSOs' licensing rules seems more than desirable.

4.3.3 Alternative model to (F)RAND licensing

In order to avoid the risks of subscribing undefined (F)RAND terms and litigating their meaning before a court, SSO members could negotiate *ex ante* the specific price terms under which licensing their rights. This model would avoid uncertainty on the level of royalties patent holders may finally charge, and might thus function as an incentive to take part in the standard setting process.

However, it has been held that, under these circumstances, SSO members would allegedly expose themselves to potential antitrust liability for price fixing under Article 101 TFEU and Section 1 of the US Sherman Act.[197] Similarly, firms

191 This test is at the core of the analysis on margin squeeze, which occurs when a vertically integrated firm provides an important input into a downstream market in which it also competes, and prices this input at such a level that "as efficient" rivals it supplies cannot make a margin for profit (Case C-280/08 *Deutsche Telekom AG v European Commission* [2010] OJ C 346).

192 J. Farrell, J. Hayes, C. Shapiro and T. Sullivan (n 92) 641.

193 A. Layne Farrar, A.J. Padilla and R. Schmalensee (n 88) 688–689. Consider, for instance, a complex piece of equipment (e.g. a computer), made up of components each covered by a patent.

194 D. Geradin, "Pricing Abuses by Essential Patent Holders in a Standard-Setting Context: a View from Europe" (2009–2010) 76 *Antitrust Law Journal* 329.

195 On the argument see, *inter alia*, J.H. Park, *Patents and Industry Standards* (Edward Elgar, Cheltenham 2010) 45; and P.D. Curran, "Standard Setting Organizations: Patents, Price Fixing, and Per Se Legality" (2003) 70 *University of Chicago Law Review* 983.

196 See D.S. Evans and A.J. Padilla, "Excessive Prices: Using Economics to Define Administrative Legal Rules" (2005) 1(1) *Journal of Competition Law and Economics* 97; M. Furse, "Excessive Prices, Unfair Prices and Economic Value: the Law of Excessive Pricing Under Article 82 EC and the Chapter II Prohibition" (2008) 4(1) *European Competition Journal* 59; D. Geradin (n 194) 329.

197 D.J. Teece and E.F. Sherry (n 101) 1955.

could face antitrust liability for implementing an illegal group boycott, in case they conditioned the standardization of a proprietary technology on the IPRs owner's acceptance of licensing rates specified in advance.[198]

Other comments have then emphasized the risk that discussing on licensing terms may ultimately lead to exhausting policy battles between SSOs' participants, which may finally compromise the standardization process.[199] Furthermore, it has also been added that *ex ante* joint negotiation may be unfavorable for those firms joining the standard-setting body later in the process, as they would have to accept conditions already established by others.[200] In light of these observations, to be thoroughly reviewed in the next chapter, *ex ante* joint negotiation of licensing terms does not seem a viable alternative to FRAND.

4.3.4 Patent pools

As a system of price negotiations, SSOs could also allow the formation of patent pools, in order to market altogether patents essential to the standard.[201] Patent pools, in particular, have been defined as price-fixing arrangements, by which two or more parties put their complementary IPRs together in a package and license them to the members of the pool and to third parties.[202]

Patent pools may benefit standard-setting activities as far as they preserve fair competition, reduce the incidence of legal suits and keep the total royalties low,

198 On group boycotts, see *Golden Bridge Technology v Motorola Inc.*, 547 F3d 266 (C App 5th Circuit, 2008). Here, the SSO's (3GPP) members were accused by Golden Bridge to have conspired (contrary to Section 1) and removed the plaintiff's technology from the standard to avoid paying the royalties. The Court of Appeals, however, rejected Golden Bridge's argument on the illegal conspiracy, holding that the informal communications were an important part of the SSO process. The case seems to suggest that the line beyond which legitimate standard setting conduct becomes actionable is beyond the limits of an SSO's formal proceeding.

199 See ETSI, "Guide on IPRs" (2013). Section 4.1 clarified that "[s]pecific licensing terms and negotiations are commercial issues between the companies and shall not be addressed within ETSI. Technical Bodies are not the appropriate place to discuss IPRs issues."

200 M. Valimaki (n 127) 689. On the *ex ante* negotiation, see also T. Winston, "Innovation and ex ante consideration of licensing terms in standard setting" (2006) EAG Discussion Paper n. 6-3.

201 See C. Shapiro, "Navigating the Patent Thicket: Cross Licensees, Patent Pools and Standard Setting" (2001) Social Science Research Network 1; R. Gilbert, "Antitrust for Patent Pools: a Century of Policy Evolution" (2004) *Stanford Technology Law Review* 3; J. Verbruggen and A. Lorincz, "Patents and technical standards" (2002) 33(2) *International Review of Intellectual Property and Competition Law* 150; and J. Lerner and J. Tirole, "Efficient Patent Pools" (2004) 94 *American Economic Review* 691. In their research, Lerner and Tirole considered the MPEG-2 ("Moving Picture Experts Group") video patent pool, where one of the most debated issues during the pool formation was the licensing fee to be charged. Some participants (Columbia University) wanted to maximize the fee level, while others (Sony, both IPRs owner and manufacturer) preferred to maximize sales of the final standard-based product.

202 On the function of patent pools, see also J. Temple Lang, "Patent pools and agreements on standards" (2011) 36(6) *European Law Review* 887. As an example of standard based on several complementary IPRs, the author recalls the UMTS (Universal Mobile Telecommunication Standard), which requires the use of around 1,500 claimed standard essential patents, held by approximately 50 different companies.

thus limiting the so-called "complements problem."[203] As an author remarks, "a patent pool facilitates technology licensing and encourages greater adoption by creating a one stop shop that lowers overall royalties and transactions costs."[204] The creation of a patent pool, in particular, would require the implementation of two different phases: the identification and the licensing of relevant IPRs. First, it would be necessary to identify those patents which are essential to the standard, which means patents that would be necessarily infringed if the standard is practiced. Then, the patent pool administrator would have to work with the IPRs holders on a workable royalty scheme. Finally, the administrator would have to propose the licensing agreements to those companies using the standardized technology, and eventually redistribute the collected royalties to the pool members according to the chosen sharing rule. In this context, as it has been held, it seems fundamental that the pool administrator be independent, innovative, internationally based, effective, and with a relevant technical background. It is further argued that a successful pool should also include enforcement mechanisms in order to ensure that unlicensed companies implementing the standardized technology will not gain an unfair advantage.[205]

However, there are different reasons that lead to doubt about patent pool effectiveness.[206] For instance, if the patent pool is only formed by IPRs owners who are not also manufacturers of the final standardized product, there may still be a risk of excessive cumulative royalties being charged. Indeed, unlike vertically integrated firms (which may have an interest to shift their profits downstream), upstream innovators may not have any intention to keep licensing prices low; they may even refuse to join a pool in the first instance. Second, in pools formed by both upstream innovators and vertically integrated firms (which may contribute to keep the royalty level low), there could still be a risk under competition law as long as the members discuss resale prices of the final standardized item. Also, in this context, some upstream innovators may simply decide to stay out of the pool and free ride on the lower rates chosen by the firms that are part of it.[207] This further

203 A. Cournot, *Recherches sur les principles mathematiques de la theorie des richesse* (Calmann Levy, Paris 1974). Cournot was the first to understand that if a good required complementary inputs supplied by different firms each of which had market power, then the suppliers may exert an externality on each other that would lead to exorbitant prices being charged.

204 R. Dini, "How to Support New Technology Development and its Commercial Success by Avoiding Royalty Stacking" (2010) 2 *Concurrences* 13–15. Further analysis of the beneficial effects of patent pools has been developed by N. Gallini, "Private agreements for coordinating patent rights: the case of patent pools" (2011) Institutions Economics and Law – IEL Paper No. 5; and A. Layne Farrar and K.M. Schmidt, "Licensing Complementary Patents: Patent Trolls, Market Structure, and Excessive Royalties" (2010) 25 *Berkeley Technology Law Journal* 1132. Farrar and Schmidt, for instance, highlight the important role played by pools and cross-licensing agreements in limiting the cumulative amount of fees charged in SSOs.

205 R. Dini (n 204). The Digital Video Broadcasting (DVB) consortium is an example of a body that actively encourages the formation of patent pools covering DVB standards. Examples of firms managing patent licensing programs include MPEG LA, Sisvel and VIA Licensing.

206 K.M. Schmidt, "Standards, Innovation Incentives and the Formation of Patent Pools" in *The Pro & Cons of Standard Setting* (Swedish Competition Authority, 2010) 57–58.

207 Ibid., 69. On the free riding problem, see also N. Gallini (n 204) 15.

means that it may be particularly difficult to form a patent pool if patent holders are asymmetric. Third, if patent pools concerned also substitute IPRs, as it may be the case,[208] their function could be detrimental to societal welfare as long as they reduce price competition among competing innovators.[209] On a further different ground, patent pools may suppress competition if their members harbor non-essential, weak or invalid intellectual property rights.[210] In other words, negative welfare consequences may derive in case pools reduce the incentives to challenge weak patents, and foreclose competition downstream or discourage innovative activities.[211] Finally, not all innovators would take part in the pool due to the expected difficulties of agreeing on the distribution of royalties and sustaining the stability of the pool. For instance, in case the pool adopted "numeric proportionality" rules to distribute the royalties among the SSO members, those firms with fewer patents of higher relevance may be reluctant to participate.[212] In light of the above, there is no guarantee that patent pools may effectively benefit the standard-setting process, by keeping royalty levels low while reducing transaction costs and avoiding costly infringement litigation. The historical development of standard-setting organizations shows that firms often fail to form a pool that includes all complementary patents.[213] Other times, a patent pool may even break up into different smaller pools, as happened for instance in relation to the DVDs (digital versatile discs) standardization work.[214] The larger the number of complementary IPRs holders, the lower the probability of developing a stable pool mechanism.[215] These considerations explain why SSOs should carefully examine the opportunity to form patent pools, despite their alleged desirable properties and despite the fact that in recent years different courts and agencies have started to consider this

208 N. Gallini (n 204) 7. As Gallini holds, "more commonly, the relationship between patents in a pool includes element of both substitutability and complementarity."

209 On the tension arising between the different members of a patent pool, see the analysis developed by A. Layne Farrar (n 52) 46.

210 N. Gallini (n 204) 12. According to the author, who applies a model based on "product and litigation rules," most patent pools with valid, essential and complementary patents can lead to positive and welfare-enhancing effects.

211 Ibid.,16.

212 M.K. Herman, "Negotiating Standards-Related Patent Licenses – How the Deal is Done" (2010) *Landslide* 39. According to the author, "mandatory pooling [...] would prevent some companies from lawfully licensing their patents in a manner that best suits their business needs."

213 For instance, shortly before the formation of the cited MPEG-2 pool, the firm Lucent chose not to participate as it believed it could better maximize its profits by licensing out of the pool. On the dynamics related to the activities of MPEG-2 pool, see J. Verbruggen and A. Lorincz (n 201) 150.

214 K.M. Schmidt (n 206) 68–70.

215 J.L. Contreras, "Rethinking RAND: SDO based approaches to patent licensing commitments" (2012) Social Science Research Network 19. Contreras argues, *inter alia*, that patent pools would be cost-prohibitive in an SSO context. Thus, he developed a "pseudo-pool approach that incorporates some of the beneficial features of patent pools while preserving the flexibility and broad activity scope that is inherent in the SDO model." Such approach is based on the *ex ante* joint negotiation model, and requires an aggregate royalty determination made by working groups to limit the risk of excessive royalties.

licensing mechanism more favorably than in the past.[216] In conclusion, what IPRs licensing policy may represent the optimal framework in standard-setting environments still remains an open question which deserves careful scrutiny.

5 Conclusion

Intellectual property rights and standards play a central role in today's global economy. IPRs represent a relevant incentive for firms to innovate and enhance dynamic efficiency. The technologies developed by innovators may then be subject to standardization processes; standards, it is well-known, may contribute significantly to economic growth, as they facilitate trade and help to achieve products' interoperability. Both standards and IPRs, therefore, aim at enhancing consumer welfare, which is crucial in competition policy's goals.

Besides the importance and meaning of standards, the chapter has shed light also on the different processes that lead to their adoption. Further, relevant questions have been addressed, concerning above all the opportunity to reward innovators in SSO contexts. Rewarding IPRs owners' investments in new technologies has beneficial effects for both consumers and competition, to the benefit of the welfare of the whole society. Equally important was the analysis of the most common policy rules. The adoption of a legal framework over a different one may well discourage or incentivize participation to SSOs by IPRs holders. Licensing rules, in particular, pose many questions on definitions and firms' liability.[217] Several arguments make it difficult to share the view of those authors supporting (F)RAND rules.[218] Above all, one question still stands unanswered: how to define the concept of fair, reasonable and non-discriminatory? The main problem concerns its meaning and determination, which is context-specific. This is evidenced by an increasing number of lawsuits and agency investigations on the implementation of (F)RAND terms.[219] What is more, the economic literature is far from developing a "magic formula." Thus, the model does not seem the most effective

216 See, for instance, *Hartford-Empire Co v United States*, 46 F Supp 541 (ND Ohio, 1942); and *United States v Line Material*, 333 US 287 (1948).

217 See S.M. Amundson, "Recent Decisions Provide Some Clarity on how Courts and Government Agencies will Likely Resolve Issues Involving Standard Essential Patents" (2014) 13(1) *Chicago-Kent Journal of Intellectual Property* 91.

218 D.J. Teece and E.F. Sherry (n 101) 1973; L. Zhang (n 138) 409; D. Geradin and M. Rato, "FRAND Commitments and EC Competition Law: A Reply to Philippe Chappatte" (2010) 6(1) *European Competition Journal* 129; D. Geradin and R.G. Brooks (n 117). Geradin, for instance, takes the FRAND obligation as an enforceable contract. The meaning of FRAND, as he holds, should not be subject to specific limitations; its initial interpretation and determination should be left to the parties. Only in case of disagreement, a court should assess the reasonableness of the offered terms, taking into consideration, *inter alia,* the factors established in *Georgia Pacific.*

219 Besides the cited cases, see also Case AT.39985 *Motorola – Enforcement of GPRS Standard Essential Patents,* C (2014) 2892 final; and Case AT.39939 *Samsung – Enforcement of UMTS Standard Essential Patents,* C (2014) 2891 final. Samsung was involved in litigation against Apple in many jurisdictions, including Italy, Japan, Korea, England, Germany, the Netherlands and France. On the "smartphone war" between these IT giants, see also M. Siragusa, "Case Comment – Italy: Tribunal of Milan – Samsung v Apple" (2012) 5(3) *Global Competition Litigation Review* R32-R33.

answer when setting licensing rules. Similarly, the *ex ante* negotiation of fees cannot be implemented as the optimal model due to the cited faults. This does not mean that innovators should be allowed to charge any desired price.[220] All these conclusions will be thoroughly justified in the next chapter, which will shed further light on the risks arising in standard setting and will explain in more detail why these models are not effective.

220 D. Geradin (n 194) 329. In Geradin's view, however, any fees for a standardized technology will be constrained by the prices charged by other firms for complementary IPRs.

Part Two

Anticompetitive conduct and standardization

4 The interaction IPRs–competition in standard setting

1 Introduction

Standardization may determine risks for both the members of standard-setting organizations (SSOs) and the organizations themselves. Indeed, standard setting represents a context where the principles of IP and competition laws may potentially conflict. On the one hand, it seems important to encourage the owners of intellectual property rights (IPRs) to participate in SSOs, and reward their investments in research and development. On the other hand, the protection of IPRs holders' interests should be balanced by the need to preserve standard-setting objectives in terms of enhanced consumer welfare. A non-optimal balance between these goals may lead to considerable losses for society as a whole.

The achievement of a proper balance implies, in the first place, the setting of a legal framework which clearly strikes *ex ante* the boundaries between legitimate and forbidden conduct. Indeed, the risk exists that innovators may mislead the other participants, compromising the whole standardization process. The implementation of a policy model preventing the rise of these risks seems to be a crucial step in the development of effective and transparent standard setting. At the same time, from a further perspective, competition law may also play a role by tackling *ex post* any misleading and unfair practices. In this regard, as explained in Chapter 1, competition enforcers should be encouraged to apply a test which aims to enhance consumer welfare. This, in turn, may stimulate consumer demand and raise production levels to the benefit of societal welfare. In light of these arguments, it is clear why US antitrust and EU competition laws may be held as potential remedies to conduct undermining the optimal functioning of standardization processes and the achievement of their goals.

This chapter aims to assess the risks in terms of antitrust liability deriving from the conduct of SSO members. Both the literature and jurisprudence have identified two particular behaviors which may raise specific concerns: patent ambush and the mere breach of defined licensing terms. These practices are often referred to as patent hold-up, due to the holding effect on other members.

After further introductory remarks on the nature of the intersection IP–competition, I will start an in-depth examination of the concept of patent ambush and of its negative consequences on standard setting, while appraising the different models proposed as solutions. I will then examine the second conduct, the mere breach of defined (i.e. FRAND) licensing terms. In this context, I will evaluate the alternative scenarios that may lead to different outcome under EU and US antitrust laws. Finally, I will consider the threat posed by the request of injunctive relief, as assessed by the EU and US courts. I will eventually suggest that a more effective policy is needed to tackle abusive conduct in SSO contexts.

2 The interplay between standards and competition

Standards, it has been said, play a crucial role in today's knowledge-based economy. They expand network externalities and allow customers to switch to alternative products, leading to more innovation.[1] From an antitrust perspective, a standard-setting situation is benign where IPRs owners participate in the meetings and try to influence, in compliance with the SSO rules and without hiding the existence of their rights, the standard-setting body to include their technology in the standard. By having their invention included in the standard, IPRs holders may be finally rewarded for their contribution to technological progress and innovation.[2]

However, it has also been clarified that the various phases of the standard-setting process may raise concerns about antitrust liability. In particular, standard setting represents a context where conflicts between antitrust and intellectual property principles may arise. This is mainly due to the alleged contradictory nature of the relationship between antitrust regimes, which aim, *inter alia*, at the protection of competition, and intellectual property regulations, whose goal is to protect original and valuable creations.[3] Cooperative standard-setting, for instance, may require horizontal competitors to agree on specifications of products, raising potential concerns on the boundaries between cooperation and collusion.[4]

In the US, the American Bar Association has developed an interesting study of many such issues.[5] In Europe, the Commission has started to pay due attention to

1 See J. Gstalter, "Open Standards and Competition Law: an Overview" (2010) 1 *Concurrences* 1–4; J.Y. Art and U. Decker, "Openness and Standards – How do (Open) Standards Affect Competition?" (2010) 1 *Concurrences* 18–20; H.J. Hovenkamp, "Competition in information technologies: standards-essential patents, non-practicing entities and FRAND bidding" (2012) University of Iowa Legal Studies Research Paper n. 12–32. On the "lock-in" effect, see also E. Ramirez and L. Kimmel, "A Competition Policy Perspective on Patent Law: the Federal Trade Commission's Report on the Evolving IP Marketplace" (2011) *The Antitrust Source* 4.

2 M.C. Naughton and R. Wolfram, "The Antitrust Risks of Unilateral Conduct in Standard Setting, in the Light of the FTC's case against Rambus Inc" (2004) 49 *Antitrust Bulletin* 701.

3 H.K.S. Schmidt, "Article 82's Exceptional Circumstances that Restrict Intellectual Property Rights" (2002) 23(5) *European Competition Law Review* 210; S.D. Anderman, *The Interface between Intellectual Property Rights and Competition Policy* (Cambridge University Press, Cambridge 2007).

4 J. Farrell, J. Hayes, C. Shapiro and T. Sullivan, "Standard Setting, Patents, and Hold-Up" (2007) 74 *Antitrust Law Journal* 603; C. Shapiro, "Setting Compatibility Standards, Co-operation or Collusion?" in R. Dreyfuss, D.L. Zimmerman and H. First, *Expanding the Boundaries of Intellectual Property – Innovation Policy for the Knowledge Society* (Oxford University Press, New York 2001) 91.

5 American Bar Association, *Handbook on the Antitrust Aspects of Standard Setting* (2nd edn, ABA Section of Antitrust Law, Chicago 2011).

the potential anticompetitive conduct adopted in the standard-setting context. In particular, the EU competition enforcer, although recognizing that standard setting may encourage "the development of new and improved products or markets and improved supply conditions,"[6] also noted that it could further lead to the exclusion of competitors and prevent the development of alternative standards.[7] Collusion among SSO participants could entail the application of Article 101 TFEU and Section 1 of the US Sherman Act. Unilateral abusive behaviors could instead be reviewed under Article 102 TFEU and Section 2 of the Sherman Act.[8]

The implementation of these practices has probably been facilitated by the policy model adopted so far by SSOs, which do not seem to have struck the right balance in the setting of their internal regulations. Therefore, a change of legal framework – in particular, licensing rules – is needed and will be eventually suggested in order to strengthen standardization processes and ensure the latter may enhance consumer welfare and societal productivity. For the sake of clarity, not only cooperative but also *de facto* standard setting may ultimately lead to harm competition and consumer welfare. The concerns arising in standardization *de facto* have been already discussed in Chapter 2 of the book, in conjunction with the studying of those cases (e.g., *Microsoft*) which testified the contrast between innovators and the marketplace; a conflict which may potentially arise outside of the context of SSOs' activities. For the purpose of this book, the next sections will focus on the antitrust issues arising in collaborative standardization, developed by formal standards institutes and private industry networks.

3 Patent ambush

Patent ambush is the most common example of anticompetitive conduct in the standardization processes and is a form of patent hold-up. Nobel Prize economist Williamson famously identified this sort of opportunistic behavior as "self-interest seeking with guile."[9] From a general perspective, hold-up occurs:

> when a gap between economic commitments and subsequent commercial negotiations enables one party to capture part of the fruits of another's investment, broadly construed. Hold-up can arise, in particular, when one party makes investments specific to a relationship before all the terms and

6 European Commission, "Guidelines on the Applicability of Article 101 TFEU to Horizontal Co-operation Agreements" [2011] OJ C 11/1, at 263.

7 Ibid., at 264. See also J. Gstalter (n 1) 1–4; and P. Chappatte, "FRAND commitments – the case for antitrust intervention" (2009) 5(2) *European Competition Journal* 324.

8 P. Hellstrom, T. Kramler and F.W. Bulst, "Holding Standardization to Competition Law Standards" (2010) 1 *Concurrences* 24–26. On the need to control anticompetitive practices in contractual licenses, see also Article 40 of the Agreement on Trade Related Aspects of Intellectual Property Rights (TRIPs), Annex 1C to the Marrakesh Agreement establishing the World Trade Organization (WTO), 33 ILM 1197 (1994).

9 O. Williamson, *The Economic Institutions of Capitalism: Firms, Markets, Relational Contracting* (The Free Press, New York 1985) 47.

> conditions of the relationship are agreed. Hold-up generally leads to economic inefficiency that contracting parties, and courts interpreting contracts, often try to avoid.[10]

In the standard-setting context, patent ambush arises when firms fail to disclose to an SSO the existence of IPRs they own over a technology that could be part of a specific standard. These firms may decide to withhold information pertaining to relevant IPRs and maintain control over their own property rights.[11] This conduct may manipulate the standard-setting process and allow the undertaking concerned to have a dominant position in the market of the standardized technology.[12] Competition is harmed as competitors (the rival IPRs owners) are excluded. The ultimate risk is that the dominant firm might be able to gain supra-competitive royalties for the sale of the selected technology from licensees.[13] Licensees may then pass the burden of such excessive fees downstream, harming the welfare of consumers and, more generally, society as a whole.[14] The existing link between consumer and societal surplus has already been scrutinized in Chapter 1.[15]

In order to understand better why IPRs owners may be tempted by patent ambush, some considerations deserve attention. A patent which is essential to implement a standard has a much higher value *ex post* than *ex ante*,[16] because at the start of an SSO process several alternative technologies may potentially be available. Once the adoption of a standard has been formalized and sunk investments (for designing, producing, distributing the product) have been made, competition ends between IPRs owners pursuing the inclusion of their technology in the standard. It is clear, then, why a patent owner may well be attracted by the opportunity to withhold conflicting IPRs and obtain the *ex post* rather than the *ex ante* value of its technology. In order to obtain supra-competitive rates for the license of its technology, the IPRs owner may threaten to block the implementation of the standard by seeking an injunction.[17] That is why Lemley and Shapiro suggested

10 J. Farrell, J. Hayes, C. Shapiro and T. Sullivan (n 4) 603–604.

11 M.A. Lemley and C. Shapiro, "Patent Hold-up and Royalty Stacking" (2007) 85 *Texas Law Review* 1991; R.A. Skitol, "Concerted Buying Power: Its Potential for Addressing the Patent Hold-up Problem in Standard Setting" (2004–2005) 72 *Antitrust Law Journal* 729; D. Geradin and M. Rato, "Can Standard Setting Lead to Exploitative Abuse? A Dissonant View on Patent Hold-Up, Royalty Stacking and the Meaning of FRAND" (2007) 3 *European Competition Journal* 125–126; G. Ohana, M. Hansen and O. Shah, "Disclosure and Negotiation of Licensing Terms Prior to Adoption of Industry Standards: Preventing Another Patent Ambush?" (2003) 24(12) *European Competition Law Review* 645; J.G. Sidak, "Patent Hold-up and Oligopsonistic Collusion in Standard-Setting Organizations" (2009) 5(1) *Journal of Competition Law and Economics* 125.

12 J. Farrell, J. Hayes, C. Shapiro and T. Sullivan (n 4) 608–609; M.C. Naughton and R. Wolfram (n 2) 701–702.

13 D.G. Swanson and W.J. Baumol, "Reasonable and Non-discriminatory (RAND) Royalties, Standards Selection, and Control of Market Power" (2005–2006) 73 *Antitrust Law Journal* 3–4.

14 On the connection between consumer and societal welfare, see J.M. Keynes, *The General Theory of Employment, Interest and Money* (Macmillan, London 1936).

15 See Chapter 1 section 2.2.1.

16 G. Ohana, M. Hansen and O. Shah (n 11) 645.

17 Ibid., 644–645; J.G. Sidak (n 11) 125.

that patent law should be changed through legislation and judicial interpretation (public collective action), so as to limit the availability of patent injunctions and contrast this form of hold-up.[18]

The development of a standardized technology may also encounter similar difficulties in case of the "complements problem," which arises in case of multiple complementary IPRs which are essential for implementing a standard. In this situation, different firms may assert their rights and ask for the payment of royalties for licensing their patents.[19] These parallel practices may eventually determine an excessive cumulative royalty burden for the implementers of the technological device. The phenomenon, known as royalty stacking, can make the whole process more difficult and costly, but may also lead to the proposed technology not being implemented at all, determining a significant deadweight loss.[20] From these arguments, it can be inferred that any solution addressing hold-up may also help in overcoming the risks deriving from the royalty stacking problem.

3.1 US v EU approach

The first examples of SSOs originated in the United States[21] and set the stage for further developments in Europe.[22] It is not surprising, therefore, that the first cases concerning SSO processes were decided by US courts and antitrust authorities.[23] In recent years, however, the European Commission has started paying careful attention to the standard-setting phenomenon.[24] Standardization activities, for

18 M.A. Lemley and C. Shapiro (n 11) 1991. In their model, the authors suggest that injunctive relief should be limited in cases where the patented components represent only a small share of the overall value of the infringer's product. At the same time, they argue, injunctions should be granted only when the IPRs owner practices the patent in competition with the alleged infringer.

19 D. Geradin and M. Rato (n 11) 126. See also A. Cournot, *Recherches sur les principles mathematiques de la theorie des richesse* (Calmann Levy, Paris 1974). According to Cournot, if several suppliers of essential raw materials or components price their products separately, the effect may be to increase the total cost to users to such an extent that the demand falls.

20 M.A. Lemley and C. Shapiro (n 11) 1991. *Cf.* with D. Geradin, A. Layne Farrar and A.J. Padilla, "The complements problem within standard setting: assessing the evidence on royalty stacking" (2008) 14 *Boston University Journal of Science and Technology Law* 144; and E. Elhauge, "Do Patent Hold-Up and Royalty Stacking lead to Systematically Excessive Royalties?" (2008) 4(3) *Journal of Competition Law & Economics* 535. According to Geradin and Elhauge, royalty stacking and hold-up seem to be bogus conjectures or (at least) are not as widespread and recurring as others held.

21 For instance, ANSI (the American National Standards Institute) was founded in 1918, when five engineering societies and three government agencies created the American Engineering Standards Committee (the present name was adopted in 1969). Today, it includes approximately 1.300 corporations, 260 industry groups and several public agencies and academic institutions.

22 E.g., CEN (*Comité Européen de Normalisation)*, CENELEC (*Comité Européen de Normalisation Électrotechnique)*, and ETSI (European Telecommunications Standards Institute) were founded respectively in 1961, 1973 and 1988.

23 See, *inter alia*, *Allied Tube & Conduit v Indian Head*, 486 US 492 (1988); *Dell Computer*, 121 Federal Trade Commission 616 (1996); *Wang Labs. v Mitsubishi Elecs.*, 103 F.3d 1571 (C App Federal Circuit, 1997).

24 See European Commission, "Towards an Increased Contribution from Standardization to Innovation in Europe" (Communication) COM 133 final, 11 March 2008; and European

instance, have been thoroughly scrutinized in the "Guidelines on the Applicability of Article 101 TFEU to Horizontal Co-operation Agreements," where the EU enforcer explicitly promotes openness and transparency for standard-setting processes.[25] As will be discussed in Chapters 5 and 6, cases and investigations both in the US and in the EU have addressed competition risks arising in this context, with specific reference to patent ambush.[26] The shared objective was to prevent firms from charging high royalties by means of "submarine patents" (i.e. by hiding the existence of conflicting IPRs).[27] However, US and EU antitrust enforcers have often elaborated different perspectives. The divergent outcomes of the investigations should be explained mainly in light of the different legal frameworks and approaches to dominance.

In particular, the approach developed by US courts and authorities to tackle unilateral conduct has been usually defined as less interventionist, when compared to their EU counterparts, and more in line with liberal principles. This may also be a reflection of the fact that the US modern antitrust framework has been highly influenced by the effect-based analysis promoted by the Chicago School. The EU competition system, instead, has for a long time been modeled on the more formal approach initially adopted by the Harvard School.[28] These differences are also reflected in the different legal frameworks.

The US antitrust provisions, indeed, do not prohibit exploitative abuses but only sanction exclusionary practices. Unlike Article 102 TFEU, in particular, Section 2 of the Sherman Act explicitly requires harm to competition for the finding of an infringement.[29] This means that, where evidence shows that the SSO would have adopted the chosen technology under all circumstances, no breach of antitrust rules can be deemed to exist. On the other side of the Atlantic, Article 102 TFEU, in prohibiting the abuse of a dominant position, does not necessarily refer to harm to the competitive process. Exploitative practices also are forbidden by EU antitrust enforcers. This might be the reason why the *Rambus* case led the EU Commission and the US Court of Appeals for the DC Circuit to develop different perspectives.[30]

Commission, "Modernising ICT Standardization in the EU – The Way Forward" (Communication) COM 324 final, 3 July 2009.

25 European Commission, "Guidelines on the Applicability of Article 101 TFEU to Horizontal Co-operation Agreements" [2011] O.J. C 11/1.

26 See *Rambus Inc.*, Case n. 9302, Federal Trade Commission (2006); *Rambus Inc. v Federal Trade Commission*, 522 F.3d 456 (C App D.C. Circuit, 2008); *Union Oil Company of California*, Case n. 9305, Federal Trade Commission (2004); *Wang Labs.* (n 23); *Dell Computer* (n 23). In the EU, see Case COMP/38.636 *Rambus* [2010] O.J. C 30.

27 G. Ohana, M. Hansen and O. Shah (n 11) 645.

28 I. Schmidt and J.B. Rittaler, *A Critical Evaluation of the Chicago School of Antitrust Analysis – Studies in Industrial Organization* (Kluwer Academic Publishers, Dordrecht 1989); H.J. Hovenkamp, "Post-Chicago Antitrust: a Review and Critique" (2001) *Columbia Business Law Review* 257; A. Weitbrecht, "From Freiburg to Chicago and Beyond: the First 50 Years of European Competition Law" (2008) 29(2) *European Competition Law Review* 81.

29 See *Spectrum Sports Inc v McQuillan*, 506 US 447 (1993), at 458.

30 *Rambus* (n 26).

Another relevant difference between the US and EU jurisdictions lies in the fact that the latter, unlike the former, does not prohibit the attempt to monopolize. This aspect might lead to the argument that patent ambush cannot be appraised as an illegitimate conduct under EU competition law as firms withholding rights in standard setting are not yet in a dominant position.[31] Without dominance, IPRs alone do not confer such a status.[32] Only after the adoption of the standard by the SSO and the subsequent implementation by the industry can an IPRs owner be held to be dominant in the standardized technology market.[33] Absent a dominant position, as the argument goes, failure to disclose alone cannot be interpreted as abusive. This notwithstanding, patent ambush may still be considered illegal under EU competition law, as it may be theoretically read as an exploitative practice. Charging excessive royalties indeed meets all the requirements for being captured by Article 102(a) TFEU.[34]

These divergent approaches to standard setting and to the conduct implemented therein will be further scrutinized in depth in Chapters 5 and 6. This chapter will focus on the various paths proposed to overcome the risk of patent ambush in standardization contexts. The evaluation of these models, together with the analysis of the US and EU jurisprudence, will ultimately lead to the identification in Part Three of the optimal solution to the ambush problem. Undoubtedly, any potential model should consider and reflect these differences between the EU and US antitrust frameworks and approaches to dominance.

3.2 How to solve the ambush issue?

Patent ambush may enable IPRs owners to extract supra-competitive royalties for the licensing of their patents.[35] As a consequence, it is very likely that licensees may eventually pass the burden to the final consumer, by means of a price increase of the products manufactured. Alternatively, patent ambush may lead to exhausting judicial battles before courts, and to the withdrawal of the standardized technology.[36] These effects are highly detrimental to consumer welfare and, more generally, societal surplus, due to the missed opportunity to launch innovative and technological goods in the marketplace. It is not only consum-

31 On the argument, see D. Geradin and M. Rato (n 11) 159; and J. Killick and P. Berghe, "Rambus: an Overview of the Issues in the Case and Future Lessons for SSOs when Designing IPR Policies" (2010) 2 *Concurrences* 6–12.

32 D. Geradin, "Pricing Abuses by Essential Patent Holders in a Standard-Setting Context: a View from Europe" (2009–2010) 76 *Antitrust Law Journal* 329.

33 Ibid. Geradin, however, notes that the existence of vertical, horizontal and institutional constraints may preclude a finding of dominance for the selected innovator under Art. 102 TFEU.

34 *Cf.* M. Glader and S. Chabert Larsen, "Article 82: Excessive Pricing – An Outline of the Legal Principles Relating to Excessive Pricing and their Future Application in the Field of IP Rights and Industry Standards" (2005) *Competition Law Insight* 3.

35 D.G. Swanson and W.J. Baumol (n 13) 3–4; J.L. Contreras, "Rethinking RAND: SDO-based Approaches to Patent Licensing Commitments" (2012) Social Science Research Network 1.

36 D.J. Teece and E.F. Sherry, "Standard Setting and Antitrust" (2003) 84 *Minnesota Law Review* 1953.

ers who would be harmed by the misleading conduct: undertakings would also realize losses in terms of waste of investments and reduced production. In view of these effects, it is clear why several authors and antitrust experts have tried to establish legal frameworks limiting the negative risks of patent ambush in the standardization processes.

The models suggested have headed towards the two directions mentioned: (a) the adoption of (F)RAND licensing terms; and (b) the requirement for *ex ante* negotiation of the royalty levels. In the next paragraphs, I will focus in depth on these approaches, looking at the positive and negative aspects of each. The considerations developed will be recalled in Part Three of the book, where the optimal model will be ultimately identified and justified.

3.3 The (F)RAND model

Different SSOs have adopted (F)RAND licensing terms in their IPRs policies, as they require relatively few overheads to enact.[37] If patent holders do not agree to comply with these conditions, the SSO may refuse to implement the standard, opt for an alternative technology or may withdraw the standard if this has already been promulgated.[38]

Teece and Sherry questioned whether the willingness to license on (F)RAND terms to all interested firms may compensate for a failure to disclose conflicting IPRs.[39] In particular, the authors argued that if a firm has subscribed (F)RAND conditions but does not reveal that it owns potentially conflicting rights, the standard-setting process, in principle, may still reach its goals. Indeed, the argument goes, if the IPRs holder agreed to license on fair reasonable and non-discriminatory terms, there is no reason to believe that the SSO will withdraw the standard, and no reason to believe that it would have acted any differently had it known of the existence of the patent. Once the standard has been adopted, whatever right a firm may assert, it would be obliged to license it under the accepted (F)RAND terms. In case IPRs owners refused to respect these conditions, the SSO may withdraw the standardized technology or take legal action for abidance by the rules subscribed. From this perspective, apparently, a patent ambush would seldom be successful, as IPRs owners would fail in holding the SSO's members and charging supra-competitive royalties.[40]

37 Among these, for instance, ETSI, JEDEC, OASIS, IEEE, IETF, IEC, ITU and ISO.

38 See C. Tapia, *Industrial Property Rights, Technical Standards and Licensing Practices (FRAND) in the Telecommunications Industry* (Carl Heymanns Verlag, Köln 2010); and M.A. Lemley, "Intellectual Property Rights and Standard-Setting Organizations" (2002) 90 *California Law Review* 1974. Lemley has mentioned examples of typical RAND clauses, for instance: "RAND to entire world required or standard is withdrawn"; "RAND, or the standard will be cancelled"; "RAND, or the standard will be referred back to the Committee for consideration"; and "RAND, or possible withdrawal of the standard" (the latter, adopted by JEDEC).

39 D.J. Teece and E.F. Sherry (n 36) 1973.

40 However, Teece and Sherry also hold that antitrust authorities should refrain from imposing stronger fines under antitrust laws, beyond those already fixed by the SSO for non-compliance.

Supporters of the (F)RAND model, however, seem to underestimate one crucial aspect concerning the exact meaning of these terms, which still remains vague. Without a clear answer to the issue, the standard-setting process may encounter several obstacles and delays before reaching the expected outcome. As held in Chapter 3, the literature on (F)RAND is far from reaching a shared view to help solve the problem.[41] SSOs, in addition, do not usually specify in their policies which fees can be considered (F)RAND, as any proposal may potentially discourage firms from participating in their processes. Firms may often have differing perspectives when interpreting if royalties are fair, reasonable and non-discriminatory.[42] In case a SSO defined, *ex ante*, the meaning of (F)RAND, IPRs holders in disagreement with it may well be tempted to avoid the membership, and enforce their rights once the standard has been formalized.[43]

In brief, without a precise idea of what (F)RAND means, there might be considerable delays in the implementation of the standardized technology. First, after the standard has been chosen, implementers may resist adoption until acceptable licensing conditions are offered. Failure of *ex post* negotiation may lead the SSO to redesign and rewrite the standard around the IPRs concerned. Innovation would be slowed down to the detriment of consumers.[44] Second, in case of any disagreement on the meaning of (F)RAND, the standard setting body could withdraw the standardized technology and block the whole standardization process. Of course, this may drastically reduce the incentive for IPRs owners to take part in SSO activities. Last, the standard-setting body may decide to litigate the meaning of (F)RAND before a court.[45] In this case, the courts could interpret "fair and reasonable fees" as the price that would have been voluntarily negotiated by SSO members before the standard could be formally adopted.[46] However, this may prove to be a very difficult task, as the interpretation of a hypothetical negotiation would require the judge to identify the expectations of the parties and the competitive conditions existing before the selection of the standard.

This could lead to further delays in the development of the standardized technology by the industry and to significant losses for both consumers and producers. A lengthy and tortuous proceeding may even make the outcome of the standard-setting process out-of-date, especially in those high-technology markets where

41 See Chapter 3 sections 4.3.1 and 4.3.2, for a thorough analysis of the methods developed to define (F)RAND licensing terms.

42 P. Treacy and S. Lawrence, "FRANDly Fire: Are Industry Standards Doing More Harm than Good?" (2008) 3(1) *Journal of Intellectual Property Law & Practice* 22; D. Geradin and R.G. Brooks, "Interpreting and Enforcing the Voluntary FRAND Commitment" (2011) 9(1) *International Journal of IT Standards and Standardization Research* 1; J.L. Contreras (n 35).

43 In other words, by refusing to join the SSO, they would be legitimized to protect and enforce their IPRs in case of infringement by users and implementers of the standardized technology.

44 G. Ohana, M. Hansen and O. Shah (n 11) 647.

45 See, *inter alia*, *Broadcom v Qualcomm*, US Dist LEXIS 62090 (D New Jersey, 2006); *Broadcom v Qualcomm*, 501 F3d 297 (C App 3rd Circuit, 2007).

46 J. Farrell, J. Hayes, C. Shapiro and T. Sullivan (n 4) 637.

competing undertakings innovate rapidly.[47] All of these problems would be exacerbated where complementary IPRs are owned by different firms, as they could each charge supra-competitive royalties for licensing the rights.[48]

In summary, (F)RAND terms are not a sufficient solution because they leave potential implementers of a technology uncertain as to the economic terms on which essential patents will be licensed to them. Such uncertainty, increased by the divergent economic theories developed by the literature, may lead key market players to avoid standard-setting processes, or to hesitate in developing technologies which may still be the subject of litigation among interested parties.[49] The fault related to the risk of litigation, furthermore, could consistently undermine the ultimate goal of competition and of any other public policy, which is the enhancement of consumer and societal welfare. From these arguments, it can be inferred that *ex post* negotiation, litigation and perhaps binding arbitration with respect to royalty rates are not the most efficient way to solve the patent ambush problem. A (F)RAND licensing model probably asks more questions than it answers, and cannot represent the optimal solution.[50]

3.4 **Ex ante** ***negotiation of royalties***

The (F)RAND scheme described above is not the only model suggested to constrain patent ambush behaviors in SSO processes. As we saw in Chapter 3, other alternatives have been proposed by the literature.[51] One of them, it has been said, would lead to allow SSO members to negotiate *ex ante* the licensing terms of relevant IPRs. According to this model, patent holders and potential licensees may discuss – before the formal adoption of the standardized technology – the level of royalties that would be paid to those firms owning rights covered by the standard. In comparison to the (F)RAND commitment, the *ex ante* negotiation option seems to have some advantages.[52] At the same time, as it has been noted, doubts exist about its legitimacy, also due to alleged concerns which may arise under antitrust law.[53]

The next sections examine in depth the pros and cons of the *ex ante* negotiation model. They will first focus on those aspects that might suggest adopting this scheme as the optimal solution to the ambush problem. They will then consider the reasons of those commentators who disagree with this proposal and opt for

47 The IT (Information Technology) and TMT (Telecommunications) sectors are clear examples, as they demand an increasingly faster standardization process to satisfy ever-shorter product cycles.

48 G. Ohana, M. Hansen and O. Shah (n 11) 647.

49 Ibid., 648. See also K. Kuhn, F. Scott Morton and H. Shelanski, "Standard setting organizations can help solve the standard essential patents licensing problem" (2013) *CPI Antitrust Chronicle* 1.

50 See *Motorola Inc v Rockwell International*, Case n. 95-575-SLR (D Delaware, 1995). Here, Motorola sued Rockwell for patent infringement. The case was finally settled, having Rockwell accepted to pay for Motorola's licenses. The main problem, however, concerned the indefinite nature of the FRAND terms, devoid of any meaning in practice.

51 See Chapter 3 section 4.3.3.

52 J. Farrell, J. Hayes, C. Shapiro and T. Sullivan (n 4) 629; R.A. Skitol (n 11) 729.

53 See, for instance, J.G. Sidak (n 11) 123.

the adoption of further alternative solutions or for the implementation of the (F)RAND licensing model.[54]

3.4.1 Advantages of ex ante *joint negotiation*

First, it seems that *ex ante* joint negotiation is more likely to identify a competitive and appropriate level of royalties than a court's decision issued *ex post* could do.[55] A judge (in charge with the interpretation of (F)RAND licensing terms) may be potentially influenced in its determination by the market power conferred on the IPRs owner by the standardized technology.[56] Thus, the *ex post* evaluation may lead to set the price at a supra-competitive level. As a consequence, it could be assumed, SSO members may either decide to reject the standard or reduce the output of products based on that standard.[57]

Second, it has been held that the *ex ante* joint negotiation is more likely to contrast effectively patent ambush behaviors than a (F)RAND licensing model could ever do.[58] In the former case, firms who fail to disclose all their rights and aim for a supra-competitive level of price would seldom be able to extract royalties beyond any rate fixed *ex ante*. In the *ex post* model, instead, patent ambush could lead to one of the negative effects previously cited, among which the withdrawal of the standard or the accumulation of consistent delays ultimately undermining the whole standardization process. These undesirable consequences would clearly affect consumer welfare and societal productivity.[59]

The positive effects of the *ex ante* joint negotiation model, as some authors argue, would be all the more evident in case of activities led by formal standard-setting organizations.[60] The latter, as already explained, usually involve a broad group of stakeholders (e.g. technology developers, implementers and users) in the elaboration of technical specifications. Under these circumstances, the standardization process may be so lengthy and complex that members may find themselves locked into the standard once it is adopted. Switching to effective alternatives may entail the loss of substantial sunk investments and the commitment to undertake further relevant costs.[61]

In the case, instead, of *fora* and *consortia*, characterized by simpler procedures and a reduced number of participants, it could be easier to switch to alternative technologies when firms try to hold up the other members. What is more, as has

54 D.J. Teece and E.F. Sherry (n 36) 1953; D. Geradin, A. Layne Farrar and J. Padilla (n 20) 173.
55 J. Farrell, J. Hayes, C. Shapiro and T. Sullivan (n 4) 629.
56 See S.K. Peterson, "Consideration of Patents during the Setting of Standards" available at: www.ftc.gov/opp/Intellect/021106peterson-pdf.
57 C. Shapiro, "Competition Policy and Innovation" (2002) OECD STI Working Paper n. 11/2002.
58 G. Ohana, M. Hansen and O. Shah (n 11) 648.
59 See above, Chapter 1 section 2.2.1.
60 G. Ohana, M. Hansen and O. Shah (n 11) 649–650.
61 Investments in the context of SSOs may take many forms: specialized investments in learning the techniques the standard involves; costly marketing campaign to create buyer awareness of the use of the technology; or investments in particular types of plant and equipment.

been observed, in these private networks hold-ups may occur less frequently, due to the shared interest of the participants in creating a market for the products from which revenues can be obtained.[62] Therefore, as the argument goes, formal standard-setting bodies represent the appropriate context for promoting *ex ante* joint negotiation of licensing terms.[63] However, this particular comment is questionable and cannot be accepted without reserve. It is true that standard setting is usually faster and more effective in private networks. Nevertheless, US jurisprudence has attested that risks deriving from hold-up may also occur in private networks.

Finally, further aspects might legitimize the view that *ex ante* joint negotiations would represent the optimal option in the setting of SSOs licensing policies. For instance, it could be held that allowing early negotiation of royalties may better incentivize implementers to be involved in standard-setting processes, especially where there are only a small number of candidate technologies. The existence of a limited number of relevant technologies covering the standard, coupled with the lack of clear licensing terms, may potentially discourage other firms from committing to the standard or to the SSO process, due to the possible risk of being "hostage" to the owner of the IPRs. A patent holder's leverage, indeed, is usually greater when its technology is the only specification in compliance with the proposed standard.[64] Joint negotiation of royalties would avoid uncertainty on the level of price licensees may be charged for the standard.

At the same time, it has been added, the *ex ante* joint negotiation model might prove to be effective even in case of multiple rival technologies. Under these circumstances, early disclosure and negotiations of licensing terms may well allow potential implementers to compare effectively the economic and technological merits of the competing solutions.[65] However, all these arguments, albeit appealing, must be confronted with further elements highlighting its faults. Many authors, indeed, evaluate the model as difficult to implement.[66]

3.4.2 Faults of ex ante *joint negotiation*

Various reasons suggest that the *ex ante* joint negotiation model – in or outside patent pool contexts – may not represent the best option when setting the IPRs policies of standard-setting organizations. Although it may appear a good solution in principle, especially when compared to the (F)RAND licensing scheme, this

62 See S.K. Peterson (n 56). The author interestingly associates *ad hoc consortia* with joint ventures.

63 G. Ohana, M. Hansen and O. Shah (n 11) 649–650.

64 The risk to be under the IPRs owner's leverage might, in particular, materialize in case of (F)RAND commitments, due to the explained indefiniteness of the licensing terms.

65 G. Ohana, M. Hansen and O. Shah (n 11) 650; J.L. Contreras (n 35).

66 J.G. Sidak (n 11) 123; D.J. Teece and E.F. Sherry (n 36) 1953; M. Naughton and R. Wolfram (n 2) 779; T. Winston, "Innovation and Ex Ante Consideration of Licensing Terms in Standard Setting" (2006) EAG Discussion Paper n. 6-3. Winston, for instance, highlights that *ex ante* licensing discussions may reduce the IPRs owners' incentive to invest in R&D. However, this negative effect should be weighed against any positive effect on social and consumer welfare.

model raises several doubts under different perspectives, and seems to be complex and rare.[67]

First, as explained earlier, there is a risk that discussions on licensing terms may lead to exhausting policy battles between the members of the standard setting bodies. It might be complex, indeed, to define a level of royalty which is acceptable to all parties of a negotiation.[68] Difficulties may arise both where there are multiple competing technologies, and when there is only one relevant technology covering the proposed standard. Furthermore, if the standard is based on different complementary technologies, negotiations might be even harder, due to the need to appraise and balance the exact contribution to the standard from each technology.[69] On the one hand, firms possessing relevant IPRs are clearly interested in fixing a level of fees which may reward them for the investments made in research and developments. On the other, those members without relevant patents have more of an incentive to keep the royalty rate low. Therefore, early negotiations between interested parties may run the risk of failure or determine consistent delays to the standard-setting process.[70]

Second, it has been noted that early negotiations may be unfavorable for those firms without relevant patents joining the SSO process in an advanced stage, after discussions on the licensing terms have been concluded.[71] These participants would have to accept contractual conditions already established by others.[72] The definition of the royalty level may thus represent the stage after which firms may be reluctant to join the standard-setting body. Therefore, the adoption of *ex ante* joint negotiations may have the undesirable effect of limiting the number of potential participants, to the detriment of the standardization process. Indeed, the greater the number of firms involved in standard setting, the higher the possibility of a successful and efficient outcome for the industry concerned.

Third, further considerations link the effectiveness of the model to the type of IPRs disclosed. It has been explained above that most standard-setting bodies,

67 J. Farrell, J. Hayes, C. Shapiro and T. Sullivan (n 4) 630–631. Despite recognizing the merits of early negotiation, the authors find the model relatively difficult.

68 See the Report of the US Department of Justice and Federal Trade Commission, "Antitrust Enforcement and Intellectual Property Rights: Promoting Innovation and Competition" (April 2007) 50.

69 On negotiations in patent pools, see C. Shapiro, "Navigating the Patent Thicket: Cross Licensees, Patent Pools and Standard Setting" (2001) Social Science Research Network 1; R. Gilbert, "Antitrust for Patent Pools: a Century of Policy Evolution" (2004) *Stanford Technology Law Review* 3; J. Lerner and J. Tirole, "Efficient Patent Pools" (2004) 94 *American Economic Review* 691; and J. Farrell, J. Hayes, C. Shapiro and T. Sullivan (n 4) 641–643. The latter question the effectiveness of a "proportionality rule," according to which the aggregate royalties could be distributed among innovators on the basis of the number of patents essential to the standard.

70 See European Telecommunications Standards Institute (ETSI), "Guide on IPRs" (2013) § 4.1; here, it is stated that "[s]pecific licensing terms and negotiations are commercial issues between the companies and shall not be addressed within ETSI. Technical Bodies are not the appropriate place to discuss IPRs issues."

71 M. Valimaki, "A Flexible Approach to RAND Licensing" (2008) 29(12) *European Competition Law Review* 689.

72 Ibid.

with few exceptions, usually expect disclosure of only issued patents.[73] Requiring full disclosure of pending IPRs may discourage firms from taking part in the standard-setting process. This is because other undertakings may take advantage in different ways from the revealed technical know-how pending the application, and may compromise the investments made by the IPRs applicant.[74] This notwithstanding, if SSOs require full disclosure of pending IPRs applications, the adoption of the *ex ante* joint negotiation scheme may actively discourage the participation of innovators. Negotiating *ex ante* the value of a right which has not been granted yet may prove to be an unfeasible task.[75]

Besides these observations, further relevant criticism has been made about the functioning of the *ex ante* joint negotiation model. Promotion of early discussions on licensing terms may indeed represent a disincentive to participate to the activities of standard-setting bodies even from a different point of view.[76] If the adoption of the (F)RAND model might enable a patent owner to hold-up the SSO's participants, the implementation of the *ex ante* joint negotiation scheme may instead lead patent holders to avoid membership of the SSO. Indeed, outside patent pools, IPRs owners may, in theory, exert weaker power in negotiating the price with several implementers and industry participants who usually have an interest in keeping the royalty rate low.[77] The lower the fees to be paid to the licensor, the higher the profit from the sale of the final product. From this perspective, SSO policies implementing early negotiation of royalty rates could have a negative effect on the incentive for IPRs holders to take part in the processes. Limited participation to standard-setting bodies would deprive standardization of the opportunity to maximize dynamic efficiency, due to the risk to implement technologies of lower value and quality.[78] These observations lead to the conclusion that, although imposing low prices on patent owners may benefit buyers and consumers in the short term, in the long term this may reduce the incentives to invest and be part of SSO processes.[79] The ultimate consequence would be detrimental to both consumers and producers: the former would buy lower-quality, less innovative products, and

73 M.A. Lemley (n 38) 1904–1905.

74 M.C. Naughton and R. Wolfram (n 2) 764–765.

75 Rather, as explained in Chapter 7, the unilateral appraisal of the pending IPRs values may be interpreted by innovators as a more reasonable requirement.

76 J.G. Sidak (n 11) 141–142.

77 Ibid. For instance, this could happen where there are few innovators involved in the process. On the interaction between licensors and licensees, see A. Layne Farrar, "Business Models and the Standard Setting Process" in *The Pro & Cons of Standard Setting* (Swedish Competition Authority, 2010) 42.

78 See T.O. Barnett, "Maximizing Welfare through Technological Innovation" (2008) 15 *George Mason Law Review* 1199.

79 See T. Winston (n 66); and G. Ohana, M. Hansen and O. Shah (n 11) 649. The latter, however, hold that the risk of disincentives for licensors' participation is low, and that any reduction in the participation of IPRs owners may be counter-balanced by the greater certainty resulting from *ex ante* joint negotiation.

may likely reduce consumption; the latter, as a consequence, would suffer from reduced production levels.[80]

3.4.3 Collusion: bogus issue or real concern?

Finally, and most importantly, several authors have raised doubts about the legitimacy of this model due to potential concerns raised under Section 1 of the US Sherman Act and Article 101 TFEU.[81] As Naughton and Wolfram observed, "SSO participants cannot agree on royalty rates in specific quantitative terms without running the risk of liability for price fixing."[82] For instance, under certain circumstances, there might be the risk that patent holders in the context of negotiations of the royalty rates could agree on fixing high and supra-competitive fees for the license of relevant IPRs. Such a conduct would probably lead to raise prices of the final product, as licensees would have all the interest to pass the burden to the final purchaser. This would undoubtedly harm the welfare of consumers. Further concerns may also arise in case of illegal group boycotts, which occur if members conditioned the standardization of proprietary technologies on the IPRs owner's acceptance of low licensing rates specified in advance, implementing a sort of oligopsonistic collusion or a buyers' cartel.[83]

The risk of collusive conduct, however, cannot be presumed but must be appraised with careful attention, due to the specific context in which the interested firms operate.[84] In the SSO environment, members may pursue different strategies, also depending on the existence of patent pools. This is because firms involved in standard setting may either play the role of licensors-innovators, licensees-users or vertically integrated firms. Therefore, higher level of royalties for IPRs may either benefit or bear heavily on the parties concerned.[85] That is why standard-setting contexts must be distinguished from the typical market situation in which collusion benefits producers and harms the interests and welfare of consumers.[86] This being stated, in order to appraise the likelihood of collusive mechanisms in

80 See Chapter 1 sections 2.2 (on consumer welfare) and 2.3 (on dynamic efficiency).

81 J.G. Sidak (n 11) 123; M. Naughton and R. Wolfram (n 2) 779; D.J. Teece and E.F. Sherry (n 36) 1953. Sidak, in particular, recalls the letter of the US "Standards Development Organizations Advancement Act," and argues that price negotiations in standard setting should be appraised under a *per se* rule of illegality.

82 M.C. Naughton and R. Wolfram (n 2) 779.

83 D.J. Teece and E.F. Sherry (n 36) 1955; J.G. Sidak (n 11) 143. The conduct is known as "holdout."

84 On the analysis of collusive conduct in the EU, see Case 56/65 *Société Technique Minière v Maschinenbau Ulm* [1966] ECR 235; Case T-528/93 *Metropole Television SA v European Commission* [1996] ECR II-649; Case T-374/94 *European Night Services v European Commission* [1998] ECR II-3141.

85 G. Ohana, M. Hansen and O. Shah (n 11) 649.

86 On the dynamics of collusive behaviors, see V. Korah, *An Introductory Guide to EC Competition Law and Practice* (9th edn, Hart Publishing, London 2007) Ch. 2; R. Whish and D. Bailey, *Competition Law* (7th edn, Oxford University Press, Oxford 2012) Ch. 13; S. Bishop and M. Walker, *The Economics of EC Competition Law* (3rd edn, Sweet & Maxwell, London 2010) 164; R.J. Van den Bergh and P.D. Camesasca, *European Competition Law and Economics: a Comparative Perspective* (2nd edn, Sweet & Maxwell, London 2006) Ch. 5.

standard setting and the resulting harm, further aspects must be scrutinized. In particular, it would be important to identify and understand better the dynamics characterizing price negotiations within standard-setting bodies.[87] The analysis could, in theory, focus on two possible, though not the only, scenarios.

On the one hand, in case the SSO assembles several firms without relevant IPRs and only one or few patent holders, it is likely that negotiations could lead to a low royalty rate. The many licensees – exerting greater pressure on the patent holder – would probably succeed in lowering the licensing price, hence limiting the costs of manufacturing the final product. Licensees may act as a buying group, implementing a sort of joint purchasing agreement.[88] In case the IPRs holder refused to license at the suggested rate and no alternative were available, the SSO may either block the whole process or try to design around the patented technology. Under these alternative perspectives, it is unlikely that antitrust authorities could be concerned about price discussions.[89] The imposition of low rates on IPRs holders would appear to benefit consumers – at least in the short term – in so far as the savings granted to the licensees would be passed downstream.[90] In addition, as some authors argue, it is unlikely that antitrust enforcers would be concerned about the effects of foreclosure. Indeed, the negotiated price would likely be available without exception for all the implementers participating in the standard-setting process.[91]

On the other hand, the SSOs may attract participation from several IPRs owners, each of them with potentially relevant technologies. In this scenario, negotiations on royalty rates between members might be more balanced, and patent holders might exert a greater influence on potential licensees.[92] There is a slight risk that putative licensors may collude so as to raise the level of royalties to be paid for their technologies. Each of them could agree on a price rate under which it would not license its IPRs. In this respect, the Antitrust Division of the US Department of Justice and the Federal Trade Commission have clearly stated that "summary condemnation would be justified if IP holders were to reach naked agreements on the licensing terms they will propose to an SSO that permits multilateral negotiations, thus, in effect, rigging their selling bids."[93] The collusive conduct would allow the selected IPRs owners to benefit from higher revenues. Instead, users and implementers, as well as those non-selected vertically integrated innovators manufacturing downstream, would have to pay high levels of royalties,

87 G. Ohana, M. Hansen and O. Shah (n 11) 651–655.

88 On the argument, see R.A. Skitol (n 11) 735.

89 M.A. Lemley (n 38) 1947. *Contra,* T.F. Cotter, "Patent Holdup, Patent Remedies and Antitrust Responses" (2009) 34 *Journal of Corporation Law* 1151. Cotter seems to consider a *per se* rule of illegality.

90 However, Sidak [(n 11) 124] argues that pass-through is not automatic, but requires information on the calculation of royalty payments, the demand and supply elasticity facing the licensees, and the structure of the industry further downstream (between the manufacturer and consumer).

91 G. Ohana, M. Hansen and O. Shah (n 11) 653–654.

92 Ibid., 650.

93 Report of the US Department of Justice and Federal Trade Commission (n 68) 51–52.

the burden of which could still be passed to the ultimate consumer by means of final price increases. This last possibility, in theory, could make firms complacent about supporting the collusive mechanism. In addition, if the standard required adoption of different complementary technologies, those licensees playing the role of (vertically integrated) licensors might benefit from advantageous bilateral cross-licensing.[94]

However, this is only a hypothetical scenario. No element can ensure that patentees would agree on the collusive mechanism, and that the standard-setting body would not be able to extract lower fees. Even if the described circumstances occurred, the SSO could still decide either to reject the standard or design around the patented technologies. Of course, in the event that several IPRs holders were part of the collusive mechanism, it could be a complex and lengthy process for the SSO to develop open, non-proprietary standards, without infringing any of the essential patented technologies. This notwithstanding, even this possibility cannot be excluded.

Perhaps, a more plausible concern could arise in case licensees found in the *ex ante* joint negotiation the optimal context to hide collusive intents, aimed at raising downstream sale prices.[95] Put differently, users and implementers, besides discussing the fees level to be paid to IPRs owners, could also agree to fix higher prices for the sale of final products to consumers.[96] This may also happen between vertically integrated firms discussing prices in patent pools. The US Federal Trade Commission notably stated that if rivals crossed the line from negotiating fee levels and started "discussing and fixing the price of the products they sell, summary condemnation is almost certainly warranted."[97]

However, the risk of fixing downstream prices does not seem peculiar to the early negotiation model only, but could arise in any phase of the standard-setting process and under any IPRs policy (even under a (F)RAND regime). These considerations, therefore, suggest that the *ex ante* joint negotiation system should not be excluded *a priori* only on the ground that it may facilitate risky or suspicious price discussions under the auspices of SSOs.

In any case, it could be also argued that, even if courts or authorities interpreted early negotiations among SSO members as being suspect, they could still consider exemptions under Article 101(3) TFEU or appraise the conduct (in the US) under the rule of reason rather than under a *per se* rule of illegality.[98] In the EU,

94 On the functioning of the various business models in standardization, see A. Layne Farrar (n 77) 42. Cross-licensing, it must be noted, may potentially occur also in case of standards based on single technologies. The non-selected vertically integrated firms (in need of the IPRs license) may indeed negotiate with the selected innovator to waive the fees on the basis of cross-licensing involving IPRs and technologies examined in other different standard-setting contexts.

95 On the argument, see J.G. Sidak (n 11) 164.

96 Report of the US Department of Justice and Federal Trade Commission (n 68) 50; Antitrust Modernization Commission (AMC), "Final Report and Recommendations" (April 2007) 121.

97 D. Platt Majoras, "Recognizing the Pro-competitive Potential of Royalty Discussions in Standard Setting, Remarks at Standardization and the Law: Developing the Golden Mean for Global Trade" (Speech at Stanford University, Stanford – 23 September 2005).

98 R.A. Skitol (n 11) 737–739.

the Commission has already exempted certain forms of horizontal price fixing between rivals, as price setting in those circumstances was essential to achieve the pro-competitive benefits of cooperation.[99] However, in its recent analysis of horizontal cooperation agreements, the authority has clearly banned price fixing in SSOs in the belief that it would seldom achieve any benefit for competition.[100] On the contrary, in the United States, different agencies believe that early negotiation could be appraised under the rule of reason, as price discussions may have procompetitive effects and mitigate the risks of hold-up.[101] In order to deny the existence of potential concerns under antitrust laws, some commentators have even argued (less convincingly) that licensees should be considered as a single entity, which cannot be deemed to conspire with itself.[102]

3.4.4 Failure of the model

In light of the arguments on the *pro* and *cons* of the model, it can be concluded that *ex ante* joint negotiation (in or outside patent pool contexts) does not probably represent the optimal solution in the setting of SSO IPRs policies. Leaving aside the highly debated risk of collusion, other relevant considerations justify this conclusion. The most relevant lies on the fact that joint discussion of licensing terms between licensees and licensors, potentially leading to lower prices, may ultimately discourage IP owners from taking part in SSOs. The main effect deriving from reduced participation in SSOs would be a loss in terms of dynamic efficiency.[103] On the one hand, IPRs owners may limit investments in research and development, redirecting their resources to other more profitable targets. On the other, SSOs would only be able to standardize non-optimal technologies.

In order to overcome these obstacles, some authors have even tried to elaborate a slightly different model, based on the *ex ante* bilateral negotiation with a non-discrimination requirement. Under this regime, IPRs owners would be involved in bilateral negotiations with potential licensees before the standard is chosen.[104]

99 See Article 4 of Regulation (EEC) n 1617/93 (establishing a group exemption for price agreements between airlines). See also Article 3 of Regulation (EEC) n 4056/86 (granting an exemption for price agreements between liner conferences).

100 European Commission, "Guidelines on the Applicability of Article 101 TFEU to Horizontal Co-operation Agreements" [2011] OJ C 11/1, at 274. Here, it is stated that "[a]ny agreements to reduce competition by using the disclosure of most restrictive licensing terms prior to the adoption of a standard as a cover to jointly fix prices either of downstream products or of substitute IPRs or technology will constitute restrictions of competition by object."

101 Report of the US Department of Justice and Federal Trade Commission (n 68) 53–56; and Antitrust Modernization Commission (AMC) (n 96) 117. *Contra*, see J.G. Sidak [(n 11) 126], who holds that price fixing within the SSO context should be appraised under a rule of *per se* illegality.

102 See M.R. Patterson, "Inventions, Industry Standards, and Intellectual Property" (2002) 17 *Berkeley Technology Law Journal* 1043; and M.A. Carrier, "Why Antitrust Should Defer to the Intellectual Property Rules of Standard Setting Organizations: a Commentary on Teece and Sherry" (2003) 87 *Minnesota Law Review* 2030.

103 J.G. Sidak (n 11) 141–142.

104 A. Layne Farrar, G. Llobet and A.J. Padilla, "Preventing Patent Hold Up: An Economic Assessment of Ex Ante Licensing Negotiations in Standard Setting" (2009) 37(4) *AIPLA Quarterly*

This may, of course, reduce patent owners' fear of low prices being imposed by the majority of implementers. At the same time, the non-discrimination clause would ensure that reasonable ("first best") royalty rates would be charged to all licensees, even those negotiating *ex post*.

However, this model poses various questions as to how it may be practically implemented. Indeed, as Contreras has suggested, various factors usually lead potential licensees to postpone any bilateral price negotiation after the standard is chosen.[105] For instance, sometimes implementers may simply not have the opportunity to negotiate *ex ante*, either because they were not aware of the standard before its adoption, they were not active in the relevant product market at the time or because they were not part of the SSO process. Other times, implementers may find it too costly and time consuming to negotiate *ex ante* and bilaterally with each IPRs owner, especially when they are taking part in different standardization bodies at the same time. Implementers could also be discouraged by the risk of embarking on bilateral negotiation with IPRs owners whose disclosed patents may later be found to be invalid or non-essential. A further reason then may justify implementers' inaction; some patent owners (so-called "sleeping dogs") engaged in standard setting do not actively seek to license or enforce their IPRs, but may merely use them for defensive purposes in case of litigation. Finally, it should not be forgotten that it may be particularly difficult to conclude bilateral negotiations on the value of those pending IPRs which, once granted, may be considered essential to the standard.

All these uncertainties and the fear of the cited negative effects probably explain why standard-setting organizations have so far been reluctant about the possibility to adopt the *ex ante* joint or bilateral negotiation models,[106] and have rather opted for the adoption of (F)RAND licensing terms. However, the considerations made thus far have clarified that also this option cannot be implemented without raising further concerns. Hence, the question on how to solve the ambush problem still stands.

3.5 Conclusive remarks on patent ambush

The very first examples of patent ambush are to be found in the US. This explains why the first investigations have been decided by US courts and antitrust authorities.[107] This form of hold-up has only attracted the attention of the European Commission in the last decade, which has started to take into due consideration

Journal 462; R. Gilbert, "When Standards Require IP: FRAND v Negotiation" in *The Pro & Cons of Standard Setting* (Swedish Competition Authority, 2010) 80; R. Gilbert, "Deal or No Deal? Licensing Negotiations in Standard-setting Organizations" (2011) 77 *Antitrust Law Journal* 855.

105 J.L. Contreras (n 35) 7–9.

106 E.g., VITA explicitly clarifies that the "negotiation or discussion of license terms among WG Members or with third parties is prohibited at all VSO and WG meetings" (see VITA, "Standards Organization – Policies and Procedures" (2011), § 10.3.4).

107 *Inter alia*, *Allied Tube* (n 23); *Dell Computer* (n 23); *Wang Labs.* (n 23).

this particular conduct arising in the context of standard setting.[108] Patent ambush raises various concerns, as it may lead to a manipulation in the SSO process and confer on IPRs holders a dominant position in the market of the standardized technology.[109] The main risk is that the dominant firm may be able to extract excessive fees from licensees for licensing its rights.[110] Licensees may then pass this burden onto the final consumer by means of price increases. The outcome would be harmful to consumer welfare and, ultimately, societal surplus. These effects would be exacerbated in case of complementary technologies, as each IPRs owner might implement ambush.[111] Different solutions have been proposed by the literature, from a (F)RAND regime to *ex ante* joint or bilateral negotiation. However, various reasons suggest that these options would raise more questions than give answers. The ambush problem will be further reviewed in Chapters 5 and 6, focused on an analysis of the US and EU case law, which will help in understanding why the rules proposed so far have raised several doubts. Chapter 7 will instead be devoted to defining a new legal framework, which may potentially address any form of hold-up in a more effective way.

4 Mere breach of (F)RAND terms

The previous sections have clarified that most SSOs have usually adopted (F)RAND licensing terms in their IPRs policies. The economic principle underlying these commitments is that essential IPRs owners should not be able to exploit the extra power gained as a result of having technology based on their rights incorporated in the standard. This regime, as it has been added, has been criticized as it leaves licensees uncertain about fee levels and may facilitate patent owners in holding-up other members.

A second concern, directly linked to the indefiniteness of (F)RAND terms, may arise where the selected IPRs owners, despite subscribing to the IPRs policy, finally breach the licensing terms. Put differently, the patent holder, albeit disclosing its relevant rights and accepting the (F)RAND regime, may finally infringe the agreement and charge unfair, unreasonable and discriminatory royalties.[112]

108 See European Commission, "Towards an Increased Contribution from Standardization to Innovation in Europe" (Communication) COM 133 final, 11 March 2008; and European Commission, "Modernising ICT Standardization in the EU – The Way Forward" (Communication) COM 324 final, 3 July 2009. At the end of 2014, the European Commission's Directorate General Enterprise and Industry launched a "Public Consultation on Patents and Standards," seeking public input on the relationship between the standardization of technical specifications and related IPRs.

109 M.C. Naughton and R. Wolfram (n 2) 701–702.

110 D.G. Swanson and W.J. Baumol (n 13) 3–4.

111 See D. Geradin and M. Rato (n 11) 126; G. Ohana, M. Hansen and O. Shah (n 11) 645.

112 See D. Geradin (n 32) 329; M. Valimaki (n 71) 690; C.B. Hockett and R.G. Lipscomb, "Best FRANDs Forever? Standard-Setting Antitrust Enforcement in the United States and the European Union" (2009) 23(3) *Antitrust* 22–23; L. Zhang, "How IPR Policies of Telecommunication Standard-setting Organizations can Effectively Address the Patent Ambush Problem" (2010) 41(4) *International Review of Intellectual Property and Competition Law* 406. On the dif-

Unlike patent ambush, therefore, the behavior is not based on the innovator's concealment of its patents. The burden of the higher costs would be likely passed from licensee manufacturers to the final consumer, by increasing the price of the final product. Similar to what has been held in relation to ambush, these negative effects would harm both consumer and societal surplus.[113]

These consequences, what is more, could be exacerbated if the standard includes various complementary technologies. Under these circumstances, indeed, each selected IPRs holder may ask for the payment of royalties, the sum of which may ultimately determine highly burdensome costs. The phenomenon, known as "royalty stacking," may occur even if the IPRs covering each component would be offered under a (F)RAND regime.[114] In case innovators charged supra-competitive fees, then the negative effects of royalty stacking could be even worse and might compromise the whole SSO process, which could become extremely costly and lead to inefficient outcome.[115]

In view of these considerations, and provided that failure to comply with IPRs policies may entail, in principle, the enforcement of contract law,[116] the question is whether the mere breach of (F)RAND terms may call EU and US courts and agencies to enforce antitrust provisions.

4.1 Analysis of the conduct: alternative scenarios

The conduct under examination does not necessarily lead to harm competition by the exclusion of rivals. Two different scenarios, indeed, must be distinguished. On the one hand, a standard-setting body may be willing to adopt a particular patented technology under all circumstances, even if it knew about the IPRs holders' intention to charge non-(F)RAND royalties. This may happen when there are no alternatives at all or when the technology appears to be far better than the others proposed.[117]

On the other hand, the organization may be interested in including the patent owner's invention as long as the latter complies with (F)RAND commitments. Under these circumstances, the SSO would reject the IPRs owner's technology

ferent categories of hold-up risk, see also F.S. Kieff and A. Layne Farrar, "Incentive Effects from Different Approaches to Holdup Mitigation Surrounding Patent Remedies and Standard Setting Organizations" (2013) 9(4) *Journal of Competition Law and Economics* 1091.

113 Sidak [(n 11) 124], however, observes that pass-through cannot be automatically presumed.

114 D. Geradin and M. Rato (n 11) 127; M.A. Lemley and C. Shapiro (n 11) 1991.

115 J.G. Sidak, "Holdup, Royalty Stacking, and the Presumption of Injunctive Relief for Patent Infringement: A Reply to Lemley and Shapiro" (2008) 92 *Minnesota Law Review* 714; J.L. Contreras (n 35) 14. See, however, E. Elhauge (n 20) 535; Elhauge's economic analysis leads him to conclude that royalty stacking is a bogus problem, as innovators would be often under-compensated.

116 On the enforcement of contract law, see Chapter 7 section 4. See also R. Hewitt Pate, "Competition and Intellectual Property in the U.S.: Licensing Freedom and the Limits of Antitrust" (Speech at *EU Competition Workshop*, Florence – 3 June 2005) 10.

117 This was the case, for instance, in the *Rambus* case. The US Court of Appeals had indeed established that there was no proof that JEDEC would have adopted alternatives had it known about Rambus' intention to charge (after holding-up JEDEC members) non-RAND rates.

if it knew about the firm's intention to charge excessive fees. This conduct may lead to the exclusion of rivals which would otherwise have been selected. This may occur because, once the standard has been adopted and the innovator has revealed its intention to charge non-(F)RAND fees, it would be unreasonable to switch to alternative technologies, as the SSO may have required members to make burdensome sunk investments (e.g. in learning the techniques the standard involves or in particular types of plant and machinery).[118]

4.2 US v EU approach

Breach of (F)RAND terms alone (in the absence of ambush) may involve different legal consequences, depending on the antitrust framework under which the conduct is appraised.[119] US antitrust law, it is well known, by requiring harm to the competitive process for the finding of an infringement does not forbid purely exploitative abuses, but only prohibits exclusionary practices.[120] Therefore, without exclusion, no liability lies under Section 2 of the Sherman Act.[121] As held by the US Court of Appeals in *Rambus*, "to obtain higher prices normally has no particular tendency to exclude rivals and thus to diminish competition."[122] This means that, in case the innovator demonstrates that the SSO would have developed its technology under all circumstances, no infringement can be deemed to exist for breach of (F)RAND prices.

On the other side of the Atlantic, Article 102 TFEU states that a dominant undertaking imposing "unfair purchase or selling prices or other unfair trading conditions" may be subject to liability.[123] The provision does not explicitly require harm to the competitive process to find abuse. Besides exclusionary conduct, therefore, purely exploitative practices are caught and sanctioned.[124] Article 102 TFEU could hence be used to regulate the level of fees charged by essential patent owners, even in the absence of exclusionary behaviors.[125]

This view has been endorsed by the European Commission in its public statements on the *Qualcomm* investigation, where it held that:

118 E.g., Qualcomm was charged by the US Court of Appeals as there was reason to believe that ETSI would have adopted alternatives had it known about its intention to breach FRAND terms.

119 On the enforceability of (F)RAND terms, see M. Valimaki (n 71) 690.

120 See *Spectrum Sports* (n 29), at 458.

121 H.J. Hovenkamp, "Patent Continuations, Patent Deception, and Standard Setting: the Rambus and Broadcom Decisions" (2008) University of Iowa Legal Studies Research Paper n. 08-25.

122 *Rambus* (n 26), at 15.

123 Case 27/76 *United Brands v European Commission* [1978] ECR 207; Case 26/75 *General Motors v European Commission* [1975] ECR 1367; Case 30/87 *Bodson v Pompes Funebres* [1988] ECR 2479; Case 226/84 *British Leyland v European Commission* [1986] ECR 3263; Case COMP/A.36.568/D3 *Scandlines Sverige AB v Port of Helsingborg* [2006] 4 CMLR 22.

124 Besides excessive prices, Article 102 TFEU fines, *inter alia,* loyalty rebates, discrimination, refusal to deal, as well as tying and bundling. These practices may potentially be implemented in standard-setting environments.

125 C.B. Hockett and R.G. Lipscomb (n 112) 22.

> [i]n the context of standardization, a finding of exploitative practices by Qualcomm in the WCDMA licensing market contrary to Article 82 of the EC Treaty may depend on whether the licensing terms imposed by Qualcomm are in breach of its FRAND commitment.[126]

In brief, the differences of legal framework (reflecting the more liberal US system and the more interventionist EU approach) may contribute to explain why the *Rambus* and *Qualcomm* cases, both dealing with the implementation of (F)RAND terms, eventually led the EU and US enforcers to adopt divergent perspectives.[127]

4.3 Competition: a means to curtail excessive prices?

The analysis of the conduct of firms charging high royalties recalls a well-known dispute concerning the role of competition rules in curtailing excessive prices, which has long been a contentious subject. As stated above, EU competition enforcers have traditionally developed a restrictive approach towards the issue. However, the antitrust authorities in the United States have not usually considered high pricing as a danger to competitive environments. Rather, as held by Judge Scalia of the US Supreme Court:

> [t]he mere possession of monopoly power, and the concomitant charging of monopoly prices, is not only not unlawful; it is an important element of the free-market system. The opportunity to charge monopoly prices—at least for a short period—is what attracts "business acumen" in the first place; it induces risk taking that produces innovation and economic growth. To safeguard the incentive to innovate, the possession of monopoly power will not be found unlawful unless it is accompanied by an element of anticompetitive conduct.[128]

That being stated, commentators argued that, in order to scrutinize better the merits of a system allowing excessive pricing, three main grounds should be examined.[129] First, it is observed, enforcement which targets excessive prices may

126 European Commission, "Commission Initiates Formal Proceedings against Qualcomm" (1 October 2007) Press Release MEMO/07/389.

127 See the US cases *Rambus* (n 26); and *Qualcomm* (n 45). In the European Union, see *Rambus* (n 26); and Case 39247 *Texas Instruments v Qualcomm* [2009]. However, as it will be better explained in Part II Chapter 6, the EU Commission finally closed the *Qualcomm* case without reaching a decision, as during the investigations complainants had withdrawn their claims.

128 *Verizon Communications v Trinko*, 540 US 398 (2004). See also *Blue Cross and Blue Shield United of Wisconsin v Marshfield Clinic*, 65 F3d 1406 (C App 7th Circuit, 1995), at 1413; *United States v Aluminum Co of America*, 148 F2d 416 (C App 2nd Circuit, 1945), at 430; *Ball Memorial Hospital v Mutual Hospital*, 784 F2d 1325 (C App 7th Circuit, 1986), at 1339; *Berkey Photo v Eastman Kodak*, 603 F2d 263 (C App 2nd Circuit, 1979), at 296. On the concept of monopoly power, see *United States v E.I. du Pont de Nemours*, 351 US 377 (1956).

129 D. Gilo and A. Ezrachi, "Excessive Pricing, Entry, Assessment, and Investment: Lessons from the Mittal Litigation" (2010) 76(3) *Antitrust Law Journal* 873.

discourage undertakings to invest their resources in innovation. In other words, firms usually making investments in innovative research and development may find this unprofitable and may redirect their resources to other business targets.[130] The effect may be detrimental to consumers. The latter benefit not only from low prices, but also from new and innovative products.[131]

Second, it might be complex to establish when a price is excessive, as the application of one economic principle over another may lead to divergent outcomes.[132] Several authors have tried to develop criteria and formulas in order to clarify when a price may be deemed excessive or supra-competitive.[133] In the European Union, the Court of Justice has identified the price–cost margin principle, and has argued that:

> [t]he questions … to be determined are whether the difference between the costs actually incurred and the price actually charged is excessive, and, if the answer to this question is in the affirmative, whether a price has been imposed which is either unfair in itself or when compared to competing products.[134]

In the court's view, there must be a reasonable relationship between the value of the product and its price. However, the literature suggests that there is still no consensus as to the optimal criteria to define when a rate is excessive or supra-competitive. The determination of costs in case of IPRs licensing, for instance, may result more problematic than expected.[135]

Finally, the argument goes, intervention would seldom be necessary, as high prices may well encourage other firms to enter the market and charge lower rate. Put differently, the charging of excessive prices does not usually lead to the exclusion of competitors. Provided that entry is feasible, it may attract other firms to enter the market to the benefit of the competitive environment. In light of these considerations, competition law would appear to be ill-suited to establish when a firm is charging excessive rates.

130 Ibid. See also D. Geradin (n 32) 329; and D. Geradin, "Reverse Hold-ups: the (Often Ignored) Risks Faced by Innovators in Standardization Area" in *The Pro & Cons of Standard Setting* (Swedish Competition Authority, 2010) 101.

131 On the concept of dynamic efficiency, see M.E. Porter, *Competitive Strategy: Techniques for Analyzing Industries and Competitors* (The Free Press, New York 1980).

132 On the topic, see J. Gstalter (n 1) 1–4. The author observes that "as shown by the *Qualcomm* case, determine whether a price is unreasonably high and in breach of a FRAND commitment is not an easy task for antitrust enforcers."

133 Swanson and Baumol [(n 13) 10], Farrar, Padilla and Schmalensee [A. Layne Farrar, A.J. Padilla and R. Schmalensee, "Pricing Patents for Licensing in Standard-Setting Organizations: Making Sense of FRAND Commitments" (2007) 74 *Antitrust Law Journal* 671] are among those authors considering different models in order to understand when prices, in the standard setting context, may be considered excessive or reasonable (i.e. (F)RAND). See Chapter 3 section 4.3.

134 *United Brands* (n 123), at 250–252. On the analysis of these criteria, see D. Geradin (n 32) 329.

135 See D. Gilo and A. Ezrachi (n 129); D.G. Swanson and W.J. Baumol (n 13) 10; A. Layne Farrar, A.J. Padilla and R. Schmalensee (n 133) 671; L. Zhang (n 112) 399. Economic theory usually suggests that the appropriate measure is a firm's marginal cost or average variable cost.

The latter argument may not apply when considering standard setting. SSOs, indeed, may represent themselves as an obstacle to entry, as they finally lead to develop one firm's technology rather than rivals' alternatives. The selected IPRs owner, therefore, encouraged by the sunk investments made by the industry, may try to charge supra-competitive prices without incurring the risk of attracting massive competitors' entry. The only firms (manufacturers and vertically integrated innovators) which may consider entry in a market "seized" by the selected IPRs owner could be, in theory, those that are not under a locked-in effect, and which did not take part in the standard-setting process. Instead, the SSO's participants, having presumably incurred the high costs standardization brings, may well find it unprofitable to re-invest capitals in the development of a competing technology.

It is undoubted that all these criticisms deserve analysis. The commentators that scrutinized the issue have notably emphasized the difficulties courts or authorities face when appraising price levels.[136] In addition, antitrust intervention may appear all the more undesirable when considering the effects (i.e. disincentives to invest) enforcement could determine. US legislators may have foreseen these risks when they enacted the Sherman Act.[137] Their EU counterparts, instead, were probably much more concerned about the need to ensure homogenous market conditions in the Union and may have interpreted price control as an effective means to reach that goal.[138] By so doing, they may have underestimated the self-correcting properties of free markets. Price regulation, as it could be argued, may rather be rational in those industries (e.g. natural monopolies) which are not conducive to competition.[139]

This being stated, the question is whether cooperative standard-setting processes lead to develop products which may then still be subject to free market forces and competitive pressure. The answer is probably in the negative: after a first phase which may see rival technologies competing on the merits, competition ends with the adoption of the standard (according to the "winner takes all" nature of standardization). Therefore, there might still be a good reason to monitor price levels, especially in those markets where specific barriers limit or discourage entry. Under these circumstances, in which self-correction would seldom occur, intervention by antitrust enforcers may well preserve the consumers' interest in lower prices being charged.[140]

However, given that competition authorities seem ill-suited for price level analysis, which tool may they enforce to constrain high-pricing conduct? Part Three of the book will help to find an answer to this much-debated problem.[141]

136 See, *inter alia*, D. Geradin (n 32) 329.
137 Sherman Act (1890), 15 US Code §§ 1–7.
138 On excessive pricing, see *Port of Helsingborg*, *General Motors*, *Bodson* and *British Leyland* (n 123).
139 M. Crew and P. Kleindorfer, *The Economics of Public Utility Regulation* (MIT Press, Cambridge, MA 1987).
140 *Cf.* D. Sinclair, "Abuse of dominance at a crossroads – potential effect, object and appreciability under Article 82 EC" (2004) 25(8) *European Competition Law Review* 491.
141 See Chapter 7 section 6.1.

5 Threat of injunctive relief

In the previous sections, the instrument of injunction has been briefly cited as an equitable remedy IPRs owners may invoke in order to block the activities of a standard-setting process and prevent implementers from developing the selected technology.[142] This, as it has been argued, may happen in case a conflict arises between licensors and licensees on the level of (F)RAND royalties to pay. In order to reduce the anticompetitive effects of hold-up, some authors have proposed to limit the right of IPRs owners to seek injunctive relief. For instance, Lemley and Shapiro suggested that the right to seek injunctions should be limited in cases where the value of the patented feature is only a small part of the value of the final product. At the same time, as they explain, injunctive relief should also be denied when the IPRs owner is a non-practicing entity, which means firms not involved in the manufacturing of the final standardized good.[143]

More generally, the question under which conditions an IPRs holder can be granted an injunction for the infringement of a (F)RAND-encumbered essential patent has become one of the most debated issues, at the intersection of patent law and competition law. Different courts, authorities and even standard-setting bodies have recently started to pay an increasing attention to the matter. From the analysis of various cases, it seems that patent holders are less likely to obtain injunctive relief in relation to (F)RAND-encumbered patents, especially when a licensee has agreed to pay fair and reasonable fees. This does not mean that the mere act of seeking an injunction should be automatically considered as a breach of competition law. The specific conditions to be met in order to obtain or avoid injunctions may vary depending on the jurisdiction. However, there is increasing consistency between national judges when it comes to consider the good faith of the parties involved. Below, I will briefly survey some of the landmark disputes.

5.1 The Orange Book Standard *case*

In this case, the German Federal Supreme Court argued that a defendant, against whom an action seeking an injunction has been filed on the basis of patent infringement, may raise the antitrust defense that the patent holder (plaintiff) is abusing its dominant position by refusing to license its IPRs on non-discriminatory and non-obstructive conditions.[144] The abuse of dominance may be established as long as the defendant has already made the patent holder an unconditional and binding offer to conclude the license contract, and (if it has already started using

142 See C. Shapiro, "Injunctions, Hold-Up and Patent Royalties" (2010) 12(2) *American Law and Economics Review* 280; J.G. Sidak (n 115) 714; and D.W. Carlton and A.L. Shampine, "An economic interpretation of FRAND" (2013) 9 *Journal of Competition Law and Economics* 550.

143 See M.A. Lemley and C. Shapiro (n 11) 1991; and J.G. Sidak (n 11) 135. *Contra*, see D. Geradin (n 130) 124. Geradin, in particular, argues that the risk of patent hold-up (defined as a conjecture) should not be tackled by limiting IPRs owners' right to seek injunctive relief.

144 Case KZR 39/06 "*Orange Book Standard*" (Bundesgerichtshof, 2009). The name of the case comes from the "Orange Book" that contained the format specifications of the (*de facto*) CD-R technology.

the standard essential patent) has also complied with those legal obligations that the contract to be concluded imposes on the use of the licensed object. In case the defendant considers the IPRs owner's license requirements as excessive or if the IPRs owner refuses to quantify the royalties, the unconditional offer requirement is satisfied by an offer to sign a contract under which the licensor shall define the level of royalties at his fair discretion. This means, according to the German court, that the party seeking a license must pay (e.g. into an escrow account) or guarantee the payment of the fees resulting from the agreement. In other words, the party must behave as if the license offer had been accepted, thus rendering account of the use of the invention, and without subjecting the effectiveness of the offer to the validity of the patent. An injunction will instead be granted in case evidence shows that the defendant was not willing to conclude a licensing agreement on non-discriminatory terms.

Germany is traditionally a major EU market for technological products. Its IP legal framework has been often considered as patent-owner friendly. In this case, as one commentator holds, the German Federal Court's decision may have made an antitrust defense against a patent injunction action extremely difficult.[145] In particular, it has been argued that the court, by narrowing the concept of abusive refusal to deal, demonstrated reluctance to let injunctive relief actions become the subject of review under competition law. By doing so, as the argument goes, it may have undermined "the direct effect of the rules prohibiting the abuse of market power, and thus jeopardised the aim of the competition rules, which is to secure freedom of competition and openness of the markets."[146]

5.2 Samsung v Apple *in the Netherlands*

Further interesting remarks derived from the Dutch legal framework, where in 2012 a court rejected Samsung's application for an injunction to prevent Apple from selling its products in the Netherlands and for the award of damages.[147] Samsung argued that the US firm had infringed its (F)RAND-encumbered patents, concerning the technology essential to the 3G standard developed in the EU by ETSI. Apple had also challenged the validity of Samsung's patents. The court first confirmed that a mere (F)RAND promise given to an SSO does not constitute a binding license offer, and that an IPRs holder has the right to enforce its (F)RAND-encumbered patents. It then held that a patentee would not be allowed to do so when seeking the injunction would constitute abuse of power or breach of good faith.[148] Therefore, the District Court of The Hague rejected the claim as

145 H. Ullrich, "Patents and Standards – A Comment on the German Federal Supreme Court Decision Orange Book Standard" (2010) 41(3) *International Review of Intellectual Property and Competition Law* 340.

146 Ibid., 349.

147 *Samsung Electronics v Apple*, Doc. n. 400367/HA ZA 11-2212 (The Hague District Court, 2012).

148 On the analysis of the case, see A. Jones, "Standard-essential Patents: FRAND Commitments, Injunctions and the Smartphone Wars" (2014) 10(1) *European Competition Journal* 10.

(i) Samsung had only made one offer[149] without replying to Apple's counter-offer, and (ii) Apple had not acted as an unwilling licensee. It concluded that the threat of an injunction, under the special circumstances examined, would put Apple under pressure to accept non-(F)RAND licensing terms.[150]

5.3 The referral of **Huawei v ZTE** *to the CJEU*

More recently, another German court made a preliminary reference to the CJEU, asking for clarification on the use of injunctive relief by innovators owning standard essential patents.[151] The case involved ZTE and the IPRs owner Huawei, both members of ETSI. Under ETSI licensing policy, IPRs holders were obliged to grant irrevocable licenses to third parties on FRAND terms. Having failed to come to an agreement over the licensing terms, Huawei claimed before the German court that its patent, essential for the 4G/LTE ("Long Term Evolution") mobile communication standard, had been infringed and consequently asked for injunctive relief. Opposing the plaintiff's lawsuit, the defendant argued that the refusal to grant a FRAND license amounted to an abuse of the patent owner's dominant position. If the German court had applied the *Orange Book Standard* test to this case, then no reference would have been necessary, as the defendant in this case never made an explicit offer or payment in relation to a hypothetical licensing agreement.[152] However, the court decided to refer the case to the CJEU in light of the recent EU Commission's statement in *Samsung*, where it held that:

> the Commission takes the preliminary view that the seeking of an injunction for SEPs can constitute an abuse of a dominant position in the exceptional circumstances of this case – where the holder of a SEP has given a commitment to license these patents on FRAND terms and where the company against which an injunction is sought is willing to negotiate a FRAND license.[153]

149 I.e., a royalty of 2.4 percent of the entire price of the final Apple product.

150 A similar approach has been adopted by Italian, French and UK courts. See, *inter alia*, Case n. 45629-1-2011 *Samsung Electronics v Apple Inc.* (Tribunal of Milan, 2012); and *IPCom v Nokia*, [2012] EWHC 1446 (Ch). In *IPCom,* for instance, the High Court of England & Wales refused to grant an injunction sought by IPCom against Nokia in relation to a patent essential to the 3G standard. The request, aimed at preventing Nokia from selling its products in the UK, was rejected as Nokia had declared itself willing to take a license on FRAND licensing terms in relation to valid patents.

151 Case n. 4b O 104/12 *Huawei v ZTE* (Landgericht Düsseldorf, 2013).

152 See also Case n. 2 O 240/11 *General Instrument v Microsoft Deutschland* (Landgericht Mannheim, 2012); and Case n. 2 O 41/13 *Vringo v ZTE* (Landgericht Mannheim, 2013). In *Vringo,* for instance, the court decided to grant an injunction to the patent holder Vringo, due to the fact that ZTE had never made any offer to conclude a licensing agreement. Rather, ZTE had merely stated its will to take a license under FRAND terms in case the patent was held valid and infringed by a court.

153 European Commission, "Samsung – Enforcement of ETSI standards essential patents (SEPs)" (21 December 2012) Press Release MEMO/12/1021.

The German district court, therefore, decided to refer a few questions to the CJEU, concerning the applicability and the scope of the *Orange Book Standard* test. In particular, the court asked whether the mere willingness to negotiate a FRAND license (without proposing a binding unconditional offer) is sufficient to reverse a patent infringement action and establish an abuse of the patent owner's dominant position. Besides posing these questions, the court also suggested a possible solution. In this context, it argued that the mere willingness of the infringer to negotiate should not be sufficient to establish a dominant abuse and reverse the patent owner's request for an injunction. On the one hand, the infringer should make a binding offer for a license agreement, including all the contractual conditions typically adopted in the relevant industry practice. On the other hand, the court remarked that the infringer should be allowed to make an offer conditional to the validity of the standard essential patent.[154]

Following the referral to the Court of Justice, the Advocate General (AG) issued his advisory Opinion, which may well represent a significant clarification on the subject if followed by the CJEU.[155] According to the Opinion, before seeking an injunction the patent owner must inform the infringer about the infringement, specifying the patents concerned and presenting a written offer for a license on FRAND terms. Such an offer should contain the precise amount of the royalty and the way in which that amount is calculated. If the infringer does not accept that offer, it must promptly submit to the patent holder a reasonable counter-offer relating to the clauses with which it disagrees. An injunction can be granted if the infringer does not reply in a serious and diligent manner within a reasonable time. According to the Advocate General, seeking an injunction does not constitute an abuse if the infringer's conduct is purely tactical or dilatory.

The conduct instead cannot be considered as tactical or dilatory if, despite the failure of negotiations, the infringer agrees to be bound by a court or arbitral decision on the licensing terms. In that event, the patent owner can legitimately ask the infringer to provide a bank guarantee for the payment or to deposit a provisional amount for past and future use of the patents. The Opinion further adds that the infringer, after concluding a license agreement, still has the right to challenge the validity or essential nature of the patents at issue.

According to the Advocate General, such a test, which clearly differs from the *Orange Book Standard* approach, may strike a better balance between the interests of all the different parties involved.

154 S. Gallasch, "The Referral of Huawei v ZTE to the CJEU: Determining the Future of Remedies in the Context of Standard-essential Patents" (2013) 34(8) *European Competition Law Review* 443; Association Internationale pour la Protection de la Propriete Intellectuelle (AIPPI), "Availability of injunctive relief for FRAND-committed standard essential patents" (2014) Report of the Special Committee Q222. On the effects of injunctions on the dynamics of price negotiations, see G. Langus, V. Lipatov and D. Neven, "Standard Essential Patents: Who is Really Holding Up (and When)?" (2013) 9(2) *Journal of Competition Law and Economics* 253.

155 Case C-170/13 *Huawei Technologies Ltd v ZTE Corp* (not yet reported).

5.4 The European Commission's decisions in Samsung *and* Motorola

In 2014, the European Commission closed two investigations against the ICT giants Samsung and Motorola, both concerning a potential breach of Article 102 TFEU.[156] The proceedings were launched in order to examine whether the firms had abused their dominant position by seeking injunctions in relation to their standard essential patents, despite commitments to apply FRAND terms.[157]

In *Motorola*, the Commission found that the firm had infringed competition law by seeking and enforcing an injunction in Germany against Apple on the basis of a patent essential to the GPRS standard. Motorola's conduct was implemented even though Apple had agreed to obtain a license under FRAND licensing terms, as determined by a German court. As the Commission argued, the acceptance of binding third-party determination for the terms of a FRAND license in the event that bilateral negotiations fail is a clear indication that a potential licensee is willing to enter into a FRAND licensing agreement.[158] Motorola also required Apple to renounce to the right to challenge the validity of its standard essential patents. In this regard, the Commission held that implementers of standards and ultimately consumers should not have to pay for invalid or non-infringed patents, and that implementers should therefore be able to establish the validity of patents and contest alleged infringements.[159] The authority further clarified that its decision does not compromise the general right of IPRs holders to seek injunctive relief in patent infringement cases. It rather specified that injunctions should not be granted in case the patentee has committed to FRAND terms and the potential licensee is willing to enter into a FRAND license agreement. The Commission eventually found an infringement of Article 102 TFEU; however, it did not impose any fine against Motorola, but rather ordered the firm to eliminate the negative effects of its conduct.

In *Samsung*, the Commission accepted Samsung's commitment not to seek any injunctions – in Europe and for a period of five years – on the basis of its standard essential patents included in smartphones and tablets against companies willing to accept specified licensing terms.[160] The decision followed Samsung's efforts to enforce its patents related to the UMTS standard, despite a commitment to license under FRAND terms. Samsung had started to seek injunctive relief before various EU courts against Apple, on the basis of alleged infringement of its 3G (third generation) technology. During the investigation, it withdrew its claims and

156 Case AT.39985 *Motorola – Enforcement of GPRS Standard Essential Patents*, C (2014) 2892 final; and Case AT.39939 *Samsung – Enforcement of UMTS Standard Essential Patents*, C (2014) 2891 final.

157 On the EU Commission's approach to the issue of injunctive relief for standard essential patents, see also the merger Case COMP/M.6381 *Google/Motorola Mobility* [2012] OJ C 75, at 107. Google's purchase of Motorola Mobility included the acquisition of more than 17,000 patents.

158 *Motorola* (n 156).

159 Ibid., at 59. *Cf.* Case n. 7 O 122/11 *Motorola Mobility v Apple Inc* (Landgericht Mannheim, 2011).

160 *Samsung* (n 156). In relation to the smartphone industry, it has been estimated that an average smartphone may read on at least 250,000 standard-essential and non-essential patents.

offered commitments, which were finally accepted and made legally binding. The licensing framework consists of a mandatory negotiation of up to 12 months and, if negotiations fail, a determination of FRAND by a third party (e.g. by a court or arbitration panel).

5.5 eBay v MercExchange

On the other side of the Atlantic, the US Supreme Court dealt with the thorny issue of injunctive relief in the *eBay* case.[161] As it has been argued, *eBay* was not an antitrust case but an equity decision concerned with private remedies generally.[162] The judgment of the Supreme Court overruled a line of rulings, adopted at the Federal Circuit level, which had made injunctions almost a matter of right in the context of patent infringement disputes. Here, the Court argued that a decision on whether a patentee is entitled only to damages or to injunctive relief against patent infringement must be based on four traditional principles of equity. A plaintiff must demonstrate that: (a) it has suffered an irreparable injury; (b) remedies available at law (monetary damages) are inadequate to compensate for the injury; (c) a remedy in equity is warranted; and (d) the public interest would not be harmed by a permanent injunction. As Justice Thomas added:

> when the patented invention is but a small component of the product the companies seek to produce and the threat of injunction is employed simply for undue leverage in negotiations, legal damages may well be sufficient to compensate for the infringement and an injunction may not serve the public interest.[163]

In the Court's view, injunctions can potentially hold up an entire industry or at least make it less competitive.[164] The fact that the patent at issue has already been FRAND encumbered should demonstrate that the IPRs owner's reasonable expectation was the right to obtain reasonable fees, rather than to exclude. Thus, patents subjected to FRAND terms should never be enforced by injunction, at least not when the defendant has accepted to pay a fair and reasonable fee.[165] As it has been held, one of the most important legal consequences of *eBay* was for the

161 *eBay Inc v MercExchange LLC*, 547 US 388 (2006).

162 H.J. Hovenkamp (n 1); E. Elhauge (n 20) 536; J.G. Sidak (n 11) 139; A. Layne Farrar (n 77) 48; M.A. Lemley and A.D. Melamed, "Missing the Forest for the Trolls" (2013) Stanford Law School Working Paper Series n. 443; S. Michel, "Bargaining for RAND royalties in the shadow of patent remedies law" (2011) 77 *Antitrust Law Journal* 889; C. Shapiro (n 142) 282. The latter two examine negotiations between the parties in the shadow of litigation and the threat of injunction.

163 *eBay* (n 161), at 396–397. E.g., consider a patent on a circuit layout of a complex microprocessor.

164 Ibid.

165 R.D. Keeler, "Why Can't We Be (F)RANDS? The Effect of Reasonable and Non-discriminatory Commitments on Standard Essential Patent Licensing" (2013) 32 *Cardozo Arts and Entertainment Law Journal* 329; J.L. Contreras (n 35) 17; C. Shapiro (n 142) 282; D.C. Andrews, "Why Patentees Litigate?" (2011) 12 *The Columbia Science and Technology Law Review* 240.

non-practising or non-manufacturing entities (NPEs).[166] These firms may have the potential to destabilize and harm the entire standard-setting industry as they have different incentives from other members. Because non-producing entities can profit from IPRs only by licensing them, it is very difficult for them to demonstrate that damages are an inadequate remedy, as *eBay* instead requires. Consequently, since the *eBay* case, many NPEs have failed to obtain injunctive relief and have been rather limited to damages.[167]

5.6 The FTC's Google *order*

In the course of 2012, the US Federal Trade Commission started an investigation against Google and its subsidiary Motorola for an alleged violation of Section 5 of the FTC Act, which prohibits unfair methods of competition and unfair acts or practices.[168] According to the authority, the infringement was caused by Motorola's attempt to obtain injunctive relief and exclusion orders against other companies (Apple and Microsoft) before various district courts and the US International Trade Commission, despite its commitment to give them a license under FRAND terms. The FTC claimed that this conduct likely limited competing products, increased costs for both consumers and competitors, destabilized the standard-setting process, and therefore breached Section 5.[169]

Under the consent agreement which settled the dispute, Google and Motorola agreed to cease and desist from making future claims for injunctive relief on the basis of an alleged infringement of their FRAND-encumbered patents. According to the order, in particular, the IPRs owner must provide a potential licensee with a written offer to license enclosing all material terms for the standard essential patents at issue. In case of an initial disagreement over the meaning of FRAND terms, a potential licensee may try to have the dispute resolved through a request for a binding arbitration or court's determination of FRAND. Google would be allowed to seek an injunction in case a licensee refused to accept the FRAND licensing terms as determined by a judge or by an arbitration panel or in case the potential licensee has specified that it will not agree to a license on any terms, or if the licensee is not subject to US jurisdiction. The consent order does not bind holders of essential IPRs other than Google and Motorola. A defendant, however,

166 A. Layne Farrar and K.M. Schmidt, "Licensing Complementary Patents: Patent Trolls, Market Structure, and Excessive Royalties" (2010) 25 *Berkeley Technology Law Journal* 1123. The authors, however, held that the remedy of injunctive relief should not depend on a firm's business model. As they explain, NPEs may sometimes charge lower royalties than vertically integrated firms. Rather, the risk of excessive fees depends on the existence of sunk investments or weak patents.

167 C.V. Chien and M.A. Lemley, "Patent Holdup, the ITC, and the Public Interest" (2012) 98(1) *Cornell Law Review* 1; M.A. Lemley and A.D. Melamed (n 162). The latter, in their paper, develop a thorough examination of the business models adopted by NPEs ("trolls") and practicing entities.

168 *Motorola Mobility LLC & Google Inc*, FTC Docket n. C-4410, Decision and Order (2013).

169 Ibid., at 5–6.

may refer to the FTC's position to defeat a request for injunction if sued for infringing a FRAND-encumbered patent.[170]

The FTC's decision, in brief, seems to leave open the possibility for the interested parties to solve the licensing dispute by a mutual negotiation, judicial determination or binding arbitration. More importantly, it recognized that the law of injunctions in patent disputes must be flexible and responsive to the case where opportunistic IPRs owners use the threat of an injunction in order to obtain royalties well in excess of the real value of their patents.[171] The use of Section 5 of the FTC Act in this context seems appropriate, due to the risk that an action brought under Section 2 of the Sherman Act may fail.[172] On a further different ground, it must be argued, no insight came from the authority as to the meaning of FRAND licensing terms and the risks related to its implementation.

5.7 The **Microsoft v Motorola** *legal battle*

Following the *eBay* ruling, the Ninth Circuit confirmed that (F)RAND-encumbered patents should never be enforced by injunction, at least not when the infringement defendant has accepted to pay (F)RAND royalty rates.[173]

In this case, Motorola had made promises to the International Telecommunication Union (ITU) to license its standard-essential patents on a worldwide and non-discriminatory basis to an unrestricted number of applicants, and to apply reasonable terms and conditions. As a consequence, it had received the benefit of having its patents included in the standards. Motorola could have withheld the promise at the price of having the ITU avoid its IPRs when setting the standards, but chose not to.[174] Upon Motorola's request for non-RAND royalties, Microsoft filed a breach of contract action; Motorola replied by suing Microsoft for patent infringement.[175] Motorola also sued Microsoft in Germany, where it was able to obtain injunctive relief and block Microsoft from selling allegedly infringing products in the German territory. This was due to the fact that German law does not recognize third-party contractual rights, so Microsoft could not assert that Motorola's RAND commitments entitled Microsoft to a license.[176] In its suit before the US district court, therefore, Microsoft further asked a preliminary

170 S. Amundson, "Recent Decisions Provide Some Clarity on How Courts and Government Agencies Will Likely Resolve Issues Involving Standard Essential Patents" (2014) 13(1) *Chicago-Kent Journal of Intellectual Property* 106.

171 See also T. Cotter, "The Comparative Law and Economics of Standard-Essential Patents and FRAND Royalties" (2013) University of Minnesota Law School Research Paper n. 13-40; and D. Geradin, "Ten Years of DG Competition Effort to Provide Guidance on the Application of Competition Rules to the Licensing of Standard-Essential Patents: Where Do We Stand?" (2013) Tilburg Centre of Law and Economics Discussion Paper n. 2013-11.

172 See also *In Re Robert Bosch GmbH*, FTC Docket n. C-4377, 2012 WL 5944820 (2012).

173 *Microsoft v Motorola Inc*, 696 F3d 872 (C App 9th Circuit, 2012). The US International Trade Commission (ITC), however, has adopted a more flexible approach in granting exclusion orders.

174 H.J. Hovenkamp (n 1).

175 *Microsoft v Motorola Inc*, 871 F Supp 2d 1089 (WD Washington, 2012), at 1094–1095.

176 *Microsoft v Motorola* (n 173), at 879.

injunction preventing Motorola from enforcing any injunctive relief obtained in Germany.[177]

In evaluating the different claims, the district court considered the following four factors: (1) likelihood of success on the merits; (2) irreparable harm absent the requested injunction; (3) the balance of hardships; and (4) the public interest.[178] The court eventually concluded that these factors justified an order prohibiting Motorola from enforcing any injunction obtained from the German court. Judge Robart further remarked the importance of "ensuring standard essential patents are accessible to all comers under RAND terms" and of "permitting Microsoft's customers [...] to conduct business uninterrupted."[179]

On appeal, the Ninth Circuit upheld the decision of the district court and confirmed that a patentee's commitment to license essential IPRs on RAND conditions establishes a contract governing the patentee's ability to enforce the patent; thus, a third-party beneficiary can bring a claim for breach of that contract.[180] As the Court of Appeal held, "injunctive relief against infringement is arguably a remedy inconsistent with the licensing commitment."[181]

5.8 Judge Posner and the Federal Circuit in Apple v Motorola

In line with the reasoning of the Ninth Circuit and of the Supreme Court, in *Apple v Motorola*, Judge Posner held that, by committing to (F)RAND licensing terms, Motorola had agreed to license the essential patents to anyone willing to pay a (F)RAND royalty, so that injunctions could no longer be granted unless the licensee refused to pay a royalty meeting the (F)RAND requirement. In the words of Judge Posner:

> I don't see how, given FRAND, I would be justified in enjoining Apple from infringing the [standard-essential patent] unless Apple refuses to pay a royalty that meets the FRAND requirement. By committing to license its patents on FRAND terms, Motorola committed to license the [standard-essential patent] to anyone willing to pay a FRAND royalty and thus implicitly acknowledged that a royalty is adequate compensation for a license to use that patent. How could it do otherwise? How could it be permitted to enjoin Apple from using an invention that it contends Apple must use if it wants to make a cell phone with UMTS telecommunications capability—without which it would not be a cell phone.[182]

177 *Microsoft v Motorola* (n 175), at 1096.
178 Ibid., at 1102–1103.
179 Ibid., at 1098–1103.
180 *Microsoft v Motorola* (n 173), at 885.
181 Ibid., at 884–885. See also *Microsoft v Motorola Inc*, Case n. 10-1823, 2012 WL 5993202 (WD Washington, 2012), at 6–8. A few months later, the district court confirmed that Motorola could not obtain any injunction for its essential patents in any country, as it was not able to prove irreparable harm.
182 *Apple Inc v Motorola Inc*, 869 F Supp 2d 901 (ND Illinois, 2012).

In the appeal of that case, the Federal Circuit followed a similar approach, recalling first the value of the precedents established by the US jurisprudence. As the Court argued:

> the framework laid out by the Supreme Court in *eBay*, as interpreted by subsequent decision of this court, provides ample strength and flexibility for addressing the unique aspects of FRAND committed patents and industry standards in general.[183]

It then recognized that there is no *per se* rule prohibiting injunctive relief for the holders of standard essential patents that are subject to FRAND terms. An injunction, in particular, may be usually justified where an infringer unilaterally refuses a FRAND rate or unreasonably delays negotiations to the same effect. At the same time, as it argued, a patentee subject to FRAND commitments may have difficulty in establishing irreparable harm. The court eventually denied Motorola an injunction against Apple, on the grounds that money damages were adequate to fully compensate for any infringement.[184] These conclusions, it is worth noting, have been echoed and upheld by other US courts in infringement cases related to standard essential patents.[185]

5.9 A view from the Asian legal framework

The availability of injunctive relief for FRAND-committed standard essential patents has been recently debated in Asia. In this context, different courts and authorities seem to have followed the approach developed in the US and the EU. One example is represented by the recent decision of a Japanese court in the well-known patents war *Samsung v Apple*.[186] The dispute concerned a Japanese patent considered essential to the 3GPP ("third generation partnership project") standard[187] and for which Samsung committed to FRAND licensing terms. The

183 *Apple Inc v Motorola Inc*, 757 F3d 1286 (C App Federal Circuit, 2014).

184 Ibid. For an analysis of the different types of damages (e.g. ordinary, enhanced or punitive) and their related scope and legal basis, see F.S. Kieff and A. Layne Farrar (n 112) 1091.

185 See *Barnes & Noble v LSI Corp*, 849 F Supp 2d 925 (ND California, 2012); and *Realtek Semiconductor Corp v LSI Corp*, Case n. 12-3451, 2013 WL 2181717 (ND California, 2013). In the latter case, for instance, Judge Whyte held that LSI had breached its FRAND promise by failing to offer a license to Realtek or to negotiate one before starting proceedings for obtaining an exclusion order from the US International Trade Commission (ITC). Such a conduct was interpreted by the judge as "a clear attempt to gain leverage in future licensing negotiations." See, however, also *Apple Inc v Motorola Inc*, Case n. 11-178, 2012 WL 7989412 (WD Wisconsin, 2012); here, Judge Crabb dismissed Apple's FRAND-based claim on the basis that the SSOs (ETSI and IEEE) licensing policies did not explicitly deprive the patent owner of the right to seek injunctive relief.

186 Cases n. 2013 (Ra) 10007, 2013 (Ra) 10008 and 2013 (Ne) 10043 *Samsung Electronics v Apple Inc* (Japanese IP High Court Tokyo, 2013).

187 The 3GPP results from the collaboration of different groups of telecommunication associations. It concerns *inter alia* the development of a globally applicable third generation mobile phone system specification, based on evolved GSM (global system for mobile communications) specifications.

Japanese court established that Samsung's request for injunctive relief amounted to an abuse of rights, as Apple had agreed to take a license under FRAND terms. The court also confirmed that an injunction may be granted only in case of unwilling licensees who make or sell the standardized product without willingness to pay FRAND rates. The Korean IT giant was eventually awarded damages on the basis of fair and reasonable fees, as determined by the court.

The conduct of Samsung has been recently scrutinized by the Korean Fair Trade Commission.[188] Here, the outcome was slightly different and led to the rejection of Apple's claims according to which Samsung had breached competition law by seeking injunctions on a FRAND-encumbered patent. The Korean authority concluded that Samsung's enforcement strategy did not infringe the Korean Monopoly Regulation and Fair Trade Law, as Apple had, *inter alia*, failed to engage in good faith negotiation. As the authority explained, Apple engaged in reverse hold-up (also known as "hold-out")[189] as it did not demonstrate any intention to pay FRAND fees until the conclusion of the legal battle. In an attempt to justify this interpretative approach, the Korean Commission referred to other investigations, like the case closed by the European Commission with the acceptance of Samsung's commitment.

More in line with established case law, a Chinese court found the firm InterDigital liable for breaching China's antimonopoly law and failing to license certain patents on fair and reasonable terms.[190] The court established liability on the basis of (1) excessive fee proposals made to Huawei for Chinese standard essential patents; (2) the request of grant-backs from Huawei; (3) the tying of essential patents to non-essential patents; and (4) the request of an exclusion order against Huawei before the US International Trade Commission, pending negotiations on the licensing of the relevant patents. On a further ground, the court held that InterDigital was required to license its Chinese essential IPRs on FRAND terms, even in the absence of explicit commitments by the firm towards a Chinese body.[191] It eventually set a FRAND rate for the firm's essential patents.

5.10 Further remarks on injunctive relief

The analysis of the EU, US and Asian cases on the availability of injunctions for (F)RAND-committed standard essential patents has evidenced a rather consistent approach. Despite some differences exist as to the specific terms and conditions (see the German legal framework), courts and authorities have clarified that IPRs holders may find it difficult to seek injunctive relief for patent infringements when they have committed to (F)RAND terms and "the good faith potential licensees" have accepted to pay fair and reasonable royalties.

188 *Samsung Electronics Co, Ltd* (Korean Fair Trade Commission, Decision of 26 February 2014).

189 On the concept of reverse hold-up, see F.S. Kieff and A. Layne Farrar (n 112) 1091.

190 Cases n. 305–306 *Huawei v InterDigital* (Guangdong Higher People's Court, 2013).

191 According to the court, this was because InterDigital had joined other SSOs (e.g. ETSI). On Chinese (F)RAND case law, see also *Nokia/Microsoft* (MOFCOM, Decision of 8 April 2014).

Of course, this does not mean that seeking an injunction against a recalcitrant firm would always be anticompetitive.[192] In the US, for instance, the Patent Code establishes that no patent owner should be denied relief for the infringement of a patent.[193] In the EU, furthermore, a firm's right of access to the courts is an essential right, guaranteed by the Charter of Fundamental Rights.[194] Besides, the EU Directive on the enforcement of IPRs stated that: "Member States shall ensure that, where a judicial decision is taken finding an infringement of an IPR, the judicial authorities may issue against the infringer an injunction aimed at prohibiting the continuation of the infringement."[195] This interpretative approach is also consistent with that established by the Agreement on Trade Related Aspects of Intellectual Property Rights (TRIPs), which similarly holds that "… the judicial authorities shall have the authority to order a party to desist from an infringement, inter alia to prevent the entry into the channels of commerce in their jurisdiction of imported goods that involve the infringement of an intellectual property right …."[196]

This notwithstanding, the seeking of injunctive relief under certain circumstances may potentially amount to a form of abuse of dominance. The choice of the appropriate legal test may vary, depending also on the jurisdiction concerned. For instance, in the EU case *ITT Promedia*, the Court of First Instance held that dominant firms are generally free to start litigation against their competitors, unless wholly exceptional circumstances occur.[197] As it further held, to establish abuse under Article 102 TFEU, it must be shown that litigation (i) cannot reasonably be considered as an attempt to establish the rights of the undertaking concerned; and (ii) was conceived as part of a plan to eliminate competition.[198] An abusive litigation test has been thoroughly examined and justified as the optimal legal standard by part of the literature.[199] Other tests that have been examined, in order to apply Article 102 TFEU to the seeking of injunctions for (F)RAND-encumbered standard essential patents, refer to (i) the abusive refusal to supply,[200]

192 See C. Graham and J. Morton, "Latest EU developments in standards, patents and FRAND licensing" (2014) 36(11) *European Intellectual Property Review* 703; and A. Jones (n 148) 28–29.

193 Manual of Patent Examining Procedure (1948), 35 USC § 271(d).

194 Article 47, Charter of Fundamental Rights of the European Union, [2010] OJ C 83/389.

195 Article 11, Directive of the European Parliament and the Council 2004/48/EC, [2004] OJ L 195/16.

196 See Article 44(1) of the Agreement on Trade Related Aspects of Intellectual Property Rights (TRIPs), Annex 1C to the Marrakesh Agreement establishing the World Trade Organization (WTO), 33 ILM 1197 (1994). At the same time, however, Article 44(2) also allows the Members to "… limit the remedies available against such use to payment of remuneration …."

197 Case T-111/96 *ITT Promedia NV v European Commission* [1998] ECR II-2937.

198 Ibid. See also Case T-119/09 *Protégé International Ltd v European Commission* [2012] OJ C 319.

199 See N. Petit, "Injunctions for FRAND Pledged SEPs: The Quest For An Appropriate Test of Abuse Under Article 102 TFEU" (2013) 9(3) *European Competition Journal* 677.

200 Here, the substantive conditions were set in Joined Cases C 241-242/91 P, *Radio Telefis Eireann & Independent Television Publications v European Commission* [1995] 4 CMLR 718; and Case C-418/01 *IMS Health GmbH v NDC Health GmbH* [2004] 4 CMLR 28.

(ii) the abusive anticompetitive foreclosure,[201] (iii) the abusive bargaining,[202] and (iv) the above-mentioned willing licensee test.[203]

In this context, further guidance is expected from the Court of Justice of the EU, which was recently asked to shed light on the issue in the cited *Huawei v ZTE* case. Perhaps, additional elucidations on the use of injunctions in patent cases may also derive from SSOs, which may clarify – once and for all – which steps IPRs holders must take before seeking injunctive relief. However, the difficulties faced by some SSOs (e.g. ETSI) in their recent attempts to discuss the use of injunctions with members, reveal that broad consensus is unlikely.[204] Besides, a change of approach is also expected from the US International Trade Commission, which has so far declined to follow *eBay* when granting injunctions against patent infringing products. As a consequence, exclusion orders have increasingly been sought by non-practicing entities that hold US patents.[205]

This being said, it is evident that, in order to avoid any risk of injunctions, IPRs owners and implementers should have a clearer picture of the licensing terms to be applied. The implementation of (F)RAND licensing policies, so widely adopted by standard-setting organizations operating in the ICT industry, seems to be at the root of all the disputes. It is clear that any given definition of (F)RAND is specific to each case, based on the number of patents, their technical significance and other factors. Therefore, in the absence of absolute and unequivocal criteria to define fair, reasonable and non-discriminatory licensing terms, there is the serious risk that parties may litigate each time on both the meaning of (F)RAND and the right to claim for injunctive relief.

Despite the fact that several judges and authorities (e.g. Judge Robart in the well-known *Microsoft v Motorola* dispute)[206] have tried to identify a workable path to be followed in future judgments, one question still stands: Is litigation the optimal way to eliminate the conflicts arising in standard setting activities? Litigation, it must be remembered, may require considerable time – in the range of years – and financial expenses. These may well be interpreted as social costs which may eventually disrupt the whole standardization system and compromise the achievement of its proposed goal (i.e. bringing new technologies to the market in a timely manner to the benefit of consumer and societal welfare).[207]

201 See, *inter alia*, Case C-209/10 *Post Danmark A/S v Konkurrenceradet* [2012] 4 CMLR 23.

202 This test was scrutinized in M. Mariniello, "European Antitrust Control and Standard Setting" (2013) Bruegel Working Paper n. 2013/01.

203 See *Huawei Technologies* (n 155); *Motorola* (n 156); and *Samsung* (n 156).

204 C. Graham and J. Morton (n 192) 705; AIPPI (n 154). However, it is noteworthy that IEEE has recently included *ad hoc* rules to limit the right to seek prohibitive orders (see IEEE-SA, "Standards Board Bylaws" (2015) § 6.2).

205 C.V. Chien and M.A. Lemley (n 167) 2. The ITC issues exclusion orders under 19 USC § 1337.

206 *Microsoft v Motorola Inc*, Case n. 10-1823, 2013 WL 2111217 (WD Washington, 2013).

207 According to M.A. Lemley and A.D. Melamed (n 162), a recent estimate found that only the "smartphone war" has already led the parties involved in the disputes (from Samsung, to Apple and Nokia) to spend around $1 billion in legal fees.

6 Conclusion

Standard setting may enhance innovation and boost competition by ensuring that products from multiple manufacturers are compatible and interoperable.[208] However, it may also raise concerns under both US antitrust and EU competition laws. This is because, as I have argued, standard setting represents a context where the principles of IP and competition laws may potentially conflict. The literature has identified risks of both exploitative and exclusionary conduct, which could be implemented by firms taking part in the SSO environment. The analysis of these practices may change in accordance with the legal framework considered. This is the reason behind the existing gap between the EU and US approaches to standards. The more interventionist EU approach must be compared to the more liberal US legal environment. Both jurisdictions prohibit exclusionary practices by dominant firms. Only the EU legal framework, in fact, is concerned by purely exploitative behaviors.

This notwithstanding, given the fundamental role of standards in our economy, it is also important to encourage innovators to participate in standardization. In this context, both EU and US courts and authorities are called to enforce a legal framework which strikes the right balance between investment incentives and competition objectives. On the one hand, any abuse of market power in standard setting has the potential to cause significant harm to society. On the other hand, any form of control of market power must weigh up between prohibiting abuses and preserving investment incentives, particularly in high technology industries. Arguably, the law is struggling to find the right compromise, which also affects the right to seek injunctive relief. A non-optimal balance would generate losses in long-term consumer surplus and productivity. The IPRs policies proposed by the literature and implemented by the SSOs cannot be interpreted as an effective means to tackle the risks of abusive conduct in standard setting. The (F)RAND model has led to several disputes, concerning both the grant of injunctions and the determination of fair and reasonable rates.

Besides the need to strike *ex ante* the optimal policy, the chapter has also mentioned the importance of an effective enforcement system of antitrust. Its role, as an *ex post* potential tool to remedy abusive behaviors, will be further scrutinized in Chapter 7. It suffices here to remember that the ultimate outcome should lead to maximize societal welfare and productivity in the long run.

In the next sections, before suggesting an optimal policy framework, the book will thoroughly examine four landmark cases on standard setting, decided by EU and US enforcers. These cases may well be considered as the evidence for the indefiniteness and inefficiency of the (F)RAND licensing model.

208 See C.B. Hockett and R.G. Lipscomb (n 112) 19; C. Koenig and K. Spiekermann, "EC competition law issues of standard setting by officially-entrusted versus private organizations" (2010) 31(11) *European Competition Law Review* 449; and P. Chappatte (n 7) 322.

5 The US approach in the standards–market power dichotomy

1 Introduction

The approach developed by the US courts and antitrust authorities to tackle abuse of dominance has usually been defined as less interventionist in comparison to that adopted by their European Union (EU) counterparts.[1] The absence of antitrust rules forbidding exploitative practices by dominant firms should be interpreted in light of the more liberal US legal framework. Other elements can be considered as evidence of the existing gap between US and EU laws: from the relatively high thresholds (in comparison to the EU benchmark) for market shares necessary to raise concerns under Section 2 of the Sherman Act, to the concept of "special responsibility" to which dominant firms are subjected in the EU only. What is more, EU competition law and jurisprudence do not seem to place as much importance on the role of "free market forces" as their US counterparts. As held by US courts, the issue "is not to protect businesses from the working of the market; it is to protect the public from the failure of the market."[2] These arguments should be reconciled with the US interpretation of the role played by monopolistic firms, which are seen as important means – *Verizon*[3] *docet* – to increase the national wealth by enhancing innovation and advancing the welfare of the whole society.

The more liberal US approach can also be observed in relation to the case law on standard setting, which has developed sooner and more rapidly than in the EU. The differences in the treatment of standard-setting conduct could be explained mainly in light of these preliminary considerations.

After discussing the relevant legal framework, the next sections will explore the US jurisprudence on standard setting and will explain how the different legal background is reflected in the case law. The analysis will focus on the earliest and most representative disputes, from *Rambus* and *Unocal* to *Dell* and *Qualcomm*. Their scope, significance and impact on the doctrinal environment justify a case-by-case

1 D. De Smet, "The Diametrically Opposed Principles of US and EU Antitrust Policy" (2008) 29(6) *European Competition Law Review* 359.

2 *Spectrum Sports Inc v McQuillan*, 506 US 447 (1993), at 458.

3 *Verizon Communications v Trinko*, 540 US 398 (2004).

approach in the analysis of the core issues. In particular, one question needs to be addressed. What lessons can be learned from the divergent outcomes of these disputes? In the pursuit of a plausible answer, the chapter will examine both the relevant conduct and the elements of intent, causation and effects. As will be shown, concrete legal problems exist in the field of US standardization, from the lack of clear policy rules to hold-up. The chapter will clarify why the IPRs policies proposed so far by several SSOs have asked more questions than they answer, and why these rules do not represent effective means to preserve the efficient development of standards.

2 Legal framework

Before taking into consideration the legal arguments developed by the US jurisprudence, it is worth mentioning the relevant provisions that have been applied to standardization cases. The focus is on the rules of the Sherman Act and the Federal Trade Commission Act.

With respect to the former, Section 2 of the Sherman Act addresses conduct concerning monopolization and attempted monopolization. In particular, Section 2 condemns "[e]very person who shall monopolize, or attempt to monopolize, or combine or conspire with any other person or persons, to monopolize any part of the trade or commerce among the several States, or with foreign nations."[4] The concepts of monopolization and attempt to monopolize should be interpreted separately. Monopolization, indeed, requires possession of monopoly power and the willful acquisition or maintenance of it, an element of anticompetitive conduct. It means to acquire or maintain monopoly through improper means. The attempt to monopolize, instead, requires the anticompetitive conduct, a specific intent to monopolize, and the dangerous probability of achieving monopoly power. Unlike monopolization, it is not necessary to succeed and gain monopoly. Section 2, in brief, regulates undertakings with market power, and can be considered as the corresponding provision to Article 102 TFEU.[5] Basically, undertakings are not allowed to implement unlawful or abusive behaviors to become a monopolist, attempt to gain monopoly power or use such conduct if they are already a monopoly.

The second relevant provision is represented by Section 5 of the Federal Trade Commission Act. It outlaws unfair methods of competition and unfair or deceptive acts or practices. In particular, it establishes that "unfair methods of competition in or affecting commerce, and unfair or deceptive acts or practices in or affecting commerce, are hereby declared unlawful."[6] An act or practice is deceptive if it involves a representation, omission or practice that is likely to mislead consumers acting reasonably under the circumstances, and the representation, omission or

4 15 USC § 2.
5 Formerly, Article 82 of the EC Treaty.
6 15 USC § 45.

practice is material.[7] Deception does not require intent to deceive, nor does it require harm to competition.[8] An act or practice, furthermore, is unfair if it causes injury to consumers and is substantial, not outweighed by countervailing benefits to consumers and competition, and consumers themselves could not reasonably have avoided it.[9] Under the Federal Trade Commission Act, the authority has the exclusive power to enforce Section 5, while there is no room for private actions. Section 5 could be interpreted as a provision necessary to fill the gaps left in US antitrust enforcement and address conduct escaping the application of Section 2 of the Sherman Act. As held by Commissioner Leibowitz, "the framers of the FTC Act gave the Agency a mandate – one unique to the Commission – to use Section 5 to supplement and bolster the antitrust laws by providing, in essence, a jurisdictional 'penumbra' around them."[10] This means that violations of the Sherman Act are also violations of section 5 FTCA, but section 5 covers some practices that are beyond the scope of the Sherman Act.

Section 5, as I shall argue, could be potentially applied in the context of standard setting to tackle not only exclusionary but also purely exploitative practices not addressed by the Sherman Act. For instance, the conduct of patent holders merely breaching the promise to license under defined terms, in the absence of exclusion, might well be sanctioned as a deceptive behavior. Of course, a precondition for enforcing Section 5 should be the existence of specific policy rules clearly explaining the duties participants must comply with.

In conclusion, Section 5 and Section 2 are at the basis of the enforcement activity of US courts and authorities. In applying these provisions, the meaning and scope of the principles stated in the "Standards Development Organization Advancement Act" could not be ignored.[11] Here, indeed, the US Congress highlighted the importance of co-operative and transparent standardization processes, based on openness, balance of interests and consensus.

3 Conduct

Two different practices in the US standard-setting context have been considered under legal provisions: patent ambush and the mere breach of (F)RAND licensing conditions. Both behaviors, already scrutinized in Chapter 4, have been deeply investigated in the last decades by US jurisprudence, which attested to the existence of a real problem. US courts and authorities, however, have often shown conflicting perspectives in examining hold-up. What is more, they have extensively – and perhaps controversially – discussed the various elements related to conduct, from causation to intent and effects, required for a finding of an infringement

7 See, for instance, *Federal Trade Commission v Pantron I*, 33 F3d 1088 (C App 9th Circuit, 1994), at 1095; *Federal Trade Commission v Minuteman Press*, 53 F Supp. 2d 248 (EDNY, 1998), at 258.

8 *Federal Trade Commission v World Travel Vacation Brokers*, 861 F2d 1020 (C App 7th Circuit, 1988), at 1029.

9 *Federal Trade Commission v Verity International*, 443 F3d 48 (C App 2nd Circuit, 2006).

10 *Rambus Inc*, FTC Docket n. 9302, Opinion of Commissioner Leibowitz (2 August 2006), at 18.

11 *Standards Development Organization Advancement Act of 2004*, 15 USC § 4301 (2004).

under Section 2 of the Sherman Act. In the analysis of these aspects, I shall start discussing those disputes that, more than others, have contributed to the development of relevant legal principles in the US standard-setting environment.

3.1 Patent ambush

A patent ambush, as it has been said, may arise in the situation where implementers of a standardized technology, unaware *ex ante* of the existence of potentially blocking patents or patent applications, invest resources in the implementation of a standard that infringes the hidden patents. In this context, the holder of the "submarine" patents may assert *ex post* its claims against the alleged infringement. As Shapiro clarifies, once the standardized technology has been adopted and the patent ambush has been successful, the patent owner may either ask for supra-competitive royalties or try to block the development of the technology on the ground of an injunction or other exclusionary relief.[12] Various cases can be mentioned when appraising patent ambush in US standard setting. *Wang*, for instance, was one of the earliest examples, and concerned a case of false representation made by a member as to its real intention of seeking patent rights on a standardized design.[13] The next sections will focus only on those landmark disputes that fomented the debate on the standards–IPR dichotomy, from *Dell* to *Rambus* and *Unocal*.[14]

3.1.1 Deception and the breach of Section 5 in Dell

Although it was never fully litigated, *Dell*[15] deserves specific attention as one of the most relevant early disputes. Ultimately settled by consent decree, the case might be considered as a fundamental precedent among the federal antitrust enforcement actions brought for alleged unilateral abuse of private standard-setting procedures. Unlike other cases, the Commission here focused on deceptive conduct under Section 5, while it did not formally allege monopolization or attempted

12 C. Shapiro, "Navigating the Patent Thicket: Cross Licenses, Patent Pools and Standard-Setting" (2001) Social Science Research Network 1. On the scope of injunctive relief, see also S. Gallasch, "The Referral of Huawei v ZTE to the CJEU: Determining the Future of Remedies in the Context of Standard-essential Patents" (2013) 34(8) *European Competition Law Review* 443; T.F. Cotter, "Reining in Remedies in Patent Litigation: Three (Increasingly Immodest) Proposals" (2013) 30 *Santa Clara High Technology Law Journal* 1; and S. Michel, "Bargaining for RAND royalties in the shadow of patent remedies law" (2011) 77 *Antitrust Law Journal* 889.

13 *Wang Labs. v Mitsubishi Elecs.*, 103 F3d 1571 (C App Federal Circuit, 1997).

14 Besides these disputes, the Qualcomm/Broadcom legal battle also gave rise to a case of patent ambush in the context of the Joint Video Team standards institute (see *Qualcomm Inc v Broadcom Corp*, US Dist LEXIS 28211 (SD California, 2007); and *Qualcomm Inc v Broadcom Corp*, 548 F3d 1004 (C App Federal Circuit, 2008)). However, for the purposes of this book, the chapter will take into account only that portion of the dispute which concerned the mere breach of FRAND terms.

15 *Dell Computer*, 121 Federal Trade Commission 616 (1996).

monopolization under Section 2 of the Sherman Act. This may be the reason why it did not precisely identify a relevant market.[16]

In *Dell*, the company was deemed guilty by the Commission of false representation towards the Video Electronics Standards Association (VESA). As a member of the organization, Dell was asked to certify under VESA policy that it had no IPRs that could cover the proposed VL-bus standard.[17] Dell's representative had certified that, to the best of his knowledge, the company did not have any conflicting patents. This notwithstanding, after the adoption of the standard by VESA, Dell asserted its IPR against all those manufacturers producing the technology.[18]

3.1.1.1 VESA'S PREFERENCE FOR NON-PROPRIETARY STANDARDS

The Commission in its decision established that there was evidence that VESA would have implemented a different non-proprietary design had Dell disclosed its rights, due to its strong preference for standards not based on proprietary technology. This means that Dell's acquisition of market power was not inevitable, due to the existence of equally effective non-proprietary standards that were competing in the selection process.[19] The conclusion of the authority was based on the analysis of the circumstances and of VESA policy, according to which members were required to identify potentially conflicting patents in order to avoid the adoption of standards infringing those patents. To this extent, the participants had to explicitly certify the existence of any potentially conflicting IPRs, also in accordance to an alleged good faith duty of disclosure. VESA policy clearly manifested the preference for non-proprietary standards.[20] Dell's failure to act in good faith, as the Commission concluded, led to justified enforcement action to prevent harm to competition and consumers.[21]

3.1.1.2 FAULTS OF THE DISSENTING OPINION

The decision of the majority, however, was contested under several aspects by one of the Commissioners, who expressed her arguments in the dissenting statement. Firstly, the Commissioner noted that the adoption of Dell's standard could be only explained by the high quality and efficiency of the product, rather than by a false representation to the SSO. The firm's behavior, it was argued, was legitimate as it had neither proposed nor sponsored the standard, nor had it exerted pressure

16 M.C. Naughton and R. Wolfram, "The Antitrust Risks of Unilateral Conduct in Standard Setting, in the Light of the FTC's case against Rambus Inc" (2004) 49 *Antitrust Bulletin* 706.

17 The VL-bus mechanism had the function of transferring instructions between a computer's CPU and its peripherals. This technology has been used by computers using 486 chips.

18 Dell threatened to sue certain VESA members, on the ground of the patent previously granted, after manufacturers had sold about 1.5 million PCs reading on the VL-bus standard.

19 *Dell* (n 15), at 624.

20 Ibid.

21 Ibid.

on the standard-setting body for the selection of its technology.[22] The argument, however, seemed to be fictitious, in so far as a successful patent ambush does not necessarily require an active line of conduct in the SSO selection process. Rather, a patent ambush could simply derive from the omission of information on the existence of related IPRs.

Secondly, it was held that the representative's actions in submitting the certification did not bind the corporation. There was no proof, in the Commissioner's view, that the representative was aware of the existence of the patent or of the infringement.[23] This argument was correctly rejected by the majority. Corporations act through their agents; when an agent acts in his capacity, he acts for the corporations.[24] Were the Commissioner's point of view accepted, it would be useless even to start standard-setting processes as the will of representatives could not be finally imputed to the members of the organization.

Other considerations concerned the fact that the complaint had not apparently identified other equally valuable existing technologies which VESA could have adopted had it known of Dell's patent.[25] In relation, instead, to the alleged lock-in effect of Dell's patent ambush, the Commissioner argued that computer manufacturers could have readily shifted to a new standard after the adoption of the VL-bus technology.[26] These observations seemed contradictory, as the Commissioner referred at the same time to an alleged lack of evidence for alternative technologies in the selection process and to the existence of alternative standards to which manufacturers could have readily switched. Nevertheless, the majority correctly recognized that it would have not been reasonable to switch to alternatives, as the market had overwhelmingly adopted the standard and had incurred considerable costs.[27]

In brief, the arguments of the dissenting Commissioner did not seem generally convincing. This notwithstanding, the majority could have brought stronger evidence in relation to the existence of alternative standards available to VESA.[28] On a further ground, the majority did not always develop a clear line of reasoning, especially by referring to those elements (e.g., market power) which are only required under Section 2 of the Sherman Act, but not under Section 5.

3.1.1.3 PROHIBITIONS OF THE SETTLEMENT AGREEMENT

A settlement agreement was finally adopted according to which Dell was prohibited from seeking royalties and enforcing its VL-bus patent against any firm using the standard.[29] The remedy was consistent with the equitable estoppel doctrine,

22 *Dell Computer*, 121 FTC 616, Dissenting Statement of Commissioner M.L. Azcuenaga, at 628.
23 Ibid.
24 *Dell* (n 15), at 624.
25 *Dell* (n 22), at 640.
26 Ibid., at 641.
27 *Dell* (n 15), at 624.
28 *Dell* (n 22), at 628–633.
29 *Dell* (n 15), at 620–621, §§ 2–4.

according to which courts should preclude IPRs owners from enforcing those patents which have not been properly disclosed by them.[30] In explaining the measure, the FTC noted that Dell's behavior conferred market power, unreasonably restrained competition and harmed the IT industry by discouraging undertakings from manufacturing products based on the VL-bus standard. In addition, by raising the costs of standardization, thc conduct reduced the willingness to participate to SSO.[31]

3.1.1.4 MERITS OF THE COMMISSION'S LINE OF REASONING

It is undoubtedly the case that *Dell* represented a notable attempt to develop legal principles in addressing what by then had become a serious concern in the standard-setting field. Despite the criticism of the Commission's arguments, the case was an opportunity to clarify crucial aspects related to the functioning of standard-setting bodies and the role of antitrust enforcement.

For instance, in considering the public comments on the decision made by different SSOs, the majority rejected the view that private litigation could represent a more specific tool to address this type of dispute. The Federal Trade Commission, in particular, established that the existence of potential harm to consumers also justifies enforcement actions under Section 5 of the FTC Act.[32] The authority recognized that enforcement may have the final detrimental effect of discouraging participation in standard setting. Nevertheless, since members may use SSOs as vehicles to alter and undermine their objectives and finally harm competition and consumers,[33] it seems reasonable to consider public enforcement as proper and justified.[34]

Even more important was the answer given by the majority to one of the questions raised by SSOs in their public comments: did the Commission intend to establish a general duty to search for patents in case of firms engaged in a standard-setting process? The answer must be in the negative, as a duty to search may only be deemed to exist where a standard-setting body explicitly sets its provisions in this direction.[35] Clear policy rules are needed to set out any specific duty. In this case, the duty to search directly derived from VESA's affirmative search requirement, which created a justified expectation by its members that each firm would act in good faith to identify and disclose any conflicting patents. Nonetheless, the Commission noted that other SSOs may adopt different provisions that do not create such expectation.

Of course, a duty to search relevant IPRs may be interpreted by patent owners as too burdensome and may hence discourage them from participating in standard setting. As it has been held in the previous sections, this may explain

30 On the equitable estoppel doctrine, see Chapter 7 section 5.1.
31 *Dell* (n 15), at 624.
32 Ibid., at 626.
33 See, e.g. *Allied Tube & Conduit v Indian Head*, 486 US 492 (1988).
34 *Dell* (n 15), at 626.
35 Ibid., at 625.

why few SSOs have adopted search provisions. However, it is clear that in case an organization is mainly interested in non-proprietary standards (as in the field of the internet) such a duty might ultimately play a more central role in the IPRs policy.

Finally, *Dell* also opened an important debate on whether the breach of a search or disclose duty should be intentional, and whether inadvertent non-disclosure should not be prohibited. These questions will be better addressed in the section on intent, where I will deal also with the theories examining the concept of negligence. The considerations developed therein will then be recalled in Chapter 7, in the comparison with EU standardization case law. As it will be explained, direct evidence of anticompetitive intent is not expressly a substantive requirement for an Article 102 TFEU violation.

Before delving into the intentional element, however, it seems still necessary to further explore the dynamics of hold-up and any obstacles it may create for standardization. To this end, the next sections will focus on the concerns arising in *Unocal*, *Rambus* and *Qualcomm*. Each of these disputes reveals different peculiarities of the US legal system which justify a case-by-case approach in the examination of the most relevant issues.

3.1.2 *UNOCAL*'S SUBVERSION OF A GOVERNMENTAL BODY

A violation of Section 5 of the Federal Trade Commission Act was also alleged in *Union Oil Company of California* (*Unocal*), which represented another challenge for the US *de jure* standards development process.[36]

Unlike *Dell*, *Rambus* and *Qualcomm*, *Unocal* did not concern a private but a governmental standard-setting body, the California Air Resources Board (CARB). The Commission accused the company of having subverted the regulatory standard-setting process of CARB. The latter had started proceedings to elaborate legal rules and standards regulating the composition of low-emissions reformulated gasoline.[37] Unocal was actively involved in the process. However, as stated by the complaint counsel, it adopted a misleading behavior towards the governmental body and the other participants by affirming that its emissions research results were not covered by any rights but were in the public domain. In other words, Unocal did not disclose that it had pending patent claims on these research results and did not reveal its intention to enforce the proprietary interests. The behavior led Unocal to acquire market power in the related market illegitimately.[38]

36 *Union Oil Company of California*, Case n. 9305, Federal Trade Commission (2004).

37 Reformulated gasoline was required by the Environmental Protection Agency (EPA) in many metropolitan areas of the United States to reduce urban smog caused by automobile emissions.

38 *Union Oil Company* (n 36), Complaint at § 2. In the US, it is worth noting, most pending patent applications are published 18 months after filing, and all of them become public records once the patent is granted.

3.1.2.1 RISK OF SUBSTANTIAL HARM TO CONSUMERS

According to complaint counsel, the firm's misrepresentation led the public body to adopt a formula that infringed its patents, on which Unocal then sought royalties.[39] Had Unocal disclosed the existence of its pending patents claims, either CARB would have opted for alternatives or Unocal would have been able to enforce its proprietary interests only under less attractive economic terms.[40] Therefore, in the complaint counsel's view, Unocal's false and misleading statements, on which CARB and the other members reasonably and detrimentally relied, led to harmful competition and conferred on it monopoly power.[41] In addition, Unocal's patent ambush was harmful to both competition and consumers in the related downstream market.[42] Indeed, Unocal's enforcement of its patent portfolio would have caused substantial consumer injury.[43] Companies producing CARB gasoline would have been required to pay royalties to the firm, the bulk of which would have been later passed on to consumers in the form of wild gasoline price fluctuations and supply uncertainties.[44] The conduct, then, would have led to decreased incentives to produce and supply low-emissions reformulated gasoline. On the effects these cost fluctuations would have had on consumers, a governmental agency importantly noted that "[c]onsumer welfare is the goal of antitrust enforcement across all industries"; and further added, "even small price increases can strain the budgets of many consumers [...] and of small business, and, as a result, can have a direct and lasting impact on the entire economy."[45]

3.1.2.2 WEAK ATTEMPT AT DEFENSE

On the defense side, Unocal first denied the substantive allegations of the complaint by counter-arguing that the industry considered its research results to be so valuable that they would have been standardized even in case of early disclosure.[46] The company also claimed that CARB may have viewed Unocal's patents enforceability as too uncertain, thus it would have never adopted different regulations and standards on knowledge that the firm had merely lodged an application for a patent.[47] These observations may potentially present interesting points in support of the company's defensive line. However, if the arguments were valid,

39 Ibid., at §§ 1–6.
40 Ibid., at § 90.
41 Ibid., at § 76.
42 Ibid.
43 Ibid., at §§ 97–98.
44 *Union Oil Company of California*, FTC Docket n. 9305, Statement of the Commission (2 August 2005). The FTC, in particular, estimated that Unocal's enforcement of these patents could potentially lead to over $500 million of additional consumer costs per year.
45 See US Congress Research Service, "Midwest Gasoline Prices: a Review of Recent Market Developments" (June 2000).
46 *Union Oil Company of California*, FTC Docket n. 9305, Respondent's Post-Trial Brief (14 March 2005), at 257 § IV.B.2.C.
47 Ibid., at 41 and 102.

it is not clear why Unocal decided to adopt the misleading strategy, intentionally hiding the existence of its IPRs.[48]

On a further ground, although admitting that certain claims of its pending applications had been allowed by the US Patent Office, Unocal added that it had no duty to disclose to CARB whether it had IPR or whether it would assert these rights.[49] At all times, it argued, it acted in accordance to a business justification.[50] However, these arguments – to be examined under a different perspective in *Rambus* – do not seem completely convincing, especially if considered in the context of a public body which required a cooperative attitude among the members. Unocal did not simply refuse to reveal the existence of its IPRs, it actively misled CARB despite a clear duty to disclose.

3.1.2.3 ENACTMENT OF THE CONSENT ORDER

An administrative law judge rejected the complaint on different procedural grounds.[51] Besides citing jurisdictional factors, it applied the *Noerr-Pennington* doctrine[52] and claimed that Unocal's conduct had to be granted antitrust immunity as it consisted in indirect petitioning to the government aimed at influencing the passage or enforcement of law. However, the Federal Trade Commission reaffirmed its jurisdiction over the issues of the dispute and rejected the antitrust immunity motion.[53] The case was finally closed with a consent order in which the firm – as in the *Dell* case – agreed to cease enforcement of its patents.[54]

3.1.2.4 CORE PRINCIPLES OF THE DISPUTE

Unocal undoubtedly deserves attention as it made clear, in line with the reasoning developed in *Dell*, the FTC's intention to scrutinize carefully the activities of SSOs. Even in the context of governmental actions, their participants may implement potentially anticompetitive conduct, based upon an intentional failure to disclose the existence of IPRs on which a proposed standard may read on. These practices, as the authority recognized, may be detrimental to the welfare of consumers, who are the true victims of licensing cost increases. However, one could wonder whether the Federal Trade Commission in *Unocal* would have reached the same conclusions had CARB policy been more ambiguous on its principles and

48 J. Farrell, J. Hayes, C. Shapiro and T. Sullivan, "Standard Setting, Patents, and Hold-Up" (2007) 74 *Antitrust Law Journal* 655.

49 *Union Oil Company of California*, FTC Docket n. 9305, Respondent's Reply (2 April 2003), at 9.

50 Ibid., at 64.

51 *Union Oil Company of California*, FTC Docket n. 9305, Initial Decision of the Federal Trade Commission's Administrative Law Judge (25 November 2003).

52 See *Eastern RR. Presidents Conference v Noerr Motor Freight*, 365 US 127 (1961); and *United Mine Workers v Pennington*, 381 US 657 (1965). Here, the Supreme Court held that the First Amendment right to petition the government provides a qualified immunity from antitrust liability.

53 *Union Oil Company* (n 36).

54 *Union Oil Company of California*, FTC Docket n. 9305, Consent Order (2005).

corresponding duties. In other words, it could be questioned whether a legitimate business justification would have been granted in case of unclear policy rules. The answer is in the analysis of the *Rambus* case, which provided interesting, albeit often controversial, observations on the boundaries between SSO functions and members' duties.

3.1.3 Rambus*: a tale of standards in the standard*

The case against the semiconductor designer Rambus for allegedly subverting the JEDEC (Joint Electron Device Engineering Council), by means of an alleged anticompetitive patent ambush, highlights several difficult issues that firms may face when they join SSO processes. As a more sophisticated and complex sequel to the Commission's actions against Dell and Unocal, *Rambus* gained considerable attention for it is undoubtedly the most dramatic example of the tension between the IPRs of patent owners who take part in SSOs, on the one hand, and the pro-competitive and innovation enhancing character of private standard-setting bodies, on the other.[55] After a short synopsis of the factual allegations, the section will use the case as a platform to discuss whether the conduct examined should be considered legitimate, exclusionary or merely deceptive, and for identifying an optimal standard of conduct in an SSO context.[56]

3.1.3.1 JEDEC POLICY AND GOALS: AT THE ORIGINS OF THE DISPUTE

Rambus designed, licensed and marketed to downstream manufacturers high-speed connection dynamic random access memory (DRAM) and synchronous DRAM (SDRAM) technologies, which could be considered as the most common form of semiconductor computer memories (electronic data storage devices) in use in several downstream products. In the course of the 1990s, the company joined JEDEC and withdrew from it a few years later.

JEDEC, in its Manual of Organization and Procedure, established its primary purpose and function in promoting the development and standardization of terms, definition, product characterization, test methods, manufacturing support function and mechanical standards for solid state products.[57] JEDEC had basically a policy of open standards, a policy promoting standards freely available to all industry members or not subject to excessive and unreasonable licensing conditions. To this extent, JEDEC firstly intended to impose on its members a duty to disclose the existence of any IPRs which a standard considered by the organization might read on. Second, in case the technology chosen to be included in a standard was covered by a member's patent, it also included a duty to declare

55 M.C. Naughton and R. Wolfram (n 16) 704.

56 *Rambus Inc.*, Case n. 9302, Federal Trade Commission (2006); *Rambus Inc v Federal Trade Commission*, 522 F3d 456 (C App DC Circuit, 2008); *Federal Trade Commission v Rambus Inc*, 129 S Ct 1318 (2009).

57 *Rambus Inc.*, FTC Docket n. 9302, Initial Administrative Complaint (18 June 2002), at § 14. See also JEDEC, "Manual of Organization and Procedure, JM21-R" (2015) § 1.

whether the company would license the technology under royalty-free or RAND conditions. In case of a refusal of such license conditions, JEDEC did not allow the incorporation of the technology into the proposed standard. However, as better explained in the next sections, the problem lay in the clarity and awareness of these principles by the members of the body.

In two different phases, the JEDEC committee, in charge of the development of memory devices standards, implemented first and second generation SDRAM technology, which accounted in the late 1990s for the large majority of all computer memory applications. In this period of time, Rambus had already obtained a number of patents that, according to the company, covered the SDRAM technology included in the JEDEC standard.[58] As a result, Rambus informed all manufacturers using the standardized technology that their products were infringing Rambus's patent rights. Consequently, the company demanded royalties, which were finally obtained for about half of the total worldwide production of SDRAM technology.

The litigation began when Rambus sued several undertakings for having refused to pay the royalties demanded.[59] Almost in parallel with private litigation, the Federal Trade Commission opened proceedings on the conduct of the microchip designer, giving rise to one of the most interesting and controversial investigations in the field of US standardization.

3.1.3.2 *RAMBUS* AND THE INITIAL DEBATE

In the belief that government intervention was warranted to protect the broader marketplace, the Commission filed an administrative complaint against Rambus for unfair methods of competition and unfair or deceptive acts or practices under Section 5 of the FTC Act.[60] The complaint, initially dismissed by an administrative law judge, led the authority to condemn Rambus in its 2006 decision, which eventually limited the theory of liability under Section 2 of the Sherman Act.[61] The FTC's decision, however, was finally overturned two years later by the US Court of Appeals, which sided with Rambus in holding that the behavior constituted neither monopolization nor attempted monopolization.[62]

58 Rambus' IPRs, in particular, covered SDRAM and DDR (Double Data Rate) SDRAM technologies.

59 See, *inter alia*, *Rambus Inc v Hynix Semiconductor*, Case n. C 05-00334 RMW, US Dist. LEXIS 60838 (ND California, 2008); *Hynix Semiconductor v Rambus Inc.*, Case n. CV-00-20905 RMW, 2006 WL 2038357 (ND California, 2006); *Rambus Inc v Samsung Electronics*, Case n. CV-05-02298 RMW (ND California, 2005); *Samsung Electronics v Rambus Inc.*, 439 F Supp 2d 524 (ED Virginia, 2006); *Rambus Inc v Micron Technology*, Case n. C 06-00244 RMW (ND California, 2006); *Micron Technology v Rambus Inc*, Case n. 3:06-CV-00132-REP (ED Virginia, 2006); *Micron Technology v Rambus Inc.*, 189 F Supp 2d 201 (D Delaware, 2002); *Rambus Inc v Infineon Technologies*, 164 F Supp 2d 743 (ED Virginia, 2001); *Rambus Inc v Infineon Technologies*, 318 F3d 1081 (C App Federal Circuit, 2003); *Rambus Inc v Infineon Technologies*, 124 US 227 (2003).

60 *Rambus* (n 57).

61 *Rambus Inc*, Case n. 9302, Federal Trade Commission (2006).

62 *Rambus Inc v FTC*, 522 F3d 456 (C App DC Circuit, 2008). The Court of Appeals' findings were not contested by the Supreme Court, which rejected the request to review the case.

3.1.3.2.1 Initial administrative complaint The initial administrative complaint was one of the longest, most detailed complaints in the Commission's history. Distilled to its essence, it alleged that the US microchip designer had engaged in monopolization, attempted monopolization and unfair methods of competition by intentionally subverting JEDEC standard-setting process in order to ensure that the standardized technology would read on Rambus's IPR. Rambus's deceptive conduct, as the Commission observed, consisted of hiding the existence of both its issued and pending essential patent applications, and led the company to deliberately manipulate an otherwise open-standard, pro-competitive and objective process. As a consequence, JEDEC finally functioned as a vehicle that conferred on Rambus monopoly power and the opportunity to harm competition and consumers.[63]

As suggested in the complaint, a company's conscious subversion of the objectives of a standard setting body combined with the requisite harm to competition can trigger antitrust exposure.[64] Moreover, it was also established that literal compliance by Rambus with the SSO's rules on disclosure could not be interpreted as a valid defense. On this specific aspect, complaint counsel held that even if there was no technical violation of JEDEC disclosure rules, this fact alone would not permit Rambus to escape antitrust liability. This can only be because Rambus apparently failed to fulfill a general good faith duty.

The main issue, therefore, did not concern the question on whether the US firm's conduct technically violated the SSO's disclosure rules. It rather concerned the broader question of whether the behavior infringed an obligation of good faith and fair dealing, and whether such violation could ground a claim for monopolization and unfair competition.[65] In the view of complaint counsel, Rambus breached this second broader duty. The alleged existence of such a general duty, stepping beyond the strict limits of JEDEC rules, led complaint counsel to conclude that the US firm should be charged for deception and misrepresentation, in light of both its silence and the affirmative false statements. In relation to this general good faith duty, different members had testified in a deposition that there was a strong expectation of good faith among them, in order to reach JEDEC's main goal of developing open standards.[66]

Nevertheless, complaint counsel also argued that the US firm infringed specific JEDEC rules, according to which standardization activities should have not been misused to exclude competitors.[67] Second, it was noted that Rambus infringed those JEDEC principles established to promote the incorporation of free non-

63 *Rambus Inc*, FTC Docket n. 9302, Complaint Counsel Opposition to Summary Decision, at 11.

64 Ibid., at 35.

65 See also *Allied Tube* (n 33). In this case, the court noted that, although the defendant "did not violate any rules of the Association," it "nonetheless did subvert the consensus standard-making process of the Association … at least partially motivated by the desire to lessen competition"; it also held that "the antitrust validity of these efforts is not established, without more, by defendant's literal compliance with the rules." The case concerned the issue of "vote stacking," where some SSO members recruited other participants to vote in favour of their interests.

66 *Rambus* (n 63), at 18.

67 Ibid., at 24.

proprietary standards or the adoption of proprietary standards to be licensed for free or under RAND terms.[68] The objective of Rambus's conduct was identified in the illegitimate achievement of monopoly power. In light of these considerations, complaint counsel requested an order preventing Rambus from enforcing against producers and users of SDRAM technology any rights deriving from the applications filed before the company's withdrawal from JEDEC.[69]

3.1.3.2.2 Rambus's defense On the defense side, Rambus did not contest its monopolistic position, but argued instead that it had promptly informed JEDEC that it would not discuss the existence of issued and pending patent applications at the SSO's meetings. It claimed that complaint counsel had failed to show that other JEDEC participants were relying on the firm's misrepresentations and omissions. Rather, as it was noted, Rambus had fairly warned them about its position and such warning had been ignored. The US firm further questioned the appropriateness of imposing liability in case the defendant fully complied with the SSO's policy. Accordingly, no charge for deception and misrepresentation against Rambus should have been ever made.[70]

On the existence of a disclosure duty, Rambus further contended that, even if it was required to disclose limited information (e.g., on the mere existence of patent applications), such minimal disclosure would have never given JEDEC enough information to appraise its relevance in relation to the standard. On the other hand, as it was argued, limited disclosure could still have represented an advantage for competitors, giving them the possibility to jeopardize Rambus's IP strategy.[71] In the analysis of this issue, Lemley has addressed the question of whether there is a degree of disclosure that may satisfy both the trade secret of a patent applicant and the duty to disclose as a SSO's member.[72] The question is whether, assuming a company discloses only the existence and scope of its application but not the technical know-how, such company would still be able to protect the information as trade secret.

Rambus's observations (which relate to the question) may sound contradictory or at least unclear, in so far as they mean that information disclosed in the SSO context could represent an advantage for the strategy of competitors, but could never be properly assessed by the SSO in relation to the proposed technology. It is not clear, in particular, the reason why a standards institute, unlike competing firms, would not be able to evaluate the importance and scope of information that

68 Ibid.

69 *Rambus* (n 57).

70 *Rambus Inc*, FTC Docket n. 9302, Memorandum in Support of *Rambus*'s Motion for Summary Decision (28 February 2003), at 37. As Rambus remarked, before withdrawing from JEDEC, it had sent a letter to the SSO stating that "[o]ur presence or silence at committee meetings does not constitute an endorsement of any proposal under the committee's consideration nor does it make any statement regarding potential infringement of Rambus' intellectual property."

71 *Rambus Inc*, FTC Docket n. 9302, Trial Brief of Respondent *Rambus* (22 April 2003), at 38–39.

72 M.A. Lemley, "Intellectual Property Rights and Standard-Setting Organizations" (2002) 90 *California Law Review* 1889. See also Chapter 3 section 4.2.

could bring an advantage to rivals when disclosed. It cannot be excluded that JEDEC may have been able to identify, in the limited IPRs details provided by Rambus, a threat to the SSO process, and may have consequently shifted to the proposal of a different technology to ensure the adoption of a non-proprietary standard.

3.1.3.3 DECISION OF THE COMMISSION

The arguments of Rambus, supported by the administrative law judge, were rejected in the final Commission's decision which found Rambus guilty of monopolization under Section 2 of the Sherman Act.[73] The authority found that the US microchip designer had unlawfully monopolized various technology markets through the deliberate manipulation of a standard-setting process. Rambus, as it said, "engaged in exclusionary conduct that significantly contributed to its acquisition of monopoly power in four related markets."[74]

In reaching its decision, the Commission contested the arguments proposed by the administrative law judge[75] and Rambus in the course of the proceedings. The authority rejected the judge's argument that complaint counsel had failed to demonstrate both the existence of a JEDEC disclosure duty and a valid legal theory based on Section 5 of the FTC Act. It observed that "[t]he complaint in this case alleged not just a breach of a duty to disclose under JEDEC rules, but a course of conduct that was materially deceptive under all of the circumstances in which the standard setting occurred."[76]

3.1.3.3.1 Meaning of JEDEC rules The Commission, then, contested the judge's assumption that JEDEC rules were unclear and ambiguous. The judge, in particular, had stated that JEDEC had not properly clarified the content of its policy-related duties and had consequently failed to create any expectations in relation to potential contrasts between the standard and the members' IPRs.[77] This position was ultimately rejected by the authority, which counter-argued that "JEDEC's policies … and practices, considered as a whole, gave JEDEC's members reason to believe the standard-setting process would be cooperative and free from deceptive conduct."[78] By failing to disclose its patents, it added, Rambus had intentionally subverted JEDEC policy and secured monopolies in four technology markets.[79] These opposite views clearly highlight a possible friction between the alleged expectations of SSO members and the IPRs owners' interests. This leads to the question whether the general expectations of the participants should prevail over

73 *Rambus* (n 61).
74 Ibid., at 118–119.
75 *Rambus Inc.*, FTC Docket n. 9302, Initial Decision of the Administrative Law Judges (17 February 2004), slip opinion.
76 *Rambus* (n 61), at 51.
77 *Rambus* (n 75), at 258.
78 *Rambus* (n 61), at 52.
79 I.e., latency, burst length, data acceleration and clock synchronization technology markets.

the need to apply only clear rules properly made known. Perhaps, more reasonably, it could be argued that any optimal balance should not disregard the need to set clear policy frameworks. The general expectations of the members should rely on the clear meaning of written policy principles properly disclosed. An ambiguous policy may mislead as to the duties members are expected to respect, and may finally discourage innovators' interest in standards. Only when a company subscribes to specific policy duties, a regime of liability should then prevail over the need to preserve patentees' rights.[80] From this perspective, it seems that the Commission's approach was rather rigid and unpersuasive.

3.1.3.3.2 Exclusionary and deceptive conduct On a further ground, the Commission shed light on the boundaries between merely deceptive and exclusionary behaviors. On this issue, there is some support for the notion that deceptive conduct can be a proper foundation for liability under Section 2 of the Sherman Act.[81] In this respect, the FTC held that the US firm's failure to disclose amounted to deception qualifying as exclusionary conduct under Section 2. It also appraised the behavior as deceptive under Section 5 of the FTC Act. In particular, the authority observed that standard-setting bodies may opt not to require members' disclosure of patent applications. However, if a disclosure policy is adopted, non-disclosure "followed by adoption of a standard incorporating the intellectual property, and royalty demands against those practicing the standard – may be considered a material omission and may constitute deceptive conduct under Section 5."[82]

Nevertheless, it also noted that, unlike deception under Section 5, Section 2 requires conduct to have been intentional and to have hindered competition. The authority found that Rambus's deceptive behavior met both of the criteria. Thus, as the FTC observed, "[w]hatever the potential breadth of Section 5 of the FTC Act in these circumstances, [the] analysis in this opinion rests on the traditional criteria for evaluating allegations of monopolization under Section 2 of the Sherman Act."[83]

The judge's argument that the conduct could not be considered exclusionary and deceptive due to a legitimate business justification was rejected.[84] As the FTC explained, if protecting trade secrets was critical to Rambus and given the latter had clear knowledge of the disclosure duty, it was legitimate to question why the company did not refrain earlier from participating in JEDEC.[85] Rambus was not able to explain how its non-disclosure policy could be pro-competitive in a context

80 On a "dynamic liability rule," see J.H. Park, *Patents and Industry Standards* (Edward Elgar, Cheltenham 2010) 204.

81 M.S. Royall, "Standard Setting and Exclusionary Conduct: The Role of Antitrust in Policing Unilateral Abuses of Standard-Setting Processes" (2003–2004) 18 *Antitrust* 46. As Royall argues, "there is precedent for imposing antitrust liability for deceptive acts that cause harm to the competitive process."

82 *Rambus* (n 61), at 34.

83 Ibid., at 30.

84 *Rambus* (n 75), at 287–291.

85 *Rambus* (n 61), at 69.

of cooperation among participants. Rather, the aim and the final effect were "to manipulate the standard setting process at JEDEC and gain market power."[86] In any event, in the FTC's view, the business justification could have not outweighed the anticompetitive effects.[87]

However, these arguments do not seem completely convincing. First, the question is not whether Rambus had the right to protect its business secrets and to amend its patent applications. The question instead is whether Rambus had the right to do so in the described context, as member of a body promoting open standards on a cooperative basis. It needs to be assessed whether the business justification could be interpreted as a mere pretext for the exclusionary refusal to disclose information, or as the right to protect legitimate trade secrets. The answer, of course, depends on whether Rambus could be entitled to enjoy these rights after having agreed to abide by JEDEC rules. This, in turn, depends on whether these rules were clear and properly made known to the participants.[88]

The prevalence of one view over the other could also depend on the degree of importance given to the aims of protecting a standard-setting process or the patentee's interests in standard setting. For the sake of clarity, it is possible or likely that Rambus may have unfairly exploited to its advantage the ambiguity of JEDEC rules. Nonetheless, the existence of clear policy principles seems to be the first crucial step for effectively implementing any regulation. From a further point of view, the existence of exclusionary effects – required for an infringement of Section 2 – was not certain. In this sense, the Commission was unable to prove that JEDEC would have chosen an alternative standard had it known about Rambus's patents. For these reasons, the authority's approach raises more than a doubt.

3.1.3.3.3 Remedy The Commission did not immediately establish the appropriate remedy for Rambus's infringement. The parties were allowed to brief their respective opinions in relation to remedy. To this end, the FTC emphasized its interest in the parties' views regarding the adoption of reasonable royalty rates. In the final order, it decided on worldwide non-exclusive compulsory licensing, and set the royalty rates Rambus could charge to the firms manufacturing and using its technology.[89] In particular, the FTC did not impose on Rambus royalty-free conditions, as there was insufficient evidence that JEDEC would have opted for alternative technologies had Rambus disclosed its patents. It rather ordered Rambus to license at reasonable royalty rates, in accordance to what the

86 Ibid., at 70–71.

87 The FTC, hence, rejected also the judge's opinion (supported by *Aspen Skiing v Aspen Highlands Skiing*, 472 US 585 (1985)) according to which a legitimate business justification trumps any further analysis on potential anticompetitive effects.

88 See *Image Technical v Eastman Kodak*, 125 F3d 1995 (C App 9th Circuit, 1997), where it was held that a patent-based refusal to deal is presumptively legal but rebuttable by evidence of pretext. On the importance to set clear policy regulations for the SSOs participants, see also C. Hardee, "Single-firm opportunism and the FTC's Rambus defeat: implications for Section 2 of the Sherman Act" (2010) 18 *Texas Intellectual Property Law Journal* 97.

89 *Rambus Inc*, FTC Docket n. 9302, Opinion of the Commission on Remedy (5 February 2007).

Commission believed would have resulted from negotiations with manufacturers before JEDEC's selection.[90] In this respect, the authority arbitrarily chose this criterion as the optimal method to define RAND.

3.1.3.3.4 Concluding remarks The decision of the Commission in *Rambus*, which was not binding on the courts, marked the first time that conduct of this nature had ever been held to breach antitrust laws. However, it also demonstrated that the application of antitrust law into standard contexts represents an area of disagreement among courts and scholars. The main outcome of the FTC's analysis is that IPRs owners in SSO processes may easily incur the risk of being held liable under antitrust law. When a duty to disclose is established, regardless of whether such a duty is explicit in the rules or derives from their interpretation, a participant that does not comply with it risks antitrust liability if its IPRs ultimately cover the proposed standard. Even if SSOs do not require disclosure, the Commission established that members "still are not free to lie or to make affirmatively misleading representations ... [W]hether the SSO requires disclosure should be judged not only by the letter of its rules, but also on how the rules are interpreted by its members ... ".[91] At the same time, the whole procedure before the FTC highlighted the need to set forth rules that clearly specify the duties of the participants. In the absence of such clear principles in the SSOs' manuals, room for ambiguity exists. Such ambiguity may lead, in the Commission's view, to imply an affirmative duty to disclose. The severity of the enforcer's approach, some authors argued, could be in theory interpreted as an attempt of using antitrust-based legal theories for filling the gaps left by patent remedies.[92]

However, the decision seems to have ignored the risk of negative effects on the willingness of patentees to participate in standard setting. Firms, indeed, may decide not to participate in the process in order to avoid antitrust liability, and may rather opt to seek enforcement of their patents once the standard has been adopted. This is the main risk of an approach that values the protection of standardization processes more than the need to ensure that clear and precise policy rules are properly made known to all members. The Commission rejected Rambus's arguments on the ground of the general interpretation given to those rules and on the basis of the expectations the other members had in the standard-setting process. It consequently opted for a rigid approach, and disregarded the cited consequence of discouraging innovators' participation in standard setting. The approach developed by the FTC, however, does not seem to define the optimal balance between patentees' interests and SSO objectives.

90 Ibid., at 16–25. The FTC's order limited Rambus's royalties for three years to 0.25% for JEDEC-compliant SDRAM and 0.5% for JEDEC-compliant DDR (Double Data Rate) SDRAM. After that period, it forbade any fee collection. See H.J. Singer and K. Smith, "What Does An Economist Have to Say About the Calculation of Reasonable Royalties?" (2009) 14 *Intellectual Property Law Bulletin* 8.

91 *Rambus* (n 61), at 35.

92 M.S. Royall, A. Tessar and A.J. Di Vincenzo, "Deterring Patent Ambush in Standard Setting: Lessons from *Rambus* and *Qualcomm*" (2009) 23(3) *Antitrust* 35. On the enforcement of private law remedies against hold-up behaviors, see also Chapter 7 section 5.

The antitrust enforcer, *inter alia*, did not properly consider also other important issues (e.g. the role of harm to competition) that deserve careful analysis when establishing liability in the context of US standard setting. In addition, although the attempt to define reasonable royalties deserves some merit, it does not yet represent the optimal path to solve licensing disputes. The Commission's analysis could have probably been more persuasive if limited to Section 5 of the FTC Act, which does not require exclusionary effects. Even in this case, the problem of the clarity of SSO regulations should have been addressed. The faults of the Commission's position were highlighted in the judgment of the Court of Appeals, which reflected the need to define a more equilibrated balance in the assessment of these conflicting interests.

3.1.3.4 *RAMBUS* AND THE US COURT OF APPEALS' REVERSAL

The decision of the Federal Trade Commission in *Rambus* was appealed before the US Court of Appeals for the District of Columbia. The court vacated the FTC's decision and held that, even if the US microchip designer had deceived JEDEC's members in order to get higher royalties, Rambus would have not necessarily infringed Section 2 of the Sherman Act.[93]

3.1.3.4.1 Monopoly versus *monopolization* The court first remembered that the mere existence of monopoly does not lead to a violation of the Sherman Act. Besides possession of monopoly power, Section 2 requires the willful acquisition or maintenance of that power, as distinguished from growth or development as consequence of a superior product, business acumen, or historical accident.[94]

Rambus, as it was stated, had not contested that it possessed monopoly power over the four technologies covering the JEDEC standard. It had instead denied that it had engaged in exclusionary conduct and had acquired monopoly power unlawfully. The relevant issue, therefore, concerned the analysis of Rambus's behavior and of its effects in the standard-setting context.[95]

In order to scrutinize the conduct properly, the court identified two relevant principles established in the US jurisprudence which had to be followed.[96] First, to engage in exclusionary conduct, a monopolist's act must have anticompetitive effects; it must harm the competitive process and consumers, while harm to one or more competitors is not sufficient.[97] Second, the antitrust plaintiff bears the burden of proving these anticompetitive effects.[98]

93 *Rambus* (n 62).

94 Ibid., at 11.

95 Ibid., at 12.

96 Ibid., at 12.

97 See *United States v Microsoft*, 253 F3d 34 (C App DC Circuit, 2001), at 58–59. See also *Verizon* (n 3), at 407; *Brooke Group v Brown and Williamson Tobacco*, 509 US 209 (1993), at 224; *Covad Communications v Bell Atlantic*, 398 F3d 666 (C App DC Circuit, 2005), at 672.

98 *Microsoft* (n 97), at 59.

3.1.3.4.2 Alternative scenarios The Commission had previously concluded that, but for Rambus's deceptive behavior, JEDEC would have either excluded Rambus's technology from the standard or made Rambus license under reasonable and non-discriminatory terms.[99] However, according to the Court, the FTC had not proved that one scenario was more likely than the other. It had also failed to demonstrate that the two possible alternative scenarios were anticompetitive.[100]

With respect to the first scenario, the court held that, if JEDEC would have chosen an alternative technology had Rambus disclosed its patents, then Rambus's deceptive conduct would have harmed competition.[101] In these circumstances, the US company would have obtained monopoly power through exclusionary conduct, not because of a "superior product, business acumen, or historical accident."[102] Hence, a declaration of antitrust liability under Section 2 of the Sherman Act would have been legitimate. However, as the court said, the Commission had failed to demonstrate that JEDEC would have opted for alternative standards had it known about Rambus's patents applications. There was not sufficient evidence to exclude that the SSO would have standardized the firm's technology in the absence of deception. What is more, the Commission itself had recognized in its decision that there was insufficient proof to retain this first scenario more likely than the other.[103]

In relation to the second scenario, in which JEDEC would have adopted Rambus's technology even if informed about its patents, the court established that the only consequence of the company's conduct was that it finally obtained higher (non-RAND) licensing fees.[104] As the court interestingly held, "an otherwise lawful monopolist's use of deception simply to obtain higher prices normally has no particular tendency to exclude rivals and thus to diminish competition."[105] The deceptive behavior under these circumstances would have led to higher prices but would have not harmed the competitive process or structure, and hence no violation of the Sherman Act could have ever been found.[106] "Rambus's alleged deception," it was explained, "cannot be said to have an effect on competition in violation of the antitrust laws; JEDEC's loss of an opportunity to seek favourable licensing terms is not as such an antitrust harm."[107] In brief, the Commission had failed to demonstrate that anticompetitive effects could derive from the mere charging of higher fees for the standardized technology. Deceptive behaviors that

99 *Rambus* (n 62), at 9.
100 Ibid., at 12.
101 Ibid., at 13.
102 Ibid.; see also *Verizon* (n 3), at 407.
103 *Rambus* (n 62), at 13.
104 On the argument, see H.J. Hovenkamp, M.A. Lemley and M.D. Janis, *IP and Antitrust: an Analysis of Antitrust Principles Applied to Intellectual Property* (Aspen Law & Business, New York 2008) Ch. 35.5.
105 *Rambus* (n 62), at 15. See also *NYNEX Corp v Discon Inc*, 525 US 128 (1998), at 136-137, where it was held that a lawful monopolist's deception of a regulatory agency to obtain higher prices from consumers was itself not an antitrust violation because the deception did not harm the competitive process.
106 *Rambus* (n 62), at 16–17.
107 Ibid., at 18. See also H.J. Hovenkamp, M.A. Lemley and M.D. Janis (n 104).

raise prices but do not harm competition cannot form the basis for a monopolization claim and are beyond the reach of antitrust laws.[108] Therefore, the court concluded that the Commission's failure to demonstrate that Rambus's conduct was exclusionary ultimately justified the dismissal of the unlawful monopolization claim.[109]

In appraising the merits of the Court of Appeals' position, it should be remembered that US antitrust laws do not consider abusive exploitative conduct. Rather, they are only focused on exclusionary behaviors under Section 2 of the Sherman Act. On the contrary, Article 102 TFEU also refers to exploitative practices, which may take the form of excessive prices.[110] In the EU, however, there is debate over the issue, as difficulties may arise in establishing when a price is low enough to ensure compliance with Article 102. Hence, the question on whether competition authorities are well-suited for price levels analysis seems more than legitimate.[111]

3.1.3.4.3 Importance of clear disclosure policy Finally, the court also expressed its "serious concerns about the strength of the evidence relied on to support some of the Commission's crucial findings" regarding JEDEC disclosure policy.[112]

It was held, in this context, that JEDEC disclosure rules "suffered from a staggering lack of defining details."[113] The ambiguity, in particular, regarded the duty to disclose both issued or pending patent applications and un-filed work in progress on potential amendments to those patent applications. Based on these observations, the court held that the Commission had taken an aggressive interpretation of rather weak evidence.[114] It thus notably recognized the need to rely on clearer regulations, to avoid the risk of ambiguous duties for SSO members. The uncertainty on policy rules could discourage participation of patentees to SSO activities, and could finally lead to an inefficient outcome of the whole standardization process. From the court's comments, it follows that it could be more difficult to prove deception without reference to clear provisions.

3.1.3.5 CONCLUSIVE REMARKS ON *RAMBUS*

The Federal Trade Commission has usually cultivated a strong role for enforcement against conduct undermining a standard-setting process, on the ground of alleged harm to competition and consumers. In *Rambus*, however, the FTC has not given much relevance to the ambiguities of JEDEC policy rules, as the

108 *Rambus* (n 62), at 14.

109 Ibid., at 19.

110 Article 102(a), Treaty on the Functioning of the European Union (TFEU), OJ [2010] C 83/89.

111 On the argument, see also Chapter 4 section 4.3 and Chapter 7 section 6.1.

112 *Rambus* (n 62), at 19.

113 Ibid., at 22. See also *Rambus Inc v Infineon Technologies*, 318 F3d 1081 (C App Federal Circuit, 2003).

114 *Rambus* (n 62), at 23. The Court of Appeals' observations were not challenged by the US Supreme Court (see *Federal Trade Commission v Rambus Inc*, 129 S Ct 1318 (2009)), which denied the FTC's "writ of certiorari."

general understanding of the members and their expectation led to presume the existence of a duty to search and disclose potentially conflicting IPRs. The Court of Appeals, instead, seems to have better defined the correct balance in assessing conflicts in standard setting. The balance, as importantly noted, should properly take into consideration the need for SSOs' participants of clear policy rules, in order to incentivize their participation to standardization processes. These observations undoubtedly presuppose that the duties to search, disclose and license IPRs should not be usually imposed on IPRs owners out of the SSO contexts. Undertakings may otherwise face the risk to be subject to unexpected restrictive conditions that would undermine their will to further developing innovative technologies. The ultimate outcome would be detrimental to dynamic efficiencies and, consequently, consumer choice and welfare. Consumers, indeed, may benefit not only when prices are low, but also when new products of better quality are launched in the market. On these grounds, therefore, it is reasonable to believe that a non-optimal balance between the pursuit of SSO objectives and the protection of IPRs owners' interests may well determine considerable welfare losses.

The importance of striking a better balance in SSO legal frameworks is all the more evident when considering a further scenario. A rigid approach, as it has been held, would likely lead a patent owner to reject participation to standard setting. This notwithstanding, the IPRs owner may still resort to a court and try to obtain an injunction for patent infringement once the standard has been selected. In these circumstances, therefore, the patent owner may attempt to enforce its rights, facing a lower risk to be found liable under antitrust law. Such a consequence would certainly undermine the work and efforts that these organizations make to enhance dynamic efficiency and societal growth. Hence, there is a need to strike a balance which may effectively attract innovators' participation in standard setting.

Of course, the setting of a balanced legal framework which clearly defines the scope of the members' duties does not eliminate the need to assess properly other important aspects. The court confirmed that, besides conduct, the firms' intention must be examined to establish antitrust liability. The existence of anticompetitive effects plays a crucial role, as well as the causal link between the conduct and the effects. All these issues will be examined in separate sections.

In conclusion, there is certainly some merit in the Court of Appeals' analysis, especially when compared to the Commission's line of reasoning. This notwithstanding, the court in *Rambus* seems to have underestimated a fundamental aspect. It has not paid sufficient attention to the faults of a (F)RAND licensing model in SSO regulations. Neither the authority nor the Court of Appeals have ever assessed the risks that such a model may entail, but have probably presumed that (F)RAND could represent a proper balance between IPRs owners' and licensees' interests. This was perhaps due to the unwillingness to examine in depth the effectiveness of alternative licensing models. Nevertheless, striking the proper balance between SSO goals and patentees' aims on consistent rewards necessarily implies the need to define the optimal licensing framework. Chapter 7 will be devoted to this important objective.

3.2 Breach of (F)RAND commitments

The second conduct deserving careful scrutiny consists of the mere breach of (F)RAND conditions by a firm whose technology has been incorporated in the standard. As was clarified in Chapter 4, the firm owning the selected technology may decide, having disclosed the existence of its rights and accepted the licensing policy, to breach that agreement and subject the grant of IPR licenses to the payment of supra-competitive royalties. Should the mere breach of licensing terms be considered as an anticompetitive conduct, or should the behavior be interpreted as legitimate? It could be argued that, if IPRs owners are allowed to demand *ex post* any royalty they want, a (F)RAND model would be deprived of its alleged function of protecting licensees from excessive prices. The risk is that the higher fees charged by the licensor may be passed down by the licensee, to the ultimate detriment of consumers.[115]

As attested by *Negotiated Data Solutions*,[116] a similar problem may arise where the buyer of another firm's IP portfolio breaches the promise previously made by the seller to license under specified prices in a standard-setting context. Here, the FTC remarked the need to respect any promise previously made by a seller on the licensing terms of essential IPRs. This may suggest that deception may not always be necessary to apply Section 5 to a conduct undermining the whole process. Therefore, the rule established in *Negotiated Data Solutions* could be interpreted as an important deviation from prior hold-up enforcement actions in *Dell*, *Unocal* and *Rambus*, where deception was instead required.

In US jurisprudence, *Qualcomm* can be considered as the most important case on the mere breach of FRAND licensing terms. The following sections are devoted to a better understanding of the courts' line of reasoning, and to assess whether and how the principles expressed therein may be reconciled with the early jurisprudence.[117]

115 On the breach of (F)RAND terms, see for instance *Motorola Inc v Rockwell International*, Case n. 95-575-SLR (D. Delaware, 1995); and *Microsoft v Motorola Inc*, US Dist. LEXIS 146517 (WD Washington, 2012). Motorola has also been recently involved in different patent disputes against the IT giant Apple, in both the United States and the EU.

116 *Negotiated Data Solutions LLC*, FTC Case n. 0510094 (2008). On the analysis of the case, see M.S. Royall and A.J. Di Vincenzo, "The FTC's *N-Data* Consent Order: A Missed Opportunity to Clarify Antitrust in Standard Setting" (2008) *Antitrust* 83.

117 *Inter alia*, see *Townshend v Rockwell International*, 55 USPQ 2d 1011 (ND California, 2000). This case, however, presents some peculiarities, since the patent holder could be legitimately exculpated as it disclosed its proposed (RAND) licensing terms in advance. The court recognized that the SSO (ITU) "was satisfied that the proposed terms submitted by 3Com evidenced willingness by 3Com to negotiate non-discriminatory, fair and reasonable terms" (at 1018). Given the absence of any royalty increase after the adoption of the standard, the court rejected the *ex post* licensing challenge that those terms were unfair.

3.2.1 Litigation in Qualcomm

Qualcomm[118] confirmed that standardization is neither a neutral nor a peaceful process. The case represented another example of the judicial uncertainty that has characterized the resolution of disputes related to SSO activities. Important questions were posed, regarding whether a patent holder's deceptive conduct, consisting in the mere breach of a FRAND promise, may be condemned under antitrust laws.

After a brief introduction to the facts of the case, the section will consider the legal arguments developed by the District Court and the US Court of Appeals that dealt with Qualcomm's behavior.

3.2.1.1 ANALYSIS OF THE COMPANY'S BEHAVIOR

The case started when Broadcom, a company active in the mobile phone industry, sued Qualcomm alleging that, by its intentional deception of private standard-setting bodies, the latter had monopolized certain markets for cellular telephone technology and components.[119] The market involved in the case concerned mobile wireless telephony, where two different non-interoperable technology paths were in widespread use: the CDMA and GSM technologies.[120] The standard used in the GSM path network was the third generation standard known as the "Universal Mobile Telecommunications System (UMTS) Standard," developed by the European Telecommunications Standards Institute (ETSI). Some of the technologies included by the SSO in the UMTS standard were supplied by Qualcomm, which held IPRs over them.[121]

In order to avoid the risk that members could subvert and manipulate the standard-setting process by exerting illegitimate control over the implementation of a standard, ETSI required participants to undertake FRAND commitments. Hence Qualcomm, as a member of ETSI, had committed to its licensing policy by accepting fair reasonable and non-discriminatory terms.

Broadcom, however, lodged a complaint before the US District Court. It alleged that Qualcomm, having agreed to abide by the ETSI licensing policy and having succeeded in the selection of the standard, breached that agreement

118 *Broadcom v Qualcomm*, US Dist LEXIS 62090 (D New Jersey, 2006); *Broadcom v Qualcomm*, 501 F3d 297 (C App 3rd Circuit, 2007). Qualcomm has also been involved in several other cases (US, EU and China), concerning patent infringements and antitrust violations – see for instance the *Nokia v Qualcomm* saga, finally settled in 2008. Further, in a different *Broadcom/Qualcomm* dispute, the Federal Circuit applied the doctrine of implied waiver, charged Qualcomm for "ambushing" the standards institute JVT and barred it from enforcing its IPRs (*Qualcomm* (n 14)).

119 The cellular telephone market is characterized by the use of different chipsets, whose function is to allow transmission of information to and from the wireless network. Industry-wide standards are necessary in order to facilitate interoperability between all the components.

120 CDMA and GSM stand respectively for "code division multiple access" and "global system for mobility." Cellular telephone service providers operate under one technology or the other.

121 Qualcomm's technology was called Wide-band CDMA. It was said to be essential to the practice of the standard. The WCDMA standard took over three years to develop.

and started licensing under non-FRAND conditions. Therefore, according to the plaintiff, the unlawful acquisition of monopoly power through deception violated the Sherman Act. In particular, Qualcomm's deceptive conduct consisted of a material omission, which misled ETSI and its members as to its real intention to charge supra-competitive prices.[122] What is more, Broadcom alleged that Qualcomm had ignored its FRAND commitments to ETSI also by charging higher royalties to competitors and customers using chipsets not directly manufactured by Qualcomm. This strategy, as Broadcom alleged, was supposed to be part of Qualcomm's business policy aiming at monopolistic power in the UMTS chipset market. The latter, it was argued, could represent a threat to the existing monopoly Qualcomm had in the CDMA chipset market.[123] Finally, Broadcom claimed that Qualcomm was maintaining its monopoly in the markets for 3G CDMA technology and chipsets in violation of the Sherman Act as: (a) most producers of UMTS mobiles were subject to Qualcomm's monopoly power in the CDMA markets; (b) Qualcomm was using leverage over customers in the CDMA markets to destroy the UMTS chipset business; and (c) Broadcom, as an innovator in WCDMA technology and UMTS chipsets, was suffering injury.[124]

In brief, Qualcomm's conduct was interpreted as able to compromise the SSO's reputation, credibility and ability to generate coalitions of intents. It was seen as a threat to the fragile equilibrium on which standardization was based.

3.2.1.2 *QUALCOMM* AND THE JUDICIAL APPROACH

The case was first decided by the District Court of New Jersey[125] and further appealed before the US Court of Appeals for the Third Circuit.[126] The following subsections will delve into the opposite views expressed by the courts. Indeed, while the judge of first instance rejected Broadcom's arguments, the Court of Appeals reversed that decision and joined the complainant's line of reasoning under several aspects.

3.2.1.2.1 Monopolization claim The District Court had dismissed the monopolization claim on the ground that Qualcomm allegedly enjoyed a legally sanctioned monopoly in its patented technology. In the court's view, this had given Qualcomm the right to exclude competition and fix the price for licensing. Similarly, the judge of first instance had further argued that Qualcomm's conduct should not be assessed under antitrust principles, as the adoption of the standard would have, in any event, eliminated competition.[127] The District Court did not consider the role

122 *Broadcom v Qualcomm*, US Dist LEXIS 62090 (D New Jersey, 2006).

123 Qualcomm, it was stated in the complaint, had a 90% share in the market for CDMA-path chipsets; thus, by charging higher royalties in that market, indirectly imposed mobile manufacturers to purchase its UMTS-path chipsets.

124 *Qualcomm* (n 122).

125 Ibid.

126 *Broadcom v Qualcomm*, 501 F3d 297 (C App 3rd Circuit, 2007).

127 *Qualcomm* (n 122), at 21; in the court's view, "[I]t is the SDO's decision to set a standard for

of FRAND as a guarantee for ETSI. Nor did it consider the possibility that ETSI would have chosen non-proprietary technology had it known about Qualcomm's intention. From this perspective, therefore, it seems that the court did not develop a thorough examination of the dynamics of standardization.

The Third Circuit reversed the District Court's judgment. After mentioning the different elements Section 2 requires in order to find an infringement under antitrust law, the Court of Appeals clarified that "unethical and deceptive practices can constitute abuses of administrative or judicial processes that may result in antitrust violations."[128] Private SSOs, as it held, have historically been scrutinized by US courts and federal authorities as they "can be rife with opportunities for anticompetitive activity."[129] At the same time, private standard setting can also advance on several levels the main antitrust goal, the promotion of consumer welfare.[130] This is because standards that ensure the interoperability of goods also enhance the sharing of information among buyers of goods from competing producers, thereby promoting the utility of all goods and developing the overall consumer market.[131] As a consequence, this would allow undertakings to decrease research and development costs and to charge less for the same product. Standards, as the Third Circuit continued, may benefit consumers by reducing the switching costs between competing products and services, thereby promoting competition among manufacturers. They may also enhance competition at an upstream level, as standard setting functions as an incentive for firms to strive and improve technologies in order to be selected. Therefore, the development of a standard "does not eliminate competition among producers but, rather, moves the focus away from the development of potential standards and toward the development of means for implementing the chosen standard."[132] These efficiencies, by enhancing consumer welfare and competition in the marketplace, demonstrate that standard-setting processes are consistent with the goals of antitrust law.[133]

The Court of Appeals, hence, held that SSOs, which could otherwise be interpreted as unlawful agreements between rivals not to manufacture or distribute

WCDMA technology, not Qualcomm's 'inducement', that results in the absence of competing WCDMA technologies." *Cf.* with the decision in *Townshend* (n 117), where the court said that "given that a patent holder is permitted under the antitrust laws to completely exclude others from practicing his or her technology, the Court finds that 3Com's technology submission of proposed licensing terms with which it was willing to license does not state a violation of the antitrust laws."

128 *Qualcomm* (n 126), at 13 (citing the US case *Allied Tube* (n 33), at 500).

129 *Qualcomm* (n 126) (citing the US case *American Society of Mechanical Engineers v Hydrolevel*, 456 US 556 (1982), at 571; here, it was established that an SSO incurs antitrust liability when it fails to implement procedures for the prevention of anticompetitive misuse of its processes).

130 As held in Chapter 1, in the US there is strong consensus for a consumer welfare standard. See *Reiter v Sonotone,* 442 US 330 (1979), at 343; *Business Electronics v Sharp Electronics*, 485 US 717 (1988), at 723; *Leegin Creative Leather Products v PSKS*, 551 US 877 (2007); *Brooke Group* (n 97).

131 *Qualcomm* (n 126), at 13 (citing the US case *Allied Tube* (n 33), at 506–507).

132 *Qualcomm* (n 126), at 14.

133 See P.E. Areeda and H.J. Hovenkamp, *Antitrust Law: an Analysis of Antitrust Principles and Their Application* (2nd edn, Aspen Publishers, New York 2004).

certain goods, do not seem to infringe *per se* antitrust principles.[134] This does not mean that there are no limits to their activities. Indeed, as it was noted, private standard setting is permitted under antitrust laws as long as it is "conducted in a non-partisan manner offering pro-competitive benefits and in the presence of 'meaningful safeguards' that prevent the standard-setting process from being biased by members with economic interests in stifling product competition."[135] This means that practices undermining the pro-competitive benefits of SSO activities run the risk of being deemed unlawful and sanctioned under antitrust law. In this context, the Third Circuit analyzed the specific risks related to deception. In particular, after a standardized technology has been adopted and the industry has invested significant resources into the standard, the industry itself will find it locked into the technology adopted. In these circumstances, the patent holder may over-exploit its bargaining position and obtain supra-competitive royalties from the industry participants.[136]

ETSI licensing policy had been implemented in order to avoid these risks.[137] The cost and performance characteristics of the competing technologies were factors highly considered in the selection procedure. Qualcomm's deception on the licensing costs granted it an unfair advantage and distorted competition by favoring the adoption of its technology to the detriment of the alternatives.[138] On the basis of these elements, the US Court of Appeals concluded that:

> in a consensus-oriented private standard setting environment, a patent holder's intentionally false promise to license essential proprietary technology on FRAND terms, coupled with an SDO's reliance on that promise when including the technology in a standard, and the patent holder's subsequent breach of that promise, is actionable anticompetitive conduct.[139]

Deceptive conduct which hides the level of royalties a participant intends to charge may harm the competitive process no less than deceptive non-disclosure of IPRs.[140] On the other hand, the District Court had erroneously concluded that

134 See also *Allied Tube* (n 33), at 500–501; and the *Standards Development Organization Advancement Act of 2004*, 15 USC § 4301 (2004).

135 *Qualcomm* (n 126), at 15 (citing, *inter alia, All v Cast Iron Soil Pipe Inst*, 851 F2d 478 (C App 1st Circuit, 1988), at 488).

136 *Qualcomm* (n 126), at 15. See also *Rambus* (n 61), at 2; *Eastman Kodak v Image Technical Services*, 504 US 451 (1992); and *Townshend* (n 117). In *Townshend*, however, the court failed to recognize that standards may confer market power on the incorporated IPR.

137 See D.G. Swanson & W.J. Baumol, "Reasonable and Non-discriminatory (RAND) Royalties, Standards Selection, and Control of Market Power" (2005–2006) 73 *Antitrust Law Journal* 9.

138 See *Qualcomm* (n 126), at 23 (citing the US case *Allied Tube* (n 33), at 501; here it was stated that SSOs need to be free "from being biased by members with economic interests in stifling product competition"); and *Rambus* (n 61) (in the FTC's view, "distorting choices through deception obscures the relative merits of alternatives and prevents the efficient selection of preferred technologies").

139 *Qualcomm* (n 126), at 24.

140 Ibid. (citing *Rambus*, where it was held that "distorting … technology choices and undermining members' ability to protect themselves against patent hold-up … caused harm to competition").

monopoly was "the natural consequence of the standard setting processes, an unsupported factual finding that ignored the possibility of a standard comprised of non-proprietary technologies."[141] It was shown that ETSI would not have adopted Qualcomm's technology had it known about its deceptive intention. With respect to deception, the District Court had even failed to recognize that Qualcomm's FRAND commitment was an essential part of its strategy to win the inclusion of its technology in the standard.[142] For these reasons, the Court of Appeals reversed the decision on the first monopolization claim and rejected the main argument posed by Qualcomm, according to which the reasonableness of its licensing policy was not a subject to scrutiny under antitrust principles.[143]

3.2.1.2.2 Attempted monopolization claim With respect to the second claim, concerning Qualcomm's attempted monopolization in the UMTS chipset market, the judge of first instance had argued that the complaint had not provided sufficient information to enable the court to infer that Qualcomm's conduct was anticompetitive.[144] This interpretation was rejected by the Third Circuit, which remembered that such a claim under Section 2 of the Sherman Act must allege "(1) that the defendant has engaged in predatory or anticompetitive conduct with (2) a specific intent to monopolize and (3) a dangerous probability of achieving monopoly power."[145]

Broadcom had described numerous practices implemented by Qualcomm. The latter, in particular, had a near monopoly in the CDMA chipset market, and was striving to obtain a new monopoly in the UMTS chipsets market. In violation of its FRAND commitments, Qualcomm was charging higher royalties both to those licensees of the WCDMA technology and to those manufacturers who did not use Qualcomm's UMTS chipsets. On the other hand, Qualcomm was providing discounts to mobile manufacturers using only its UMTS chipsets.[146] These practices harmed competition and undermined innovation. The Third Circuit considered the allegations of anticompetitive practices as sufficiently specific to satisfy the first element of an attempted monopolization claim.[147]

Broadcom had also claimed that Qualcomm acted with specific intent to obtain a monopoly in the UMTS chipset market. Several of the anticompetitive practices lacked a legitimate business justification. As clarified in *Aspen Skiing*, evidence that business conduct is not related to any apparent efficiency may constitute proof of specific intent to monopolize.[148] On the basis of these considerations, the Court

141 Ibid.
142 Ibid., at 21.
143 Ibid., at 24 (mentioning *Georgia-Pacific v United States Plywood*, 318 F Supp. 1116 (SDNY, 1970), at 1120).
144 *Qualcomm* (n 122), at 23–24.
145 *Qualcomm* (n 126), at 29. See also *Crossroads Cogeneration v Orange & Rockland Utilities*, 159 F3d 129 (C App 3rd Circuit, 1998), at 141.
146 *Qualcomm* (n 126), at 30.
147 Ibid.
148 *Aspen Skiing* (n 87), at 608.

of Appeals held that Broadcom's complaint had completely satisfied the specific intent element.[149]

Finally, in relation to the "dangerous probability" of successful monopolization, the Court argued that this factor required a fact-sensitive inquiry.[150] Broadcom had provided considerable details on Qualcomm's conduct and anticompetitive effects. It had also demonstrated that Qualcomm's practices "effectively foreclosed Broadcom's entry into the UMTS chipset market."[151] These arguments finally led the Court to accept Broadcom's position with respect to its second claim on the attempted monopolization.[152]

3.2.1.2.3 Unlawful maintenance of monopoly claim The US Court of Appeals finally considered the third relevant antitrust claim, according to which Qualcomm was maintaining monopoly in the 3G (third generation) CDMA technology and chipset markets in violation of the Sherman Act. As held before the District Court, Broadcom confirmed its view that Qualcomm was using leverage over customers in the CDMA markets to destroy the UMTS chipset business, and that it was consequently suffering injury.

The US Court of Appeals, however, decided to affirm the District Court's dismissal of that claim[153] on the ground that Broadcom lacked standing. It observed that there were insufficient factual allegations proving a causal link between Qualcomm's maintenance of its monopolies in the 3G CDMA technology and chipset markets and the alleged harm caused to Broadcom in the WCDMA technology and UMTS chipset markets. Injury to Broadcom was also considered to be extremely remote. In addition, the Third Circuit observed that Broadcom had not demonstrated that it was active in the same relevant market as Qualcomm. Hence, it concluded that Broadcom's alleged injury was not "inextricably intertwined" with Qualcomm's alleged anticompetitive conduct.[154]

3.2.1.3 CONCLUSIVE REMARKS ON *QUALCOMM*

The decision of the US Court of Appeals in *Qualcomm* confirmed once again that standard-setting processes are subject to close scrutiny under antitrust principles, where competition to implement the standard is hindered rather than promoted. The Third Circuit importantly noted that standard-setting processes are consistent with the main antitrust goal (i.e. consumer welfare). They may also enhance dynamic efficiencies and promote competition, in so far as no exogenous manipulation of the processes occurs. In the latter case, instead, standard setting may lead

149 *Qualcomm* (n 126), at 31.

150 See also *Barr Laboratories v Abbott Laboratories*, 978 F2d 98 (C App 3rd Circuit, 1992).

151 *Qualcomm* (n 126), at 32.

152 Ibid., at 32–33.

153 *Qualcomm* (n 122), at 23.

154 *Qualcomm* (n 126), at 34–35 (citing *Carpet Group International v Oriental Rug Importers Association*, 227 F3d 62 (C App 3rd Circuit, 2000), at 76–77).

to increased fees for licenses and consequently higher prices for consumers, to the ultimate detriment of societal welfare.

With respect to the analysis of the conduct, Qualcomm's deception was appraised as the kind of behavior which may seriously impair the activities of a consensus-driven standard-setting environment. Thus, in the court's view, breach of FRAND terms may harm SSOs no less than non-disclosure of IPRs.

In order to establish an infringement of Section 2, the conduct must be willful and harm competition. The Sherman Act should not be enforced against inadvertent failures to comply with SSO rules, as this may also compromise participation to standard setting by IPRs owners. At the same time, this intentional or willful conduct must lead to anticompetitive effects. These effects in *Qualcomm* were represented by the missed opportunity for ETSI to adopt non-proprietary standards, had it known about the firm's intention to deceive.

As in *Rambus*, however, the risks deriving from the adoption of (F)RAND terms were not properly assessed. The Court of Appeals, indeed, did not take into proper account the potential threat deriving from litigation on their meaning, as the bottleneck of the whole process. It merely observed that "the reasonableness of royalties is an inquiry that courts routinely undertake."[155] In this respect, it cited as an example the 15-factors test proposed and developed in *Georgia Pacific*.[156] As explained in Chapter 3, however, this test raises more than a doubt due to the interpretative problems which may likely arise in applying the various criteria.

The faults of this licensing model will be further examined in Chapter 7, aimed at setting the optimal balance between patentees' interests and standard-setting goals. The following sections, instead, will be devoted to understand better the role of causation, intent and effects for the finding of an infringement under US antitrust law. By delving into the enforcers' approach to the issue, the book aims at a two-fold goal: (a) identify any possible faults in the courts' and Commission's analysis; and (b) outline potential best practices in enforcement activities.

4 Causation

In order to establish antitrust liability under Section 2 of the Sherman Act, it is necessary to prove causation, the causal link between the effects and the behavior. Section 5 of the FTC Act, which regulates deceptive acts or practices, does not instead require neither the element of intention nor harm to competition.[157] An act or practice is deceptive if it involves a representation, omission or practice that is likely to mislead consumers acting reasonably under the circumstances, and the representation, omission or practice is material.[158] It follows that causation

155 *Qualcomm* (n 126), at 25. The rationale for awarding reasonable royalties is also established in the Manual of Patent Examining Procedure (35 USC § 284), which allows "damages adequate to compensate for the infringement, but in no event less than a reasonable royalty for the use made of the invention by the infringer."

156 *Georgia-Pacific* (n 143).

157 See, for instance, *Pantron* (n 7); and *Minuteman Press* (n 7).

158 15 USC § 45.

between conduct and anticompetitive harm must only be proved in case of Sherman Act violations. This section is devoted to the analysis of the various perspectives developed in the assessment of causation by the US courts and the Commission, both in *Rambus* and (to a minor extent) *Qualcomm*.

4.1 Proof of causation in Rambus

The thorniest issue for the FTC in *Rambus* was causation. The causation element and the standard of proof to establish anticompetitive effects have been at the core of intense discussions. As Areeda and Hovenkamp rightly evidence, to establish illegal monopolization courts require a causal link between the alleged exclusionary conduct and the attainment or maintenance of market power.[159] To what extent, however, can this causal link be inferred or assumed from the anticompetitive conduct?

4.1.1 Inference of causation

Some authors have argued that, in certain cases concerning anticompetitive conduct having natural and probable effects, proof of harm to competition is not necessary but it can be established by inference.[160] In *Rambus*, opposing counsel did not seem to have moved away from this position, in so far as it was stated that it was only necessary to show "that Rambus's failure to disclose is the type of conduct that is reasonably capable of causing JEDEC to include the undisclosed [Rambus] intellectual property in the [JEDEC] standards."[161]

This interpretation of causality, however, does not seem to be supported by established jurisprudence, and may also present relevant risks for SSO activities. By inferring causation, courts and authorities may come more easily to establish antitrust liability under the Sherman Act. This may finally represent a potential obstacle to firms' participation to standard setting processes.

4.1.2 Clear and convincing evidence standard

Rambus, instead, claimed that complaint counsel had to satisfy a far higher standard of proof to demonstrate a causal link between its alleged exclusionary conduct and any resulting anticompetitive effects. This position was endorsed by the administrative law judge.[162] The US company, in particular, referred to the necessity to prove the causal link under "the clear and convincing" evidence standard, a heavier burden than the "preponderance of the evidence test."[163]

159 P.E. Areeda and H.J. Hovenkamp (n 133), § 650. See also J. Kattan, "Antitrust Implications: Disclosure and Commitments to Standard Setting Organizations" (2002) 16 *Antitrust* 22.

160 T.J. Muris, "The FTC and the Law of Monopolization" (2000) 67 *Antitrust Law Journal* 695–701.

161 *Rambus Inc*, FTC Docket n. 9302, Complaint Counsel Post-Hearing Brief (9 September 2003), at 107.

162 *Rambus* (n 75), at 300.

163 *Rambus* (n 71), at 5 and 26.

Under the former, the judge must be persuaded by the evidence that it is highly probable that the claim or affirmative defense is true.[164] Under the "preponderance of the evidence test" it is instead required that the matter asserted seems more likely true than not.[165] Both standards are less stringent than "proof beyond a reasonable doubt" test, which requires the judge to be close to certain of the truth of the matter asserted.[166] Rambus claimed that the "clear and convincing evidence standard" was necessary to protect innovators' rights to exercise their patents and reduce disincentives to take part in SSOs.[167]

However, it could be counter-argued, a very high standard of proof may facilitate participants in their intent to subvert and manipulate legally a standard-setting process to their advantage. This would finally reduce the incentives of other firms to participate in SSOs. Given that both inference of causation and a too high standard of proof may have negative effects, a legitimate doubt arises: which approach may better address the issue? Before answering the question, it seems relevant to examine the FTC's and Court of Appeals' views.

4.1.3 Commission's analysis of causation

On the debate, the Commission concluded in its decision that the same evidence establishing that Rambus had implemented an exclusionary conduct and had gained monopoly power contributed to show a causal link between Rambus's behavior and its power. In this regard, it was stated that "the evidence links Rambus's conduct to JEDEC's adoption of SDRAM standards incorporating Rambus's patents and … links JEDEC's adoption of those standards to Rambus's acquisition of monopoly power."[168] In relation to the first connection, the FTC considered that, as there were some elements showing JEDEC would have adopted an alternative technology had Rambus disclosed its IPRs, this evidence suggested a causal link between the firm's behavior and the SSO's decision-making process.[169] In relation to the second link, it was clear in the Commission's analysis that, once JEDEC had adopted Rambus's undisclosed technology, the market was then very likely to adopt the standardized choice.[170]

164 The "clear and convincing evidence standard" was applied, for instance, in *American Cyanamid*, 72 Federal Trade Commission 623 (1967); and *VISX*, Case n. 9286, Federal Trade Commission (1999). It may be applied also in criminal procedures.

165 The "preponderance of the evidence standard" is mainly adopted in US civil cases. See *Concord Boat v Brunswick*, 207 F3d 1039 (C App 8th Circuit, 2000).

166 As the highest level of burden of persuasion, this standard is usually required in most US criminal cases.

167 *Rambus* (n 71), at 15–16.

168 *Rambus* (n 61), at 74.

169 Ibid., at 77.

170 Ibid., at 78.

4.1.4 Arguments of the US Court of Appeals

The US Court of Appeals, however, held that the Commission was wrong to find Rambus liable as it had failed to show a link between the alleged anticompetitive conduct and JEDEC's final choice of the standard.[171] The court, in contrast with the findings of the authority, concluded that, in order to establish an antitrust infringement under Section 2, a more explicit proof of causation must be given. In particular, it highlighted that the Sherman Act does not prohibit deception in standardization processes if the deceptive conduct cannot be proved to have caused the adoption of the proprietary technology as a standard.[172] In *Rambus*, there was insufficient evidence that JEDEC, had it known about the firm's patents, would have opted for different technologies. The failure to prove causation also explained why the FTC could not invoke (before the Supreme Court) the appeal decision adopted in *Qualcomm*, where the burden of proof had instead been satisfied for most of the antitrust claims.[173]

4.1.5 Preponderance of the evidence standard

The question, in conclusion, turns to which appropriate standard of proof should be adopted. In relation to the proof of causation between Rambus's conduct and JEDEC's choice of Rambus's technologies (the first causal link), Hovenkamp noted that "an antitrust plaintiff must establish that the [SSO] would not have adopted the standard in question but for the misrepresentation or omission."[174] The proof of these crucial elements must be given under the "preponderance of the evidence standard." Also with respect to proof of causation between the anticompetitive conduct and the maintenance or attainment of monopoly (the second causal link), it has been held that the plaintiff had "the burden of pleading, introducing evidence, and presumably proving by preponderance of the evidence that anticompetitive behaviour has contributed significantly to the achievement or maintenance of monopoly."[175]

The "preponderance of the evidence standard," less stringent than the "clear and convincing evidence" test, has been proposed in other US cases decided under the Sherman Act.[176] It may reflect better the need to balance innovators' interests in standard setting and the safeguard of SSO objectives. From this perspective, therefore, the application of this test in antitrust enforcement may probably be interpreted as the optimal guarantee for all the parties involved.

171 *Rambus* (n 62), at 19.

172 Ibid., at 13–14.

173 *Qualcomm* (n 126).

174 H.J. Hovenkamp, M.A. Lemley and M.D. Janis (n 104) Ch. 35.5b.

175 P.E. Areeda and H.J. Hovenkamp, *Fundamentals of Antitrust Law* (4th edn, Wolters Kluwer, New York 2012) Ch. 6.03c.

176 *E.g.*, *Concord Boat* (n 165).

4.2 Causality in **Qualcomm**

Unlike *Rambus*, *Qualcomm* did not present a thorough discussion of the causation issue.[177] No reference was made as to the appropriate standard of proof discussed above. The judge of first instance had mainly focused on procedural aspects. With respect to the monopolization claim, the District Court had not developed an in-depth analysis on causation, as it had erroneously held that Qualcomm's conduct could not be deemed unlawful. Similarly, causality was not an issue in the analysis of the other claims, on attempted monopolization and unlawful maintenance of monopoly power.[178]

Before the US Court of Appeals, Qualcomm was considered to have monopolized the market for UMTS technologies, in violation of Section 2 of the Sherman Act. The Third Circuit, in particular, held that there was sufficient evidence to believe that Qualcomm's deception had finally led to anticompetitive effects, consisting in the missed opportunity for ETSI to standardize non-proprietary technologies had it known about the firm's intention to charge higher fees.[179] In relation to the second claim on attempted monopolization, it was similarly held that Broadcom had provided relevant details on conduct and effects. It had also demonstrated that Qualcomm's practices "effectively foreclosed Broadcom's entry into the UMTS chipset market."[180] Only in the appraisal of the third claim, the Third Circuit manifested its concerns as to the causal connection between the antitrust violation and the harm to the plaintiff. It deemed insufficient the factual allegations proving a causal link between Qualcomm's maintenance of monopoly in the 3G CDMA technology and chipset markets and the alleged harm caused to Broadcom in the WCDMA technology and UMTS chipset markets.[181] These considerations ultimately lead to reason that, in comparison to the District Court's approach, the Court of Appeals seems to have interpreted better the theory of causality, on which the final decision was grounded.

5 Anticompetitive effects

The analysis of the different cases on standards has evidenced the need to discuss anticompetitive effects, which are necessary for establishing antitrust liability under Section 2 of the Sherman Act. In the US, the evaluation of monopolization charges requires a two-step process: on the one hand, the examination of the effects on competition and consumers;[182] on the other, the appraisal of

177 *Qualcomm* (n 122); *Qualcomm* (n 126).

178 *Qualcomm* (n 122). On the absence of causation in a breach of (F)RAND case, see also *Townshend* (n 117).

179 *Qualcomm* (n 126), at 29.

180 Ibid., at 32.

181 Ibid., at 34–35 (citing *Carpet Group* (n 154)).

182 See A. Pera and V. Auricchio, "Consumer Welfare, Standard of Proof and the Objectives of Competition Policy" (2005) 1 *European Competition Journal* 153.

any existing business justification which a defendant may invoke.[183] Article 102 TFEU, instead, does not seem to necessarily require harm to the competitive process. This explains why a dominant undertaking charging excessive prices may infringe EU competition law, despite the absence of exclusionary effects, and escape liability in the United States.

With respect to the possibility of presuming anticompetitive effects when a certain conduct has occurred, such a presumption may be justified only under Section 1 (and similarly, under Article 101 TFEU). A *per se* rule indeed seems to have been applied so far only to those violations that, by their very nature, affect antitrust more seriously, such as cartels. A rule of reason has been usually implemented in examining potentially risky unilateral conduct.

As to Section 5 FTCA, this does not require harm to competition in order to establish liability. Below, therefore, I will delve only into the arguments developed in *Rambus* and *Qualcomm* as to the role of effects.

5.1 Rambus, Qualcomm *and the debate on the effects*

The *Rambus* saga highlights the contrast between the firm, the Commission and the US Court of Appeals in the discussion on effects. Complaint counsel, in particular, in discussing the effects determined by the conduct, had focused on the exclusion of alternative technologies, the excessive fees level charged for SDRAM licenses and the likely consequential increase in the price of SDRAM technology. This would have further led to a decrease of the output and to a reduction in the reliance on SSO activities.[184]

The Commission endorsed this position and rejected the company's defensive brief, according to which no anticompetitive effects could have ever been deemed to exist.[185] The authority rather argued that substantial record evidence showed that JEDEC members had become locked in and were unable to avoid Rambus's royalties.[186] In the Commission's view, several firms had invested relevant resources in the standardized technology, and it would have not been reasonable to switch to alternatives. No legitimate business justification was granted. However, the assessment of the authority did not properly apply antitrust principles.

The faults in the Commission's interpretation on effects were highlighted by the Court of Appeals, which reversed the ruling of the authority on the ground that it had failed to prove anticompetitive effects. With respect to the first scenario, indeed, the Court established that there was insufficient evidence to exclude that JEDEC would have adopted Rambus's technology even where the firm had disclosed the existence of its IPRs. This led the Court to note that it was not possible to establish anticompetitive effects.[187] With respect to the second scenario,

183 See S. Salop and T. Krattenmaker, "Analyzing Anticompetitive Exclusion" (1987) 56 *Antitrust Law Journal* 71.

184 *Rambus* (n 57).

185 *Rambus* (n 71), at 72–74.

186 *Rambus* (n 61), at 99.

187 *Rambus* (n 62), at 12.

in which JEDEC would have adopted Rambus's technology under RAND terms, the only consequence of deception was that JEDEC had lost an opportunity to seek lower royalties. But this, as the Court rightly held, did not imply harm to competition. There is no antitrust violation under US law if the deceptive conduct only influences the price charged without harming the competitive process. The Commission erroneously referred to *Qualcomm* in order to define anticompetitive the charge of supra-competitive fees.[188] To the extent that the ruling in *Qualcomm* rested on the argument that deception lured the SSO away from non-proprietary technology, it could not help the Commission in view of the inability to find that Rambus's conduct caused the SSO's choice. The authority itself had left open the possibility that Rambus's technology could have been standardized in any case.[189]

In *Qualcomm*, the dispute on the existence of anticompetitive effects involved the District Court and the Third Circuit. The former had argued that the inclusion of Qualcomm's technology in the UMTS standard did not harm competition, as the ultimate consequence of any SSO process is the absence of competition.[190] However, as rightly held by the Court of Appeals, the District Court was wrong, as there was evidence that ETSI would have not adopted Qualcomm's technology had it known about its intention to deceive. Broadcom had also properly described several unlawful practices implemented by Qualcomm, which was violating its FRAND commitments by charging higher royalties and providing discounts in a discriminatory way. These practices, in the Third Circuit's view, harmed competition and were sufficient to state a claim under Section 2 of the Sherman Act.[191]

In conclusion, *Rambus* and *Qualcomm* seem to suggest that parties of a dispute will need to refer to anticompetitive effects by proving that an SSO would not have standardized a proprietary technology had it known about the existence of relevant IPRs. In addition, it may be necessary to prove that the SSO would have not opted for a proprietary technology had it known about the right holder's refusal to license under RAND terms. These appeal judgments, therefore, seem to have properly shed light on (and perhaps heightened) the burden of proving causation and anticompetitive effects of deceptive conduct.

6 Fault and strict liability

Besides effects and causation, a further element is needed in order to find an infringement under Section 2. It is necessary to prove that the conduct is willful or intentional. A monopolization claim requires the willful acquisition or maintenance of monopoly power by the firm under scrutiny.[192] In order to support an attempted monopolization claim, the plaintiff must prove a specific intent to

188 Ibid., at 17.

189 *Rambus* (n 61).

190 *Qualcomm* (n 122), at 18. On a similar ground, see also *Townshend* (n 117), at 1021.

191 *Qualcomm* (n 126), at 30.

192 See *United States v Grinnell*, 384 US 563 (1966), at 570–571. This is known also as "general intent," which refers to the intention to realize the conduct under examination.

monopolize.[193] Unlike Section 2, Section 5 of the FTC Act does not require that deception be intentional.[194] Similarly, as it will be explained in Chapter 6, direct evidence of anticompetitive intent is not explicitly required in the enforcement of Article 102 TFEU.

The following passages are devoted to the study of the intent element in *Rambus* and *Qualcomm*. Nonetheless, further interesting considerations will also be made with respect to *Dell*, decided under Section 5.

6.1 Intent element in **Rambus** *and* **Qualcomm**

In *Rambus*, by referring to intent, opposing counsel noted that the US microchip designer had engaged in a "pattern of deceptive, exclusionary conduct through which [it] consciously subverted an open standards process and thereby captured a monopoly in important technology-related markets."[195] These observations, rejected by the administrative law judge,[196] were finally endorsed by the Commission, which confirmed that Rambus had unlawfully monopolized various technology markets through the deliberate manipulation of JEDEC's activities. The authority, in particular, had observed that:

> [b]y silently using JEDEC to assemble a patent portfolio to cover the SDRAM and DDR SDRAM standards, Rambus's conduct significantly contributed to JEDEC's choice of Rambus's technologies for incorporation in the JEDEC DRAM standards and to JEDEC's failure to secure assurances regarding future royalty rates.[197]

Intent, however, could not be a relevant issue in the arguments of the US Court of Appeals. The court remembered that an infringement of Section 2 requires the willful acquisition or maintenance of monopoly power, as distinguished from growth or development as a consequence of a superior product, business acumen, or historical accident.[198] This notwithstanding, it did not broaden the willfulness issue as the Commission had even failed to prove harm to competition. This means that, in the absence of clear anticompetitive effects, it was useless to engage in the analysis of Rambus's will.

Therefore, it seems that to establish liability under Section 2 of the Sherman Act, both an intentional or willful conduct and harm to competition are necessary. Consequently, it would not be possible to find an antitrust infringement in the absence of one of these elements. Even if deception is shown to be willful, harm to

193 See *Spectrum Sports* (n 2), at 456; and *Barr Laboratories* (n 150), at 65. "Specific intent" requires the intention to realize the effects prohibited by the law.

194 15 USC § 45.

195 *Rambus* (n 63).

196 *Rambus* (n 75), at 297–299.

197 *Rambus* (n 61), at 118–119.

198 *Rambus* (n 62), at 11.

competition cannot be presumed (and vice versa). It needs to be proved under the "preponderance of the evidence standard."

As to the *Qualcomm* case, the District Court had not properly scrutinized intention, as the company was held to enjoy a legally sanctioned monopoly in its patented technology and to have the right to exclude competition.[199]

The faults of this position were rightly highlighted by the Third Circuit, which rather argued that evidence showed Qualcomm had obtained and maintained market power willfully, not on the basis of competition on the merits. These arguments led the court to uphold the appellant's monopolization claim.[200] Similarly, with reference to Broadcom's claim on attempted monopolization, the Third Circuit established that Qualcomm had acted with specific intent to obtain a monopoly in the UMTS chipset market. Several of the anticompetitive practices identified by Broadcom, moreover, allegedly lacked a legitimate business justification.[201] From this perspective, the analysis developed by the Third Circuit seems to confirm the importance of proving intention in order to establish liability under Section 2 of the Sherman Act.

6.2 **Dell** *and the inadvertent failure to disclose*

Section 5, it has been said, outlaws unfair methods of competition and unfair or deceptive acts or practices. Deception does not require either intention or harm to competition.[202] Nevertheless, the FTC's decision in *Dell* dwelled on the analysis of these elements and made some relevant points.

6.2.1 Unknowing failure to disclose

In *Dell,* the authority posed an important question: should unknowing or inadvertent failure to disclose essential IPRs be considered unlawful?[203] The decision of the authority was strictly linked to the enforcement of VESA's rules and to the facts of the case, as there was evidence that Dell's failure to disclose was not inadvertent.[204]

The FTC notably argued that no general rule condemning inadvertent failure to disclose should be applied. If such a rule were in force, it would impose on the participants a regime of strict liability according to which they would put their IPRs at risk by simply joining SSOs. Under a strict liability regime, no justification for inadvertence is admitted. Firms with hundreds of employees and thousands of patents would be tempted to ignore participation and enforce their rights at a later stage, without facing the risk of antitrust liability.[205]

199 *Qualcomm* (n 122), at 18.
200 *Qualcomm* (n 126).
201 See *Aspen Skiing* (n 87), at 608 (footnote 39).
202 *Pantron* (n 7); and *Minuteman Press* (n 7).
203 *Dell* (n 15), at 625–626.
204 Ibid.
205 On the role of intent in the non-disclosure of essential IPRs, see L. Zhang, "How IPR policies

Of course, in case a firm decides to take part in standard setting, the burden to search and disclose patents should, in theory, be placed on the patent holder, as the latter is in the optimal position to determine if its IPRs read on the standard. However, an unintentional failure to disclose should not be sanctioned, also due to the relevant difficulties that search in patent portfolios may sometimes determine. In order to escape antitrust liability, there should be proof that failure to disclose was not caused by a negligent conduct, but rather by the material impossibility to search and find conflicting patents under reasonable circumstances.

6.2.2 *Concept of negligence*

In *Dell*, it must be remembered, the dissenting Commissioner criticized the majority's arguments on intention. Besides the criticism for having failed to prove causation, the Commissioner added that the decision did not properly address the intent element. It was noted that "by finding a violation of Section 5 in the absence of any allegation of a knowing or intentional misrepresentation, the Commission effectively imposes a duty of disclosure on Dell beyond what VESA required."[206] The Commissioner further argued that "not inadvertent failure" did not necessarily mean intentional. "Negligence," as it was said, "is the legal characterization of conduct that seems closest to the standard of the majority."[207] But negligence, as the Commissioner added, brought back to the general duty of search that the majority had rejected.[208] In other words, it was held that by sanctioning negligence the authority would have admitted the existence of a generalized obligation to search and disclose essential IPRs.

Regardless of whether the issue in *Dell* concerned intent to deceive or negligence, the view of the dissenting Commissioner does not seem convincing. The concept of negligence is assessed against an objective standard, having regards usually to the circumstances and to the standard of care which would be reasonably expected of a reasonable person in similar circumstances.[209] It requires the existence of a duty, the breach of that duty, causation and harm.[210] In the context of standard setting, negligence implies a violation of a duty to identify and disclose patents. This violation, in terms of liability, cannot be compared to the infringement deriving from inadvertent behaviors, where proof is needed that firms could have not identified conflicting IPRs under reasonable circumstances.

The main question, hence, is whether a negligent conduct may be punishable in the same way as intentional deception. The answer must be in the affirmative, in so far as both intention and negligence require (unlike inadvertent acts) a mental

of telecommunication standard-setting organizations can effectively address the patent ambush problem" (2010) 41(4) *International Review of Intellectual Property and Competition Law* 392.

206 *Dell* (n 22), at 630.

207 Ibid., at 642.

208 Ibid., at 643.

209 See R. Posner, "A Theory of Negligence" (1972) 1 *Journal of Legal Studies* 29; R. Posner and W. Lande, "The Positive Economic Theory of Tort Law" (1981) 15 *Georgia Law Review* 851.

210 W.N. Hohfeld, *Fundamental Legal Conceptions* (Yale University Press, New Haven 1919) 58–59.

element: respectively, the consciousness of deceiving a standard-setting body, and the acceptance of the risks deriving from non-disclosure of potentially conflicting IPRs.

A negligent conduct may arise, for instance, when a member does not arrange all the necessary available means to discover conflicting patents. In case it is shown under the "preponderance of the evidence test" that – although the company did not have any specific intention to deceive – the member could have avoided harm by a diligent conduct, the firm should be considered liable under antitrust law.[211]

7 Conclusion

The analysis developed in *Dell*, *Unocal*, *Rambus* and *Qualcomm* demonstrates that both the Commission and the US courts have been often involved in the assessment of potentially anticompetitive conduct in standardization contexts. The important function of SSOs in furthering the development of technological markets and in enhancing consumer welfare has never been underestimated. Thus, it is clear why in most of the discussed cases the courts and – despite to a minor extent – the FTC have carefully scrutinized potentially harmful behaviors. The litigation history and published decisions in these disputes may have partially contributed to advance antitrust doctrines used to challenge hold-up.

Although in *Dell* and *Unocal* the Commission only focused on unfair competition and did not directly consider potential infringements of the Sherman Act, nevertheless the cases represented important precedents in antitrust enforcement actions brought for alleged unilateral abuse of SSO activities. *Dell*, in particular, represented one of the first instances of the FTC's willingness to enforce its powers under Section 5 to ban anticompetitive conduct in standard setting. The case clarified that no general duty to search and disclose patents should be deemed to exist. IPRs owners should be left free to decide whether to participate in SSO activities. In case a firm opts for participation, then, a duty to search and disclose may only be imposed by the SSO's rules. Such a duty, on the contrary, should not be inferred under a general principle of good faith. In order to protect the IPRs owners' interests and preserve the aims of SSOs, clear written rules should be properly made known to members. Compliance with these rules should in theory work as a safe harbor.

On a different ground, SSO members who inadvertently fail to disclose patents ultimately covering the standard should not face antitrust liability. By condemning inadvertent failure to disclose, there could be the risk to implement a too rigorous legal framework which would finally discourage patentees from participating in standard setting. Rather, intent and negligence are the appropriate standards under which liability may be established. Of course, the extent to which negligent or inadvertent failure to disclose IPRs may give rise to liability

211 J. Raz, "Responsibility and the Negligence Standard" (2010) 30 *Oxford Journal of Legal Theory* 1.

under US and EU laws "may be another source of potential divergence between the two regimes."[212]

Much more complex analysis and debate were involved in *Rambus*. The conclusions finally reached by the court seem to suggest that, in future disputes, SSOs and their participants will need to rely on much clearer rules in order to legitimately support their positions. However, regardless of the discussion on the meaning of the policy rules, it seems that the Commission's action did not produce any tangible results as the approach embraced both in developing a theory of liability and in providing causation was not supported by convincing evidence. This is the reason why the conclusive analysis in *Rambus* finally led to a much different outcome in comparison with the *Qualcomm* decision. Nevertheless, the FTC's loss on appeal is not likely to reduce the level of governmental antitrust enforcement in this area.

Qualcomm, it must be recognised, similarly gave important indications on whether a patent holder's deception may be condemned under antitrust laws. The different outcome of that case may also be explained by the different regulatory environment: whereas JEDEC rules seemed complex and ambiguous, ETSI policy on disclosure and licensing commitments appeared to be clearer.

In brief, these cases undoubtedly attest that private SSO processes can be pro-competitive and advance the promotion of consumer welfare. At the same time, however, they can facilitate SSOs' members to adopt anticompetitive conduct, especially when implementing (F)RAND terms. Deceptive behaviors in a consensus-driven standard setting environment, consisting of abuses of administrative or judicial processes, may result in antitrust violations and harm the competitive process. SSO members should therefore carefully consider their business strategy, as they may risk to be sanctioned under the Sherman Act or the FTC Act. A firm owning patents over a technology may face liability when, although disclosing its relevant rights, it finally breaches the subscribed licensing terms. This behavior may seriously harm the competitive process no less than deceptive non-disclosure (ambush) of IPRs and could be consequently held enforceable anticompetitive practice. In all events, any assessment of conduct should balance the interests of IPR owners with the objectives of standard-setting bodies. The elements of intent, causation and effects, therefore, should be properly scrutinized under a test which optimally reflects the need to overcome this tension.

Finally, from the analysis of the US case law on standard setting, it is clear that (F)RAND policies cannot represent an efficient solution. In order to overcome the risks – lengthy litigation and bottleneck of the activities – deriving from this licensing model and ensure a more transparent and fair process, a different regime should be implemented as a more workable framework.

212 C.B. Hockett and R.G. Lipscomb, "Best FRANDs Forever? Standard-Setting Antitrust Enforcement in the United States and the European Union" (2009) 23(3) *Antitrust* 23.

6 The EU approach – abuse of dominance in standard setting

1 Introduction

The EU background in standardization clearly differs from the experience developed in the United States. The US standard-setting environment has evolved sooner and more rapidly. Both the US literature and case law have heavily contributed – sometimes controversially – to identify the main issues related to standards. In the EU, instead, until a few years ago the interaction between IPRs, standards and competition was an area known to a group of legal specialists only.[1] This notwithstanding, it seems important to delve also into the experience developed at the Union level, albeit more limited and recent.

The comparative analysis does reveal interesting features, as it reflects the divergent approach adopted towards dominance abuse. In this context, several questions could be raised. For instance, it could be questioned why Rambus's arguments supporting the legitimacy of its conduct were assessed by the US Court of Appeals and the EU Commission in different ways. Which approach better reflects the optimal goal of competition? Whereas the US courts, inspired by a more liberal policy, tended to develop a more flexible analysis, the EU counterparts, more in line with an interventionist approach, have expressed greater concerns for abuse in the standard-setting environment. Further interesting considerations could be inferred from the analysis of the Commission's approach in *Qualcomm*, with specific reference to the legitimacy of high pricing behaviors of IPR owners. The bedrock for the analysis of these claims is Article 102 TFEU, which is the primary vehicle in addressing hold-up cases in the EU.

Besides considering the EU case law on standard setting, the chapter will also take into account the content and scope of the "Guidelines on the Applicability of Article 101 TFEU to Horizontal Co-operation Agreements."[2] The document highlights the position of the Commission on various issues related to standards: from the function of standard setting, to the anticompetitive risks which may

1 S. Sattler, "Standardization under EU competition rules – the Commission's new horizontal guidelines" (2011) 32(7) *European Competition Law Review* 343.

2 European Commission, "Guidelines on the Applicability of Article 101 TFEU to Horizontal Co-operation Agreements" [2011] OJ C 11/1.

potentially arise in the context of standardization agreements. In addition, a further relevant topic concerns the meaning and role of (F)RAND commitments as interpreted by the authority.

The analysis of the Guidelines and of the case law (structured on the duality *Rambus–Qualcomm*)[3] will ultimately help to understand whether the EU Commission addressed the problems arising in standard setting more effectively than its US counterpart. On a further note, it will also help to identify those questions which remain still unanswered.

2 Legal framework

To understand the approach developed by the Commission in the appraisal of standard-setting disputes, it is necessary to examine briefly the relevant legal framework. Article 102 TFEU is the legal provision to be enforced in cases of abuse by dominant firms. A dominant position has been defined as a:

> position of economic strength enjoyed by an undertaking which enables it to prevent effective competition being maintained on the relevant market by giving it the power to behave to an appreciable extent independently of its competitors, customers and ultimately of the consumers.[4]

The concept of abuse has been defined by the Court of Justice as:

> an objective concept relating to the behaviour of an undertaking in a dominant position which is such as to influence the structure of a market where, as a result of the very presence of the undertaking in question, the degree of competition is weakened and which, through recourse to methods different from those which condition normal competition [...], has the effect of hindering the maintenance of the degree of competition still existing in the market or growth of that competition.[5]

It is beyond the scope of this book to explore thoroughly the doctrinal and normative debate on the concepts of dominance and abuse.[6] It suffices here to say that Article 102 TFEU can be considered as the corresponding provision to Section 2 of the Sherman Act, although it has a wider scope. Indeed, Article 102 not only bans those (exclusionary) behaviors which aim to prevent, restrict or distort competition.[7] It also captures those (exploitative) abuses which lead to an unlawful

3 Case COMP/38.636 *Rambus* [2010] OJ C 30; Case 39247 *Texas Instruments v Qualcomm* [2009].

4 See Case 27/76 *United Brands v European Commission* [1978] ECR 207, at 65; and Case 85/76 *Hoffmann-La Roche v European Commission* [1979] ECR 461, at 38.

5 Case 322/81 *Michelin v European Commission* [1983] ECR 3461, at 70; *Akzo Chemie BV* [1985] OJ L 374/1; and Case C-62/86 *AKZO v European Commission* [1991] ECR I-3359, at 69.

6 On the issue, see R. Nazzini, *The Foundations of European Union Competition Law – The Objective and Principles of Article 102* (Oxford University Press, New York 2011) 107.

7 See J. Temple Lang, "Fundamental Issues Concerning Abuse under Article 82 EC" (Annual

advantage regardless of the competitive structure of the market. This seems to be one of the main differences between the legal frameworks in the US and the EU. A typical example of an exploitative conduct consists in charging excessive prices to final consumers, where the price has no relation to the real economic value, based on the assessment of both cost and non-cost-related factors. Charging high prices does not usually have any negative effect on the competitive process. Rather, it could encourage other firms to enter the market and contribute to the development of dynamic competition in the long run. Nevertheless, it has been identified as a form of abuse in a number of cases.[8] The aim of including this conduct under the prohibition of Article 102 might perhaps be one of the reasons why the Treaty of Rome did not make any explicit reference to "an object or effect of restricting competition."[9] However, there is still debate on the opportunity to consider this type of practice abusive, and the scarce number of related cases decided by the Commission and the EU courts does not clear up the uncertainty.

Another relevant difference between the EU and the US antitrust frameworks lies in the fact that Article 102, unlike Section 2 of the Sherman Act, does not provide for the attempt to monopolize. This feature has led some commentators to argue that patent ambush should not be considered unlawful under EU competition law.[10] Also the attested irrelevance of anticompetitive intent in the enforcement of Article 102 TFEU may mark a significant difference.[11]

Besides Article 102, the second provision deserving close scrutiny is Article 101 TFEU, which addresses anticompetitive agreements and concerted practices.[12] Albeit not applicable to *Rambus* and *Qualcomm*, it has been appraised by the Commission as potentially enforceable in the standard-setting context.

3 Patent ambush and *Rambus*

The conduct of the microchip designer Rambus, besides drawing the attention of US courts and authorities, has also been scrutinized on the other side of the Atlantic. The European Commission opened an investigation into the US firm,

Competition Policy Conference Regulatory Policy Institute Oxford – July 2005); and A. Jones, "Standard-essential Patents: FRAND Commitments, Injunctions and the Smartphone Wars" (2014) 10(1) *European Competition Journal* 16.

8 *United Brands* (n 4); Case 26/75 *General Motors v European Commission* [1975] ECR 1367; Case 30/87 *Bodson v Pompes Funebres* [1988] ECR 2479; Case 226/84 *British Leyland v European Commission* [1986] ECR 3263.

9 D. Sinclair, "Abuse of Dominance at a Crossroads – Potential Effect, Object and Appreciability under Article 82 EC" (2004) 25(8) *European Competition Law Review* 492.

10 See D. Geradin, "Pricing Abuses by Essential Patent Holders in a Standard-Setting Context: A View from Europe" (2009–2010) 76 *Antitrust Law Journal* 329; and D. Geradin and M. Rato, "Can Standard Setting Lead to Exploitative Abuse? A Dissonant View on Patent Hold-Up, Royalty Stacking and the Meaning of FRAND" (2007) 3 *European Competition Journal* 101.

11 On the scope of the test of intent, see R. Nazzini (n 6) 57. As the author argues, anticompetitive intent has been applied as a test mainly in relation to predatory pricing (e.g. see *AKZO* (n 5)).

12 See C. Townley, *Article 81 EC and Public Policy* (Hart Publishing, Oxford 2009).

giving rise to the first case of patent ambush in the EU.[13] The intervention was justified as "Rambus is active worldwide, has obtained patent protection for the relevant technologies in Europe and it is enforcing its patents against companies applying the relevant standards in Europe."[14] As the Commission argued, the firms allegedly damaged by Rambus's conduct could have not always sought relief on the basis of a US decision.[15] Hence, action by the EU enforcer was considered appropriate.

The next sections will focus on the analysis of the Commission's line of reasoning. Due to the final acceptance of Rambus's commitments, the case was closed without the adoption of a formal decision. As a consequence, only the arguments emerging from the "commitment decision" will be examined. The conclusions will clarify whether the Commission struck an optimal balance in the assessment of the conduct or whether its approach was faulty.

3.1 Policy principles and abusive conduct

During 2007, the EU Commission sent a Statement of Objections[16] to Rambus for having abused its dominant position by claiming unreasonable fees for the use of its technology.[17] Investigations had started following a joint complaint[18] lodged by two companies, Infineon and Hynix.[19] A complete history of the case is well beyond the scope of this section, as the facts have been already detailed in Chapter 5.[20] Here, it is worth focusing only on the main legal features emerging from *Rambus*, so as to appraise properly the line of reasoning developed by the Commission. These features concerned the content and clarity of JEDEC policy, the alleged existence of a good faith duty, and the abusive conduct of Rambus.[21]

13 *Rambus* (n 3).

14 European Commission, "Commission Confirms Sending a Statement of Objections to Rambus" (23 August 2007) Press Release MEMO/07/330.

15 Ibid. At the time of the EU Commission's investigation, the US Court of Appeals for the DC Circuit had not yet adopted its final decision in the *Rambus* case (see Chapter 5 section 3.1.3).

16 Through this formal step, the Commission informs the parties subject to an investigation of the objections raised against them. Sending a Statement of Objections does not prejudge the final outcome, as the Commission may still decide to close proceedings without a formal decision.

17 European Commission (n 14).

18 See Article 3 of EEC Council Regulation n 17/62, [1962] OJ 13/204.

19 However, in 2005, Infineon withdrew its complaint as a result of patent litigation settlement.

20 See Chapter 5 section 3.1.3.

21 As the Statement of Objections has not been published, the analysis of the European Commission's reasoning will be based mainly on the arguments emerging from the press release. On the considerations emerging from the *Rambus* case, see A. Emanuelson, "Standardization Agreements in the Context of the New Horizontal Guidelines" (2012) 33(2) *European Competition Law Review* 69–70; and C. Koenig and A. Trias, "Some Standards for Standardization: A Basis for Harmonization and Efficiency Maximization of EU and US Antitrust Control of the Standard Setting Process" (2010) 32(7) *European Intellectual Property Review* 328–329.

3.2 JEDEC policy and the duty of good faith

First, it seems important to highlight one more time the primary goal pursued by JEDEC.[22] JEDEC had a policy of open standards, promoting those freely available to all industry members or not subject to excessive and unreasonable licensing terms.[23] This means that JEDEC did not consider only free technologies, but had left open the possibility to implement standards subjected to RAND fees.

In *Rambus*, it is well known, the problem lay in the clarity and awareness of the policy by the members. Indeed, it seems that JEDEC principles had not been properly revealed and explained to the participants. Furthermore, JEDEC language on disclosure policy had been interpreted as broad and amorphous.[24] This view, supported by different US courts, was not endorsed by the EU Commission, which did not doubt the clarity of the rules. In addition, it seems that the EU competition enforcer also relied on the existence of a general covenant of good faith to which SSO members would be subjected. Such a duty would impose an obligation of fair dealing towards the other members in identifying and disclosing essential rights, regardless of the letter of the policy.

However, the effectiveness of a general duty of good faith is doubtful. It is true that standards institutes must rely on a high level of cooperation between the participants in order to develop their projects. It is also true that Rambus, in the specific case, might have presumed its disclosure obligations. This notwithstanding, the first step to ensure the fairness and transparency of a standard-setting process should be the enforcement of robust regulations. An ambiguous policy, instead, may mislead the SSO members as to the exact duties they are expected to fulfill. It may further discourage any participation in SSO activities from the industry concerned.[25]

In light of these arguments, it seems that the EU Commission undervalued the importance of clear policy rules for SSOs. Even in case a general good faith covenant was admitted in standardization, this should not replace the need for robust guidelines. This means that the general expectations of the members should be based on clear and strong regulations, rather than on the existence of a good faith duty alone. This approach seems to better define the right balance between the interests of IPRs owners and the objectives of SSOs.

3.3 Relevant market and conduct

Besides the content and scope of JEDEC policy, the second issue deserving due attention concerned Rambus's conduct. Rambus designed, manufactured and licensed DRAM and synchronous DRAM (SDRAM) chips, widely used by the IT

22 JEDEC, "Manual of Organization and Procedure, JM21-R" (2015) § 1.1.

23 See Chapter 5 section 3.1.3.1.

24 See *Rambus Inc v Infineon Technologies*, 318 F3d 1081 (C App Federal Circuit, 2003), at 1097.

25 See Chapter 5 section 3.1.3. On the importance of clear SSO policies, see also R.A. Skitol, "Concerted Buying Power: Its Potential for Addressing the Patent Hold-up Problem in Standard Setting" (2004–2005) 72 *Antitrust Law Journal* 733.

industry. DRAM technologies, therefore, defined the boundaries of the relevant product market, which had a global geographical scope. The DRAM technologies market, in particular, had to be distinguished from the final product market. As established by the "Technology Transfer Regulation," indeed, the relevant technology market includes "technologies which are regarded by the licenses as interchangeable with or substitutable for the licensed technology, by reason of their technologies' characteristics, their royalties and their intended use."[26]

The complainants had alleged that Rambus had implemented a deceitful behavior aimed at obtaining exorbitant fees from all DRAM chips manufacturers.[27] Such a conduct consisted in the concealment of its relevant patents, in breach of JEDEC policy which promoted disclosure of both pending and issued IPRs covering the standard. Rambus, as it was explained, had implemented this unfair strategy having failed to persuade the industry to develop the company's technology (the RDRAM architecture) as *de facto* standard.[28] In order to capture JEDEC specifications, the US chip designer was secretly amending its patent claims hand-in-hand with the SSO. After the adoption of the standard, the industry found itself locked-in, as it was not commercially viable to design, manufacture and sell alternative technologies.[29] Rambus was deemed to have abused its dominant position and to have infringed Article 102 TFEU by hindering the SSO process and by subsequently charging excessive prices.[30] The conduct was interpreted not only as exploitative but also as exclusionary, due to the alleged exclusion of potential alternatives to the standard ultimately adopted.

The complainants' position recalled the principle that "exercise of an exclusive right by the owner may, in exceptional circumstances, involve abusive conduct."[31] A dominant firm, it is well-known, cannot be deprived of the right to protect its own commercial interests. However, the behavior cannot be allowed when its actual purpose is to strengthen the dominant position and abuse it.[32] This principle was considered applicable to Rambus's strategy and to its attempt to obtain legal protection for the over-exploitation of its rights. The complainants' arguments could be, in theory, reconciled also with the view expressed in *ITT Promedia*[33] by the Court of First Instance (now the General Court). The latter held that "as access to the Court is a fundamental right [...], it is only in wholly exceptional circumstances that the fact that legal proceedings are brought is capable

26 See Article 1 of the "Commission Regulation (EC) n 772/2004 on the Application of Article 81(3) of the EC Treaty to Categories of Technology Transfer Agreements," [2004] OJ L 123.

27 See the European Commission's "Rejection Decision" addressed to Hynix (SG-Greffe (2010) D/275 C (2010) 150, Bruxelles 15/01/2010), at 3.

28 Ibid., at 4.

29 The process of developing a standard usually entails different costs, related to: (a) engineering and design work; (b) prototype manufacturing and testing; (c) provision of infrastructure for production; and (d) marketing burden.

30 Rambus had demanded royalties amounting to 0.75% and 3.5% of the price of SDRAM and DDR (Double Data Rate) chips respectively.

31 See Case C-418/01 *IMS Health GmbH v NDC Health GmbH* [2004] 4 CMLR 28, at 35.

32 *United Brands* (n 4), at 189.

33 Case T-111/96 *ITT Promedia NV v European Commission* [1998] ECR II-2937.

of constituting an abuse of a dominant position."[34] In this case, the exceptional circumstances were identified in the fact that Rambus's intention was to take advantage of its position and extract exorbitant fees.

On the other side of the spectrum, Rambus contested both the dominant position and its alleged abuse of it.[35] In the attempt to legitimize Rambus's conduct, some authors even noted that the EU competition framework (unlike US antitrust law) does not prohibit the attempt to monopolize.[36] Members withholding rights in the standard-setting context cannot be said to be in a dominant position. IPRs alone do not confer such a status. Only after the adoption of the standard by the SSO and the subsequent implementation by the industry, may the IPRs owners be held to be dominant in the market of the standardized technology.[37] Absent a dominant position, so the argument goes, failure to disclose alone cannot be interpreted as abusive. Hence, any exclusionary effects deriving from the conduct should not be appraised under Article 102. This position could be further reconciled with the view that challenged the very existence of exclusionary effects. Indeed, as confirmed by the US jurisprudence, it was not certain that JEDEC would have opted for alternatives had it known about the existence of Rambus's IPRs.[38] However, even if there was no exclusion, the conduct might still be deemed unlawful under EU competition law, as it could be theoretically interpreted as an exploitative practice. Although it is debatable whether charging excessive prices should fall under the competition law scrutiny, the behavior still meets all the requirements for being captured by the spirit of Article 102(a).[39]

3.4 Assessment of the conduct

In the Statement of Objections, the Commission expressed the view that Rambus had infringed Article 102 TFEU by claiming unreasonable royalties for the license of its rights covering DRAMS chips.[40] Similarly to the approach developed by the FTC in the United States, the EU enforcer provisionally argued that the company had implemented a patent ambush, aimed at extracting exorbitant fees to the detriment of the industry concerned. As the authority held, although Rambus was aware of JEDEC disclosure duties, it had deliberately breached them.[41] It had further misled the SSO as to its relevant IPRs, jeopardizing the whole standardization

34 Ibid., at 60. On this case, see N. Petit, "Injunctions for FRAND-pledged SEPs: The Quest for an Appropriate Test of Abuse under Article 102 TFEU" (2013) 9(3) *European Competition Journal* 678.

35 This is the approach emerging from Rambus's commitments, described in the next section.

36 D. Geradin and M. Rato (n 10) 160.

37 D. Geradin (n 10) 329.

38 In the United States, indeed, the FTC and the Court of Appeals had not excluded that JEDEC could have adopted Rambus's technology in any event (see Chapter 5 section 3.1.3).

39 *Cf.* M. Glader and S. Chabert Larsen, "Article 82: Excessive Pricing – An Outline of the Legal Principles Relating to Excessive Pricing and their Future Application in the Field of IP Rights and Industry Standards" (2005) *Competition Law Insight* 3.

40 European Commission (n 14).

41 European Commission's "Commitment Decision" in *Rambus* (n 3), at 41. Available: www.ec.europa.eu/competition/elojade/isef/case_details.cfm?proc_code=1_38636.

process.[42] Without the misleading conduct, Rambus would have not been able to charge the price demanded. In the Commission's view, indeed, JEDEC members would have preferred to implement free standards and would have consequently opted for any alternative technologies. In this regard, the Commission considered the alternatives as free, commercially and technically feasible.[43]

In developing a theory of culpability, it is also likely that the Commission took into account both Articles 102(a) and 102(b) TFEU. The former, it is well-known, addresses unfair purchase or selling prices or other unfair trading conditions. The latter prohibits those practices by dominant firms which limit production, markets, or technical development to the prejudice of the consumers. Rambus's behavior may have been charged under both these provisions, as the application of exorbitant fees also had the effect of hindering the SSO process, to the ultimate detriment of consumer welfare. Perhaps, the choice to enforce Article 102(b) might appear all the more appropriate, due to the recognized doubts about the suitability of antitrust in assessing high pricing conduct. The letter of this provision, in addition, does not explicitly refer to an exclusionary effect. As a consequence, it would have been easier to enforce in *Rambus*, due to the uncertainty on the existence of exclusion.

On a further different ground, it could be questioned whether the EU enforcer would have adopted the same restrictive approach even if it would have found no formal breach of JEDEC policy. In this regard, the answer could be in the affirmative, as the Commission also interpreted Rambus's intentional deception as a breach of a general good faith duty.[44] Thus, its misleading conduct would have been probably banned under all circumstances, regardless of the letter of the policy rules.

The position of the Commission should be read in light of its past Communication on "Intellectual Property and Standardization."[45] In that context, the authority had argued that innovators would act in bad faith when, although aware of a conflict between their rights and standards, they did not reveal the existence of the IPRs until after the selection process. This strategy, it was observed, would force competitors to accept the payment of fees higher than those which could have been obtained at an earlier stage.[46]

42 During participation to JEDEC activities, Rambus had only disclosed the existence of one patent (the so-called "703" patent) which was not covering the standard. This gave JEDEC members the impression that Rambus was complying with the SSO's rules.

43 European Commission's "Rejection Decision" (SG-Greffe (2010) D/275 C (2010) 150, Bruxelles 15/01/2010), at 48.

44 European Commission, 'Commitment Decision' in *Rambus* (n 3), at 38–39. On the role of intent in the EU, see A. Bavasso, "The Role of Intent under Article 82 EC: From Flushing the Turkeys to Spotting the Lionesses in Regent's Park" (2005) 26(11) *European Competition Law Review* 616; and R. Nazzini (n 6) 57.

45 European Commission, "Intellectual Property Rights and Standardization" (Communication) COM 445 final, 27 October 1992.

46 Ibid., at 4.2.1 and 4.4.1.

3.5 Commitments

From a procedural perspective, in case of a breach of Article 102 TFEU, the EU authority may require by decision that the company concerned brings such violation to an end.[47] The decision may include an order to "do certain acts or provide certain advantages which have been wrongfully withheld, as well as prohibiting the continuation of certain action, practices or situations which are contrary to the Treaty."[48] The Commission may then enjoin a dominant firm to refrain from implementing any measures which may lead to effects similar to those of the abusive conduct.[49] In any case, the remedy must be proportional to the identified infringement and must match its nature.[50]

In *Rambus*, however, no formal decision establishing an infringement was ever adopted, as the company had agreed to undertake commitments. In the Statement of Objections, the Commission concluded that Rambus should have remedied its conduct by charging reasonable and non-discriminatory (RAND) fees for the use of its patents. The related amount should have been determined in accordance to all the circumstances of the case.[51] To this end, the EU Commission invited Rambus to disclose its interpretation of RAND royalties.

Rambus offered all market participants two sets of worldwide license grants, one for DRAMs technologies and one for memory controllers.[52] First, it agreed to waive royalties for those DRAMs chips which were developed while it was a JEDEC member.[53] As to later developments of DRAMs (those developed after its withdrawal from JEDEC), it committed to license these under a maximum fee.[54] Likewise, with respect to memory controllers, Rambus agreed to charge a variable fee within a fixed maximum rate.[55] These commitments were submitted by Rambus under Article 9 of Regulation 1/2003 in order to meet the Commission's competition concerns.[56]

This does not mean, however, that the US chip designer had agreed with the authority's preliminary assessment of the factual and legal elements. The obligations were only interpreted by Rambus as being aimed "to provide a clear

47 See Article 7 of the Council Regulation n 1/2003, [2003] OJ L 1/1.

48 Joined Cases 6/73 and 7/73 *Commercial Solvents v European Commission* [1974] ECR 223, at 45.

49 Case T-83/91 *Tetra Pak v European Commission* [1994] ECR II-755, at 220.

50 Joined Cases C-241-242/91 P *Radio Telefis Eireann & Independent Television Publications v European Commission* [1995] 4 CMLR 718, at 93.

51 European Commission (n 14).

52 Memory controllers are integrated circuits capable of controlling DRAM memory devices.

53 These were the SDRAM and DDR (Double Data Rate) technologies.

54 The fee amounted to 1.5% per unit of selling price. These later developments included DDR2, DDR3, GDDR3 and GDDR4 DRAMs chips.

55 The SDR (Single Data Rate) memory controller fees were between 1% and 1.5% per unit of selling price. For all controllers using later generations of DRAMs, the royalties varied between 2% and 2.65% per unit of selling price. The maximum rate set by Rambus amounted to $20.

56 Council Regulation n 1/2003, [2003] OJ L 1/1. For a comparison with the US Federal Trade Commission's analysis and decision on remedies, see Chapter 5 section 3.1.3.3.

licensing structure at attractive rates for the next five years."[57] They were designed "to create a platform that will enable all sides to put aside their past differences and move towards a future environment where the industry resolves patent questions via licensing discussions rather than costly litigation."[58]

In assessing Rambus's licensing plan, the Commission first highlighted the importance of effective SSO processes for technical development. It further remarked on the need for standards developed through non-discriminatory, open and transparent procedures to safeguard against anticompetitive outcomes and enhance consumer welfare.[59] Rambus's conduct had undermined the development of a genuine and undistorted process, putting at risk the industry's confidence in the work of SSOs. Nonetheless, the commitments were deemed both appropriate and adequate to address the competition concerns and to provide potential new entrants with a clear perspective on royalty costs.[60] The industry, in other words, would have found a clear price benchmark in the disclosed rates. For these reasons, the commitments were eventually accepted.[61]

3.6 Lessons from Rambus

The analysis of Rambus's conduct by the European Commission highlighted some important elements, concerning: (a) the function of standards; (b) the role of policy rules; (c) the legal approach developed to tackle the abusive conduct; and (d) the possibility to quantify (F)RAND terms.

As to the first point, the Commission has importantly recognized the role that standards play for technical development and dynamic efficiency. Standards promote economic interpenetration on the internal market, encourage development of new markets and improved supply conditions.[62] They tend to encourage competition, lower output and sales costs, promote interoperability, enhance product quality and provide information.[63] Of course, in order to implement an effective standardization process, standards need to be developed through open, transparent and non-discriminatory procedures.[64] Furthermore, in the European Commission's position, the adoption of one standard over another

57 See the final version of the "Commitments" submitted by Rambus on 9 December 2009. Available at: http://ec.europa.eu/competition/elojade/isef/case_details.cfm?proc_code=1_38636.
58 Ibid. However, commitments were not conditional upon third parties settling patent litigation.
59 Summary of Commission Decision in *Rambus* (n 3), at 3.
60 European Commission, 'Commitment Decision' in *Rambus* (n 3), at 55.
61 On the analysis of the EU Commission's approach, see also D. Geradin, "Ten Years of DG Competition Effort to Provide Guidance on the Application of Competition Rules to the Licensing of Standard-Essential Patents: Where Do We Stand?" (2013) Tilburg Centre of Law and Economics Discussion Paper n. 2013-11.
62 European Commission, "Guidelines on the Applicability of Article 81 of the EC Treaty to Horizontal Co-operation Agreements" [2001] OJ C 3, at 169.
63 European Commission, "The Role of European Standardization in the Framework of European Policies and Legislation" (Communication) COM 674 final, 18 October 2004.
64 European Commission, "Guidelines on the Applicability of Article 81 of the EC Treaty to Horizontal Co-operation Agreements" [2001] OJ C 3.

must be justifiable, both in terms of quality and costs.[65] These considerations reflect the same views of the US authorities and courts on the importance of effective standardization.

More controversial, instead, was the well-known issue on the clarity of JEDEC policy. On the one hand, both the FTC in the US and the Commission in the EU seem to have interpreted such rules as clear and properly disclosed. In addition, they relied on the existence of a general good faith duty that would apply to all members of SSOs. On the other, the US Court of Appeals raised several doubts on the clarity of JEDEC policy and on the effectiveness of such a general covenant.[66] The position of the court seems undoubtedly more persuasive, mainly in light of the need to establish robust policy regulations and avoid misunderstandings on the members' duties.

The interpretation of JEDEC policy, then, necessarily recalls the legal approach adopted in the analysis of Rambus's behavior. In this context, the EU Commission seems to have considered the company's conduct as both exploitative and exclusionary. However, as I have argued, the existence of exclusionary effects was not certain, due to the possibility that JEDEC could have adopted Rambus's technology in any event. This consideration explains why Rambus finally escaped antitrust liability in the US, where the Sherman Act requires harm to the competitive process as a condition for its enforcement. Nevertheless, the EU Commission could still legitimately appraise the conduct as an exploitative practice under Article 102 TFEU. To this end, as explained above, the enforcement of Article 102(b) might appear more appropriate, in light of the difficulties which may arise in interpreting price levels.

However, it is likely that the Commission in the Statement of Objections considered the conduct also under Article 102(a), which bans excessive pricing. Such position may be confirmed by the fact that the authority required Rambus to remedy by charging reasonable fees, the amount of which should have been determined in accordance to the circumstances of the case. In other words, Rambus's royalties were deemed excessive. This further meant, in the authority's opinion, that the concept of (F)RAND could have been quantified. As a consequence, the US chip designer finally proposed a set of licensing fees within a determined price range.

The possibility to determine the meaning of (F)RAND royalties is certainly one of the most interesting issues emerging from this case. However, two considerations should be made. Firstly, as observed in the course of the book, the concept of fair and reasonable is not an absolute one; hence, what the Commission may have interpreted as fair and reasonable could be defined by another court or authority as still unfair or unreasonable. Secondly, even admitting the possibility to quantify (F)RAND terms on a case-by-case basis, it is plausible that an agreement on such a meaning could only be reached after litigation. However, litigation has negative effects on standardization, due to the implied costs and delays in innovation.

65 Ibid., at 171.

66 See *Rambus Inc v Federal Trade Commission*, 522 F3d 456 (C App DC Circuit, 2008).

Thus, in conclusion, the attempt to define fair and reasonable cannot be supported. The (F)RAND notion, merely leading to an "agreement to agree", is a highly problematic concept which is likely to raise disputes on its very meaning to the ultimate detriment of the whole SSO system.

4 *Qualcomm* and the breach of FRAND terms

The EU experience with standard setting and potential competition infringements is not limited to *Rambus*. Indeed, the Commission initiated proceedings also against Qualcomm,[67] active in the market of mobile phones with IPRs covering both the CDMA and WCDMA standards.[68] The EU investigation on Qualcomm's conduct followed the proceedings against the firm started by US courts for the same behavior, and already scrutinized in Chapter 5.[69] However, due to the differences of legal framework and enforcement mechanism between the EU and US systems, it is relevant to examine also how the Commission tried to approach the dispute.

4.1 "FRAND(ly)" licensing or exploitation?

During 2007, the EU enforcer decided to start investigations against Qualcomm for an alleged infringement of Article 102 TFEU,[70] after complaints lodged by six mobile phone and chipset manufacturers.[71] Similarly to what held by Broadcom in the US,[72] the complainants had alleged that Qualcomm's licensing practices for the WCDMA standard were not fair reasonable and non-discriminatory (FRAND) and were in breach of EU competition law. In this context, the complainants had alleged that charging non-FRAND royalties, in violation of the duty undertaken under the SSO (ETSI) policy, could have led to higher handset prices for consumers, a slower development of the third generation standard for mobile phone technology, and negative effects also for the development of the future fourth generation standard.[73]

The investigation, therefore, did not concern patent ambush, as Qualcomm had disclosed all its relevant IPRs. It was rather focused on the level of royalties charged by the company and on the risk that Qualcomm could have gained extra power as a result of its technology incorporated in the standard. As the

67 See *Texas Instruments v Qualcomm* (n 3); and European Commission, "Commission Initiates Formal Proceedings against Qualcomm" (1 October 2007) Press Release MEMO/07/389.

68 CDMA and WCDMA respectively stand for "Code Division Multiple Access" and "Wide-Band CDMA." WCDMA standard forms part of the 3G (third generation) EU phone mobile technology.

69 See Chapter 5 section 3.2.1.

70 The legal base of this procedural step is Article 2 of Commission Regulation n 773/2004, [2004] OJ L 123/18. Article 2 provides that the Commission may initiate proceedings with a view to adopting at a later stage a decision on substance at any point in time, but at the latest when issuing a Statement of Objections or a preliminary assessment notice in a settlement procedure.

71 These were Ericsson, Nokia, Texas Instruments, Broadcom, NEC and Panasonic.

72 *Broadcom v Qualcomm*, 501 F3d 297 (C App 3rd Circuit, 2007).

73 These allegations were also at the basis of further investigations against Qualcomm led, *inter alia*, by the Korean Fair Trade Commission (KFTC) and Japan Fair Trade Commission (JFTC).

EU authority held, "a finding of exploitative practices by Qualcomm in the WCDMA licensing market contrary to Article 82 of the EC Treaty may depend on whether the licensing terms imposed by Qualcomm are in breach of its FRAND commitment."[74] This means that the Commission was interested in understanding whether Qualcomm was dominant in the relevant market and whether it had exploited its position by charging unreasonably high prices. Furthermore, the concerns of the Commission were also based on the company's price discrimination strategy. Qualcomm, indeed, was excluding competitors by giving discounts for exclusive customers of its mobile phone chipsets. These practices could discourage firms to participate in SSOs and consequently jeopardize the innovative effort within standards.[75]

However, Qualcomm eventually signed mutual agreements with all the complainants and settled the dispute.[76] This fact prompted the authority to close the investigation, at a time when it had not yet reached any formal conclusions. This further means that the case did not ultimately lead to discuss FRAND criteria, including the numeric proportionality rule proposed by the litigants.[77] Thus, *Qualcomm* probably represented a missed opportunity for those authors still supporting the possibility to define fair reasonable and non-discriminatory terms.[78] Nevertheless, the case is relevant as it highlighted the EU Commission's interventionist approach towards high pricing and discriminatory conduct, especially in those sectors which are key to enhance innovation and welfare.

5 Guidelines on horizontal co-operation agreements

As *Qualcomm* and *Rambus* attested, and even considering the case law on the scope of injunctions, the EU experience in standard setting is more limited and not comparable to the US background. The procedural dynamics of these cases did not allow defining in-depth a well-established EU practice in tackling the risks related to standards. In order to gain a clearer insight, it seems then relevant to examine also the content and goals of the Commission's "Guidelines on the Applicability of Art. 101 TFEU to Horizontal Co-operation Agreements."[79]

74 European Commission (n 67).

75 A. Chronopoulos, "Patenting Standards – A Case for US Antitrust Law or a Call for Recognizing Immanent Public Policy Limitations to the Exploitation Rights Conferred by the Patent Act?" (2009) 40(7) *International Review of Intellectual Property and Competition Law* 790.

76 The worldwide litigation between Qualcomm and Broadcom, for instance, was settled in 2009 under condition that the former would pay Broadcom $891 million over four years.

77 S. Sattler (n 1) 347. On the concept of numeric proportionality, see Chapter 3 section 4.3.1.

78 A. Layne Farrar, "Non-discriminatory Pricing: Is Standard Setting Different?" (2010) 6(4) *Journal of Competition Law and Economics* 811. Among the authors supporting (F)RAND terms, see also R.A. Epstein, F.S. Kieff and D.F. Spulber, "The FTC, IP and SSOs: Government Holdup Replacing Private Coordination" (2012) 8(1) *Journal of Competition Law and Economics* 1.

79 European Commission (n 2). The document replaced the 2001 version ("Guidelines on the Applicability of Article 81 of the EC Treaty to Horizontal Co-operation Agreements" [2001] OJ C 3/2), which was considered too broad to offer effective guidance for SSOs.

The latter set out the principles for the assessment under Article 101 TFEU of agreements relating to horizontal cooperation between competing undertakings and between non-competitors. The Guidelines look at the economic benefits deriving from horizontal co-operation, in terms of risk sharing, cost savings, investment incentives and welfare enhancement. At the same time, they identify the potential anticompetitive risks related to these agreements, from price fixing to output reduction and market sharing.[80]

Among the most common types of horizontal co-operation,[81] the Guidelines scrutinize the activities of standard setting organizations. In particular, they appraise the function of standards, identify the markets potentially concerned and analyze the risks standardization may raise. To this end, they apply both legal and economic criteria, based on the assessment of market structure and market shares. Furthermore, the Guidelines highlight the Commission's position on the well-known dispute on (F)RAND terms. In this context, they review the possibility to determine the meaning of fair reasonable and non-discriminatory conditions. This is certainly a crucial point for standard-setting processes, as several SSOs have implemented (F)RAND terms.[82] This notwithstanding, it is not clear which interpretative criterion should ultimately prevail.

5.1 Standardization agreements

First, the Guidelines give an invaluable insight on the crucial role of standardization agreements, focused on the "definition of technical or quality requirements with which current or future products, production processes, services or methods may comply."[83] Standardization, it is observed, is key to economic interpenetration on the internal market and to the development of new and improved product markets and supply conditions; thus, it helps to eliminate restrictions on trade between Member States.[84] Standardization can take different forms, depending on the parties involved: from national or European organizations, to private *consortia* and independent firms.[85]

As to the effects, then, four markets are seen as potentially affected by standard-setting activities: (i) the product or service market to which the standard relates; (ii) the relevant technology market, in case IPRs covering the standard are marketed separately; (iii) the market for standard setting, in case different SSOs or agreements exist; and (iv) where relevant, a distinct market for testing and certification.[86] In these markets, the Guidelines note that standard setting may raise competition

80 Ibid., at 2–3.

81 E.g. R&D, production, purchasing and commercialization agreements.

82 For instance, ETSI, IEEE and OASIS usually refer to FRAND commitments. IETF, IEC, ITU and ISO consider instead RAND licensing policies.

83 European Commission (n 2), at 257.

84 Ibid., at 263.

85 On the possible forms of standardization, see Chapter 3 section 3. See also R. Schellingerhout, "Standard-setting from a Competition Law Perspective" (2011) 1 *Competition Policy Newsletter* 3.

86 European Commission (n 2), at 261.

law concerns, both in case of agreements between undertakings and agreements within a standard setting institute.[87] At the same time, however, standardization may also lead to efficiency gains. Therefore, two different types of assessment are considered, under Article 101(1) and Article 101(3) TFEU.

In the next subsections, I will delve into the approach developed by the EU Commission to tackle the anticompetitive effects arising from standard-setting agreements. As a premise, I will first examine the core policy principles emerging from the Guidelines. Due regard will also be given to the authority's position on the meaning of fair reasonable and non-discriminatory terms.

5.2 Core policy principles

The analysis of the Guidelines leads to identify some basic principles which are seen as the core of effective policies and which may constitute "safe harbors." As recognized by the Commission, there exist different competing models of standard setting which can be freely adopted by SSOs. The latter, however, must implement rules and procedures that do not infringe competition law.[88] To this end, it is essential to ensure unrestricted participation in standard setting by guaranteeing that all competitors can participate to the selection of the standard. SSOs, in particular, should develop objective and non-discriminatory procedures for allocating voting rights and selecting the technology to include in the standard.[89] The scope of this principle must be read also in light of the need to encourage effective participation of IPRs owners. Indeed, the involvement of a significant number of innovators may lead to the selection of the optimal standard, to the benefit of societal welfare.

On a further ground, SSOs should implement transparent procedures "which allow stakeholders to effectively inform themselves of upcoming, ongoing and finalised standardization work in good time at each stage of the development of the standard."[90] In case of standards involving IPRs, the Commission highlights the need to develop clear and balanced IPR policies, adapted to the particular industry and to the SSO's needs.[91] Transparency must therefore be interpreted as a crucial safeguard against anticompetitive risks.

Finally, the Guidelines examine the role of a good faith duty to disclose. In this context, it is observed, SSO members should be required to reveal those IPRs which are relevant to the standard. In this way, the standard-setting body would be able to make an informed choice of technology and ensure effective access to the standard. As further argued, "such a disclosure obligation could be based on ongoing disclosure as the standard develops and on reasonable endeavors to identify IPR reading on the potential standard."[92] With respect to these last

87 Ibid., at 258.
88 Ibid., at 279. On the issue, see also Case IV/35.006 *ETSI Interim IPR Policy* [1995] OJ C 76/5.
89 European Commission (n 2), at 280–281.
90 Ibid., at 282.
91 Ibid., at 284.
92 Ibid., at 286.

considerations, however, some doubts may arise. First, it is not clear whether the Commission implicitly recognized the necessity to implement a duty to search. On a different ground, the Commission did not precisely identify an optimal time of disclosure of essential rights. It did not even set the scope of the mentioned good faith duty. The Guidelines, thus, leave many questions open, regarding also the enforceability of the policy models. On the other side, they make some interesting observations, which will be developed further in Chapter 7. In particular, as to the subject of disclosure, the Guidelines notably state that members may preserve their trade secrets by simply stating to have IPR claims over a standard, without disclosing specific claims or applications.[93]

5.3 FRAND terms

One of the most interesting questions addressed by the Commission in the attempt to provide for more legal certainty concerns the meaning and role of FRAND. The issue, as explained in Chapter 3, is certainly crucial to standardization, due to the wide adoption of this licensing model by standard setting institutes. This being premised, the Guidelines note that:

> [i]n order to ensure effective access to the standard, the IPR policy would need to require participants wishing to have their IPR included in the standard to provide an irrevocable commitment in writing to offer to license their essential IPR to all third parties on fair, reasonable and non-discriminatory terms.[94]

The *ex ante* implementation of FRAND terms, in the Commission's view, should prevent innovators from harming SSOs processes through the charging of excessive fees or a refusal to license. In order to ensure its effectiveness, the commitment should bind also third parties who purchase the IPRs subjected to a member's FRAND promise.[95] This effect, according to the Guidelines, could be obtained by including a contractual clause between the buyer and the seller.[96]

These observations undoubtedly reveal interesting ideas. The proposal of an irrevocable commitment in writing, for instance, may give more guarantees in terms of fulfillment of the selected innovator's promise. Furthermore, the proposal to transfer to third parties also the FRAND commitment may preserve the outcome of the process. This notwithstanding, serious doubts arise as to the arguments relating to the meaning of FRAND.

93 Ibid.

94 Ibid., at 285.

95 On the scope of this argument, see European Commission, "Commission Welcomes IPCom's Public FRAND Declaration" (10 December 2009) Press Release MEMO/09/549. After acquiring Bosch's patents, IPCOM finally agreed with the Commission to adopt the commitments originally provided by Bosch and to grant irrevocable licenses to use its patents on FRAND terms.

96 European Commission (n 2), at 285. These views recall the FTC's arguments developed in the case *Negotiated Data Solutions* (above, Chapter 5 section 3.2).

First, the Guidelines note that the SSO members themselves will have to assess whether the level of fees charged fulfills the FRAND commitment.[97] Second, they argue that, in case of a dispute, "the assessment of whether fees charged for access to IPR in the standard setting context are unfair or unreasonable should be based on whether the fees bear a reasonable relationship to the economic value of the IPR."[98] It is alleged that, in order to qualify royalty fees as excessive, the conditions for an abuse of a dominant position as set out in Article 102 TFEU and in the case law of the EU courts must be fulfilled.[99] The Guidelines identify various ways to make the assessment, provided that cost-based methods seldom work due to the difficulties arising in the appraisal of IPR-related costs.[100] They suggest to compare the royalties charged by the innovator in an *ex ante* competitive environment (before the industry is locked-in) with those charged *ex post* (after the lock-in effect has occurred).[101] However, this method does not seem faultless, mainly due to the risk that licenses may have been overpriced or undervalued in the course of previous negotiations.[102] The Guidelines, then, consider the possibility "to obtain an independent expert assessment of the objective centrality and essentiality to the standard at issue of the relevant IPR portfolio."[103] However, also this system may be subject to criticism. Two independent experts appointed by the licensor and licensee, indeed, will probably have conflicting perspectives as to the level of fair and reasonable terms. Finally, the Guidelines observe that the level of fees charged for the same IPR in other comparable standards may also provide an indication.[104] Perhaps, also this method could raise some doubts, due to the risk that royalty rates charged in other standards may not necessarily reflect a fair and reasonable price. The list of criteria, as the Commission clarifies, is not exhaustive but further ways for defining FRAND might be adopted.

On a different ground, the authority leaves open the possibility for the interested parties to resolve their disputes on the issue before the competent civil or commercial courts. This means that the risks deriving from lengthy litigation, in terms of bottleneck of standardization and delays of innovative processes, were not properly scrutinized by the authority. In conclusion, the Commission's approach to FRAND terms and to the cited interpretative methods is certainly one of the most controversial matters emerging from the text of the document. This approach, however, seems to have been endorsed in the recent "European

97 Ibid., at 288.
98 Ibid., at 289. See also *United Brands* (n 4), at 250; Case C-385/07 P *Der Grune Punkt – Duales System Deutschland GmbH v European Commission* [2009] ECR I-6155, at 142; and *Attheraces v British Horse Racing Board*, [2007] EWCA 38.
99 *United Brands* (n 4).
100 European Commission (n 2), at 289.
101 Ibid.
102 On the faults of the alternative methods suggested for the appraisal of (F)RAND licensing conditions, see also Chapter 3 section 4.3.
103 European Commission (n 2), at 290.
104 Ibid.

Standardization Regulation," which encouraged the implementation of (F)RAND licensing policies.[105]

5.4 Anticompetitive conduct

The examination of the core policy principles does not exhaust the analysis of the most relevant issues. The Commission's assessment of anticompetitive practices is undoubtedly a subject which needs close scrutiny. In this context, two different perspectives are developed. On the one hand, the Guidelines consider those restrictive practices which may affect price competition, production, markets and technical development. On the other, they delve into the efficiency gains which may potentially arise from standards and which may lead to an exemption under Article 101(3) TFEU. The Commission, however, does not examine thoroughly the concept of hold-up and its inherent dynamics. It only mentions the risk that members may behave in anticompetitive ways by holding-up users after the adoption of the standard.[106]

5.4.1 Restrictive practices in standardization

Potential restrictive practices may lead to a "reduction in price competition, foreclosure of innovative technologies and exclusion of, or discrimination against, certain companies by prevention of effective access to the standard."[107]

As to the first channel, reduction or elimination of price competition may occur when firms start discussing prices in the context of standard setting.[108] These restrictions could, in theory, occur either on the supplier or on the purchaser side of the market for the standard. Standardization agreements which allow early disclosure of most restrictive licensing terms may potentially facilitate price fixing of downstream products or of substitute IPRs or technology between SSO participants. These agreements, in the Commission's view, should be interpreted as restrictions of competition by object, prohibited by Article 101(1) TFEU.[109] However, a more serious risk of price fixing may occur mainly in case of vertically integrated firms or licensees discussing sale prices of downstream products. On the contrary, and especially if outside a patent pool context, it is not certain that licensors would jointly set the royalty level for the relevant IPRs. Prior to the adoption of the standard, indeed, innovators usually compete with each other for the selection of the proprietary technology.[110]

Secondly, further concerns may arise in case of foreclosure of competing innovative technologies. This may happen when, during the selection process,

105 EU Parliament and Council Regulation n 1025/2012, [2012] OJ L 316/12, Annex II par. 4.

106 European Commission (n 2), at 269.

107 Ibid., at 264.

108 Ibid., at 265.

109 Ibid., at 274. On the effects of restrictive practices, see also M. Glader, "Open Standards: Public Policy Aspects and Competition Law Requirements" (2010) 6(3) *European Competition Journal* 611.

110 Chapter 4 section 3.4.

undertakings with competing technologies are unjustifiably excluded. Similar effects could arise in case the producers of an incumbent product collude with the SSO members to exclude new technologies from an already existing standard. Also these practices, as the Commission rightly notes, should be considered as restrictions of competition by object. Their ultimate effect would be detrimental to technical development and innovation.[111] These considerations evoke the Commission's conclusions in the case *Pre-Insulated Pipes,* where the infringement of Article 101(1) TFEU consisted in the use of "norms and standards in order to prevent or delay the introduction of new technology which would result in price reductions."[112]

Thirdly, the Guidelines identify a serious risk of anticompetitive effects in the exclusion of undertakings from access to the standard.[113] Under these circumstances, firms might be completely prevented from obtaining access to the result of the standard (the technical specifications or essential IPRs). Alternatively, they might be granted access only on prohibitive or discriminatory terms. In order to limit these risks, the Guidelines remark the importance of clear disclosure policies requiring members to reveal *ex ante* the existence of relevant IPRs. This way, SSO participants may easily identify which technologies are proprietary and may consequently make a more informed decision on the basis of more transparent procedures. Besides access to the results of the standard, access to the standard-setting process may be limited. Standard-setting agreements may indeed discriminate against particular types of participants or potential members, and exclude them from participation in the SSO's activities.[114] This could also lead to a restriction of competition contrary to Article 101(1) TFEU.[115]

However, it is further stated, in case of several competing standards or effective competition between standardized and non-standardized solutions, a limitation of access may not necessarily lead to restrictive effects on competition.[116] Similarly, if the limitation on the number of the participants was ancillary to the implementation of the standard, then the agreement would seldom lead to restrictive effects on competition in violation of Article 101(1). But even in case of negative effects determined by restricted participation, these effects could be limited or removed "by ensuring that stakeholders are kept informed and consulted on the work in progress."[117]

More in general, as the Guidelines clarify, standardization agreements which do not restrict competition by object must be assessed in their legal and economic

111 European Commission (n 2), at 266.

112 Case IV/35.691 *Pre-Insulated Pipes* [1999] OJ L 24, at 147.

113 European Commission (n 2), at 268 and 295.

114 See the Commission's decision in Case IV/31.458 *X/Open Group* [1987] OJ L 35, at 36. Here, the Commission considered that "even if the standard adopted were made public, the restricted membership policy had the effect of preventing non-members from influencing the results of the work of the group and from getting the know-how and technical understanding relating to the standards which the members were likely to acquire." This led to an infringement of Art. 101(1).

115 European Commission (n 2), at 297.

116 Ibid., at 294–295.

117 Ibid., at 295.

context, with regard to their actual and likely effects on competition.[118] Only in the absence of market power would these agreements likely fall outside of the scope of Article 101(1) TFEU. The existence of restrictive effects may depend also on whether SSO members remain free to develop alternative standards or products that do not comply with the selected standard.[119] For instance, in case an organization binds its members to produce only products in compliance with the standard, there would be a higher risk of negative effects on competition. This happened in the case *Philips/VCR*, where the parties were prohibited from manufacturing and distributing products different from those complying with the standard.[120] At the same time, it is also true that in case of standards only covering minor aspects or parts of the end product competition concerns would be less likely.[121]

5.4.2 Efficiency gains

Despite the risks of anticompetitive practices, standardization agreements may give rise to substantial efficiency gains. In order to outweigh any restrictive effects, these must be passed on to consumers.[122] In this regard, for instance, the Guidelines remark the important role played by Union-wide standards. The latter, as powerful harmonizing factors, may facilitate market integration between the Member States, ultimately leading to lower prices and increased consumer choice.[123] With respect to the standards promoting technical interoperability, the Guidelines highlight their beneficial effects in terms of increased competition between different technologies and a reduced risk of lock-in effects. Standards may also reduce transaction costs for sellers and buyers, and may have a crucial impact on innovation. To this end, "[t]hey can reduce the time it takes to bring a new technology to the market and facilitate innovation by allowing companies to build on top of agreed solutions."[124] In order to achieve these efficiency gains, the information necessary to apply the standard must be available to those wishing to enter the market. The willingness to make available the results of a standard as quickly as possible influenced the Commission's decision in *X/Open Group* to grant an exemption under Article 101(3) TFEU.[125]

On a further different ground, the Commission notably argues that restrictions on competition may be accepted as long as they are indispensable to achieve these efficiency gains.[126] This means that standardization agreements should cover no

118 Ibid., at 277.

119 Ibid., at 293. On the analysis of restrictive effects of standard setting agreements, see also J. Temple Lang, "Patent Pools and Agreements on Standards" (2011) 36(6) *European Law Review* 887; and A. Emanuelson (n 21), 69.

120 See also Case IV/29/151 *Philips/VCR* [1978] OJ L 47, at 23.

121 European Commission (n 2), at 293.

122 Ibid., at 321.

123 On standards and market integration, see L. Goerke and M. Holler, "Strategic Standardization in Europe: A Public Choice Perspective" (1998) 6(2) *European Journal of Law & Economics* 95.

124 European Commission (n 2), at 308–309.

125 *X/Open Group* (n 114), at 42.

126 European Commission (n 2), at 314–315.

more than what is strictly necessary to achieve their goals.[127] Those restrictions which go beyond the objective of achieving efficiencies do not fulfill the criteria of Article 101(3) TFEU. For instance, limited access to the standard-setting process may only be justified as long as the parties demonstrate significant inefficiencies from unlimited participation.[128] No justification, instead, may be given in case of standardization agreements limiting the use of a proprietary technology to a particular standard. Exclusive use, it is explained, could limit inter-technology competition and would not be indispensable for the achievement of any efficiency.[129] In the same vein, agreements which make a standard binding for the industry are in principle not indispensable.[130] The cited case *Philips/VCR* also gave an example of unnecessary restrictions, since the constraints imposed on the parties were not indispensable to attain any efficiency.[131]

6 Conclusion

In brief, it is undoubted that the Guidelines develop interesting concepts and innovative ideas. The implementation of transparent, unrestricted processes is considered at the basis of productive standard setting.[132] In comparison to the case law, a stronger need for more effective policies is highlighted. Thus, it is to be welcomed that the Commission apparently follows the principle that prevention is better than cure. However, the Guidelines leave several issues open. They contribute only partially to solve the tension between standards, IPRs and competition. For instance, it is not clear which is the authority's position on search requirements. In addition, the Commission did not thoroughly explain how disclosure policies may function in practice, in terms of time of disclosure and good faith duty. Also the proposed assessment of FRAND terms does not provide for more legal certainty. Likewise, doubts exist as to how a prevention-based approach could be reconciled with an effective enforcement mechanism.

As to the case law, it seems that the Commission was not able to strike an optimal balance between innovators' interests and SSO aims. However notable the analysis of the benefits of standards, the Commission undervalued the importance of robust policy rules. It further failed to detect the faults of FRAND licensing and the related high risks of litigation. Therefore, in conclusion, all these issues still need an appropriate and comprehensive examination.

127 Ibid., at 317.

128 Ibid., at 316. See also Case 39.416 *IACS – Ship Classification* [2010] OJ C 2.

129 European Commission (n 2), at 317.

130 Ibid., at 318.

131 *Philips/VCR* (n 120), at 31.

132 See also European Commission, "Towards an Increased Contribution from Standardization to Innovation in Europe" (Communication) COM 133 final, 11 March 2008; and EU Parliament and Council Regulation n 1025/2012, [2012] OJ L 316/12 ("European Standardization Regulation").

Part Three

Reconciling IPRs and competition in standard setting

7 Suggested model and enforcement

1 Introduction

The arguments developed in the first chapters have focused on the roles and objectives of IP and antitrust laws.[1] It has been argued that, although a superficial tension may exist, IPRs and competition are finally concordant in enhancing consumer welfare and innovation. The achievement of these goals may ultimately raise the welfare of the society as a whole. This notwithstanding, specific attention has also been paid to one of those fields where the interaction IP–competition may lead to potentially harmful conflicts.

In this context, the standard-setting environment has been considered, from both the EU and US perspectives.[2] In particular, it has been explained how standardization processes may lead IPR owners to over-exploit their market power and compromise the ultimate function of standards, to the detriment of consumer surplus and societal productivity. The main solutions cited by the literature in terms of policies have not proved to be effective remedies to tackle the risks arising in the field. Thus, uncertainty still exists as to the most workable regime for SSOs.

In view of these considerations, this chapter aims to strike an optimal policy framework which may ensure from an *ex ante* perspective the proper functioning of standardization, without reducing the IPRs owners' incentives to participate in SSOs. After briefly recalling the faults of the (F)RAND model and early negotiation regime, I will consider an alternative licensing policy which may prove to be far more effective. Other important remarks will be given on the need to establish search and disclosure duties, which may play a relevant influence on innovators' will to participate in standard setting.

Besides proposing a workable model, further questions will be addressed. Which role, if any, may the enforcement of contract law play in limiting the negative effects of unfair conduct by IPRs owners? Further tools of private law will also be examined as possible *ex post* remedies. Among these, the book will draw the attention to those doctrines advancing proposals of patent restrictions. Would patent law defenses and counterclaims to patent infringement be effective

1 See Chapter 1 section 2 and Chapter 2 section 2.

2 See Chapter 4 sections 3 and 4.

means to address the risks arising in standard setting? The *pro* and *contra* of these alternative theories will be considered, with particular reference to their effects on the IPRs owners' incentives to invest in innovation. Indeed, it is still debatable whether limiting the scope of IPRs protection may ultimately have a detrimental effect on long-term societal growth. Finally, due to the problems these private law remedies may raise, the book will examine whether an effective competition or antitrust system enforcing a consumer welfare test may succeed – from an *ex post* perspective – in constraining misleading behaviors.

2 Promoting innovation and protecting competition

Before looking at the optimal model reflecting IPRs owners' interests and standard-setting goals, it seems important to review in more detail one basic cornerstone, which is the need to reconcile the promotion of innovation with the protection of competition.

It is true that economic growth strongly relies on innovative capability; competition and IPRs are well-known key factors to innovation, as they both aim to strengthen innovative competition.[3] However, it has also been said that IPRs and competition may potentially give rise to controversy. In this context, US and EU antitrust enforcers have sometimes pursued the aim to reconcile innovation and competition in slightly different ways.

The next sections will delve into these different approaches and will further explore the intersection between IPRs, standardization and competition. The considerations developed therein will be paramount in order to understand and justify the optimal policy model for standard setting organizations.

2.1 US v EU perspectives

The importance of innovation for consumer and societal welfare has been clearly recognized both in the US and the EU. The recently modified Treaty on the EU, for instance, has identified the Union's aim to promote scientific and technological advance as a crucial step towards the achievement of innovation.[4] On a similar ground, both US courts and agencies have often stressed the need to enhance innovation as a means to increase the national wealth.[5]

3 M. Angelov, "The Exceptional Circumstances Test: Implications for FRAND Commitments from the Essential Facilities Doctrine under Art. 102 TFEU" (2014) 10(1) *European Competition Journal* 39–41; S. Sattler, "Standardization under EU Competition Rules – The Commission's New Horizontal Guidelines" (2011) 32(7) *European Competition Law Review* 344. On the one hand, as Sattler notes, IPRs encourage innovation by rewarding investments in R&D; they constitute, therefore, a socially optimal incentive for investing in innovative activities. On the other hand, competition drives undertakings to innovate in order to succeed and constrain rival businesses.

4 Article 3(3), Treaty on the European Union (TEU), OJ 2010 C 83/13.

5 See, for instance, *Verizon Communications v Trinko*, 540 US 398 (2004); and the Report of the US Federal Trade Commission, "The Evolving IP Marketplace: Aligning Patent Notice and Remedies with Competition" (March 2011).

However, it is clear that in order to enhance dynamic efficiency it is necessary to encourage firms to develop new innovative products. In the absence of incentives, the level of investment that maximizes the net value to society would not be undertaken, and dynamic inefficiencies would arise.[6] In this context, undertakings are usually incentivized to invest in research and development as long as they get rewarded for their economic efforts.[7] This is the well-known function of IPRs, which confer on the owners the exclusive right to exploit their inventions and grant a license to interested firms upon the payment of running royalties, lump sum fees or the grant of cross-licences.[8]

As explained by US agencies, IP laws provide a complex system of affirmative rewards by "establishing enforceable property rights for the creators of new and useful products, more efficient processes, and original works of expression."[9] On the other side of the Atlantic, the EU Commission has similarly recognized the importance of IPRs and of the licensing mechanism, which is interpreted as a crucial way for innovators to cover their costs.[10] However, dissimilarities may arise when appraising the perspectives adopted to protect competition from the over-exploitation of IPRs. For instance, US antitrust enforcers seem to have developed a more permissive approach in interpreting the role of monopolistic innovators. As held by the US Supreme Court:

> [t]he mere possession of monopoly [...] and the opportunity to charge monopoly prices—at least for a short period—is what attracts "business acumen" in the first place; it induces risk taking that produces innovation and economic growth.[11]

6 J.G. Sidak, "Patent Hold-up and Oligopsonistic Collusion in Standard-Setting Organizations" (2009) 5(1) *Journal of Competition Law and Economics* 141.

7 D. Geradin and M. Rato, "Can Standard-Setting Lead to Exploitative Abuse? A Dissonant View on Patent Hold-Up, Royalty Stacking and the Meaning of FRAND" (2007) 3 *European Competition Journal* 110. See also M. Dolmans, "A Tale of Two Tragedies – A Plea for Open Standards, and Some Comments on the RAND Report" (2010) 1 *Concurrences* 7–17. As Dolmans argues, "patent law secures to the inventor, for a limited time, the exclusive use of his invention; and thereby adds the fuel of interest to the fire of genius."

8 See Chapter 2 section 2. On the different business strategies adopted by patent owners, see M.A. Lemley and A.D. Melamed, "Missing the Forest for the Trolls" (2013) Stanford Law School Working Paper Series n. 443. Here, the authors explore the role of non-practicing entities (also called "trolls"), which are not seen as the cause of all the problems affecting the patent system.

9 Report of the US Department of Justice and Federal Trade Commission, "Antitrust Enforcement and Intellectual Property Rights: Promoting Innovation and Competition" (April 2007) 1. See also US Department of Justice and US Patent & Trademark Office, "Policy Statement on Remedies for Standards-Essential Patents Subject to Voluntary F/RAND Commitment" (January 2013). As stated in the latter document, "the DOJ and USPTO recognize that the right of a patent holder to exclude others from practicing patented inventions is fundamental to obtaining these benefits. It is incorporated into section 337 of the Tariff Act of 1930 itself, which forbids the unlawful importation into the United States ... of articles that ... infringe a valid enforceable United States patent."

10 See the European Commission, "Guidelines on the application of Article 81 of the EC Treaty to technology transfer agreements" [2004] OJ C 101, at 17.

11 *Verizon* (n 5) 398.

The EU counterparts, instead, have traditionally looked at monopolies from a more restrictive perspective, as a potential danger for the market structure and for societal welfare. Unlike the interpretation given by the US Supreme Court, the opportunity to charge monopoly prices can be scrutinized by the EU competition enforcers under Article 102(a) TFEU, which prohibits high pricing conduct.[12]

These different views, for instance, are reflected in the analysis of the jurisprudence on standard setting, with particular reference to the *Rambus* case.[13] This notwithstanding, as I will argue in the course of the chapter, the development of the right balance in standard-setting policies may help in reducing the existing gap between the EU and US perspectives when enforcing the law. This means that the very detection of the optimal equilibrium between SSO aims and innovators' interests may facilitate the implementation of similar approaches by EU and US enforcers towards standardization issues.

2.2 IPRs, competition and the standards

The considerations developed above on the need to reward innovators hold true also in case of standard setting. By having their protected inventions included in the standard, IPRs holders may be rewarded for their contribution to technological progress and innovation.[14]

With respect to standards, the EU Commission has clarified that "a stronger role for standardization in support of innovation is important for the European effort to address economic, environmental and social challenges."[15] Standards permit mass-collaboration, facilitate the dissemination of knowledge, ultimately leading to more innovation.[16] However, a few legitimate questions could be posed. Would the adoption of non-proprietary standards lead to fewer firms investing in innovation? Would the requirement on selected IPRs owners to waive their royalties lead to similar consequences? Standard setting concerns several important

12 Article 102(a), Treaty on the Functioning of the European Union (TFEU), OJ [2010] C 83/89.

13 *Cf.* the European Commission's Statement of Objections in Case COMP/38.636 *Rambus* [2010] OJ C 30; and *Rambus Inc v Federal Trade Commission*, 522 F.3d 456 (C App DC Circuit, 2008).

14 M.C. Naughton and R. Wolfram, "The Antitrust Risks of Unilateral Conduct in Standard Setting, in the Light of the FTC's case against Rambus Inc" (2004) 49 *Antitrust Bulletin* 701; D. Geradin and R.G. Brooks, "Interpreting and Enforcing the Voluntary FRAND Commitment" (2011) 9(1) *International Journal of IT Standards and Standardization Research* 1; M.R. Patterson, "Inventions, Industry Standards, and Intellectual Property" (2002) 17 *Berkeley Technology Law Journal* 1043. Patterson interestingly argues that a patent owner should be rewarded only for its invention, but not for the benefits deriving from the whole standardization (e.g. interoperability).

15 European Commission, "Towards an Increased Contribution from Standardization to Innovation in Europe" (Communication) COM 133 final, 11 March 2008.

16 See J. Gstalter, "Open Standards and Competition Law: an Overview" (2010) 1 *Concurrences* 1–4; J.J. Anton and D.A. Yao, "Standard setting consortia, antitrust, and high-technology industries" (1996) 64 *Antitrust Law Journal* 247; and M.A. Lemley and C. Shapiro, "A Simple Approach to Setting Reasonable Royalties for Standard-essential Patents" (2013) 28 *Berkeley Technology Law Journal* 1136.

industries,[17] and SSO policies may well incentivize or discourage firms from investing in expensive innovative processes.

In light of the above, it seems reasonable to argue that the automatic exclusion of IPRs from standardization would likely lead to fewer innovations and less competition within the standards, especially technically complex ones.[18] The immediate consequence could be a reduced number of standards, of a lower quality.[19] The ultimate effect would be detrimental to the welfare of consumers, and may impact negatively the societal growth.[20]

This notwithstanding, it has also been said that innovators participating in standard setting may implement unfair conduct aimed at excluding competitors and charging exorbitant fees.[21] This is due to the fact that IPRs in standards may have an undesirable impact which may ultimately frustrate competition and technical development.[22] Exploitative and exclusionary practices may hence undermine the objective of standard setting, to the detriment of innovation and societal productivity. How to strike, then, the optimal balance between IPRs and industry standards, between investment incentives and competition goals? It is true that standardization, IPRs and competition can all play a role in promoting technological development, but it seems vital to keep the balance right.[23] This is the approach endorsed by the European Commission in dealing with standardization, according to which:

> both intellectual property rights and standardization encourage innovation and facilitate the dissemination of technologies. However, as they contribute to these common objectives by different means, due regard should be paid to the interrelation between IPR and standardization.[24]

17 E.g. from telecommunications, to IT and electronic engineering. A strong consensus on royalty-free policies was achieved by the open source community in the software and internet industries (for instance, in the context of the World Wide Web Consortium – W3C).

18 J. Bessen, "Open Source Software: Free Provision of Complex Public Goods" in J. Bitzer and P. Schroder, *The Economics of Open Source Software Development* (Elsevier, Amsterdam 2006) 57–81; R. Gilbert, "When Standards Require IP: FRAND v. Negotiation" in *The Pro & Cons of Standard Setting* (Swedish Competition Authority, 2010) 85. As Gilbert argues, "a royalty of zero offers no incentive for research and development and cannot be dynamically efficient."

19 J.C. De Vellis, "Patenting Industry Standards: Balancing the Rights of Patent Holders with the Need for Industry-Wide Standards" (2003) 31 *AIPLA Quarterly Journal* 301.

20 See D. Geradin, "Pricing Abuses by Essential Patent Holders in a Standard-Setting Context: A View from Europe" (2009–2010) 76 *Antitrust Law Journal* 329. The author notes that "licensing as such is pro-competitive as it leads to dissemination of technology and promotes innovation."

21 Above, Chapter 4 sections 3 and 4.

22 K.J. Koelman, "An exceptio standardis: do we need an IP exemption for standards?" (2006) 37(7) *International Review of Intellectual Property and Competition Law* 823. In its model, Koelman considers the possibility to apply an exemption (*exceptio standardis*) to IP law protection in standard setting, in order to allow compulsory licenses and reduce the risks of abusive conduct.

23 P. Hellstrom, T. Kramler and F.W. Bulst, "Holding Standardization to Competition Law Standards" (2010) 1 *Concurrences* 24–26.

24 J. Gstalter (n 16) 1–4. See also European Commission, "Modernising ICT Standardization in the EU – The Way Forward", (Communication) COM 324 final, 3 July 2009, § 2.4.

The next sections will shed light on the issue and will identify the optimal framework for SSO policies. It will be explained that under few particular circumstances it may be reasonable to require innovators to license their IPRs for free, but only when this is necessary to preserve the fairness and transparency of the whole standardization process.

3 Robust SSO rules as effective *ex ante* tools

From the arguments developed in the previous chapters, it should be clear that the risk of unfair practices affecting standards is closely related to the effectiveness of SSO policies. The implementation of certain rules over different ones may either encourage or discourage patentees from adopting misleading conduct. Therefore, in order to avoid patent hold-up, it seems essential to implement a more robust policy framework as an *ex ante* tool.

This section is devoted to understand better which model may guarantee a fair and transparent standard setting process. After having highlighted the faults of the main policy frameworks supported by the literature and SSOs, I will argue in favor of a different option which has not been given due attention by the standard-setting environment. The analysis of this model will be focused on both licensing, search and disclosure commitments.[25]

3.1 Failure of (F)RAND and ex ante *negotiation models*

As made clear in Chapter 4, both the (F)RAND model and the early joint (or even bilateral) negotiation regime have shown different faults that preclude their adoption as optimal policy frameworks. The former has been widely implemented by the standard-setting environment,[26] although it poses many questions on definitions and firms' liability. Several arguments make it difficult to endorse the view of those authors supporting the (F)RAND regime.[27] The main problem concerns the very meaning of fair and reasonable, on which courts and SSOs have seldom elaborated.[28] The uncertainty over the level of fees that licensees will be finally charged may undermine the whole process. The model, thus, does not seem the most effective answer when setting IPRs licensing rules.

On a similar ground, the *ex ante* negotiation of royalties cannot represent the optimal model due to the cited negative effects identified by the

25 See Chapter 3 section 4, for an overview of the policy rules usually adopted by SSOs.

26 In implementing their licensing rules, ETSI, IEEE and OASIS usually refer to FRAND; on the other hand, IETF, IEC, ITU and ISO consider RAND terms.

27 D.J. Teece and E.F. Sherry, "Standard Setting and Antitrust" (2003) 84 *Minnesota Law Review* 1973; and K. Kuhn, F. Scott Morton and H. Shelanski, "Standard Setting Organization Can Help Solve the Standard Essential Patents Licensing Problem" (2013) *CPI Antitrust Chronicle* 1. The latter, however, also recognize the importance of developing parallel mechanisms, such as arbitration and alternative dispute resolution, in order to clarify when an offer is (F)RAND.

28 See Chapter 4 section 3.3.

literature.[29] Besides the alleged concern for collusive behaviors, there might be a more serious risk that discussions on licensing terms may ultimately lead to exhausting policy battles between the members, compromising or delaying the adoption of a standard.[30] Furthermore, *ex ante* joint negotiation may be unfavorable for those firms joining the SSO later in the process, as they would have to accept terms already agreed by other participants.[31] More importantly, the implementation of the joint negotiation model may discourage innovators from taking part in standard setting, for fear that the majority of industry users and implementers may impose a low price. In addition, the effectiveness of negotiations between innovators in the context of patent pools has raised serious doubts.[32] In light of these observations, the *ex ante* joint negotiation of licensing terms, in or outside patent pools, cannot be considered as a viable alternative to the (F)RAND option.

3.2 Optimal policy framework

Besides the much-debated joint negotiation system and (F)RAND model, the literature mentions a third option as a means to eliminate the risks of hold-up: the unilateral disclosure of the maximum royalty level or most restrictive non-pricing terms.[33] According to this framework, IP owners joining SSOs would have to disclose, unilaterally and before the formal adoption of the standard, the maximum level of price (not excluding royalty-free terms) or the most restrictive non-pricing conditions (e.g. restrictions on the use of the licensed property) they would charge for licensing their relevant rights. In comparison with the other models, this option seems to have various advantages, and avoids many of the concerns raised with respect to early joint negotiation and (F)RAND terms.

The next sections will explain why this mechanism seems to represent a better option as a sound licensing framework for standards institutes. In this regard, I will also address various questions concerning the implementation of the model and the enforcement of those clauses (e.g. locked-in and opt-out conditions) directly linked to it. Finally, besides the analysis of the optimal licensing rule, further

29 See, *inter alia*, J.G. Sidak (n 6) 141–142; and R. Gilbert, "Deal or no Deal? Licensing Negotiations in Standard-setting Organizations" (2011) 77 *Antitrust Law Journal* 865.

30 See Chapter 4 section 3.4.

31 M. Valimaki, "A Flexible Approach to RAND Licensing" (2008) 29(12) *European Competition Law Review* 689.

32 See Chapter 3 section 4.3.4.

33 R.A. Skitol, "Concerted Buying Power: Its Potential for Addressing the Patent Hold-up Problem in Standard Setting" (2004–2005) 72 *Antitrust Law Journal* 742; J.G. Sidak (n 6) 171; S. Sattler (n 3) 348; M.K. Herman, "Negotiating Standards-Related Patent Licenses – How the Deal is Done" (2010) *Landslide* 38–39; J.L. Contreras, "Rethinking RAND: SDO-based Approaches to Patent Licensing Commitments" (2012) Social Science Research Network 12; and G. Ohana, M. Hansen and O. Shah, "Disclosure and Negotiation of Licensing Terms Prior to Adoption of Industry Standards: Preventing Another Patent Ambush?" (2003) 24(12) *European Competition Law Review* 648. The latter, for instance, do not consider early unilateral disclosure on its own (i.e. without allowing joint negotiation) as a practicable solution.

relevant observations will regard the members' search and disclosure duties, as these may also play a crucial role in the SSOs' IPR policies.

3.2.1 Unilateral disclosure of the maximum licensing terms

The maximum cap model would consist in a voluntary mechanism for IPRs owners to disclose unilaterally the licensing terms in advance.[34] The disclosed maximum terms, to be applied in a non-discriminatory way, should also bind any future purchaser of the essential IPRs. This regime undoubtedly presents several advantages. First, *ex ante* unilateral disclosure of the level of royalties or most restrictive non-pricing conditions would overcome the risks related to the uncertainties of the (F)RAND model. The latter leaves potential implementers of a technology uncertain as to the economic terms on which IPRs will be licensed.[35] This aspect might finally lead the SSO to design around the patented technology or block the whole process. It may also lead licensees to litigate the meaning of (F)RAND before a court. That is why implementing (F)RAND terms has been interpreted as a highly inefficient means to tackle patent hold-up. The adoption of IPR policies requiring early disclosure of the licensing terms, instead, would eliminate these risks, giving members more certainties about the conditions to be applied. In addition, the SSO working groups would be able to consider not only the technical merits of the proposed solution, but also its specific costs.

Second, a unilateral disclosure requirement seems to be a better means even when compared to the *ex ante* joint negotiation.[36] The latter, it has been said, may lead to exhausting policy battles between SSO members, as it might be complex to agree on a level of price which would be acceptable for all the different players.[37] By unilaterally specifying the most restrictive terms for the licensing of relevant rights, the risk of internal conflicts would not arise. This mechanism may also prove effective in encouraging participation in SSOs from IPRs owners and other implementers. Absent joint discussions of fees, indeed, patent holders would not incur the risk (typical of the early negotiation model) of being imposed low prices by SSO members.[38] What is more, in case the standard-setting body also required disclosure of pending IPRs, patent owners may find it more reasonable to establish a cap of fees – valid for both pending and issued rights – than to negotiate the exact value of a right which has still to be granted.[39] Besides IPR owners, also implementers and other firms without relevant patents may find the model more transparent and fair. In particular, they could be more willing to take part in the

34 M. Valimaki (n 31) 689. As the author notes, both IEEE and IETF suggest that the IPR owners may provide the information unilaterally.
35 G. Ohana, M. Hansen and O. Shah (n 33) 647.
36 Under the maximum cap, IP owner and each prospective licensee would bargain separately.
37 See the Report of the US Department of Justice and Federal Trade Commission (n 9) 50.
38 On the faults of early joint negotiation of prices, see J.G. Sidak (n 6) 141–142.
39 *Cf.* M.C. Naughton and R. Wolfram (n 14) 764–765.

standard-setting process even at a late stage, without having to accept policy terms previously agreed by patentees and other competing licensees.[40]

Third, as far as the members are not involved in negotiations about licensing terms, competition agencies may find it difficult to enforce those rules forbidding price fixing. Indeed, the US Department of Justice has notably argued that with voluntary disclosure of licensing terms firms can make "better informed decisions, which could further lead to faster development, implementation, and adoption of a standard as well as fewer litigated disputes."[41] Put differently, a system based on the unilateral disclosure of the maximum terms would seldom raise concerns about potential collusive conduct. It is true, however, that such a risk appears to be of limited relevance in the early negotiation system[42] or at least less relevant than some authors[43] or authorities would argue.[44] Nevertheless, in a standard-setting body implementing a maximum cap regime, anticompetitive collusive behaviors would be even less likely, due to the absence of those negotiation mechanisms which could facilitate members' collusive plans. The only plausible risk of collusion could arise where licensees started to discuss downstream prices of products incorporating the standardized technology. However, this possibility is not peculiar to a particular IPRs regime, but may arise under any SSO policy.

Finally, a further reason may encourage the adoption of the cap. Due to the existence of specific price benchmarks and non-pricing terms, unfair behaviors, such as charging higher fees and the application of more restrictive conditions than those specified *ex ante*, would seldom be successful. This is because a maximum cap would be potentially easier to enforce before a court than an undefined licensing framework (as one based on FRAND terms). This notwithstanding, as better explained in the next sections, there is still some debate in the literature as to whether SSO policy rules may be interpreted and legitimately enforced as effective contractual provisions.

For the sake of clarity, the unilateral disclosure model may be criticized in theory, due to alleged obstacles that may affect the standard-setting process.[45] Part of the criticism lies in the fact that IPRs owners may be bound too early by the licensing scheme, and would be required to make maximum term quantifications without fully knowing the specific contribution their technology may bring towards innovation and welfare.[46] Nevertheless, this does not seem to be

40 See M. Valimaki (n 31) 689.

41 See T.O. Barnett, "Response to Institute of Electrical and Electronics Engineering Inc.'s Request for Business Review Letter" (US Department of Justice, Antitrust Division, 30 April 2007).

42 As already noted, there is no certainty that IPR owners' collusion, in the context of *ex ante* joint negotiations, would finally lead to higher fees being set (see above, Chapter 5 section 3.4).

43 E.g., J.G. Sidak (n 6) 123.

44 See European Commission, "Guidelines on the Applicability of Article 101 TFEU to Horizontal Co-operation Agreements" [2011] OJ C 11/1.

45 M. Valimaki (n 31) 689. See also M.K. Herman (n 33) 38–39.

46 M. Valimaki (n 31) 689; P. Chappatte, "FRAND Commitments and EC Competition Law: A Rejoinder" (2010) 6(1) *European Competition Journal* 176; D. Geradin, A. Layne Farrar and A.J. Padilla, "The Complements Problem Within Standard Setting: Assessing the Evidence on Royalty Stacking" (2008) 14 *Boston University Journal of Science and Technology Law* 172.

an insurmountable issue, especially when compared with the faults arising in the (F)RAND and negotiation models.[47] As I will suggest, indeed, the problem may be solved by setting the optimal time of disclosure of relevant IPRs.

3.2.2 Unilateral disclosure and SSO policies

Despite all the merits of the unilateral early disclosure model, the majority of SSOs have usually implemented (F)RAND licensing terms in their IPRs policies.[48] This is probably because they may have (questionably) appraised unilateral early disclosure as a potential disincentive for IPRs holders and industry implementers to take part in SSOs. Only in the very last years have organizations started to consider the adoption of IPR policy rules promoting disclosure of the maximum cap for licensing relevant rights.

The VMEbus International Trade Association (VITA), for instance, has recently adopted a patent policy requiring members to declare the highest royalty rate for all patent claims the member owns or controls, and which may become essential to implement the standard.[49] At the same time, VITA also requires its participants to agree on granting to all members a perpetual patent license – for their patent claims essential to the standard – on fair reasonable and non-discriminatory conditions.[50] Besides VITA, the Institute of Electrical and Electronics Engineers (IEEE) mentions a maximum royalty cap in its licensing policy. IEEE specifies that IPRs owners may provide, on a voluntary basis, a "not to exceed" license fee or rate commitment. This notwithstanding, the SSO also states that patent holders may be required to submit a letter of assurance in which they declare to commit to FRAND terms or to royalty-free conditions.[51]

Two more standard-setting organizations include licensing policy rules regulating unilateral disclosure. The European Telecommunications Standards Institute (ETSI), besides encouraging its members to commit to FRAND licensing terms, also states that unilateral and voluntary early disclosure of royalties is not prohibited by ETSI directives.[52] The Internet Engineering Task Force (IETF), then, not only promotes RAND or royalty-free licensing terms, but also encourages members to include more specific licensing information in their IPRs disclosure.[53]

All these models may be considered as hybrid IPRs systems combining (F)RAND commitments with unilateral disclosure mechanisms. Thus, they still undervalue the risks arising from a vague licensing policy. This notwithstanding, they may also be interpreted as important steps towards the possible oncoming

47 See above, section 3.1. See also Chapter 4 sections 3.3 and 3.4.

48 Among these, ETSI, JEDEC, VITA, OASIS, IEEE, IETF, IEC, ITU and ISO.

49 See VITA, "Standards Organization – Policies and Procedures" (2011) § 10.3.2.

50 Ibid., § 10.3.1.

51 See IEEE-SA, "Standards Board Bylaws" (2015) § 6.2. It is worth noting that a royalty-free license may still impose other non-price terms and conditions.

52 ETSI, "Guide on IPRs" (2013) § 4.1.

53 Internet Engineering Task Force (IETF), "Intellectual Property Rights in IETF Technology" (2005) § 6.5.

adoption of a maximum cap regime by the whole standard-setting environment. Further elements, as better explained below, support this position.

3.2.3 Maximum cap in the views of US and EU antitrust enforcers

The merits of the model under examination seem to have been recognized by antitrust agencies and authorities both in the US and in the EU. In outlining its position on various SSO patent policies, the Antitrust Division of the US Department of Justice has already clarified that a maximum royalty cap (coupled with a statement on most restrictive non-royalties terms and other disclosure obligations) may well "reduce the likelihood of unexpected licensing terms that threaten the success of future ... standards" and "expand the scope of competition between alternative technological solutions during the standard setting process."[54] In that context, the Antitrust Division also explained that a policy explicitly forbidding the joint negotiations of prices among members clearly overcomes the risks of collusive conduct.[55] This notwithstanding, the authority also added that, even if information exchanges occurred, these would not be appraised under a *per se* rule of illegality, but under the rule of reason.[56] This position – supported by different US agencies[57] – was confirmed in a further intervention, where the Department of Justice argued that "unless the standard setting process is used as a sham to cloak naked price fixing or bid rigging, the Department analyses action during the standard setting process under the rule of reason."[58] Turning back to unilateral disclosure, the Antitrust Division observed that with a voluntary disclosure of licensing terms firms can make "better informed decisions, which could further lead to faster development, implementation and adoption of a standard as well as fewer litigated disputes."[59]

On the other side of the Atlantic, the EU Commission, in its recent "Guidelines on Horizontal Cooperation Agreements,"[60] has clearly acknowledged the alleged merits of (F)RAND commitments.[61] It has then clarified that agreements intended "to jointly fix prices either of downstream products or of substitute IPR or

54 See T.O. Barnett, "Response to VMEbus International Trade Association's Request for Business Review Letter" (US Department of Justice, Antitrust Division, 30 October 2006).

55 Ibid., § 4.

56 Ibid., fn 27.

57 US Department of Justice and Federal Trade Commission (n 9) 53–56; and Antitrust Modernization Commission (AMC), "Final Report and Recommendations" (April 2007) 117. *Contra*, see J.G. Sidak (n 6) 188.

58 See T.O. Barnett (n 41).

59 Ibid. See also the US case *Townshend v Rockwell International*, 55 USP Q 2d 1011 (ND California, 2000). Here, the IPR owner had disclosed *ex ante* its licensing terms. However, the inclusion in the SSO's (ITU) policy of RAND terms gave the plaintiff the pretext to argue that those terms were not RAND. This seems to confirm that (F)RAND licensing policies may easily lead to litigation, and should thus be interpreted as highly inefficient means.

60 For a thorough analysis of the Guidelines, see above Chapter 6 section 5.

61 European Commission, "Guidelines on the Applicability of Article 101 TFEU to Horizontal Co-operation Agreements" [2011] OJ C 11/1, at 283, 285 and 287.

technology will constitute restrictions of competition by object."[62] Besides these relevant statements, the EU competition enforcer has also taken into consideration the possibility to implement IPRs policy rules promoting unilateral disclosure. In this context, it has recognized that standard-setting agreements providing for unilateral *ex ante* disclosure of most restrictive licensing terms (including a maximum royalty cap) would not, in principle, restrict competition within the meaning of Article 101(1) TFEU. Rather, early disclosure would enable SSOs to take informed decisions on the alternative technologies and to appraise not only the technical merits but also their cost.[63]

These considerations confirm that a maximum cap regime may well prove to be effective in limiting hold-up and guaranteeing a more transparent process. Successful standardization may incentivize follow-on innovation, to the ultimate benefit of consumers and societal growth. However, neither the EU nor the US antitrust enforcers have ever shed light on other important questions. Firstly, there is still uncertainty on the optimal way to implement the cap, in terms of time and way of disclosure. Secondly, it is not clear which rules, if any, should complement this licensing model. Finally, further doubts concern the way a maximum cap regime may be enforced.

3.2.4 *Practical implementation of the maximum cap*

Once the advantages of the maximum cap regime have been defined and the views expressed by the enforcement authorities have been highlighted, it is necessary to evaluate its practical implementation. Several questions arise on the functioning of the model. The main issues deserving attention concern both the time and way of disclosure.[64]

3.2.4.1 TIME OF DISCLOSURE

First, in case of a maximum cap framework, SSOs should establish the timescale for disclosing the royalties and most restrictive non-pricing conditions. Time, indeed, is an inherent decisive feature in every standardization process. Different options may be taken into consideration. For instance, SSOs could require IPRs owners to disclose their terms as soon as they join the organizations. This option would give SSOs a wide lapse of time to appraise the different levels of rates proposed by innovators. However, early disclosure may be problematic under other perspectives. At early stages, indeed, standard-setting organizations may not yet have a clear idea of which technology should be developed. In other words, too many alternative projects may be under discussion. Under these circumstances,

62 Ibid., at 274.

63 Ibid., at 299. On the potential benefits of unilateral *ex ante* disclosure policies, see also European Commission, "Modernising ICT Standardization in the EU – The Way Forward" (Communication) COM 324 final, 3 July 2009, § 2.4; N. Kroes, "Being Open About Standards" (Speech at *OpenForum Europe*, Bruxelles – 10 June 2008) 4. *Contra*, see M.K. Herman (n 33) 38–39.

64 On the issue, see G. Ohana, M. Hansen and O. Shah (n 33) 644.

it would not be reasonable to require the participants to fulfill any disclosure commitments.[65]

Another option would require innovators to disclose their maximum licensing terms just before the formal adoption of the standard. However, this choice may sound unfeasible, as the SSO members may have already incurred sunk costs during the process for researching on the optimal standard (e.g. costly marketing analysis to examine buyers' interest in the use of the technology).[66] In case the royalties for the technology promoted by the industry were ultimately deemed excessive, the investments made earlier would be lost. Hence the need to have a clear understanding of the costs well before the final vote on the standard.

Given these reasons, IPRs holders should be required to submit their licensing terms before the first SSO resolution on the projects examined. In other words, it is crucial that the standard-setting environment be well oriented towards the development of specific technical proposals. At the same time, the submission should be made well before the final choice on the standard. More importantly, the cap should be submitted together with disclosure of the relevant rights. Indeed, it would be unreasonable to reveal licensing terms without disclosing all the IPRs they refer to.

Finally, the time of disclosure should bind innovators and work as a "locked-in" clause. This means that, after revealing the existence of conflicting rights and related commercial terms, IPRs holders should be banned from withdrawing from the organization. Until that moment, it would be still reasonable to let innovators exercise a sort of "opt-out" option. This way, the industry concerned would not risk losing the investment made in developing the proprietary standard due to the unexpected withdrawal of the IPRs owner. At the same time, members would have the opportunity to evaluate better the *pro* and *contra* of being part of the standard-setting process, as well as their will to license potentially conflicting rights. The locked-in and opt-out system, what is more, does not seem to raise competition law concerns. By providing an opt-out option, no one could argue that the IPR policy merely leads to an automatic compulsory licensing mechanism.[67]

3.2.4.2 MEANS OF DISCLOSURE

Besides the time of disclosure, it is also imperative to establish how innovators should convey their terms. Some authors, for instance, mention submitting licensing plans in a sealed envelope.[68] This mechanism may present some advantages, especially in case of late opening of the envelope. This method may eliminate any

65 See J. Farrell, J. Hayes, C. Shapiro and T. Sullivan, "Standard Setting, Patents, and Hold-Up" (2007) 74 *Antitrust Law Journal* 627–628.

66 Ibid.

67 See the Case IV/35.006 *ETSI Interim IPR Policy* [1995] OJ C 76/5. Here, the European Commission rejected the "licensing by default" rule, according to which IPRs owners had to agree *ex ante* (as a condition to participate) that their rights would be incorporated in the standard when deemed essential. The Commission interpreted such provision as a disincentive to innovate.

68 G. Ohana, M. Hansen and O. Shah (n 33) 655.

potential risk of pressure made by the industry on innovators to lower their rates, and may thus ensure the highest level of transparency. Furthermore, by keeping the licensing terms secret until the final vote it would be possible to reduce the risk of price discussions and avoid potential antitrust enforcement.[69] This notwithstanding, by implementing this option, the standard-setting body would be aware of the licensing costs only at a very late stage. As explained above, industry users and manufacturers may have already invested resources in the development of a specific technology. Therefore, it is clear that this mechanism would not fulfill the SSOs' need to be informed about licensing rates well in advance. As an alternative, members could be required to submit their terms in a sealed envelope to be disclosed only after a preliminary evaluation of the technical proposals, but still well before the voting stage. This option may be interesting where the organizations wish to attract various technical solutions to a problem, and immediate disclosure of commercial terms might dissuade proponents from coming forward.[70]

A sound disclosure system may consist of submitting (together with the disclosure of essential rights) an irrevocable and unconditional commitment in writing. The irrevocability of the licensing proposal should be interpreted as prohibition to raise the price submitted or ask for more restrictive non-pricing terms. This may avoid the risk of "gamesmanship," where those patentees supported by the industries may exploit their position and try to extract higher royalties. At the same time, however, it seems reasonable to leave innovators the right to submit subsequent declarations with lower rates and less restrictive conditions. IPRs owners, in other words, should be left free to make their commercial terms more attractive even after the submission of the cap. This system may be indirectly helpful in limiting the risk of royalty stacking, which may occur in case of complementary technologies.[71] Leaving innovators the right to lower the fees may indeed reduce the risk of exorbitant cumulative rates, especially when the practice of cross-licensing cannot prevent this problem.

Any written proposals, then, should be unconditional and applied in a non-discriminatory way to all firms requiring licenses for implementing the standardized technology. This mechanism has been partly considered by few organizations.[72]

69 However, as explained in Chapter 4 section 3.4, the risk of collusion in SSOs seems to be low. Such a risk could mainly concern manufacturers discussing resale prices of final products.

70 G. Ohana, M. Hansen and O. Shah (n 33) 651. The authors mention as an example the case of the SDMI Project (a quasi-SSO), which implemented a disclosure system based on sealed envelopes.

71 See *Microsoft v Motorola Inc*, Case n. 10-1823, 2013 WL 2111217 (WD Washington, 2013), at 11–12. *Contra*, see E. Elhauge, "Do Patent Hold-Up and Royalty Stacking Lead to Systematically Excessive Royalties?" (2008) 4(3) *Journal of Competition Law and Economics* 535. The author holds that, similarly to hold-up, also "royalty stacking does not lead to royalties that exceed the optimal rate […] but in fact tends to produce royalties that are at or below the optimal rate."

72 See VITA, "Standards Organization – Policies and Procedures" (2011). Section 10.3.2 states that "[t]he Declaration is irrevocable. If a subsequent Declaration covering previously disclosed information is submitted, the subsequent Declaration may only supersede the prior Declaration if the subsequent Declaration is less restrictive upon prospective licensees than the former Declaration. Otherwise, the former Declaration continues to apply." However, this policy raises some doubts, as it still refers to the need to license under the ambiguous FRAND terms.

It may only benefit the competitiveness of SSO processes and may ultimately lead to lower prices for consumers. Besides, by preserving patentees' right to decide the subject of disclosure and the related terms, it may still work as a safeguard for innovators' interests in standards.

3.2.5 Search and disclosure commitments

The described licensing mechanism is at the core of a policy which seems to be the optimal choice. However, the analysis and implementation of licensing models alone would be of limited help in the pursuit of the best policy system. In order to properly define the boundaries between the members' duties and powers, it is also crucial to deal with further regulations, covering search and disclosure commitments.

3.2.5.1 DUTY TO SEARCH

The function and limits of search rules have already been identified in Chapter 3. In that context, it has been explained that these provisions may be adopted to require members to search for potentially conflicting rights within their IPR portfolios.[73] Here, it is worth re-examining the main objections made against the implementation of those rules, in order to understand whether or not they could be part of the optimal policy framework. First, as I have argued, the adoption of a duty to search may impose on members a high burden which could deter them from participating in standard setting.[74] Undertakings usually send engineers, not patent lawyers to represent them before the organizations. While engineers have a deeper understanding of the subject matter to be discussed, they do not have extensive knowledge of their firms' IPR portfolios. It may happen, therefore, that engineers are not prepared to fulfill any search requirement, especially when a member has hundreds of patents which may potentially conflict with the standard.[75] A second factor may have a negative influence on the innovators' will to search for relevant rights. Standardization is a process *in itinere*, where different proposals could be considered before the adoption of the final version of the standard. Therefore, it may be difficult to determine when a firm is required to search for potentially conflicting IPRs.[76] Finally, a further practical reason may lead SSOs to omit a duty to search in their regulations. Imposing a search commitment for potentially conflicting rights may be quite costly to members with large IPRs portfolios.[77]

In brief, it is true that the use of extensive search rules could help to achieve high level of transparency. At the same time, however, the implementation of

73 M.C. Naughton and R. Wolfram (n 14) 759.

74 Ibid., 761.

75 M.A. Lemley, "Intellectual Property Rights and Standard-Setting Organizations" (2002) 90 *California Law Review* 1907.

76 D.J. Teece and E.F. Sherry (n 27) 1947.

77 Ibid., 1951.

search requirements may severely reduce the number of IP owners participating in standard setting. Reduced participation would probably lead to standards of a lower quality or to a higher risk of patent litigation.[78] In light of these factors, the effectiveness of these provisions seems more than doubtful. In order to preserve the advantages of the maximum cap regime and strike the right balance between innovators' interests and standard-setting aims, search commitments should not be part of SSO regulations.

3.2.5.2 DUTY TO DISCLOSE

The maximum cap framework, as an optimal licensing option, must be complemented by an effective disclosure system. Licensing provisions alone would not be able to guarantee an efficient standardization process. Given the alleged risks connected to the implementation of search requirements, it is legitimate to question how disclosure rules should be shaped by SSOs. In Part I, I discussed the role of disclosure policies, which are adopted by the vast majority of SSOs.[79] Disclosure rules usually require participants to reveal the existence of essential IPRs within their actual knowledge, without imposing any specific search activities. They may also encourage the disclosure of other firms' relevant rights of which a member is aware. Their main function is to reduce the risks of unfair conduct.[80] As done before with respect to search commitments, it seems important here to highlight those conclusions and appraise the effectiveness of the various disclosure systems. In particular, it is essential to understand which mechanism may better complement the maximum cap framework. From this perspective, two different issues deserve careful attention: the time and subject of disclosure.

3.2.5.2.1 Time of disclosure First, in relation to the time of disclosure, it is clear that innovators should not be required to reveal immediately the existence of relevant IPRs. SSOs, in other words, should refrain from imposing a duty to disclose in the initial stages. As evidenced in the previous section, at the beginning of the activities, SSOs may have unclear and undefined ideas of the project to be developed.[81] At the same time, however, disclosure should not be made too close to the formal adoption of the standard, as in the meantime industry manufacturers may have undertaken investments towards the development of a specific proposal. The same considerations developed above on the "timely" disclosure of the maximum

78 See Chapter 3 section 4.1. In relation to the costs of patent litigation, according to M.A. Lemley and A.D. Melamed (n 8), one recent estimate found a median of $6 million for substantial patent cases that go to trial in the United States.

79 On the effectiveness of disclosure policies, see also K. Hussinger and F. Schwiebacher, "The value of disclosing IPR to open standard setting organizations" (2013) ZEW Discussion Paper n. 13-060. The authors correctly hold that disclosure of essential IPR may vary in scope. As they argue, such disclosure is valued positively by financial markets only if it includes the associated patents, rather than merely affirming the existence of unspecified essential IPRs.

80 J. Farrell, J. Hayes, C. Shapiro and T. Sullivan (n 65) 624.

81 Ibid., 628.

cap should apply here. Therefore, disclosure of essential IPRs should be made, together with a submission of the cap, as soon as the standard-setting body takes its first steps toward the development of a particular project.[82] Depending on the choice of each organization, these steps could be formalized through a first resolution or a vote in the course of SSO meetings. This mechanism may preserve both the optimal functioning of standardization and the need to enable IPR holders to identify those rights in conflict with the standard. As has often been emphasized during the course of this book, striking the optimal framework implies the well-known need to balance between innovators' interests and standard-setting objectives.

3.2.5.2.2 Subject of disclosure The second issue deserving due attention concerns the subject of disclosure. In Chapter 3, the distinction between the disclosure of pending and of issued IPRs has been at the core of the analysis.[83] In that context, it has been noted that only few organizations require members to disclose both issued and pending rights,[84] due to both practical and policy reasons. On the one hand, SSOs are aware of the difficulties of determining whether a pending right may potentially conflict with a standard.[85] On the other hand, it has been argued that requiring firms to disclose pending applications may compromise their trade secret rights.[86] In light of these arguments, SSOs do not usually require innovators to reveal pending IPRs potentially related to the standard. However, as I have observed, disclosure of pending applications would not necessarily compromise the applicants' trade secret. By revealing only the existence and scope of a patent application, but not the technical know-how of the invention, innovators may still preserve their interests.[87] Indeed, it is doubtful that the substance of an invention could be inferred without access to the related technical know-how. Therefore, the mere disclosure of the existence and scope of pending IPRs may still preserve the applicants' trade secrets. At the same time, it may grant SSOs sufficient details to make the optimal choice and limit the risks of unfair conduct. That is why disclosure requirements should also include partial descriptions of pending IPRs.

3.2.5.2.3 Pending IPRs under the maximum cap This choice is all the more reasonable when adopted to complement a maximum cap framework. Under this licensing model, indeed, non-disclosure or description of pending IPRs may

82 On the importance of defining the optimal time of disclosure, see European Commission, "Commission Welcomes Changes in ETSI IPR Rules to Prevent 'Patent Ambush'" (12 December 2005) Press Release IP/05/1565.

83 See Chapter 3 section 4.2.

84 Among these, for instance, JEDEC, ETSI, W3C and ITU.

85 M.C. Naughton and R. Wolfram (n 14) 763–764.

86 R.J. Taffet, "Patented Technology and Standard Setting: A Standard Development Organization View" in American Bar Association, *A Year in the Life of a High Tech Standard Setting Organization* (ABA Section of Antitrust Law, Chicago 2002) 5.

87 M.A. Lemley (n 75) 1943. *Contra*, see D.G. Swanson and W.J. Baumol, "Reasonable and Non-discriminatory (RAND) Royalties, Standards Selection, and Control of Market Power" (2005–2006) 73 *Antitrust Law Journal* 51–53.

compromise the whole standardization process. Assuming that a standard-setting body implementing the maximum cap did not require any disclosure of pending rights, one legitimate question could be raised. What would happen if the IPRs applications covering the standard were ultimately granted? Under these circumstances, it could be supposed, SSOs may impose to license the undisclosed IPRs under the same terms submitted with the cap, so as to preserve the effectiveness of the process.

However, this solution does not seem workable, but could be used by innovators to their advantage in order to over-exploit their rights. It may happen that a member submits extremely high licensing terms, together with disclosure of the issued IPRs these terms refer to. In this situation, the SSO would likely decide to opt for a different standard and avoid the payment of prohibitive royalties. However, it cannot be excluded that the standard ultimately chosen may cover one of those pending undisclosed IPRs, formally subjected to the same restrictive terms submitted with the cap. In these circumstances, the SSO member whose (initially pending) rights conflict with the standard may legitimately claim for payment of the exorbitant royalties specified in advance. It is in view of this fault that this system cannot be adopted. A maximum cap cannot be successfully implemented without shaping a more robust regime for pending IPRs.

In order to achieve the optimal compromise, standards institutes should better implement a cap regime covering only those rights properly disclosed. In other words, the licensing terms submitted by innovators should apply only with respect to those issued and pending rights revealed in due time to the SSO committees. All those IPRs which were not disclosed, either intentionally or unknowingly, should fall out of the maximum cap. In particular, SSO policies should require IPRs owners to waive any claim and license any hidden rights for free. This rule should also apply to those members who had initially denied the existence of any relevant IPRs and had thus omitted to submit a maximum cap. Such a mechanism seems to be necessary in order to preserve the whole standard-setting system. The clear advantage is that it would allow SSOs to develop standards without being hindered by the late disclosure of essential rights.

On the other hand, it could be argued that imposing a free license for hidden IPRs may conflict with the policy choice to omit search requirements and may also represent a draconian measure.[88] Innovators could be discouraged from taking part in standard setting. However, the model may still work as an incentive for IPR holders to participate and reveal the existence of their pending or issued rights related to the standard. By failing to participate and disclose, innovators would lose the opportunity to be rewarded for their investments in innovation. Indeed, with respect to the rights disclosed in due time, the selected innovator may ask for the maximum price or most restrictive non-price terms proposed *ex ante*.

88 D.G. Swanson and W.J. Baumol (n 87) 55. The authors believe that capping the appropriate royalty at zero in cases of non-disclosure would be counterproductive, as "a zero-royalty policy might arguably amount to an excessive penalty that (at least with regard to unintentional failures to disclose) could appreciably reduce incentives to innovate."

The very opportunity to apply the desired licensing conditions should balance the negative effects of a fee waiver for any hidden rights. In addition, the choice to avoid any formal and binding search requirement may be well accepted by the members and should be interpreted as part of the delicate balance between innovators' interests and standard setting goals. It is clear, however, that the pursuit of this balance could also warrant a rigorous policy requiring members to return any collected fees in case of alleged essential IPRs which are later found to be invalid or non-essential by a court (i.e. over-disclosure).

4 Enforcement of contract law as *ex post* possible remedy

Once the structure of the optimal policy framework has been defined and its advantages highlighted, it is legitimate to question how such a model may be enforced. Indeed, SSO policy rules are not laws and are not enforceable by themselves, but on the basis of legal principles.[89] In this context, contract law could be considered as a potential tool to preserve – from an *ex post* perspective – the outcome of SSO processes.[90] This holds true as far as the rules subscribed by the members are interpreted as contractual provisions. In other words, the SSO's legal framework should be interpreted as an agreement between the organization and the participants.

There are different ways to turn SSO policies into enforceable contracts. The participants, for instance, may subscribe to a document which binds them to comply with IPR guidelines. As an alternative, they may commit themselves to comply with any SSO bylaws. In addition, it would be also possible to rely simply on sufficient factual circumstances without the need of any written documents.[91]

4.1 Breach of contract

Under these perspectives, IPR owners taking part in standard setting may breach that agreement by either infringing the established cap or refusing to license the essential rights.

Firstly, IPRs holders would potentially incur the risk of being sued for breach of contract if they required the payment of royalties for those essential rights not properly disclosed. The latter, it has been said, should be licensed for free, to preserve the fairness and transparency of the standard-setting environment. A further concern could also arise when IPRs owners tried to apply, for the rights disclosed in due time, more restrictive terms than those specified *ex ante*. In brief,

89 J.H. Park, *Patents and Industry Standards* (Edward Elgar, Cheltenham 2010) 46.

90 On the argument, see B.H. Kobayashi and J.D. Wright, "Federalism, Substantive Pre-emption, and Limits on Antitrust: An Application to Patent Holdup" (2009) 5(3) *Journal of Competition Law and Economics* 469; R. Hewitt Pate, "Competition and Intellectual Property in the U.S.: Licensing Freedom and the Limits of Antitrust" (Speech at *EU Competition Workshop*, Florence – 3 June 2005).

91 J.H. Park (n 89) 46. See also M.A. Lemley (n 75) 1909–1911. As Lemley argues, "because the IP policies are at base agreements by members of the SSO to abide by certain rules regarding IP ownership, their enforceability is initially a question of contract law."

innovators could be deemed responsible if they failed to fulfill the subscribed licensing conditions.[92]

Secondly, contract law may apply if the selected member ultimately refused to sell any license for the relevant IPRs. Under these circumstances, there would be no direct breach of the maximum cap, but a mere infringement of the duty to license. This notwithstanding, also this case may entail the enforcement of contract law for breach of a contractual provision accepted by the parties of the agreement.

4.2 Limitations

However, as it has been argued, the application of the theory of contract to cooperative standard setting may be problematic under different grounds.[93] On the one hand, the contract would be between the single participant and the standard-setting body. In case of infringement, all those firms that were not part of the organization and are interested in obtaining a license from the selected innovator would lack standing to make a claim. They should be considered as incidental beneficiaries; they generally are not allowed to enforce the contract.[94] With respect to the other members, they similarly could not be considered part of the infringed contract. However, in their capacity as intended beneficiaries, members could require the SSO to enforce the agreement on their behalf. If this was not practical, and depending on the legal system concerned, they could be even granted standing to sue.[95] As one commentator observed, "contract law remedies are therefore deficient in deterring patent ambush and widen the access to the standard because they are only available to a restricted number of claimants."[96]

On a further different ground, the enforcement of contract law for breach of IPR policies would not fully compensate the damage caused by the infringement.[97] A member who failed to obtain a license under the terms disclosed *ex ante* may be compensated for the expected gain from the contract. This is usually the net value – after subtraction of the licensing fees – it could have obtained by use of the standard. However, a remedy for contract damage does not usually consist in injunctive relief.[98] It is thus clear that the damage suffered by the whole society, in

92 See J. Gstalter (n 16) 1–4. As the author argues: "promotion of competition through open standards is at the confluence of contractual law, competition law, IPR law and other public policy instruments."

93 J.H. Park (n 89) 46–47.

94 M.A. Lemley (n 75) 1914–1916.

95 Ibid., 1914–1915.

96 A. Chronopoulos, "Patenting Standards – A Case For US Antitrust Law or A Call for Recognizing Immanent Public Policy Limitations To The Exploitation Rights Conferred by the Patent Act?" (2009) 40(7) *International Review of Intellectual Property and Competition Law* 801.

97 M.A. Lemley (n 75) 1916–1917.

98 J.H. Park (n 89) 47. On the scope of injunctive relief, see also *eBay Inc v MercExchange LLC*, 547 US 388 (2006). As held by the Supreme Court, in order to obtain an injunction, "a plaintiff must demonstrate: 1) that it has suffered an irreparable injury; 2) that remedies available at law, such as monetary damages, are inadequate to compensate for that injury; 3) that, considering the balance

terms of losses from the missed implementation of the standard, would be seldom repaid.

4.3 Effectiveness

Although the application of contract law to enforce SSOs rules has the cited limitations, it may still be considered as an *ex post* possible remedy to unlawful conduct. This tool is not likely to fully compensate the infringement; however, it may still work as deterrent to unfair innovators.

The effectiveness of contract law is all the more evident when applied in the context of the proposed policy model. Indeed, the potential enforceability of the maximum cap under contract law is the main difference between the breach of an established cap and the infringement of (F)RAND conditions. Under a (F)RAND regime, characterized by the absence of specific price benchmarks, it could be more complex and lengthy to assert one's right before a civil court.[99] Various authors have already acknowledged that courts may be reluctant to deal with (F)RAND definitions.[100] Furthermore, the economic literature focusing on the meaning of these terms has developed divergent theories which have only increased uncertainty rather than solve the issue.[101] In light of these remarks, the maximum cap regime, complemented by the proposed disclosure system, could have more chances to be promptly enforced as a contract than a (F)RAND model may ever have. This would also explain why the implementation of this mechanism should be preferred to any other framework in setting SSO IP rules.

of hardships between the plaintiff and defendant, a remedy in equity is warranted; and 4) that the public interest would not be disserved by a permanent injunction."

99 *Contra*, see D. Geradin and M. Rato (n 7) 119–120; and D. Geradin and R.G. Brooks (n 14). The authors consider (F)RAND terms as a workable and enforceable contract. As Geradin argues, if the parties do not agree on the royalties, courts should only assess whether the offered terms are within the "range of reasonableness," without setting any specific amount and becoming price regulators. To this end, courts may apply the *Georgia Pacific* criteria. However, as he continues, IPR owners would seldom charge exorbitant royalties, as by doing so they would risk to be ignored by the SSO environment for follow-on innovation of the standardized technology.

100 M. Valimaki (n 31) 690; G. Ohana, M. Hansen and O. Shah (n 33) 647.

101 See, *inter alia*, A. Layne Farrar, A.J. Padilla and R. Schmalensee, "Pricing Patents for Licensing in Standard-Setting Organizations: Making Sense of FRAND Commitments" (2007) 74 *Antitrust Law Journal* 671; D. Geradin and M. Rato (n 7) 112; D.G. Swanson and W.J. Baumol (n 87) 10; M.A. Lemley and C. Shapiro, "Patent Hold-up and Royalty Stacking" (2007) 85 *Texas Law Review* 1991; H.J. Singer and K. Smith, "What Does An Economist Have to Say About the Calculation of Reasonable Royalties" (2009) 14 *Intellectual Property Law Bulletin* 11; M. Mariniello, "Fair, Reasonable and Non-discriminatory (FRAND) Terms: A Challenge for Competition Authorities" (2011) 7(3) *Journal of Competition Law and Economics* 523; and A. Layne Farrar, G. Llobet and A.J. Padilla, "Payments and Participation: The Incentives to Join Cooperative Standard Setting Efforts" (2014) 23(1) *Journal of Economics & Management Strategy* 24. The latter, for instance, reject the view that a reasonable royalty should be based on the *ex ante* incremental value of a chosen technology.

5 Enforcement of further private law remedies

Contract law is not the only remedy of private law which could be enforced in case of misleading conduct of SSO members holding IPRs. Part of the literature mentions further tools or legal theories which may be applied.[102] These remedies have been established in the United States and refer to: (a) the equitable estoppel doctrine; (b) the implied license theory; (c) the fraud defense; and (d) the patent misuse claim.

5.1 Equitable estoppel

Equitable estoppel is a remedy which could be used in the SSO context to tackle the risks deriving from misleading conduct.[103] It can be a potential tool to regulate the duty to disclose essential IPRs. Three conditions are required for applying the doctrine: (i) the innovator, through misleading conduct, leads the alleged infringer to infer that the innovator will not enforce its rights; (ii) the alleged infringer reasonably relies on the misleading conduct; and (iii) due to the reliance, the alleged infringer will be prejudiced if the innovator is allowed to enforce its rights.[104] These three factors must be intended as cumulative.[105] When all of them are established, the doctrine aims to prevent the misleading innovator from enforcing its rights.[106] To this end, the intent of the IPR holder is not relevant.

Equitable estoppel may find application both in case of IPRs owners which actively mislead the SSO and in case of a mere omission to speak, provided that the organization imposes on members a clear duty to disclose.[107] What is more, besides the case of failure to disclose, the doctrine could be enforced under further circumstances. Indeed, as the literature clarified, the equitable estoppel could also be applied when a member, after having disclosed its relevant rights and having promised to waive any claim, ultimately tried to enforce them.[108]

102 J.H. Park (n 89) 47–48; M.A. Lemley (n 75) 1918–1919.

103 J. Verbruggen and A. Lorincz, "Patents and Technical Standards" (2002) 33(2) *International Review of Intellectual Property and Competition Law* 149.

104 *A.C. Aukerman Company v Chaides Construction*, 960 F2d 1020 (C App Federal Circuit, 1992).

105 See *Symbol Techs. v Proxim*, Case n. Civ. 01-801-SLR, 2004 WL 1770290 (D Delaware, 2004) (rejecting an estoppel defense when the firm had no duty to disclose its patent rights).

106 *Potter Instrument Co v Storage Technology Corp.*, 207 USPQ 763 (ED Virginia, 1980); *Stambler v Diebold*, 11 USPQ 2d 1709 (EDNY, 1988) (holding that estoppel precluded plaintiff from succeeding on a patent infringement claim brought after having failed to disclose its patent interests in the context of an ANSI standards committee).

107 See M.S. Royall, "Standard Setting and Exclusionary Conduct: The Role of Antitrust in Policing Unilateral Abuses of Standard-Setting Processes" (2003–2004) 18 *Antitrust* 46. As the author argues, "courts have held that equitable estoppel may apply even if the patent holder, as opposed to affirmatively misrepresenting facts about its patents to the standards organization, merely conceals relevant patent-related information, provided it can be shown that the patent holder had a duty to disclose such information." This confirms that the implementation of clear policy rules – properly made known to the members – is the precondition for enforcing any legal tool against alleged unfair conduct.

108 J.H. Park (n 89) 48.

As already explained, in the context of SSOs implementing a maximum cap framework, IPRs holders would be encouraged to disclose any essential (pending or issued) rights. Such a mechanism would enable them to establish the level of fees or other non-price conditions desired, without the risk of lengthy negotiations with the firms interested in a license. Hence, the risk of ambush and, more in general, of any other unfair behavior would be limited. This notwithstanding, in the unlikely case of misleading conduct, the doctrine of equitable estoppel could represent a further tool to address the problem.

However, it is also true that this remedy "cannot come to the rescue of all entities worthy of protection because it requires a privity relationship of the patentee to each individual infringer."[109] In other words, limitations exist on the application of equitable estoppel, as only those parties which can prove to have been misled and to have reasonably relied on the innovator's promise can benefit from the enforcement of the doctrine.[110] Non-members would clearly fall outside the category of beneficiaries. SSOs could, in theory, plug this loophole by providing in their agreements that the public should benefit as third party. In fact, this would not be a workable solution, due to the difficulty of enforcing contractual provisions characterized by an indefinite and too broad scope.[111] In addition, it is doubtful whether the "privity relationship" condition could be fulfilled and demonstrated even under these specific circumstances.

5.2 Implied license

Implied license has been mentioned by part of the literature as a variation of equitable estoppel and as another possible remedy to address misleading conduct in SSO contexts.[112] While equitable estoppel may apply where the innovator leads other members to believe that no right will be enforced, implied license requires different conditions. Indeed, courts may apply the principle when the IPRs holder, having disclosed its relevant rights and having submitted the licensing terms, ultimately breaches that agreement. Under these circumstances the innovator does not mislead the other members to believe that his rights will not be enforced. The IPRs holder merely refuses to license under the disclosed licensing conditions. If the innovator tried to enforce the rights by filing an infringement suit, the alleged infringer may require the court to apply the theory of implied

109 A. Chronopoulos (n 96) 802.

110 On the argument, see also J.M. Mueller, "Patenting Industry Standards" (2001) 34 *John Marshall Law Review* 924; and R.P. Merges and J.M. Kuhn, "An Estoppel Doctrine for Patented Standards" (2009) 97 *California Law Review* 41–48. The latter try to overcome this doctrinal fault and refer to a "gradually developing reliance interest" of members as they proceed to invest in the standard.

111 D. Lim, "Misconduct in Standard Setting: the Case for Patent Misuse" (2011) 51(4) *IDEA* 578.

112 J.H. Park (n 89) 49–50; M.A. Lemley (n 75) 1925; R.H. Stern, "Rambus v Infineon: the Superior Aptness of Common Law Remedies than Antitrust for Standardization Skulduggery" (2001) 23(10) *European Intellectual Property Review* 499.

license.[113] The latter, it must be noted, differs from the remedy of contract law as it should finally lead the alleged infringer to obtain a license.[114]

5.3 Fraud

The law of fraud has been interpreted as providing a legitimating supplement to the law of contracts. Its main objective has been identified in addressing use of access to information in transactions where possession of the information may influence the behavior of the parties of a business. In other words, it provides redress in those circumstances where one party takes unfair advantage of its superior access to certain kinds of information. This behavior may destabilize a system, as it may make other parties unwilling to keep bargains. Under this perspective, the law of fraud seems both to satisfy our moral sensibilities and to legitimate the socio-economic system. In few words, it "plays an important mediating role, it helps to maintain allegiance to, and thus stability of, the socio-economic system."[115]

In a standard-setting context, it is legitimate to ask when a duty to disclose information to the other members arises. When is silence permissible, and when does failure to disclose amount to a misrepresentation? It seems that the fraud defense may provide a remedy in case of members breaching their policy duty. In comparison to an antitrust claim, it may usually have more chances to succeed, as it does not require establishing market power in a defined market.

The fraud theory, which was applied in the context of the *Rambus* litigation,[116] can be either actual or constructive. Constructive fraud requires the "breach of duty by one in a confidential or fiduciary relationship to another that induces justifiable reliance by the other to his or her prejudice."[117] In the context of standard setting, the existence of such a direct relationship between an IPRs holder and another member is unlikely. Rather, actual fraud may be in theory a more common problem for SSOs.

In order to raise an actual fraud action, a party must establish the following elements: (1) a false representation (2) of a material fact (3) made with knowledge of that material fact (4) with the intent to induce reliance (5) where the other party takes action in justifiable reliance and (6) results in damages.

113 See *Wang Labs v Mitsubishi Elecs.*, 103 F3d 1571 (C App Federal Circuit, 1997). Here, the court held that Mitsubishi was entitled to an irrevocable royalty-free implied license.

114 J.H. Park (n 89) 50. As Park argues, the implied license theory, the equitable estoppel and contract law are all remedies used in a defensive way.

115 See R.H. Stern (n 112) 497. The author makes an interesting analysis of the development of the law of fraud, recalling the "theory of social contract" and the concept of "the state of the nature." He eventually considers its application to the *Rambus* litigation.

116 *Rambus Inc v Infineon Technologies*, 164 F Supp 2d 743 (ED Virginia, 2001); and *Rambus Inc v Infineon Technologies*, 318 F3d 1081 (C App Federal Circuit, 2003). See also R.H. Stern (n 112) 495; and M.S. Royall, A. Tessar and A.J. Di Vincenzo, "Deterring 'Patent Ambush' in Standard Setting: Lessons from *Rambus* and *Qualcomm*" (2009) 23(3) *Antitrust* 34.

117 J.H. Park (n 89) 52.

As to the first element, this may consist either in an affirmative statement or in concealment. In standard setting, a false representation may be established when a member fails to disclose its relevant IPRs or misleads other members as to its will to license under a maximum cap. With respect to the second element, materiality exists if the defrauded party would have acted differently had it known about the fact. This means that the SSO would have opted for a different standard had it known about the conduct.[118] Knowledge of the material fact, then, exists when the defrauded party proves that the IPRs holder actually knew about the conflict with the standard. The defrauded party must also prove that the conduct was intentional to induce reliance by other parties. This means that the alleged defrauder must have had a clear understanding of its duties and intentionally breached them. The existence of these duties may also help in proving justifiable reliance on the defrauder's false representation. Finally, the defrauded party must prove the existence of monetary or economic loss caused by the misrepresentation, which may include the cost of obtaining a license or designing around the IPRs. The alleged infringer may prove damages if the IPR owner is successful in its infringement suit.

However, similar to the other private law remedies, the fraud defense also has some limits. The alleged defrauder must have some duty to the defrauded party. This means that the remedy could be potentially invoked by the participants of the organization, but it cannot be claimed by non-members.[119]

5.4 Patent misuse

Equitable estoppel, the implied license theory and fraud do not exhaust the list of further potential tools which could be enforced in the SSO environment. Besides these remedies, which complement the enforcement of contract principles, one further option must be considered: patent misuse. The patent misuse doctrine represents a public policy defense against patent enforcement by IPRs owners.[120] When applied, it leads to substantive limitations of patent exploitation justified by public policy reasons.[121]

Patent misuse occurs when a patent holder, through his conduct "impermissibly broadens the patent … so as to extend the patent [owner's] statutory rights."[122] When the misuse defense is endorsed in a suit for patent infringement, the patent is declared unenforceable for as long as the adverse effects of the misuse

118 Ibid.

119 On the scope of the fraud claim, see A. Chronopoulos (n 96) note 85; M.S. Royall, A. Tessar and A.J. Di Vincenzo (n 116) 34; R.H. Stern (n 112) 497; and M.S. Royall (n 107) 46, citing *Walker Process Equip. v Food Mach. & Chem.*, 382 US 172 (1965), where proof of actual fraud was required to enforce Section 2 of the Sherman Act. In *Walker Process*, in particular, the US Supreme Court held that when a patent owner obtains a monopoly through "knowing and wilful fraud" that monopoly will be subject to challenge under the antitrust laws.

120 A. Chronopoulos (n 96) 784; D. Lim (n 111) 557.

121 *Mallinckrodt Inc v Medipart Inc*, 976 F2d 700 (C App Federal Circuit, 1992); *Princo Corp v International Trade Commission*, 616 F3d 1318 (C App Federal Circuit, 2010).

122 R.P. Taylor, "Standard Setting: A Growing Morass" (2002) *Intellectual Property Antitrust* 556.

last. Consequently, the patent owner cannot enforce its rights against any other infringer. This holds true even if the defendant has suffered no injury from the unlawful conduct.[123]

5.4.1 Effectiveness

In comparison with the other cited remedies, the patent misuse doctrine has been considered as a more effective tool in balancing IPRs protection and limitation.[124] Different authors, what is more, interpret the misuse defense as an effective means to address misleading conduct in SSOs.[125] For instance, it could be used against patent ambush, considered as an impermissible exploitation of the economic scope of the patent and contrary to the public interest.[126] By applying the patent misuse principle, a court would make the patent unenforceable and would preserve the outcome of standard setting. In particular, "rendering the patent unenforceable in cases of deceptive continuations from participants in SSOs would facilitate the creation of standards that are accessible by the greatest possible number of competitors."[127]

From a further perspective, and unlike most of the cited remedies, the misuse theory protects an entire category of infringers: all users of the selected standard.[128] This is because misuse does not require continuity or privity between patentees and the alleged infringers, but applies even when innovators do not have any direct relationship with industry users. Finally, with respect to antitrust claims, the enforcement of the misuse doctrine would relieve a court of the duty to deal with the thorny issue of punitive damages. Indeed, this remedy merely leads to suspend patent enforceability, until the misconduct is purged.[129]

Despite the cited advantages, however, there is still uncertainty as to the scope and purpose of patent misuse.[130] For instance, as some authors noted, antitrust analysis of IPR misuse may have absorbed the doctrine.[131] This view may

123 See M.J. Adelman, *Patent Law Perspectives* (2nd edn, Bender, New York 1982); T.F. Cotter, "Four Questionable Rationales for the Patent Misuse Doctrine" (2011) 12(2) *Minnesota Journal of Law, Science and Technology* 457; and W.J. Nicoson, "Misuse of the Misuse Doctrine in Infringement Suits" (1962) 9 *UCLA Law Review* 76. On the analysis of patent law remedies for hold-up, see also E. Ramirez and L. Kimmel, "A Competition Policy Perspective on Patent Law: the Federal Trade Commission's Report on the Evolving IP Marketplace" (2011) *The Antitrust Source* 1.

124 See Note, "Is the Patent Misuse Doctrine Obsolete?" (1997) 110 *Harvard Law Review* 1922.

125 J.M. Mueller (n 110) 935; D. Lim (n 111) 580.

126 A. Chronopoulos (n 96) 814.

127 Ibid., 813.

128 D. Lim (n 111) 580.

129 *B.B. Chemical v Ellis*, 314 US 495 (1942); *Morton Salt Co v GS Suppinger Co*, 314 US 488 (1942). In *Morton Salt*, the Court formulated the term "patent misuse" and its sanction of unenforceability. It further explained the patent misuse doctrine as an exercise of its powers of equitable discretion.

130 M.A. Lemley, "The Economic Irrationality of the Patent Misuse Doctrine" (1990) 78 *California Law Review* 1599; and T.F. Cotter (n 123) 457. *E.g.*, Cotter examines four different rationales that may support the doctrine: a) "optimal antitrust deterrence"; b) "social welfare"; c) "public domain"; and d) "optimal deterrence of anticompetitive conduct that lies beyond the reach of antitrust."

131 J.R. Bennet, "Patent Misuse: Must an Alleged Infringer Prove an Antitrust Violation?" (1989) 17

ultimately lead one to argue that there is the risk of enforcing two similar remedies against the same conduct. As a counter-argument, perhaps, it could be said that patent misuse is broader than antitrust liability, as it extends to some sorts of conduct antitrust laws would not reach.[132] On a different ground, the argument that the misuse doctrine unduly impairs the value of patents should be rejected, in light of the fact that unenforceability is only a temporary effect.[133]

5.4.2 Main criticism

Besides these observations, a more serious dispute is on whether this remedy may be effectively applied in standard setting. Courts, it has been noted, have found it difficult to apply the doctrine when members merely concealed their rights.[134] In other cases, they have rejected the claim that charging unreasonably high royalties constitutes patent misuse.[135] More in general, some authors believe that applying the misuse doctrine in standard setting "disregards the value of a patented technology and its contribution to the industry."[136]

The more challenging criticism concerns the applicability of patent misuse to the case of exorbitant royalties. In other words, it is disputable whether a court may enforce this remedy even when there is no concealment of IPRs but only a request for excessive fees. This may happen when an innovator, after having disclosed the relevant rights and submitted the maximum cap, ultimately breaches that cap. In the previous sections, it has been explained that this conduct may be in theory addressed by enforcing contract law.[137] Would the enforcement of the misuse principle be similarly appropriate? The behavior should be distinguished from the case where IPRs owners ask for royalties beyond the expiration (*i.e.*, the life) of the patent; under these circumstances, fewer doubts exist about the reasonableness of a misuse claim.[138]

In order to answer the question, it is first necessary to recall a basic but important concept. In a society pursuing the maximization of societal welfare and

AIPLA Quarterly Journal 1; J. Webb and L. Locke, "Intellectual Property Misuse: Developments in the Misuse Doctrine" (1991) 4 *Harvard Journal of Law and Technology* 257; G.E. Frost, "Patent Misuse as a Per Se Antitrust Violation" in J. Rahl and E. Zaidins, *Conference on the Antitrust Laws and the Attorney General's Committee Report* (Federal Legal Publication, New York 1955) 113.

132 R.C. Feldman, "The Insufficiency of Antitrust Analysis for Patent Misuse" (2003) 55 *Hastings Law Journal* 399.

133 D. Lim (n 111) 582.

134 M.G. Cowie and J.P. Lavelle, "Patents Covering Industry Standards: The Risks to Enforceability Due to Conduct Before Standard-Setting Organizations" (2002) 30 *AIPLA Quarterly Journal* 115.

135 *W.L. Gore & Assoc v Carlisle,* 529 F.2d 614 (C App 3rd Circuit, 1976), at 622–623.

136 L. Zhang, "How IPR Policies Of Telecommunication Standard-Setting Organizations Can Effectively Address the Patent Ambush Problem" (2010) 41(4) *International Review of Intellectual Property and Competition Law* 407.

137 See above, section 4.

138 *Brulotte v Thys,* 379 US 29 (1964), at 32 (stating that "a patentee's use of a royalty agreement that projects beyond the expiration date of the patent is unlawful per se"). See also the Report of the US Department of Justice and Federal Trade Commission (n 9) 97.

dynamic efficiency, IPRs owners should be allowed to choose a trading party and fix the desired price for licensing their rights. Without such incentives, firms would seldom invest substantial resources in innovation. Only under exceptional circumstances should these rights be legitimately constrained. This being stated, standard setting may well justify some limitations, especially in case of misleading conduct by IPRs holders. The existence of public interests underlying the widespread adoption of a standard may give further reasons for a liability approach. It is in view of these remarks that the charging of excessive fees, in breach of the maximum cap submitted, should also justify the enforcement of a patent misuse defense.

The implementation of a maximum cap itself would help in overcoming the uncertainties about the applicability of patent misuse to the case of excessive royalties. In this context, the uncertainty arising around the meaning of (F)RAND licensing terms has already been discussed.[139] It would then be absurd for a court to establish the existence of misuse without having such a concept made clear. When adopting a maximum cap model, instead, the breach of the specific price benchmark may well enable a court to develop a more reasonable justification for the enforcement of the misuse legal remedy.

To sum up, the patent misuse doctrine may well play a role in the pursuit of a balance between the innovators' interests and standard-setting aims. Albeit some doubts may rise on the scope of its application,[140] its effectiveness has been proved by the literature.[141] It is true, however, that this doctrine is circumscribed to the US legal framework. The EU jurisdiction has not yet developed a patent misuse theory. One commentator has suggested "a pro-competitive application of national unfair competition laws, under which the prominence would be given on the interests of the consuming public."[142] This approach, it could be argued, would allegedly allow filling the gaps of a patent system which exhaustively enumerates all the various exceptions to IPRs protection.[143]

However, it should not be forgotten that the EU legal framework already provides one specific tool to control excessive prices: Article 102 of the Treaty on the Functioning of the European Union. Further relevant remarks on the scope of this rule will be given in the next sections.

5.5 Conclusive remarks on alternative private remedies

Contract law is not the only private remedy which could be potentially enforced in case of misleading conduct by innovators. Further tools exist, particularly in the US legal framework. Among these, equitable estoppel, the implied license theory,

139 D. Lim (n 111) 587.

140 Further doubts may arise also on whether the doctrine may apply to the case of refusal to license.

141 See, *inter alia*, J.M. Mueller, "Patent Misuse through the Capture of Industry Standards" (2002) 17 *Berkeley Technology Law Journal* 623.

142 A. Chronopoulos (n 96) 816.

143 Ibid. On the scope of the patent misuse doctrine, see also V. Chiappetta, "Living with Patents: Insights from Patent Misuse" (2011) 15 *Marquette Intellectual Property Law Review* 1.

fraud and the patent misuse defense have been discussed. All these remedies and principles, in theory, may function as a deterrent against unfair behaviors in standard setting. However, they do present some limitations of different nature.[144] For instance, leaving aside the misuse claim, it seems that only SSO members could benefit from their application.

This being stated, I have also explained that the implementation of a maximum licensing cap may facilitate a more effective enforcement of these tools. At the same time, and more importantly, it may discourage innovators from implementing any unfair behavior.

6 Enforcement of competition as *ex post* effective remedy

The examination of the abovementioned remedies of civil law does not exhaust the studying of all the legal principles which may find application. Given the limitations these tools present, it seems necessary to look at further potentially effective remedies. In this context, it is legitimate to question how the breach of the cap or the mere refusal to license may be treated under US and EU competition laws. The analysis developed in Part II has already attested that both US and EU antitrust enforcers have often scrutinized unlawful practices in standard setting. Thus, it may be argued that the enforcement of antitrust rules could be well interpreted as an *ex post* potential remedy to any unfair or misleading conduct.[145]

This section is devoted to understanding better how antitrust regulations may help in preserving the activities of SSOs implementing a maximum cap regime. In the analysis of the issue, I will also deal with a further related topic, concerning the application of excessive prices.

6.1 Breach of the maximum cap

At first sight, a breach of the maximum cap may lead to consequences similar to those established by some courts with respect to the breach of (F)RAND terms.[146] Therefore, if there is evidence that the SSO would have not adopted the patented technology but would have opted for an alternative had it known about the intention to breach the cap, the behavior may be prohibited under both EU and US antitrust laws. On the one hand, US enforcers may only interpret the conduct as exclusionary under Section 2 of the Sherman Act.[147] On the other hand, their EU counterparts could fine the breach of the maximum cap (which

144 See R.H. Stern (n 112) 495.

145 See U. Petrovcic, *Competition Law and Standard Essential Patents: A Transatlantic Perspective* (Kluwer Law International, London 2014) Ch. 8; and D. Telyas, *The Interface Between Competition Law, Patents and Technical Standards* (Kluwer Law International, London 2014) Ch. 14.

146 E.g. *Rambus v FTC* (n 13); *Broadcom v Qualcomm,* 501 F3d 297 (C App 3rd Circuit, 2007).

147 On the analysis of the differences between EU and US antitrust enforcement in standard setting, see for instance C. Koenig and A. Trias, "Some Standards for Standardization: A Basis for Harmonization and Efficiency Maximization of EU and US Antitrust Control of the Standard Setting Process" (2010) 32(7) *European Intellectual Property Review* 331; and J.H. Park (n 89) 51. In

could be theoretically interpreted also as a "constructive refusal to license") both as exclusionary and exploitative conduct. In case no exclusionary effect is found and it is proved that the SSO would have chosen the selected technology under all circumstances, no concern would arise under the Sherman Act.[148] The latter, indeed, does not prohibit exploitative practices. In the EU, however, the conduct might still be charged as abusive exploitation under Article 102 TFEU.[149]

6.1.1 Competition as a means to regulate prices

The issue recalls the heated debate on whether competition authorities are well suited to deal with price regulation, a problem which has been partly scrutinized in Chapter 4. Excessive prices, it is well-known, clearly affect consumer welfare. Consumers are induced to limit their purchase of goods and services, to the ultimate detriment of societal growth. This is because industrial productivity is usually affected by reduced consumption levels. These negative effects would more likely occur in those markets where high barriers do not facilitate entry by competitors, that is where competition is static.

The investments made by the industry involved in standard setting may well be interpreted as a consistent obstacle. Indeed, in case the selected IPR owner breached the maximum cap, implementers and users would seldom reinvest their resources in the development of a new technology, as they would find themselves locked into the standard (lock-in effect). Intervention by a competition authority – besides that of a civil court under private law – may also prove effective in preventing patentees from exploiting market power and harming consumers. However, in light of the mentioned difficulty of appraising when a price is excessive, it is legitimate to question which tool a competition enforcer may adopt to address the issue. Article 102(a) TFEU, in prohibiting the imposition of unfair purchase or selling prices, raises the cited doubts.[150]

The conduct might be better addressed by Article 102(b) TFEU.[151] This provision prohibits conduct implemented by dominant undertakings and limiting production, markets, or technical development to the prejudice of the consumers. The behavior of a patentee breaching the promise to charge within a maximum fee or apply licensing terms within the specified most restrictive conditions may

considering antitrust liability in the context of formal (*de jure*) standardization, Park identifies the attempted monopolization claim as the most likely tool under Section 2 of the Sherman Act.

148 J.H. Park (n 89) 50–51; R. Gilbert, "Competition Policy for Industry Standards" in R.D. Blair and D.D. Sokol (eds.), *The Oxford Handbook of International Antitrust Economics* (Oxford University Press, New York 2015) 554.

149 See European Commission, "Commission Initiates Formal Proceedings against Qualcomm" (1 October 2007) Press Release MEMO/07/389.

150 Article 102(a), Treaty on the Functioning of the European Union, OJ [2010] C 83/89. On the application of this provision, see Case 27/76 *United Brands v European Commission* [1978] ECR 207; Case 26/75 *General Motors v European Commission* [1975] ECR 1367; Case 30/87 *Bodson v Pompes Funebres* [1988] ECR 2479; and Case 226/84 *British Leyland v European Commission* [1986] ECR 3263.

151 Article 102(b), Treaty on the Functioning of the European Union, OJ [2010] C 83/89.

be caught by the spirit of the article. After being selected by the SSO process and after the acceptance of the standard by the industry, the patentee would likely acquire a dominant position in the market of the protected technology. This fact alone would meet the pre-condition for a finding of an abuse under Article 102 TFEU. The breach of the cap, then, could clearly limit the production of the selected technology, as the industry concerned would seldom agree on terms higher than those established *ex ante*. The ultimate effect would be detrimental to consumers and societal growth.

In the US, instead, the absence of exploitative abuses in the Sherman Act reduces the scope of the antitrust enforcers' intervention. In relation to high pricing conduct, US courts' decisions have held that "[a] pristine monopolist … may charge as high a rate as the market will bear."[152] On a similar basis, it has been noted that a natural monopolist that acquired and maintained its monopoly "without excluding competitors by improper means is not guilty of 'monopolizing' in violation of the Sherman Act … and can therefore charge any price that it wants … for the antitrust laws are not a price-control statute … ."[153]

This notwithstanding, the breach of a maximum cap in the absence of exclusionary effects may be potentially caught by Section 5 of the FTC Act.[154] This provision, which prevents unfair methods of competition and deceptive practices, was enforced in *Negotiated Data Solutions*.[155] In that case, the licensor had first purchased certain patents from a SSO member. It had then tried to charge fees higher than those previously agreed by the initial owner of those patents. This means that, leaving aside the enforceability of contract rules and of the other civil law remedies, Section 5 may represent an important means to support the FTC's monitoring over unfair conduct. That case may further suggest that a maximum cap should bind any third party later purchasing relevant IPRs. In other words, a maximum cap commitment should travel with the standard essential patent it refers to, in order to ensure certainty on the costs of implementing the chosen standard.[156]

6.2 Refusal to license

Besides the breach of the maximum cap, a further different conduct should be examined: the mere refusal to license. The selected innovator, as noted before, may merely decide to refuse any license. Under these circumstances, there would

152 *Berkey Photo v Eastman Kodak*, 603 F2d 263 (C App 2nd Circuit, 1979), at 297.

153 *Blue Cross and Blue Shield United of Wisconsin v Marshfield Clinic*, 65 F3d 1406 (C App 7th Circuit, 1995), at 1413, citing *National Reporting v Alderson Reporting*, 763 F2d 1020 (C App 8th Circuit, 1985); *United States v Aluminum Co of America*, 148 F2d 416 (C App 2nd Circuit, 1945), at 430; *Ball Memorial Hospital v Mutual Hospital*, 784 F2d 1325 (C App 7th Circuit, 1986), at 1339; *Berkey Photo v Eastman Kodak* (n 152).

154 15 USC § 45.

155 *Negotiated Data Solutions LLC*, FTC Case n. 0510094 (2008). The case concerned the abuse of the IEEE's "Fast Ethernet Standard" by Negotiated Data Solutions LLC and Vertical Networks Inc.

156 On the application of this principle, though in a different model, see J.L. Contreras (n 33) 19.

be no request for a higher level of royalties. Of course, this situation is unlikely, as rational IPR holders (especially pure innovators) are usually keen to be rewarded for their efforts in innovation. By refusing to license, they would clearly lose the opportunity to recover their investment. This notwithstanding, there may be exceptional reasons leading members to deny the licenses.[157] If this happened, besides the enforcement of private law remedies, it could be questioned how antitrust enforcers may intervene.

6.2.1 *Alternative perspectives*

The problem partially recalls the observations made in Part I of the book, on refusal to deal or license by IPR holders.[158] In that context, the legal principles examined referred to the IP–antitrust tension from a general perspective, as unrelated to the standard setting environment.[159] It could be argued that, in the analysis of the tension, the considerations may change depending on whether the innovator is part or not of a standard-setting process. This view seems to be supported by part of the literature, which noted that "patent issues of formal standards are different from those of informal standards because constraints placed on the holders of patents essential to standards are greater in formal standards than in informal standards."[160] Put differently, innovators developing informal (*de facto*) standards do not have to comply with any SSO policy. Consequently, the enforcement of antitrust principles in case of refusal to deal could in theory reflect these different contexts.

6.2.2 *The IPRs–competition dichotomy*

Before answering the question, it is necessary to draw the attention to some basic concepts mentioned at the beginning of the book. IPRs, it is well known, are exclusive rights which grant the holder the exclusive control of the protected subject matter. In the absence of exceptional circumstances, the innovator should have the right to refuse to deal or license. These arguments have been endorsed – albeit to different extents – by both US and EU courts, which have clarified that a mere refusal to license does not usually constitute an antitrust infringement. The right to exclude rivals is indeed the very essence of exclusive property rights.[161] By imposing a duty to license or to deal, courts may reduce the incentive to innovate, to the ultimate detriment of societal welfare.[162] However, the

157 For instance, it could be supposed, an innovator may lately decide to develop further its technology and try to exploit it in the context of more remunerative future projects.

158 See Chapter 2 sections 3 and 4.

159 See C. Koenig and K. Spiekermann, "EC Competition Law Issues of Standard Setting by Officially-Entrusted Versus Private Organisations" (2010) 31(11) *European Competition Law Review* 452; D. Geradin and M. Rato (n 7) 154; M. Valimaki (n 31) 690.

160 J.H. Park (n 89) 23–24.

161 Ibid.

162 See M. Angelov (n 3) 37.

analysis of the case law on the interaction IP–competition has also led to identify those elements which represent the exceptions justifying an order to license. In the US, courts have mainly referred to the *Aspen Skiing* principle,[163] the essential facility doctrine[164] and the monopoly leveraging theory.[165] In the EU, instead, the Commission and the courts have often taken into consideration the concept of "exceptional circumstances."[166] These legal principles have been properly examined in Chapter 2. It suffices here to remember that their application has been considered as limited by both EU and US antitrust enforcers.[167] In only a limited number of cases, indeed, an innovator has been charged for refusal to deal or license.[168]

6.2.3 Refusal to license in standard setting

This being premised, the question is whether a refusal to license of a member of a standard setting organization may be considered under the same legal principles mentioned above, or whether such refusal may justify the adoption of a more rigid approach from competition law enforcers. A more severe analysis could, in theory, be invoked in consideration of the conduct of the member that refuses to license after having subscribed the rules of the standard-setting body. However, there is no solid ground for altering the conditions established by the EU and US jurisprudence in the enforcement of those principles. Thus, for instance, reference to the "exceptional circumstances" by the EU enforcers should still be grounded on the same cumulative factors: (a) the indispensability of the license to launch a particular business; (b) the elimination of competition in case of refusal; (c) the absence of objective justifications for the refusal; and (d) the development of a "new product or service" for which there is a potential consumer demand.[169]

Perhaps, it could be argued that, in SSO contexts where the selected patent owner is a vertically integrated firm producing downstream in competition with other firms, the requirement of the development of an "entirely new product or

163 *Aspen Skiing v Aspen Highlands Skiing*, 472 US 585 (1985).

164 *MCI Communications Corp v AT&T Corp.*, 708 F2d 1081 (C App 7th Circuit, 1983); *Alaska Airlines v United Airlines*, 948 F2d 536 (C App 9th Circuit, 1991).

165 *Berkey Photo v Eastman Kodak* (n 152).

166 See Case 238/87 *Volvo AB v Erik Veng (UK)* [1989] 4 CMLR 122; Case 53/87 *Consorzio Italiano della Componentistica di Ricambio per Autoveicoli and Maxicar v Regie Nationale des Usines Renault* [1990] 4 CMLR 265; Joined Cases C 241-242/91 P *Radio Telefis Eireann & Independent Television Publications v European Commission* [1995] 4 CMLR 718; Case T-504/93 *Tierce Ladbroke SA v European Commission* [1997] ECR II-923; Case C-7/97 *Oscar Bronner GmbH Co KG v Mediaprint Zeitungs* [1998] ECR I-7791; and Case C-418/01 *IMS Health GmbH v NDC Health GmbH* [2004] 4 CMLR 28.

167 See, for instance, *Image Technical Services v Eastman Kodak*, 125 F.3d 1195 (C App 9th Circuit, 1997); and Case T-201/04 *Microsoft v European Commission* [2007] ECR II-03601.

168 On the issue, see D. Geradin, "Limiting the Scope of Article 82 of the EC Treaty: What can the EU Learn from the US Supreme Court's Judgment in *Trinko* in the Wake of *Microsoft*, *IMS*, and *Deutsche Telekom*" (2004) 41 *Common Market Law Review* 1519; L. Zhang, "Refusal to License Intellectual Property Rights under Article 82 EC in Light of Standardisation Context" (2010) 32(8) *European Intellectual Property Review* 402; and K.J. Koelman (n 22) 827.

169 On the application of this test in the EU legal framework, see M. Angelov (n 3) 37.

service" not offered by the IPR holder may not be met. In other words, under these circumstances, a refusal to license would usually prevent the other SSO implementers and manufacturers from producing the standardized technology in competition with the vertically integrated IPR owner. It is true, however, that a competition enforcer may potentially stretch the concept of "new product" and consider the possible prevention of "follow-on innovation" in the standard as a sufficient justification to enforce competition law. This is what apparently happened in the *Microsoft* litigation,[170] which raised several debates on the scope of the "new product" requirement established by EU jurisprudence.[171] The mentioned test could be encompassed by the spirit and letter of Article 102(b) TFEU, which bans those practices limiting production, markets or technical development. Similarly to what held on excessive pricing, Article 102(b) TFEU is probably the most suitable provision to address also refusal to deal. In case, then, the IPR owner tried to seek an injunction to block an implementer, also other legal tests could be potentially invoked to prove an abuse of dominance, from the "abusive litigation" to the "willing licensee" tests.[172] Perhaps, SSOs adopting a maximum cap regime may require IP owners to waive any right to seek injunctions, unless the implementers refused to pay the cap. With respect to the US framework, then, Section 2 of the Sherman Act is the relevant legal rule. However, the existence of objective justifications or the lack of alternative standards (i.e. no harm to the competitive process) would make unlikely the enforcement of antitrust principles under this provision.

To sum up, refusal to license in the standard-setting context does not justify a change in the analytical approach to the issue. It is in view of these remarks that the EU concept of "exceptional circumstances" and the principles developed by the US jurisprudence may find application only in the cited limited cases.[173] This notwithstanding, the existence of limitations does not preclude the enforcement of further tests and remedies. For instance, refusal to license by an SSO member could also be appraised in the US under Section 5 of the FTC Act, which prohibits entities from engaging in unfair or deceptive acts.[174]

In any case, it is worth restating, it is unlikely that the selected IPR holder would refuse to license its rights and lose the opportunity to get rewarded. This situation may hypothetically occur out of the standard-setting context, between an innovator and a firm seeking a license who fail to agree on the royalty level. However, in the context of an organization adopting a maximum cap rule, refusal to license would be highly improbable. Under this regime, the innovator itself makes the explicit choice of the level of royalties or of the other non-pricing terms desired. Compliance with the cap would consequently make less relevant the thorny issues (e.g. relating to the scope of the "exceptional circumstances," or to the right to seek injunctive relief) which may arise from a refusal to license.

170 See Case C-3/37.792 *Microsoft* [2007] OJ L32; and *Microsoft v European Commission* (n 167).

171 See *Radio Telefis Eireann* (n 166); and *IMS Health* (n 166).

172 See Chapter 4 section 5.

173 J.H. Park (n 89) Ch. 3 and Ch. 4.

174 15 USC § 45.

6.3 Conclusive remarks on the role of competition

In conclusion, antitrust regulations may represent a further tool – besides civil law remedies – to constrain *ex post* the negative effects of unfair conduct and discourage other competitors from further developing similar strategies.[175] It is true that some theoretical limitations exist, with particular reference to the case of refusal to deal. This notwithstanding, as it has been said, refusal to license after having subscribed the policy rules is unlikely. What is more, with particular reference to the US jurisdiction, Section 5 FTCA may still fill the gaps left by the Sherman Act. Therefore, it seems that an effective competition framework based on the enforcement of a consumer welfare test may well come abreast of a robust IPR policy in the effort to preserve standard-setting processes.[176] Perhaps, in comparison to the other private law remedies, antitrust seems to be an even better enforcement tool, due to the prominent role given to consumer protection. This being stated, a crucial concept should be remarked one more time. A maximum cap, as the optimal compromise between innovators' interests and standard setting goals, would undoubtedly have more chances to be fulfilled than a (F)RAND commitment may ever have. This would certainly make less relevant the implementation of a good faith duty by SSOs. As a logical consequence, it would also reduce the risk of intervention by courts or authorities enforcing antitrust regulations.

7 Conclusion

The main goal of this chapter was to find a solution to the tension arising in standard setting between IP and competition laws. As it has been explained, an optimal balance between patentees' interests and standardization goals should be shaped on the following principles: (a) duty to disclose issued IPRs; (b) duty to describe the scope-function of pending rights; and (c) duty to license disclosed IPRs under the maximum cap and undisclosed essential rights for free. Under this legal framework, patentees would be required to disclose *ex ante* the maximum level of royalty or the most restrictive non-pricing terms to be applied in case of selection. Such a model, to be implemented in a non-discriminatory manner, would cover both issued and pending IPRs. Those rights which were not disclosed (either intentionally or inadvertently) should instead be licensed for free. This licensing restriction seems to be necessary in order to preserve the whole standardization process. The maximum cap rule, more importantly, would help in tackling *ex ante* the hold-up issue, typically arising under (F)RAND terms. Indeed, the opportunity itself to fix the licensing terms desired should encourage IPR owners to fulfill their commitments and refrain from misleading the other members. Nonetheless, in case of deception, the model would be potentially easier to enforce before a court. Contract law, antitrust and the further private law remedies (fraud, implied

175 *Contra*, see J.H. Park (n 89) 51. The author finally argues that "antitrust laws can be used in limited circumstances in relation to standards incorporating patents."

176 On the benefits of the consumer welfare enforcement test, see Chapter 1 section 2.2.1.

license, equitable estoppel and patent misuse) developed in the US may all benefit in terms of enforceability from the implementation of a maximum cap.

Finally, with respect to the merits of the other rules completing the model, the exclusion of a general duty to search essential IPRs (either issued or pending) and to fully disclose relevant pending rights may well encourage innovators to take part in standard setting. The effect to incentivize participation in SSOs is all the more important when considering the potential obstacles arising from non-participation.[177] Patentees who decide to stay outside the standardization process, indeed, may develop their own technical solutions. As one author has argued, an IPR owner "that is not a member of or that has not participated in an SSO's standards development effort has no obligation to abide by the SSO's patent policy, but may, nonetheless, hold patents necessary to implement the resulting standard." [178] Therefore, in case the standard ultimately developed conflicts with the rights of non-members patentees, the latter may be obliged to grant a license to standard users only under those exceptional circumstances identified in Chapter 2. By encouraging through the cited policy rules a more significant participation, the risk of blocking patents would be substantially reduced.

All these advantages would have been probably observed had the SSOs implemented the suggested framework. Under these circumstances, it is unlikely that Rambus or Qualcomm would have acted in an unfair or misleading way. Rather, they would have seen the opportunity to charge the desired licensing price and get rewarded for their innovation. Furthermore, by disclosing a specific licensing cap, they would have had no possibility to hold-up the other members. As a consequence, the standard-setting bodies would have been able to bring their technologies in the marketplace in the most effective and timely way.

In conclusion, the described policy model would ensure licensees more transparent and effective SSO processes, without reducing the IPR owners' incentive to innovate. This would hold true from an *ex ante* perspective, in the first place. It would also hold true *ex post,* since antitrust and private law defenses may both have roles to play in ensuring protection against market-wide harm resulting from the breach of the cap. In the area of standard setting, as elsewhere, private defenses and antitrust doctrines need not to be viewed as mutually exclusive, but as bodies of law which may lead to complementary remedies. Their ultimate effect would be beneficial to consumer and societal welfare, which are the true goals of standardization.

177 H.J. Hovenkamp, "Competition in Information Technologies: Standards-essential Patents, Non-practicing Entities and FRAND Bidding" (2012) University of Iowa Legal Studies Research Paper n. 12-32. Hovenkamp considers the position of those IP owners which are non-practicing entities (NPEs, i.e. do not manufacture the final product) and which may refuse to cooperate in standard setting. NPEs are in a position to obtain larger fees if they did not subscribe to any licensing policy.

178 M.K. Herman (n 33) 36. See also P. Chappatte, "FRAND Commitments – The Case for Antitrust Intervention" (2009) 5(2) *European Competition Journal* 327; and A. Layne Farrar, G. Llobet and A.J. Padilla (n 101) 24.

8 General conclusions

Competition and IPRs are both necessary for a market to work efficiently and to achieve dynamic competition. In terms of objectives, the tension between them is apparent. Properly applied, strong intellectual property protection creates the competitive environment necessary to allow firms to profit from their inventions. This encourages innovative thinking and improves dynamic efficiency, to the ultimate benefit of consumer and societal welfare. Antitrust and IP laws, thus, should be seen as encouraging firms to engage in competition, and in particular competition that involves risk and long-term investments. On the other side of the spectrum, it seems also important to strike the right balance between investment incentives and competition objectives. Indeed, any abuse of market power may cause significant harm to the well-being of society. At the same time, any form of control of market power should preserve the incentives for firms to invest in the market. The crucial aim is to develop a proper balance which avoids risks of substantial losses in long-term societal welfare. To this end, EU and US competition laws should deter IPRs owners from obtaining greater power than that inherent in the relevant IPR grant.

This being the premise, the field of standard setting is clearly a context where IPRs and competition law may potentially conflict. Patent hold-up represents the most serious risk for SSOs, and provides a solid foundation for concerns about consumer and societal welfare. This opportunistic conduct has led IPR holders to gain illegitimate economic advantages at the expense of the whole standardization system. The cause of the problem must be identified in the unclear policies widely adopted so far by SSOs. Such uncertainty raises several questions as to the best path between reducing antitrust risks and protecting IPRs. EU and US antitrust enforcers have adopted a set of key judgments in an attempt to define the rights and obligations of all parties. *Qualcomm, Rambus* and the case law on the scope of injunctions certainly provide more guidance than was in existence until a few years ago. However, these cases did not answer all the questions that SSO members may raise. One core question, in particular, still needs a comprehensive answer: how can we solve the hold-up problem, and strike the optimal balance between standardization goals and innovators' interests?

This book has made clear that, in order to solve the tension between IPRs and competition in standard setting, an improved regulatory system must be developed. Such a model should be based on the *ex ante* unilateral disclosure of the maximum price and other non-pricing licensing terms. Further rules on the disclosure of issued and pending rights should be included, as part of the delicate balance between industry standards and the interests of IPRs holders. Striking the optimal compromise, however, also means that undue restrictions on innovators should be avoided. This means that members need not feel compelled to do more than is required, particularly when this would weaken their IPRs. The adoption of an improved policy model based on unilateral early disclosure may also prove effective when appraised from an *ex post* perspective. A maximum cap regime, indeed, would be easier to enforce in case of misleading or deceptive practices. In this regard, the conclusive chapter has developed an in-depth examination of the different legal tools which could be potentially applied. Competition law is certainly one effective remedy against hold-up. It is true that, when comparing the EU and US frameworks, full convergence of transatlantic trends in antitrust jurisprudence is unlikely in the immediate future because of the different cultures, histories, economic conditions and antitrust statutes existing in the US and the EU. However, an expansive use of Section 5 of the FTC Act may (at least partially) reduce the differences between US and EU enforcement practices in standardization cases. In addition, convergence between the EU and US frameworks could also be achieved by promoting more private enforcement actions in the EU.

Current and future challenges demand an in-depth reflection on the scope and the role of standardization in the emerging global context. As standardization activities are increasingly global, both firms and standards institutes will need to pay greater attention to the legal frameworks and enforcement systems that may apply to them. This book has developed a thorough examination of the main risks arising in standard setting, which may weaken its contribution to innovation, consumer welfare and societal growth. The path proposed to update the current policies and optimize enforcement practices may hopefully help the standard-setting environment – so far affected by a flawed evolutionary process – to navigate through the existing uncertainty.

Bibliography

Articles

R. Ahdar, "Consumers redistribution of income and the purpose of competition law" (2002) 23(7) *European Competition Law Review* 341.

C. Ahlborn, "Competition policy in the new economy: is European competition law up to the challenge?" (2001) 22(5) *European Competition Law Review* 156.

C. Ahlborn, D.S. Evans and A.J. Padilla, "The logic and limits of the 'exceptional circumstances test' in *Magill* and *IMS Health*" (2005) 28 *Fordham International Law Journal* 1109.

D. Aitman and A. Jones, "Competition law and copyright: has the copyright owner lost the ability to control his copyright?" (2004) 26(3) *European Intellectual Property Review* 137.

B. Allan, "Article 82: a commentary on DG Competition's Discussion Paper" (2006) *Competition Policy International* 43.

S. Amundson, "Recent decisions provide some clarity on how courts and government agencies will likely resolve issues involving standard essential patents" (2014) 13(1) *Chicago-Kent Journal of Intellectual Property* 91.

S. Anderman, "Does the Microsoft case offer a new paradigm for the exceptional circumstances test and compulsory copyright licenses under EC competition law?" (2004) 1(2) *Competition Law Review* 7.

S. Anderman, "EC competition law and intellectual property rights in the new economy" (2002) *Antitrust Bulletin* 285.

S. Anderman, "Microsoft v Commission and the interoperability issue" (2008) 30(10) *European Intellectual Property Review* 395.

D.C. Andrews, "Why patentees litigate?" (2011) 12 *The Columbia Science and Technology Law Review* 219.

M. Angelov, "The exceptional circumstances test: implications for FRAND commitments from the essential facilities doctrine under Article 102 TFEU" (2014) 10(1) *European Competition Journal* 37.

J.J. Anton and D.A. Yao, "Standard setting consortia, antitrust, and high-technology industries" (1996) 64 *Antitrust Law Journal* 247.

J. Appeldoorn, "He who spareth his rod, hateth his son? Microsoft, super-dominance and Article 82 EC" (2005) 26(12) *European Competition Law Review* 653.

P.E. Areeda, "Essential facilities: an epithet in need of limiting principles" (1989) 58 *Antitrust Law Journal* 841.

P.E. Areeda, "Introduction to antitrust economics" (1983) 52 *Antitrust Law Journal* 523.

J.Y. Art and U. Decker, "Openness and standards – how do (open) standards affect competition?" (2010) 1 *Concurrences* 18.

S. Baches Opi, "The application of the essential facilities doctrine to intellectual property licensing in the European Union and the United States: are intellectual property rights still sacrosanct?" (2001) 11 *Fordham Intellectual Property, Media and Entertainment Law Journal* 409.

D.A. Balto and A.M. Wolman, "Intellectual property and antitrust: general principles" (2003) 43 *IDEA: The Journal of Law and Technology* 395.

T.O. Barnett, "Maximizing welfare through technological innovation" (2008) 15 *George Mason Law Review* 1191.

J. Baron and T. Pohlmann, "Who cooperates in standards consortia – rivals or complementors?" (2013) 9(4) *Journal of Competition Law and Economics* 905.

J.H. Barton, "The balance between intellectual property rights and competition: paradigms in the information sector" (1997) 18 *European Competition Law Review* 440.

A. Bavasso, "The role of intent under Article 82 EC: from flushing the turkeys to spotting the lionesses in Regent's Park" (2005) 26(11) *European Competition Law Review* 616.

R. Bekkers and A. Updegrove, "IPR policies and practices of a representative group of standard setting organizations worldwide" (2012) Social Science Research Network 1.

J.R. Bennet, "Patent misuse: must an alleged infringer prove an antitrust violation?" (1989) 17 *AIPLA Quarterly Journal* 1.

M.A. Bergman, "The Bronner case – a turning point for the essential facilities doctrine?" (2000) 21(2) *European Competition Law Review* 59.

M. Bolhuis, "Open standards and the internet – the way forward" (2010) 1 *Concurrences* 21.

O. Borraz, "Governing standards: the rise of standardization processes in France and in the EU" (2007) 20(1) *Governance: an International Journal of Policy, Administration and Institutions* 57.

D.W. Carlton, "Does antitrust need to be modernised?" (2007) 21 *The Journal of Economic Perspectives* 155.

D.W. Carlton and A.L. Shampine, "An economic interpretation of FRAND" (2013) 9 *Journal of Competition Law and Economics* 531.

M.A. Carrier, "Why antitrust should defer to the intellectual property rules of standard setting organizations: a commentary on Teece and Sherry" (2003) 87 *Minnesota Law Review* 2019.

P. Chappatte, "FRAND commitments – the case for antitrust intervention" (2009) 5(2) *European Competition Journal* 319.

P. Chappatte, "FRAND commitments and EC competition law: a rejoinder" (2010) 6(1) *European Competition Journal* 175.

B. Chiao, J. Lerner and J. Tirole, "The rules of standard setting organizations: an empirical analysis" (2007) 38(4) *Rand Journal of Economics* 905.

V. Chiappetta, "Living with patents: insights from patent misuse" (2011) 15 *Marquette Intellectual Property Law Review* 1.

C.V. Chien and M.A. Lemley, "Patent holdup, the ITC, and the public interest" (2012) 98(1) *Cornell Law Review* 1.

A. Chronopoulos, "Patenting standards – a case for US antitrust law or a call for recognizing immanent public policy limitations to the exploitation rights conferred by the Patent Act?" (2009) 40(7) *International Review of Intellectual Property and Competition Law* 782.

J.L. Contreras, "Technical standards and *ex ante* disclosure: results and analysis of an empirical study" (2013) 53 *Jurimetrics* 163.

J.L. Contreras, "Rethinking RAND: SDO-based approaches to patent licensing commitments" (2012) Social Science Research Network 1.

T.F. Cotter, "Patent hold-up, patent remedies and antitrust responses" (2009) 34 *Journal of Corporation Law* 1151.

T.F. Cotter, "Four questionable rationales for the patent misuse doctrine" (2011) 12(2) *Minnesota Journal of Law, Science and Technology* 457.

T.F. Cotter, "Reining in remedies in patent litigation: three (increasingly immodest) proposals" (2013) 30 *Santa Clara High Technology Law Journal* 1.

T.F. Cotter, "Four principles for calculating reasonable royalties in patent infringement litigation" (2011) 27 *Santa Clara Computer & High Technology Law Journal* 725.

M.G. Cowie and J.P. Lavelle, "Patents covering industry standards: the risks to enforceability due to conduct before standard-setting organizations" (2002) 30 *AIPLA Quarterly Journal* 95.

P.D. Curran, "Standard setting organizations: patents, price fixing, and per se legality" (2003) 70 *University of Chicago Law Review* 983.

M.M. Dabbah, "Conduct, dominance and abuse in 'market relationship': analysis of some conceptual issues under Article 82 EC" (2000) 21(1) *European Competition Law Review* 45.

E. Derclaye, "The IMS Health decision and the reconciliation of copyright and competition law" (2004) 29(5) *European Law Review* 687.

D. De Smet, "The diametrically opposed principles of US and EU antitrust policy" (2008) 29(6) *European Competition Law Review* 356.

J.C. De Vellis, "Patenting industry standards: balancing the rights of patent holders with the need for industry-wide standards" (2003) 31 *AIPLA Quarterly Journal* 301.

R. Dini, "How to support new technology development and its commercial success by avoiding royalty stacking" (2010) 2 *Concurrences* 13.

M. Dolmans, "A Tale of two tragedies – a plea for open standards, and some comments on the RAND Report" (2010) 1 *Concurrences* 7.

M. Dolmans, "Standards for standards" (2002) 26(1) *Fordham International Law Journal* 163.

ECLF Working Group on Horizontal Agreements, "Comments on the Draft Guidelines on the applicability of Article 101 of the Treaty on the Functioning of the European Union to horizontal cooperation agreements" (2010) 6(2) *European Competition Law Journal* 507.

C.D. Ehlermann, "The contribution of EC competition policy to the single market" (1992) 29 *Common Market Law Review* 257.

E. Elhauge, "Do patent hold-up and royalty stacking lead to systematically excessive royalties?" (2008) 4(3) *Journal of Competition Law and Economics* 535.

A. Emanuelson, "Standardization agreements in the context of the new horizontal guidelines" (2012) 33(2) *European Competition Law Review* 69.

R.A. Epstein, F.S. Kieff and D.F. Spulber, "The FTC, IP and SSOs: government holdup replacing private coordination" (2012) 8(1) *Journal of Competition Law and Economics* 1.

D.S. Evans and A.J. Padilla, "Excessive prices: using economics to define administrative legal rules" (2005) 1(1) *Journal of Competition Law and Economics* 97.

J. Farrell and M.L. Katz, "The economics of welfare standards in antitrust" (2006) 2 *Competition Policy International* 3.

J. Farrell, J. Hayes, C. Shapiro and T. Sullivan, "Standard setting, patents, and hold-up" (2007) 74 *Antitrust Law Journal* 603.

J. Farrell and R.P. Merges, "Incentives to challenge and defend patents: why litigation won't reliably fix patent office errors and why administrative patent review might help" (2004) 19 *Berkeley Technology Law Journal* 943.

J. Farrell and G. Saloner, "Standardization, compatibility, and innovation" (1985) 16 *Rand Journal of Economics* 70.

J. Farrell and G. Saloner, "Coordination through committees and markets" (1988) 19(2) *Rand Journal of Economics* 235.

J. Farrell and C. Shapiro, "How strong are weak patents?" (2008) 98(4) *American Economic Review* 1347.

R.C. Feldman, "The insufficiency of antitrust analysis for patent misuse" (2003) 55 *Hastings Law Journal* 399.

M. Furse, "The role of competition policy: a survey" (1996) 17(4) *European Competition Law Review* 250.

M. Furse, "Excessive prices, unfair prices and economic value: the law of excessive pricing under Article 82 EC and the Chapter II prohibition" (2008) 4(1) *European Competition Journal* 59.

M. Furse, "The essential facilities doctrine in Community law" (1995) 16(8) *European Competition Law Review* 469.

S. Gallasch, "The referral of Huawei v ZTE to the CJEU: determining the future of remedies in the context of standard-essential patents" (2013) 34(8) *European Competition Law Review* 443.

J. Galloway, "The pursuit of national champions: the intersection of competition law and industrial policy" (2007) 28(3) *European Competition Law Review* 172.

D. Geradin, "Limiting the scope of Article 82 of the EC Treaty: what can the EU learn from the US Supreme Court's judgment in *Trinko* in the wake of *Microsoft*, *IMS*, and *Deutsche Telekom*" (2004) 41 *Common Market Law Review* 1519.

D. Geradin, "Pricing abuses by essential patent holders in a standard-setting context: a view from Europe" (2009–2010) 76 *Antitrust Law Journal* 329.

D. Geradin and R.G. Brooks, "Interpreting and enforcing the voluntary FRAND commitment" (2011) 9(1) *International Journal of IT Standards and Standardization Research* 1.

D. Geradin and M. Rato, "Can standard setting lead to exploitative abuse? A dissonant view on patent hold-up, royalty stacking and the meaning of FRAND" (2007) 3 *European Competition Journal* 101.

D. Geradin and M. Rato, "FRAND commitments and EC competition law: a reply to Philippe Chappatte" (2010) 6(1) *European Competition Journal* 129.

D. Geradin, A. Layne Farrar and A.J. Padilla, "The complements problem within standard setting: assessing the evidence on royalty stacking" (2008) 14 *Boston University Journal of Science and Technology Law* 144.

D. Geradin and A. Layne Farrar, "Patent value apportionment rules for complex, multi-patent products" (2011) 27 *Santa Clara Computer & High Technology Law Journal* 763.

R. Gilbert, "Antitrust for patent pools: a century of policy evolution" (2004) *Stanford Technology Law Review* 3.

R. Gilbert, "Deal or no deal? Licensing negotiations in standard setting organizations" (2011) 77 *Antitrust Law Journal* 855.

D. Gilo and A. Ezrachi, "Excessive pricing, entry, assessment, and investment: lessons from the Mittal litigation" (2010) 76(3) *Antitrust Law Journal* 873.

D.H. Ginsburg, T.M. Owings and J.D. Wright, "Enjoining injunctions: the case against antitrust liability for standard essential patent holders who seek injunctions" (2014) *The Antitrust Source* 1.

M. Glader, "Open standards: public policy aspects and competition law requirements" (2010) 6(3) *European Competition Journal* 611.

M. Glader and S. Chabert Larsen, "Article 82: excessive pricing – an outline of the legal principles relating to excessive pricing and their future application in the field of IP rights and industry standards" (2005) *Competition Law Insight* 3.

L. Goerke and M. Holler, "Strategic standardization in Europe: a public choice perspective" (1998) 6(2) *European Journal of Law & Economics* 95.

C. Graham and J. Morton, "Latest EU developments in standards, patents and FRAND licensing" (2014) 36(11) *European Intellectual Property Review* 700.

J. Gstalter, "Open standards and competition law: an overview" (2010) 1 *Concurrences* 1.

B. Gurel, "An external method for establishing the balance in intellectual property rights' scope: Article 102 of the TFEU" (2010) 3 *Global Antitrust Review* 50.

C. Hardee, "Single-firm opportunism and the FTC's Rambus defeat: implications for Section 2 of the Sherman Act" (2010) 18 *Texas Intellectual Property Law Journal* 97.

P. Hellstrom, T. Kramler and F.W. Bulst, "Holding standardization to competition law standards" (2010) 1 *Concurrences* 24.

M.K. Herman, "Negotiating standards-related patent licenses – how the deal is done" (2010) *Landslide* 35.

K. Heyer, "Welfare standards and merger analysis: why not the best?" (2006) 2 *Competition Policy International* 29.

C.B. Hockett and R.G. Lipscomb, "Best FRANDs forever? Standard setting antitrust enforcement in the United States and the European Union" (2009) 23(3) *Antitrust* 19.

H.J. Hovenkamp, "Post-Chicago antitrust: a review and critique" (2001) *Columbia Business Law Review* 257.

J. Hurd and J. Isaak, "IT standardization: the billion dollar strategy" (2005) 3 *International Journal of IT Standards & Standardization* 68.

J. Hurwitz, "The value of patents in industry standards: avoiding license arbitrage with voluntary rules" (2008) 36(1) *AIPLA Quarterly Journal* 1.

P. Jebsen and R. Stevens, "Assumptions, goals and dominant undertakings: the regulation of competition under Article 86 of the European Union" (1996) 64 *Antitrust Law Journal* 443.

A. Jones, "Standard essential patents: FRAND commitments, injunctions and the smartphone wars" (2014) 10(1) *European Competition Journal* 1.

G. Julian Arnold, "International compulsory licensing: the rationales and the reality" (1993) 33 *IDEA: The Journal of Law and Technology* 349.

J. Kattan, "Antitrust implications: disclosure and commitments to standard setting organizations" (2002) 16 *Antitrust* 22.

R.D. Keeler, "Why can't we be (F)RANDs? The effect of reasonable and non-discriminatory commitments on standard essential patent licensing" (2013) 32 *Cardozo Arts and Entertainment Law Journal* 317.

F.S. Kieff and A. Layne Farrar, "Incentive effects from different approaches to holdup mitigation surrounding patent remedies and standard setting organizations" (2013) 9(4) *Journal of Competition Law and Economics* 1091.

J. Killick and P. Berghe, "Rambus: an overview of the issues in the case and future lessons for SSOs when designing IPR policies" (2010) 2 *Concurrences* 6.

C.P. Kindleberger, "Standards as public, collective and private goods" (1983) 36(3) *Kyklos* 377.

J.B. Kirkwood and R.H. Lande, "The fundamental goal of antitrust: protecting consumers, not increasing efficiency" (2008) 84 *Notre Dame Law Review* 191.

B.H. Kobayashi and J.D. Wright, "Federalism, substantive pre-emption, and limits on antitrust: an application to patent holdup" (2009) 5(3) *Journal of Competition Law and Economics* 469.

K.J. Koelman, "An exceptio standardis: do we need an IP exemption for standards?" (2006) 37(7) *International Review of Intellectual Property and Competition Law* 823.

C. Koenig and K. Spiekermann, "EC competition law issues of standard setting by officially-entrusted versus private organizations" (2010) 31(11) *European Competition Law Review* 449.

C. Koenig and A. Trias, "Some standards for standardization: a basis for harmonization and efficiency maximization of EU and US antitrust control of the standard setting process" (2010) 32(7) *European Intellectual Property Review* 320.

V. Korah, "EEC competition policy – legal form or economic efficiency" (1986) 39 *Current Legal Problems* 85.

V. Korah, "The interface between intellectual property and antitrust: the European experience" (2002) 69 *Antitrust Law Journal* 801.

K. Krechmer, "The meaning of open standards" (2006) 4(1) *The International Journal of IT Standards and Standardization Research* 43.

K. Kuhn, F. Scott Morton and H. Shelanski, "Standard setting organization can help solve the standard essential patents licensing problem" (2013) *CPI Antitrust Chronicle* 1.

R.H. Lande, "Wealth transfers as the original and primary concern of antitrust: the efficiency interpretation challenged" (1982) 34 *Hastings Law Journal* 65.

R.H. Lande, "Proving the obvious: the antitrust laws were passed to protect consumers (not just to increase efficiency)" (1999) 50 *Hastings Law Review* 959.

G. Langus, V. Lipatov and D. Neven, "Standard essential patents: who is really holding up (and when)?" (2013) 9(2) *Journal of Competition Law and Economics* 253.

A. Layne Farrar, A.J. Padilla and R. Schmalensee, "Pricing patents for licensing in standard setting organizations: making sense of FRAND commitments" (2007) 74 *Antitrust Law Journal* 671.

A. Layne Farrar, "Non-discriminatory pricing: is standard setting different?" (2010) 6(4) *Journal of Competition Law and Economics* 811.

A. Layne Farrar and K.M. Schmidt, "Licensing complementary patents: patent trolls, market structure, and excessive royalties" (2010) 25 *Berkeley Technology Law Journal* 1121.

A. Layne Farrar, "Is the patent ambush prerequisite met? Assessing the extent of ex ante IPR disclosure within standard setting" (2011) Social Science Research Network 1.

A. Layne Farrar, G. Llobet and A.J. Padilla, "Preventing patent hold up: an economic assessment of ex ante licensing negotiations in standard setting" (2009) 37(4) *AIPLA Quarterly Journal* 445.

A. Layne Farrar, G. Llobet and A.J. Padilla, "Payments and participation: the incentives to join cooperative standard setting efforts" (2014) 23(1) *Journal of Economics & Management Strategy* 24.

H. Leibenstein, "Allocative efficiency vs. 'x-efficiency'" (1966) 56 *American Economic Review* 392.

M.A. Lemley, "The economic irrationality of the patent misuse doctrine" (1990) 78 *California Law Review* 1599.

M.A. Lemley, "Antitrust and the internet standardization problem" (1996) 28 *Connecticut Law Review* 1041.

M.A. Lemley, "Intellectual property rights and standard setting organizations" (2002) 90 *California Law Review* 1889.

M.A. Lemley, "Ten things to do about patent hold-up of standards (and one not to)" (2007) 48 *Boston College Law Review* 149.

M.A. Lemley and C. Shapiro, "Patent hold-up and royalty stacking" (2007) 85 *Texas Law Review* 1991.

M.A. Lemley and C. Shapiro, "A simple approach to setting reasonable royalties for standard-essential patents" (2013) 28 *Berkeley Technology Law Journal* 1135.

J. Lerner and J. Tirole, "A model of forum shopping" (2006) 96 *American Economic Review* 1091.

J. Lerner and J. Tirole, "Efficient patent pools" (2004) 94 *American Economic Review* 691.

F. Leveeque and Y. Meniere, "Technology standards, patents and antitrust" (2008) 9(1) *Competition and Regulation in Network Industries* 29.

D. Lim, "Misconduct in standard setting: the case for patent misuse" (2011) 51(4) *IDEA* 557.

M.M. Lim, "ADR of patent disputes: a customized prescription, not an over-the-counter remedy" (2004) 6 *Cardozo Journal of Conflict Resolution* 155.

I. Liotard and R. Bekkers, "European standards for mobile communications: the tense relationship between standards and intellectual property rights" (1999) 21(3) *European Intellectual Property Review* 110.

J.E. Lopatka and W.H. Page, "Bargaining and monopolization: in search of the boundary of Section 2 liability between *Aspen* and *Trinko*" (2005) 73 *Antitrust Law Journal* 115.

P. Lowe, "The design of competition policy institutions for the 21st century – the experience of the European Commission and DG Competition" (2008) 3 *Competition Policy Newsletter* 1.

M. Maher, "An analysis of internet standardization" (1998) 3 *Virginia Journal of Law and Technology* 5.

M. Mariniello, "Fair, reasonable and non-discriminatory (FRAND) terms: a challenge for competition authorities" (2011) 7(3) *Journal of Competition Law and Economics* 523.

K.D. McDonald, "Afterword: looking for antitrust law at the IP intersection" (2011) 77 *Antitrust Law Journal* 1017.

R.P. Merges and J.M. Kuhn, "An estoppel doctrine for patented standards" (2009) 97 *California Law Review* 1.

E.M. Meth, "Final offer arbitration: a model for dispute resolution in domestic and international dispute" (1999) 10 *American Review of International Arbitration* 383.

S. Michel, "Bargaining for RAND royalties in the shadow of patent remedies law" (2011) 77 *Antitrust Law Journal* 889.

J.S. Miller, "Standard setting, patents and access lock-in: RAND licensing and the theory of the firm" (2007) 40 *Indiana Law Review* 351.

G. Monti, "Article 81 EC and public policy" (2002) 39(5) *Common Market Law Review* 1057.

J.M. Mueller, "Patent misuse through the capture of industry standards" (2002) 17 *Berkeley Technology Law Journal* 623.

J.M. Mueller, "Patenting industry standards" (2001) 34 *John Marshall Law Review* 897.

M. Muller, "The European Commission's decision against Microsoft: a violation of the antitrust agreements between the United States and the European Union?" (2005) 26(6) *European Competition Law Review* 309.

T.J. Muris, "The FTC and the law of monopolization" (2000) 67 *Antitrust Law Journal* 693.

I. Nagy, "Refusal to deal and the doctrine of essential facilities in US and EC competition law: a comparative perspective and a proposal for a workable analytical framework" (2007) 32(5) *European Law Review* 664.

M.C. Naughton and R. Wolfram, "The antitrust risks of unilateral conduct in standard setting, in the light of the FTC's case against Rambus Inc." (2004) 49 *Antitrust Bulletin* 699.

R. Nazzini, "Article 81 between time present and time past: a normative critique of 'restriction of competition' in EU law" (2006) 43 *Common Market Law Review* 497.

E.S.K. Ng, "Patent trolling: innovation at risk" (2009) 31(12) *European Intellectual Property Review* 593.

E.S.K. Ng, "Evolving landscape of patent remedies in a changing marketplace" (2012) 24 *Singapore Academy of Law Journal* 634.

E.S.K. Ng, "Smartphone patent litigation: lessons from the Apple-Samsung saga" (2014) 9(3) *Journal of Intellectual Property* 1.

W.J. Nicoson, "Misuse of the misuse doctrine in infringement suits" (1962) 9 *UCLA Law Review* 76.

Note, "Is the patent misuse doctrine obsolete?" (1997) 110 *Harvard Law Review* 1922.

S.W. O'Donnell, "Unified theory of antitrust counterclaims in patent litigation" (2004) 9 *Virginia Journal of Law and Technology* 1.

OECD Secretariat, "The objectives of competition law and policy and the optimal design of a competition agency" (2003) 5 *OECD Journal of Competition Law and Policy* 7.

N. Oettinger, "In Re Independent Service Organizations antitrust litigation" (2001) 16 *Berkeley Technology Law Journal* 323.

G. Ohana, M. Hansen and O. Shah, "Disclosure and negotiation of licensing terms prior to adoption of industry standards: preventing another patent ambush?" (2003) 24 (12) *European Competition Law Review* 644.

B. Ong, "Anticompetitive refusal to grant copyright licenses: reflections on the IMS saga" (2004) 26(11) *European Intellectual Property Review* 505.

W.H. Page, "Mandatory contracting remedies in the American and European *Microsoft* cases" (2009) 75(3) *Antitrust Law Journal* 787.

L. Parret, "Shouldn't we know what we are protecting? Yes we should! A plea for a solid and comprehensive debate about the objectives of EU competition law and policy" (2010) 6(2) *European Competition Journal* 339.

M.R. Patterson, "Inventions, industry standards, and intellectual property" (2002) 17 *Berkeley Technology Law Journal* 1043.

A. Pera and V. Auricchio, "Consumer welfare, standard of proof and the objectives of competition policy" (2005) 1 *European Competition Journal* 153.

N. Petit, "Injunctions for FRAND pledged SEPs: the quest for an appropriate test of abuse under Article 102 TFEU" (2013) 9(3) *European Competition Journal* 677.

K. Petrakis, "The role of arbitration in the field of patent law" (1997) 52 *Dispute Resolution Journal* 24.

R. Pitofsky, D. Patterson and J. Hooks, "The essential facilities doctrine under US antitrust law" (2002) 70 *Antitrust Law Journal* 443.

R. Pittman, "Consumer surplus as the appropriate standard for antitrust enforcement" (2007) 3(2) *Competition Policy International* 205.

M.E. Porter, "Competition and antitrust: toward a productivity-based approach to evaluating mergers and joint ventures" (2001) 46 *Antitrust Bulletin* 919.

R. Posner, "A theory of negligence" (1972) 1 *Journal of Legal Studies* 29.

R. Posner and W. Lande, "The positive economic theory of tort law" (1981) 15 *Georgia Law Review* 851.

E. Ramirez and L. Kimmel, "A competition policy perspective on patent law: the Federal Trade Commission's report on the evolving IP marketplace" (2011) *The Antitrust Source* 1.

J. Raz, "Responsibility and the negligence standard" (2010) 30 *Oxford Journal of Legal Theory* 1.

C. Ritter, "Refusal to deal and essential facilities: does intellectual property require special deference compared to tangible property?" (2005) 28(3) *World Competition* 281.

M.S. Royall, "Standard setting and exclusionary conduct: the role of antitrust in policing unilateral abuses of standard-setting processes" (2003–2004) 18 *Antitrust* 44.

M.S. Royall and A.J. Di Vincenzo, "The FTC's *N-Data* consent order: a missed opportunity to clarify antitrust in standard setting" (2008) *Antitrust* 83.

M.S. Royall, A. Tessar and A.J. Di Vincenzo, "Deterring 'patent ambush' in standard setting: lessons from *Rambus* and *Qualcomm*" (2009) 23(3) *Antitrust* 34.

C.F. Rule and D.L. Meyer, "An antitrust enforcement policy to maximize the economic wealth of all consumers" (1988) 33 *Antitrust Bulletin* 677.

S. Salop and T. Krattenmaker, "Analyzing anticompetitive exclusion" (1987) 56 *Antitrust Law Journal* 71.

S. Sattler, "Standardization under EU competition rules – the Commission's new horizontal guidelines" (2011) 32(7) *European Competition Law Review* 343.

R. Schellingerhout, "Standard setting from a competition law perspective" (2011) 1 *Competition Policy Newsletter* 3.

F.M. Scherer, "Antitrust, efficiency and progress" (1987) 62 *New York University Law Review* 998.

H.K.S. Schmidt, "Article 82's exceptional circumstances that restrict intellectual property rights" (2002) 23(5) *European Competition Law Review* 210.

C. Shapiro, "Navigating the patent thicket: cross licensees, patent pools and standard setting" (2001) *Social Science Research Network* 1.

C. Shapiro, "Injunctions, hold-up and patent royalties" (2010) 12(2) *American Law and Economics Review* 280.

J.G. Sidak, "Patent hold-up and oligopsonistic collusion in standard-setting organizations" (2009) 5(1) *Journal of Competition Law and Economics* 123.

J.G. Sidak, "Holdup, royalty stacking, and the presumption of injunctive relief for patent infringement: a reply to Lemley and Shapiro" (2008) 92 *Minnesota Law Review* 714.

D. Sinclair, "Abuse of dominance at a crossroads – potential effect, object and appreciability under Article 82 EC" (2004) 25(8) *European Competition Law Review* 491.

H.J. Singer and K. Smith, "What does an economist have to say about the calculation of reasonable royalties" (2009) 14 *Intellectual Property Law Bulletin* 7.

M. Siragusa, "Case comment – Italy: Tribunal of Milan – Samsung v Apple" (2012) 5(3) *Global Competition Litigation Review* R32.

R.A. Skitol, "Concerted buying power: its potential for addressing the patent hold-up problem in standard setting" (2004–2005) 72 *Antitrust Law Journal* 727.

P. Staniszewski, "The interplay between IP rights and competition law in the context of standardisation" (2007) 2(10) *Journal of Intellectual Property Law and Practice* 666.

R.H. Stern, "Rambus v Infineon: the superior aptness of common law remedies than antitrust for standardization skulduggery" (2001) 23(10) *European Intellectual Property Review* 495.

G. Stigler, "The existence of x-efficiency" (1976) 66 *American Economic Review* 213.

C. Stothers, "Refusal to supply as abuse of a dominant position: essential facilities in the European Union" (2001) 22(7) *European Competition Law Review* 256.

J. Stuyck, "EC competition policy after modernization: more than ever in the interest of consumers" (2005) 28 *Journal of Consumer Policy* 1.

D.G. Swanson and W.J. Baumol, "Reasonable and non-discriminatory (RAND) royalties, standards selection, and control of market power" (2005–2006) 73 *Antitrust Law Journal* 1.

R.P. Taylor, "Standard setting: a growing morass" (2002) *Intellectual Property Antitrust* 545.

D.J. Teece and E.F. Sherry, "Standard setting and antitrust" (2003) 84 *Minnesota Law Review* 1913.

J. Temple Lang, "Patent pools and agreements on standards" (2011) 36(6) *European Law Review* 887.

P. Treacy and S. Lawrence, "FRANDly fire: are industry standards doing more harm than good?" (2008) 3(1) *Journal of Intellectual Property Law & Practice* 22.

B.A. Tulis, "Final offer baseball arbitration: contexts, mechanics & application" (2010) 20 *Seton Hall Journal of Sports and Entertainment Law* 85.

J. Turney, "Defining the limits of the EU essential facilities doctrine on intellectual property rights: the primacy of securing optimal innovation" (2005) 3 *Northwestern Journal of Technology and Intellectual Property* 179.

H. Ullrich, "Patents and standards – a comment on the German Federal Supreme Court decision Orange Book Standard" (2010) 41(3) *International Review of Intellectual Property and Competition Law* 337.

M. Valimaki, "A flexible approach to RAND licensing" (2008) 29(12) *European Competition Law Review* 686.

M. Valimaki, "Two types of openness in information technology standards and competition policy" (2010) 1 *Concurrences* 5.

H. Vedder, "Competition law and consumer protection: how competition law can be used to protect consumers even better – or not?" (2006) 17 *European Business Law Review* 83.

J. Verbruggen and A. Lorincz, "Patents and technical standards" (2002) 33(2) *International Review of Intellectual Property and Competition Law* 125.

S. Vezzoso, "The incentives balance test in the EU Microsoft case: a pro-innovation economics-based approach?" (2006) 27(7) *European Competition Law Review* 382.

T.C. Vinje, "The final word on Magill" (1995) 6 *European Intellectual Property Review* 297.

J. Webb and L. Locke, "Intellectual property misuse: developments in the misuse doctrine" (1991) 4 *Harvard Journal of Law and Technology* 257.

A. Weitbrecht, "From Freiburg to Chicago and beyond: the first 50 years of European competition law" (2008) 29(2) *European Competition Law Review* 81.

R. Werle, "Institutional aspects of standardisation: jurisdictional conflicts and the choice of standardisation organisations" (2001) 8(3) *Journal of European Public Policy* 392.

O. Williamson, "Economies as an antitrust defence: the welfare trade-offs" (1968) 58 *American Economic Review* 18.

S.M. Willimsky, "The concept(s) of competition" (1997) 1 *European Competition Law Review* 54.

L. Zhang, "Refusal to license intellectual property rights under Article 82 EC in light of standardisation context" (2010) 32(8) *European Intellectual Property Review* 402.

L. Zhang, "How IPR policies of telecommunication standard-setting organizations can effectively address the patent ambush problem" (2010) 41(4) *International Review of Intellectual Property and Competition Law* 380.

Books

M.J. Adelman, *Patent Law Perspectives* (2nd edn, Bender, New York 1982).

G. Amato, *Antitrust and the Bounds of Power: the Dilemma of Liberal Democracy in the History Market* (Hart Publishing, Oxford 1997).

American Bar Association, *Handbook on the Antitrust Aspects of Standard Setting* (2nd edn, ABA Section of Antitrust Law, Chicago 2011).

American Bar Association, *A Year in the Life of a High Tech Standard Setting Organization* (ABA Section of Antitrust Law, Chicago 2002).

S.D. Anderman, *EC Competition Law and Intellectual Property Rights* (Oxford University Press, Oxford 2000).

S.D. Anderman, *The Interface between Intellectual Property Rights and Competition Policy* (Cambridge University Press, Cambridge 2007).

P.E. Areeda and H.J. Hovenkamp, *Antitrust Law: an Analysis of Antitrust Principles and Their Application* (2nd edn, Aspen Publishers, New York 2004).

P.E. Areeda and H.J. Hovenkamp, *Fundamentals of Antitrust Law* (4th edn, Wolters Kluwer, New York 2012).

D. Bainbridge, *Intellectual Property* (8th edn, Longman, Harlow 2010).
R. Baldwin, M. Cave and M. Lodge, *Understanding Regulation* (2nd edn, Oxford University Press, Oxford 2012).
C. Bellamy and G. Child, *European Union Law of Competition* (7th edn, Oxford University Press, Oxford 2013).
L. Bently and B. Sherman, *Intellectual Property Law* (4th edn, Oxford University Press, Oxford 2014).
S. Bishop and M. Walker, *The Economics of EC Competition Law* (3rd edn, Sweet & Maxwell, London 2010).
J. Bitzer and P. Schroder, *The Economics of Open Source Software Development* (Elsevier, Amsterdam 2006).
R.D. Blair and D.D. Sokol (eds.), *The Oxford Handbook of International Antitrust Economics* (Oxford University Press, New York 2015).
R. Bork, *The Antitrust Paradox* (Basic Books, New York 1978).
G.B. Born, *International Commercial Arbitration* (2nd edn, Kluwer Law International, London 2014).
A. Brown, J. Cornwell, S. Kheria, C. Waelde and G. Laurie, *Contemporary Intellectual Property: Law and Policy* (3rd edn, Oxford University Press, Oxford 2013).
W.R. Cornish, D. Llewelyn and T. Aplin, *Intellectual Property: Patents, Copyrights, Trademarks and Allied Rights* (8th edn, Sweet & Maxwell, London 2013).
A. Cournot, *Recherches sur les Principles Mathematiques de la Theorie des Richesse* (Calmann Levy, Paris 1974).
M. Crew and P. Kleindorfer, *The Economics of Public Utility Regulation* (MIT Press, Cambridge, MA 1987).
H. de Vries, *Standardization: a Business Approach to the Role of National Standardization Organizations* (Kluwer Academic Publisher, Dordrecht 1999).
H. de Vries and I. Oshri, *Standards Battles in Open Source Software* (Palgrave Macmillan, London 2008).
B. Doern and S. Wilks, *Comparative Competition Policy: National Institutions in a Global Market* (Clarendon Press, Oxford 1996).
R. Dreyfuss, D.L. Zimmerman and H. First, *Expanding the Boundaries of Intellectual Property: Innovation Policy for the Knowledge Society* (Oxford University Press, New York 2001).
A.L. Durham, *Patent Law Essentials – a Concise Guide* (4th edn, Praeger Publishers, Westport 2013).
T.M. Egyedi and K. Blind, *The Dynamics of Standards* (Edward Elgar, Cheltenham 2008).
C.D. Ehlermann and M. Marquis, *European Competition Law Annual 2007: a Reformed Approach to Article 82 EC* (Hart Publishing, Oxford 2008).
A. Ezrachi and U. Bernitz, *Private Labels Brands and Competition Policy* (Oxford University Press, Oxford 2009).
J. Faull and A. Nikpay, *The EU Law of Competition* (3rd edn, Oxford University Press, Oxford 2014).
J. Galbraith, *American Capitalism: the Concept of Countervailing Power* (Houghton Mifflin, Boston 1952).
D.J. Gerber, *Law and Competition in Twentieth Century Europe: Protecting Prometheus* (Clarendon Press, Oxford 1998).
M.A. Gollin, *Driving Innovation: Intellectual Property Strategies for a Dynamic World* (Cambridge University Press, Cambridge 2008).
I. Govaere, *The Use and Abuse of Intellectual Property Rights in E.C. Law* (Sweet & Maxwell, London 1996).

R.M. Grant, *Contemporary Strategy Analysis* (8th edn, Wiley, New Jersey 2013).

P. Grindley, *Standards, Strategy and Policy: Cases and Stories* (Oxford University Press, Oxford 1995).

A.S. Gutterman, *Innovation and Competition Policy* (Kluwer Law International, London 1997).

B. Hawk (ed.), *International Antitrust Law & Policy: Fordham Corporate Law Institute* (Juris Publishing, New York 2001).

D. Helm and T. Jenkinson, *Competition in Regulated Industries* (Oxford University Press, Oxford 1998).

W.N. Hohfeld, *Fundamental Legal Conceptions* (Yale University Press, New Haven 1919).

H.J. Hovenkamp, *Federal Antitrust Policy: the Law of Competition and its Practice* (4th edn, Thomson Reuters, St. Paul 2011).

H.J. Hovenkamp, M.A. Lemley and M.D. Janis, *IP and Antitrust: an Analysis of Antitrust Principles Applied to Intellectual Property* (Aspen Law & Business, New York 2008).

K. Jacobs (ed.), *Advanced Topics in Information Technology Standards and Standardization Research* (IDEA Group Publishing, Hershey 2006).

A. Jones and B. Sufrin, *EU Competition Law: Text, Cases & Materials* (5th edn, Oxford University Press, New York 2014).

J.M. Keynes, *The General Theory of Employment, Interest and Money* (Macmillan, London 1936).

C. Koenig, A. Bartosch and J.D. Braun, *EC Competition and Telecommunications Law* (Kluwer Law International, London 2002).

V. Korah, *An Introductory Guide to EC Competition Law and Practice* (9th edn, Hart Publishing, London 2007).

V. Korah, *Intellectual Property Rights and the EC Competition Rules* (Hart Publishing, London 2006).

H.W. Kuhn and A.W. Tucker (eds.), *Contributions to the Theory of Games* (Princeton University Press, Princeton 1953).

H. Laddie, P. Prescott, M. Vitoria, *The Modern Law of Copyright and Designs* (4th edn, Butterworths, London 2011).

B. Lelong and A. Mallard, *Reseaux: Dossier sur la Fabbrication des Normes* (Hermes Science Publications, Paris 2000).

B. Lundqvist, *Standardization under EU Competition Rules and US Antitrust Laws: the Rise and Limits of Self-Regulation* (Edward Elgar, Cheltenham 2014).

C. May, *A Global Political Economy of Intellectual Property Rights: the New Enclosures?* (Routledge, New York 2000).

M. Motta, *Competition Policy: Theory and Practice* (Cambridge University Press, Cambridge 2004).

R. Nazzini, *The Foundations of European Union Competition Law – the Objective and Principles of Article 102* (Oxford University Press, New York 2011).

O. Odudu, *The Boundaries of EU Competition Law: the Scope of Article 81* (Oxford University Press, Oxford 2006).

J.H. Park, *Patents and Industry Standards* (Edward Elgar, Cheltenham 2010).

U. Petrovcic, *Competition Law and Standard Essential Patents: a Transatlantic Perspective* (Kluwer Law International, London 2014).

J. Phillips, *Trademark Law – a Practical Anatomy* (Oxford University Press, Oxford 2003).

M.E. Porter, *Competitive Strategy: Techniques for Analyzing Industries and Competitors* (The Free Press, New York 1980).

R. Posner, *Antitrust Law* (2nd edn, University of Chicago Press, Chicago 2001).

J. Rahl and E. Zaidins, *Conference on the Antitrust Laws and the Attorney General's Committee Report* (Federal Legal Publication, New York 1955).

F.M. Scherer and D. Ross, *Industrial Market Structure and Economic Performance* (Houghton Mifflin, Boston 1990).

I. Schmidt and J.B. Rittaler, *A Critical Evaluation of the Chicago School of Antitrust Analysis – Studies in Industrial Organization* (Kluwer Academic Publishers, Dordrecht 1989).

S.K. Schmidt and R. Werle, *Co-ordinating Technology: Studies in the International Standardization of Telecommunication* (MIT Press, Cambridge, MA 1998).

J. Schumpeter, *Capitalism, Socialism and Democracy* (Allan & Unwin, London 1943).

A. Smith, *The Wealth of Nations* (Strahan and Cadell, London 1776).

Swedish Competition Authority, *The Pro & Cons of Standard Setting* (2010).

C. Tapia, *Industrial Property Rights, Technical Standards and Licensing Practices (FRAND) in the Telecommunications Industry* (Carl Heymanns Verlag, Köln 2010).

D. Telyas, *The Interface between Competition Law, Patents and Technical Standards* (Kluwer Law International, London 2014).

P. Torremans, *Holyoak and Torremans Intellectual Property Law* (7th edn, Oxford University Press, Oxford 2013).

C. Townley, *Article 81 EC and Public Policy* (Hart Publishing, London 2009).

R. Van den Berghe and P.D. Camesasca, *European Competition Law and Economics: a Comparative Perspective* (2nd edn, Sweet & Maxwell, London 2006).

K. Weiermair and M. Perlman, *Studies in Economic Rationality* (University of Michigan, Ann Arbor 1990).

R. Whish and D. Bailey, *Competition Law* (7th edn, Oxford University Press, Oxford 2012).

O. Williamson, *The Economic Institutions of Capitalism: Firms, Markets, Relational Contracting* (The Free Press, New York 1985).

Reports, guidelines, communications and press releases

European Union

European Commission, "Commission Initiates Formal Proceedings against Qualcomm" (1 October 2007) Press Release MEMO/07/389.

European Commission, "Commission Confirms Sending a Statement of Objections to Rambus" (23 August 2007) Press Release MEMO/07/330.

European Commission, "Commission Welcomes Changes in ETSI IPR Rules to Prevent 'Patent Ambush' " (12 December 2005) Press Release IP/05/1565.

European Commission, "Commission Welcomes IPCom's Public FRAND Declaration" (10 December 2009) Press Release MEMO/09/549.

European Commission, "Samsung – Enforcement of ETSI Standards Essential Patents (SEPs)" (21 December 2012) Press Release MEMO/12/1021.

European Commission, "Guidelines on the Assessment of Horizontal Mergers under the Council Regulation on the Control of Concentrations between Undertakings" [2004] OJ C31/5.

European Commission, "Guidelines on the Assessment of Non-horizontal Mergers under the Council Regulation on the Control of Concentrations between Undertakings" [2008] OJ C 265/07.

European Commission, "Guidelines on the Application of Article 81 of the EC Treaty to Technology Transfer Agreement" [2004] OJ C101/2.

European Commission, "Guidelines on the Applicability of Article 81 of the EC Treaty to Horizontal Co-operation Agreements" [2001] OJ C 3.

European Commission, "Guidelines on the Applicability of Article 101 TFEU to Horizontal Co-operation Agreements" [2011] OJ C 11/1.

European Commission, "Guidelines on the Application of Article 81(3) of the EC Treaty" [2004] OJ C101/97.

European Commission, "DG Competition Discussion Paper on the Application of Article 82 of the Treaty to Exclusionary Abuses" (Public Consultation, December 2005).

European Commission, "Towards an Increased Contribution from Standardization to Innovation in Europe" (Communication) COM 133 final, 11 March 2008.

European Commission, "Intellectual Property Rights and Standardization" (Communication) COM 445 final, 27 October 1992.

European Commission, "Modernising ICT Standardization in the EU – The Way Forward" (Communication) COM 324 final, 3 July 2009.

European Commission, "The Role of European Standardization in the Framework of European Policies and Legislation" (Communication) COM 674 final, 18 October 2004.

Ministerial Declaration on eGovernment, 18 November 2009. Available at: https://ec.europa.eu/digital-agenda.

United States

Antitrust Modernization Commission (AMC), "Final Report and Recommendations" (April 2007).

T.O. Barnett, "Response to Institute of Electrical and Electronics Engineering Inc.'s Request for Business Review Letter" (US Department of Justice, Antitrust Division, 30 April 2007).

T.O. Barnett, "Response to VMEbus International Trade Association's Request for Business Review Letter" (US Department of Justice, Antitrust Division, 30 October 2006).

US Congress Research Service, "Midwest Gasoline Prices: a Review of Recent Market Developments" (June 2000).

US Department of Justice and Federal Trade Commission, "Horizontal Merger Guidelines" [Revised 1997], reprinted in 4 Trade Reg Rep (CCH) § 13, 104 (April 1997).

US Department of Justice and US Patent & Trademark Office, "Policy Statement on Remedies for Standards-Essential Patents Subject to Voluntary F/RAND Commitment" (January 2013).

US Department of Justice and Federal Trade Commission, "Antitrust Enforcement and Intellectual Property Rights: Promoting Innovation and Competition" (April 2007).

US Federal Trade Commission, "The Evolving IP Marketplace: Aligning Patent Notice and Remedies with Competition" (March 2011).

United Kingdom

UK Competition Commission, "Merger References: Competition Commission Guidelines" (June 2003, CC 2).

UK Competition Commission, "Market Investigation References: Competition Commission Guidelines" (June 2003, CC 3).

UK Department of Trade and Industry, "Productivity and Enterprise: a World Class Competition Regime" (Cm 5233, 2002).

Research papers and speeches

Association Internationale pour la Protection de la Propriete Intellectuelle (AIPPI), "Availability of injunctive relief for FRAND-committed standard essential patents" (2014) Report of the Special Committee Q222.

J.L. Contreras and D.L. Newman, "Developing a framework for arbitrating standards-essential patent (SEP) disputes" (2014) American University WCL Research Paper n. 2014-20.

T. Cotter, "The comparative law and economics of standard-essential patents and FRAND royalties" (2013) University of Minnesota Law School Research Paper n. 13-40.

P. Dehez and S. Poukens, "The Shapley value as a guide to FRAND licensing agreements" (2013) CORE Discussion Paper n. 2013/12.

N. Gallini, "Private agreements for coordinating patent rights: the case of patent pools" (2011) Institutions Economics and Law – IEL Paper n. 5.

B. Ganglmair and E. Tarantino, "Patent disclosure in standard setting" (2011) NET Institute Working Paper n. 11-15.

D. Geradin, "Ten years of DG Competition effort to provide guidance on the application of competition rules to the licensing of standard-essential patents: where do we stand?" (2013) Tilburg Centre of Law and Economics Discussion Paper n. 2013-11.

R. Hewitt Pate, "Competition and intellectual property in the U.S.: licensing freedom and the limits of antitrust" (Speech at *EU Competition Workshop*, Florence – 3 June 2005).

H.J. Hovenkamp, "Patent continuations, patent deception, and standard setting: the Rambus and Broadcom decisions" (2008) University of Iowa Legal Studies Research Paper n. 08-25.

H.J. Hovenkamp, "Competition in information technologies: standards-essential patents, non-practicing entities and FRAND bidding" (2012) University of Iowa Legal Studies Research Paper n. 12-32.

K. Hussinger and F. Schwiebacher, "The value of disclosing IPR to open standard setting organizations" (2013) ZEW Discussion Paper n. 13-060.

N. Kroes, "Being open about standards" (Speech at *Open Forum Europe*, Bruxelles – 10 June 2008).

N. Kroes, "European competition policy: delivering better markets and better choices" (Speech at *European Consumer and Competition Day*, London – 5 September 2005).

M.A. Lemley, "Ex ante versus ex post justifications for intellectual property" (2004) UC Berkeley Public Law Research Paper n. 144.

M.A. Lemley and A.D. Melamed, "Missing the forest for the trolls" (2013) Stanford Law School Working Paper Series n. 443.

R. Lyons, "Could politicians be more right than economists? A theory of merger standards" (2002) University of East Anglia Centre for Competition & Regulation Working Paper n. CCR 02-1.

M. Mariniello, "European antitrust control and standard setting" (2013) Bruegel Working Paper n. 2013/01.

D. Platt Majoras, "Recognizing the pro-competitive potential of royalty discussions in standard setting, remarks at standardization and the law: developing the golden mean for global trade" (Speech at Stanford University, Stanford – 23 September 2005).

S.K. Peterson, "Consideration of patents during the setting of standards." Available at: www.ftc.gov/opp/Intellect/021106peterson-pdf.

S.C. Salop, "Question: what is the real and proper antitrust welfare standard? Answer:

the true consumer welfare standard" (Paper presented to the Antitrust Modernization Commission – 4 November 2005).

C. Shapiro, "Competition policy and innovation" (2002) OECD STI Working Paper n. 11/2002.

J. Temple Lang, "Fundamental issues concerning abuse under Article 82 EC" (Annual Competition Policy Conference – Regulatory Policy Institute Oxford – July 2005).

Unilateral Conduct Working Group, "Report on the objectives of unilateral conduct laws, assessment of dominance/substantial market power, and state-created monopolies" (6th Annual Conference of the International Competition Network (ICN) – Moscow, May 2007).

H.B. Wellford, "Antitrust issues in standard setting" (Speech at *2nd Annual Seminar on IT Standardization and Intellectual Property*, China Electronics Standardization Institute, Beijing – 29 March 2007).

T. Winston, "Innovation and ex ante consideration of licensing terms in standard setting" (2006) EAG Discussion Paper n. 6-3.

Standard setting organizations policies, guidelines and reports

ANSI, "Essential Requirements: Due Process Requirements for American National Standards" (2015).

CEN-CENELEC, "Guidelines for Implementation of the Common IPR Policy on Patent" (2011).

ETSI, "ETSI Guide on IPRs" (2013).

ETSI, "ETSI Rules of Procedure" (2014).

IEEE-SA, "Standards Board Bylaws" (2015).

IETF, "Intellectual Property Rights in IETF Technology" (2005).

ISO/IEC, "Standardization and Related Activities – General Vocabulary" (2004).

ITU/ISO/IEC, "Guidelines for Implementation of the Common Patent Policy for ITU-T/ITU-R/ISO/IEC" (2015).

ITU (Telecommunication Standardization Bureau), "Understanding Patents, Competition and Standardization in an Interconnected World" (2014).

JEDEC, "Manual of Organization and Procedure, JM21-Q" (2015).

OASIS, "Intellectual Property Rights (IPR) Policy" (2013).

VITA, "Standards Organization – Policies and Procedures" (2011).

W3C, "Patent Policy" (2004).

Index

For Product Safety Concerns and Information please contact our EU representative GPSR@taylorandfrancis.com
Taylor & Francis Verlag GmbH, Kaufingerstraße 24, 80331 München, Germany

www.ingramcontent.com/pod-product-compliance
Ingram Content Group UK Ltd.
Pitfield, Milton Keynes, MK11 3LW, UK
UKHW010958180926
475701UK00004B/429
* 9 7 8 1 1 3 8 6 1 4 4 8 2 *